The Diary of Lt. Melvin J. Lasky

Transatlantic Perspectives

Series Editors: Christoph Irmscher, Indiana University Bloomington, and Christof Mauch, Ludwig-Maximilians-Universität, München

This series explores European and North American cultural exchanges and interactions across the Atlantic and over time. While standard historical accounts are still structured around nation states, *Transatlantic Perspectives* provides a framework for the discussion of topics and issues such as knowledge transfer, migration, and mutual influence in politics, society, education, film, and literature. Committed to the presentation of European views on America as well as American views on Europe, *Transatlantic Perspectives* offers room for the publication of both primary texts and critical analyses. While the series puts the Atlantic World at center stage, it also aims to take global developments into account.

Volume 7
The Diary of Lt. Melvin J. Lasky: Into Germany at the End of World War II
Edited by Charlotte A. Lerg

Volume 6
Anglo-American Relations and the Transmission of Ideas: A Shared Political Tradition?
Edited by Alan P. Dobson and Steve Marsh

Volume 5
The Arkansas Regulators
Friedrich Gerstäcker, translated by Charles Adams and Christoph Irmscher

Volume 4
The Underground Reader: Sources in the Trans-Atlantic Counterculture
Edited by Jeffrey H. Jackson and Robert Francis Saxe

Volume 3
From Fidelity to History: Film Adaptations as Cultural Events in the Twentieth Century
Anne-Marie Scholz

Volume 2
Women of Two Countries: German-American Women, Women's Rights and Nativism, 1848–1890
Michaela Bank

Volume 1
Journey Through America
Wolfgang Koeppen

The Diary of Lt. Melvin J. Lasky
Into Germany at the End of World War II

Edited by Charlotte A. Lerg

berghahn
NEW YORK · OXFORD
www.berghahnbooks.com

First published in 2023 by
Berghahn Books
www.berghahnbooks.com

© 2023, 2024 Charlotte A. Lerg
First paperback edition published in 2024

All rights reserved. Except for the quotation of short passages
for the purposes of criticism and review, no part of this book
may be reproduced in any form or by any means, electronic or
mechanical, including photocopying, recording, or any information
storage and retrieval system now known or to be invented,
without written permission of the publisher.

Library of Congress Cataloging-in-Publication Data

Names: Lasky, Melvin J., author. | Lerg, Charlotte A., editor.
Title: The Diary of Lt. Melvin J. Lasky: Into Germany at the End of World War II / edited by Charlotte A. Lerg.
Description: New York: Berghahn Books, [2022] | Series: Transatlantic Perspectives; 7 | Includes bibliographical references and index.
Identifiers: LCCN 2022027937 (print) | LCCN 2022027938 (ebook) | ISBN 9781800736955 (hardback) | ISBN 9781800736962 (ebook)
Subjects: LCSH: Lasky, Melvin J.—Diaries. | United States. Army. Army, 7th—History—Sources. | Military historians--United States--Diaries. | Germany—Social conditions—1945–1955—Sources. | United States. Army, Europe. Historical Division—Biography. | World War, 1939–1945—Personal narratives, American. | World War, 1939–1945—Campaigns—Western Front—Sources. | Europe—Description and travel.
Classification: LCC D769.26 7th .L37 2022 (print) | LCC D769.26 7th (ebook) | DDC 940.54/1273092 [B] —dc23/eng/20220712
LC record available at https://lccn.loc.gov/2022027937
LC ebook record available at https://lccn.loc.gov/2022027938

British Library Cataloguing in Publication Data

A catalogue record for this book is available from the British Library.

ISBN 978-1-80073-695-5 hardback
ISBN 978-1-80539-342-9 paperback
ISBN 978-1-80073-696-2 web pdf
ISBN 978-1-80539-449-5 epub

https://doi.org/10.3167/9781800736955

Contents

List of Illustrations	vi
List of Abbreviations	vii
Introduction. Journal of a Conscript *Charlotte A. Lerg and Maren Roth*	1
Chapter 1. Melvin J. Lasky's Biography and Diary *Maren Roth*	9
Chapter 2. Not a Beginning but an End: Melvin J. Lasky, Diarist *George Blaustein*	21
Chapter 3. Between Denazification and Reconstruction: US Occupation Policies and Practice in Germany 1945 *Jana Aresin*	29
Chapter 4. "Clio Continues to Serve": Melvin J. Lasky as Combat Historian *Charlotte A. Lerg*	38
Chapter 5. (Military) Masculinity and a Feminized Europe: The Gender Politics of the Lasky Diary *Katharina Gerund*	49
Chapter 6. Melvin J. Lasky, Chronicler of Europe's Twentieth Century *Michael Kimmage*	59
Melvin J. Lasky Diary	67
Appendix A. List of Primary Literature in the Diary	303
Appendix B. List of Names in the Diary	306
Appendix C. Names and Ranks of Lasky's Fellow Soldiers	315
Index	316

Illustrations

Figure 1. Second Lieutenant Melvin J. Lasky en route to Germany, © Lasky Center, Munich.   66

Figure 2. Changing the tire on the road to Strasbourg, © Lasky Center, Munich.   77

Figure 3. Material for the Maison Rouge report from Lasky's personal papers, © Lasky Center, Munich.   90

Figure 4. Darmstadt reduced to rubble, © Lasky Center, Munich.   143

Figure 5. Nazi graffiti "scrawled across the Gothic facades of the Römerberg" in Frankfurt, © Lasky Center, Munich.   146

Figure 6. American Pro Station in Frankfurt, © Lasky Center, Munich.   159

Figure 7. Posing in front of the Feldherrnhalle in Munich, once a central location of the 1923 Beer Hall Putsch, © Lasky Center, Munich.   182

Figure 8. Posing in the "Führerstube" in Landsberg, © Lasky Center, Munich.   201

Figure 9. Children along the road near Hungerburg, © Lasky Center, Munich.   205

Figure 10. Poster in Nuremberg proclaiming the city to be "guilty," © Lasky Center, Munich.   212

Figure 11. Posing in front of the Brandenburg Gate, Berlin, © Lasky Center, Munich.   249

Figure 12. Posing in the rubble of Goethe's birth house, Frankfurt, © Lasky Center, Munich.   255

Figure 13. Victory Shrine and the bombed out Reichstag, Berlin, © Lasky Center, Munich.   293

Abbreviations

AEF	American Expeditionary Forces
AFN	American Forces Network (US military radio station)
AG	Aktien-Gemeinschaft (shareholder corporation)
AMG	Allied Military Government
APO	Army Post Office
AWOL	Absent Without Official Leave
BBC	British Broadcasting Corporation
CCF	Congress for Cultural Freedom
CG	Commanding General
CI	Counter Intelligence
CIA	Central Intelligence Agency
CIC	Counter Intelligence Corps
CP	Control Post or Communist Party (see context for correct application)
DDT	Dichlorodiphenyltrichloroethane
DKW	Dampf Kraft Wagen ([steam-powered wagon] German Car Company)
DP	Displaced Persons
DSCC	Defense Supply Center, Columbus
DUKW "Duck"	six-wheeled, amphibious truck, US Army (no actual abbreviation but based on letter designation to different types of vehicles as used by General Motors)
ETOUSA	European Theatre of Operations, US Army

FAB	Freiheits-aktion Bayern ([Freedom Action Bavaria] Bavarian resistance group)
FFI	Forces Françaises de l'Intérieur (French resistance fighters)
G1–G5	US Army units: G-1 (personnel), G-2 (military intelligence), G-3 (operations), G-4 (logistics), G-5 (civil-military operations)
GDR	German Democratic Republic
Gestapo	Geheime Staatspolizei ([Secret State Police] Nazi secret police)
GI	General Infantry
GPU	Gosudarstvennoye politicheskoye upravlenie ([State Political Directorate] Soviet secret police)
HQ	Headquarters
IG	Interessensgemeinschaft (common interest association) or Inspector General (see context for correct application)
K-ration	Combat food ration named for Ancel Keys, who designed it for the US Army
LCI	Landing Craft Infantry
MG	Military Government
MGO	Military Government Official
MHD	Military History Detachments
MP	Military Police
NB	Nota Bene
NKWD	Naródnyy komissariát vnútrennikh del ([People's Commissariat for Internal Affairs] Soviet ministry of the interior)
NS	National Socialist
NSDAP	Nationalsozialistische Deutsche Arbeiter Partei (National Socialist German Workers' Party)
O5	O+5th letter of the alphabet: E = OE = Ö for Österreich ([Austria] Austrian resistance group)

OCS	Officer Candidate School
o.d.	off duty
PG/Pg.	Parteigenosse (party comrade) euphemism for member of the NSDAP
Pro-station	Prophylaxis Station (US Army Facilities to test for VDs)
PW/PoW	Prisoner of War
PWB	Psychological War Branch (British and US Army joint division)
PX	Post Exchange Store
RCA	Radio Corporation of America (US Electronics Corporation)
SD	Sicherheitsdienst ([security service] intelligence agency of the SS)
SHAEF	Supreme Headquarters Allied Expeditionary Force
SS	Schutzstaffel ([protection squad] NS paramilitary organization)
T-Force	Target Force
UNRRA	United Nations Relief and Rehabilitation Administration
USO	United Service Organizations
V-mail	Victory Mail
V-Mann	Verbindungs-Mann (informant)
VD	Venereal Disease
WAC	Women's Army Corps

Introduction

Journal of a Conscript

Charlotte A. Lerg and Maren Roth

FIRST INDORSEMENT. JOURNAL OF A CONSCRIPT—in 1945, twenty-five-year-old Melvin J. Lasky boldly inscribed these words on the cover of his 250-page typescript.[1] Lasky began his diary on 22 January 1945 in Fort Totten, New York while waiting to be shipped to Europe with the US Army, and concluded it in Frankfurt, Germany almost a year later, on 19 December 1945. He chronicled his time as an American GI en route to, and into Germany, filling page after page with the narrowly spaced text of his Army-issued typewriter. However, what may once have been the ambitious book project of a young aspiring author and intellectual, was left unpublished and soon forgotten. A brief excerpt appeared in the left-leaning intellectual magazine *Common Sense* in June 1945, which seems to have been the only instance of any part of the diary being published at the time. Entitled "Travel Diary in Germany," the entries from 7 and 11 April 1945 were printed anonymously—presumably because Lasky feared Army reprimands (Anonymous 1945). Asked to comment on what he thought had been Lasky's plans for the diary, his longtime assistant Marc Svetov replied: "He might've thought he would publish [it], but I think events just transpired, and he had other ambitions" (Marc Svetov, email message to Maren Roth, 14 May 2015).

After Lasky left the military in 1946, his career picked up, at first gradually and then, starting in 1947, more quickly as events in Allied-occupied Berlin took him on the path that he is best known for today: He was one of the initiators of the Congress for Cultural Freedom (CCF) and became the editor of two highly acclaimed—albeit partially CIA-funded—literary journals; a transatlanticist, liberal anti-communist of the consensus era, and a cultural cold warrior par excellence. In fact, while Lasky features in quite a few studies of the transatlantic intellectual scene of the Cold War, he tends to be a figure on the sidelines, at best pulling strings in the background.[2] While this might indeed have been the role he thrived in, so far, we know little about his mindset and about what shaped his ideas and his identity.[3] To understand Lasky's career, his views on Germany, the United States, and transatlantic relations, reading his war diary is highly instructive. Sociologist Daniel Bell once remarked that his longtime friend Melvin J. Lasky always remained but a "visiting member" among the so-called New York intellectuals. He went to Europe and stayed there—that made all the difference (Bell 2010, 45).

Content and Themes

Written on the verge of the most politically active phase of his life, Lasky's 1945 diary illustrates formative moments and reveals personal insights into the mindset of a young man who was convinced of his own intellectual potential, but not quite sure yet how best to put it to use. The diary gives a first glimpse of the political and cultural views he would go on to assert. They emerge from his prewar youth and education, his social milieu, and his political conditioning, mostly in New York City, complemented by the experiences he gathered while serving with the US Army. As Michael Kimmage shows in his contribution to this volume: the diary clearly "bears the New York intellectuals' stamp," and a personal "trajectory" to that effect appeared to be already in place when Second Lieutenant Lasky embarked for Europe in 1945: "'America' discovering 'Russia' was a precious spectacle!" he reports from Berlin to his mentor Dwight Macdonald. At the same time, the experience of the war, specifically the experience of being part of the occupation forces, clearly impacted his commitment to Europe in general, and to Germany in particular. The diary enables us to see this pivotal development unfold. Lasky also filled his journal with literary allusions and remarks, leaving us a record of his personal cultural frame of reference. The everyday encounters, reflections, and emotions Lasky consigned to the page become, as George Blaustein puts it in his chapter, "the precondition for the postwar transatlantic exchanges."

Beyond the persona the author was to become, Lasky's diary also speaks to us on a different level. His particular positioning renders his text a multifaceted hybrid, composed by a somewhat reluctant soldier, who, on the one hand was a committed American and on the other hand, self-consciously strove for intellectualism and a transcendent notion of European culture. From this vantage point, Lasky offers unabashed observations of military life, the occupation, and views on victory and defeat that run much deeper than what we find in the average soldier's ego-documents.[4] Jana Aresin's chapter places Lasky's evaluations in the larger context of debates on denazification and early reeducation. She shows how he acutely identified key problems and predicaments.

The curiosity and journalistic ambitions that drove Lasky in his explorations of a world in the last throws of a world war had an official dimension as well. As a trained historian, he had managed to secure a position within the Army's Historical Branch. He thus had the access, the freedom, and the gear (typewriter, camera) necessary for in-depth assessments and investigations of his surroundings. He spoke a good amount of German, which also set him apart from many of his peers. Availing himself of these opportunities to explore and investigate his surroundings, he accompanied his observations with a reflective commentary in his diary on historiography and documentary method.

For all his critical ruminations and insightful observations, however, Lasky was also a young man, abroad for the first time, in the company of other young men. "We would be tourist-conquerors," he observed poignantly as they entered Heidelberg in April 1945. The men seem constantly caught between the thrill of adventure and the deeply distressing realities of war and destruction. In this respect, the diary presents a much more unmediated account of the experiences and encounters. Moods and tone change throughout the document, sometimes suddenly. Tales of juvenile antics and sexual exploits are followed by melancholy descriptions of cities reduced to rubble or profound reflection about the fate and guilt of the German people. This affective dimension of the document adds a further layer to the diary as a rich source for examining the cultural history of the immediate postwar moment. In that vein, Katharina Gerund's chapter explores the deeply gendered nature of the text. She flags the distinct "male gaze" of the composition and traces the various manifestations of military masculinity both in actual everyday practices as well as on the meta level, where war-torn Europe appears feminized.

Melvin J. Lasky's war diary can be read from many different perspectives and with numerous research interests in mind. From military history to cultural studies, from literary criticism to historiography, it presents the reader with material for a plethora of possible approaches. The accompanying essays open up the most prominent of these dimensions. They invite readers to focus on individual aspects while guiding students towards different methodologies and interpretations. Scholars of both World War II and the Cold War can find cues in the document, as well as historians of cultural diplomacy, reconstruction, or gender, and those studying transatlantic relations and the emergence of the so-called American Empire. Overall, because of Lasky's individual biography, this diary compellingly illustrates the historical moment when World War II slowly transformed into the Cold War. It sheds light on the close ties between the United States' experience of fighting Nazism, the complex occupation policies, and the emerging cultural imaginaries that shaped the second half of the twentieth century.

Publication History and Editing Process

For almost sixty years no one knew about the war diary. It was discovered only after Lasky's death on 19 May 2004, when his assistant Marc Svetov, while organizing and sorting through Lasky's papers, unexpectedly found it in three neatly stacked ring binders "hidden ... behind the closed doors of the bookcase" (Marc Svetov, email message to Maren Roth, 22 May 2018). In a report for the family on what he had found, Svetov noted his enthusiasm about this "historical and literary document worth having in print."[5] There were some aspects he felt needed editing and amending, for example, "where Mel generalizes too much in a pompous manner and appears too vain for a reader's comfort."[6] He also pointed out that, to him, Lasky at times presented the German viewpoint almost too apologetically, a position that he did not find very comprehensible for an American Jew who throughout his diary, time and again, emotionally commented on the suffering of the Jews during the Holocaust as well as on their difficult postwar situation. The typescript shows signs of a first editorial process, undertaken by Svetov, who indicated passages to be left out or explanatory information to be added. However, nothing came of it until 2007, when a few short excerpts appeared in the journal of the Berlin-based American Academy (Lasky 2007). Seven years later, a friend of the family, Professor Emeritus of Ancient History Wolfgang Schuller (1935–2020), edited a much-abridged version of the diary to appear in translation for a German readership (Lasky 2014). It was geared towards, and emphatically resonated with, the generation who, like Schuller himself, had lived through the time, growing up as children in the rubble. One of them, born in 1931, penned a moving personal response to Schuller: he had felt "truly touched and comforted" by the way Lasky had "navigated his way through hatred, rubble, war, precondition and personal experience," guided by what the writer of the letter deemed a well-calibrated *Menschlichkeitskompaß* (humanitarian compass) (Letter to Wolfgang Schuller, 23 March 2015 and kindly forwarded to Maren Roth, 2 April 2015). The book was positively reviewed in all major German newspapers.[7] These reactions hint at a further dimension that documents such as this war diary can have—as catalysts of personal and public memory, as they become part of a larger narrative (Sollors 2014).

The task of editing the full original English version of the text for both an academic readership and an interested public fell to the Lasky Center for Transatlantic Studies in Munich. This is where the original diary ended up as part of Lasky's personal papers, which were donated to Ludwig Maximilian University in 2008.

The original typescript was first transcribed and furnished with basic *annotations*, which included identification of names and places as well as deciphered military language and other colloquialisms and common abbreviations.[8] Information regarding names and contexts directly relevant to the events described in the diary are referenced in the endnotes. The numerous, often casual cultural references, especially from literature, historiography, and art, have been indexed and listed in appendices A and B. The compilation of such a separate collection of cultural references drawn from the text provides an interesting overview and affords added attention to the cultural framework at play.

The diary reflects the many uncertainties and insecurities of the time. This ought to be kept in mind when reading the primary text. Not everything Lasky observed, inferred, or speculated, proved correct later on; a considerable amount of the information he relates is based on hearsay. This incompleteness of knowledge available at the time is an essential and characteristic element of the original text. Thus, in-text annotations have been kept to a minimum. People and historical circumstances directly relevant to the events unfolding in the main text are explained in the endnotes, though hearsay and conjecture remain without comment. The accompanying chapters provide explanations of the larger historical contexts. The decision to keep interspersed foreign language terms and sentences without translation also highlights the aim to retain the original character of the document and the way it captures the polyphone confusion and chaos of that particular historical moment.

We present the document as completely as possible, though in order to keep the manuscript to a publishable length, some cuts had to be made. Places in the text where sections have been omitted are indicated by ellipses in square brackets. Any parentheses or ellipses without brackets are part of the historical text. Marc Svetov's original order has helped tremendously in compiling the manuscript. It provided a preliminary pagination and separated diary text from letters that had been mixed in with the material. Some letters remain, though, as occasionally Lasky used his diary to draft letters.

The *parameters for abridging* the text have been determined with readability, relevance, and consistency in mind. They are as follows:

- Lengthy citations from literature or newspapers, copied verbatim from books, some of them in German, have been cut.
- Sections that were clearly drafts for other texts (with the exception of some letters) were cut, along with unclear, mostly incomprehensible notes, jotted down for later use. The subject matter of these notes is generally covered in the text a few pages later.
- Some cuts were made on scenes that proved repetitive when considered in the context of the diary as a whole.
- One larger section describing a tour of the Scandinavian countries between 5 and 11 October has been taken out completely. While it would

have been valuable to keep, it constitutes the largest self-contained section that made sense to cut without losing the coherence of the narrative. Some later references to the trip remain.

In the interest of smoother reading, the following *formatting measures* have been applied:

- Dates are rendered in a uniform format: day month year (+ place where the information was available)
- Abbreviations are standardized and explained in a separate list.
- Any words and sentences in foreign languages (mostly German, some French, Russian, etc.) are left in the original without translation and are italicized. Lasky uses both, anglicized and local spellings for place names. This inconsistency has been maintained on purpose.
- Titles of books, songs, plays, etc., are italicized. As some references are rough or incomplete, full titles and publication dates are listed alphabetically in Appendix A.
- Obvious grammatical errors and typos are corrected tacitly, except for purposefully capitalized words (e.g., War, History, They). These are kept in the original form to allow for the added layer of meaning Lasky implied. Words spelled incorrectly to highlight a certain accent or dialect are also left untouched to preserve the authenticity of the text. For the same reason, racial slurs and curse words have not been expunged.

The complete original typescript as well as a full transcript are available for researchers at the Lasky Center for Transatlantic Studies, Munich.

Acknowledgments

Over the course of the editing process, we have received invaluable assistance from a number of colleagues. We would like to particularly thank Pavla Šimková (Munich) for diligently overseeing the transcription process. She also competently led a group of students who helped with background research for the project. Fred Reuss (Washington, DC) has been kind enough to proofread the first version of the transcribed typescript. Thank you also to Erica Lansberg (Lehigh Valley, PA) who with great diligence has been an immense help in preparing the original document for publication and to Benedikt Kastner (Munich) for assisting in the formatting of the contextual chapters. The chapter contributors have shown great patience and we are truly grateful for their time and insight. Moreover, we would like to extend our gratitude to the two anonymous peer reviewers for their constructive criticism and to Amanda Horn and Elizabeth Martinez at Berghahn Books (New York). Finally, we are indebted to Christof Mauch (Munich), who put this project on track.

Charlotte A. Lerg, Assistant Professor of American history at Ludwig-Maximilians-University, Munich), is Managing Director of the Lasky Center for Transatlantic Studies. She is a board member of the Bavarian American Academy, has held research fellowships at the Library of Congress as well as at the German Historical Institute (Washington, DC), and has taught at the universities of Münster, Jena, and Bochum. Recent publications include *Universitätsdiplomatie* (2019) and *Campaigning Culture* (2017) edited with Giles Scott-Smith. Lerg is also co-editor of the series *History of Intellectual Culture (HIC): International Yearbook of Knowledge and Society*.

Maren Roth is Research Associate and Director of the Lasky archive at the Lasky Center for Transatlantic Studies. She has been awarded research fellowships by the Bavarian American Academy as well as the Gerda Henkel Foundation and has taught at the universities of Munich and Augsburg. Publications include *Erziehung zur Demokratie. Amerikanische Demokratisierungshilfe im postsozialistischen Bulgarien* (2005) and *Cold War Politics. Melvin J. Lasky. New York—Berlin—London* (with Charlotte A. Lerg, 2010). Roth is currently writing a biography of Lasky's early years.

Notes

1. Cf. Melvin J. Lasky, "'First Indorsement' Journal of a Conscript," Melvin J. Lasky Papers, Lasky Center for Transatlantic Studies, Munich (subsequently quoted as Lasky Papers), New York Box 1, Folder 1.

2. For a general impression of Lasky's public image see for example his *New York Times* obituary ("Melvin J. Lasky, Cultural Cold Warrior" 2004). See also: Hochgeschwender 1998; Scott-Smith 2002; Scott-Smith and Lerg 2017. For a publication that focuses exclusively on the connections to the CIA, but at times jumps to conclusions, see Saunders 1999. For an overview of the research on the issue see Pullin 2013.

3. Maren Roth is currently working on a biography of Lasky's early life. For a first look see for example, Roth 2014.

4. Among the soldiers' diaries and memoirs of World War II appear military leaders like George Patton (Patton 1947) as well as lesser-known names (e.g., Tomikel 2000). Most examples are edited collections of various shorter accounts (e.g., Wallis and Palmer 2009; Miller and Miller 2016). There is only one other diary comparable to Lasky's in that it was also written by a combat historian (Pogue 2001).

5. Marc Svetov, Comment on "Melvin Lasky's Diary of a Conscript 1945–1946," 23 January 2005, Lasky Papers, New York Box 1, Folder 1.

6. Ibid.

7. Reviews in *Jüdische Allgemeine*, *Frankfurter Allgemeine Zeitung*, *Nürnberger Nachrichten*, *Neue Zürcher Zeitung*, *Die Welt*, and *Süddeutsche Zeitung*.

8. Full names and ranks of Lasky's fellow soldiers in the 7th Army Information and Historical Section are taken from the listing in ETOUSA Historical Division Records 1941–46. NARA Record Group 498 File No. 161. See Appendix C for a full list.

References

Anonymous. 1945. "Travel Diary in Germany." *Common Sense* (June): 32–33.

Bell, Daniel. 2010. "Mel." In *Cold War Politics. Melvin J. Lasky: New York—Berlin—London*, ed. Charlotte A. Lerg and Maren Roth, 45–47. Munich: Lasky Center for Transatlantic Studies.

Hochgeschwender, Michael. 1998. *Freiheit in Der Offensive? Der Kongress für Kulturelle Freiheit und die Deutschen*. München: Oldenbourg.

Lasky, Melvin J. 2007. "Military History Stood on Its Head: From the Lasky War Diary." *The Berlin Journal: A Magazine from the American Academy in Berlin* 14 (Spring): 22–29.

———. 2014. *Und alles war still. Deutsches Tagebuch 1945*. Edited by Wolfgang Schuller. Berlin: Rowohlt.

Miller, Myra, and Marshall Miller, eds. 2016. *Soldiers' Stories: A Collection of WWII Memoirs*. Riverton, UT: Book Wise Publishing.

New York Times. 2004. "Melvin J. Lasky, Cultural Cold Warrior, Is Dead at 84." 22 May 2004, Section B, 16.

Patton, George S., Jr. 1947. *War as I Knew It*. Boston: Houghton Mifflin Company.

Pogue, Forrest C. 2001. *Pogue's War: Diaries of a WW II Combat Historian*. Lexington: University Press of Kentucky.

Pullin, Eric. 2013. "The Culture of Funding Culture: The CIA and the Congress for Cultural Freedom." In *Intelligence Studies in Britain and the US: Historiography since 1945*, ed. Christopher R. Moran and Christopher J. Murphy, 47–64. Edinburgh: Edinburgh University Press.

Roth, Maren. 2014. "'In einem Vorleben war ich Europäer.' Melvin J. Lasky als transatlantischer Mittler im kulturellen Kalten Krieg." *Jahrbuch für Historische Kommunismusforschung*: 139–56.

Saunders, Frances Stonor. 1999. *Who Paid the Piper? The CIA and the Cultural Cold War*. London: Granta Books.

Scott-Smith, Giles. 2002. *The Politics of Apolitical Culture: The Congress for Cultural Freedom and the Political Economy of American Hegemony 1945–1955*. London: Routledge.

Scott-Smith, Giles, and Charlotte A. Lerg, eds. 2017. *Campaigning Culture and the Global Cold War: The Journals of the Congress for Cultural Freedom*. London: Palgrave Macmillan.

Sollors, Werner. 2014. *The Temptation of Despair: Tales of the 1940s*. Cambridge, MA: Harvard University Press.

Tomikel, John. 2000. *Diary of a Soldier During the Occupation of Germany Shortly After World War II*. Corry: Allegheny Press.

Wallis, Sarah, and Svetlana Palmer, eds. 2009. *We Were Young and at War: The First-hand Story of Young Lives Lived and Lost in World War II*. New York: Harper Collins.

Chapter 1
Melvin J. Lasky's Biography and Diary
Maren Roth

I feel that I must, out of a slowly growing inner need, write something about the *Life of a Conscript* some day . . .
—Melvin J. Lasky

Melvin J. Lasky was born Matthes Jonah Chernilowsky on 15 January 1920, the son of Polish Jews who had immigrated from Łódź to New York City around 1910. He lived in the Bronx with his parents Samuel and Esther, who were the owners of a small garment factory in lower Manhattan, as well as with his younger sisters Floria and Joyce. In the early 1920s the family decided to change its name from Chernilowsky to the shorter and less complicated Lasky (Joyce Lasky Reed, email message to author, 29 June 2009). Growing up in the 1920s and 1930s, Lasky's childhood and youth were shaped by three influential factors that governed his family's life (author's interviews with Oliver Lasky, 7 May 2009 in Munich and with Vivienne Freeman Lasky, 13 March 2011 in Providence, Rhode Island). The first one was the central role assigned to reading books and various newspapers, most importantly the *New York Times*. Secondly, there were the discussions that the family used to have with members of the extended family, which could become quite heated. During these discussions, the family would debate not only the latest developments in American domestic politics but also political developments overseas, especially in Europe. Thirdly, Lasky's socialization was influenced by the high esteem the family had of the German language and German culture in general. His father kept classical works of German literature in the original language in the family library and was well versed in Goethe's dramas and Wagner's operas. "My father," Lasky's sister Joyce remembered, "was a great lover of German culture . . . was one of the rare Jews that never held naziism [*sic*] against German culture" (author's interview with Joyce Lasky Reed, 18 March 2009 in Chevy Chase, Maryland). These early influences, intellectual stimulation, and the importance his parents placed upon the education and social advancement of all of their children, suited the character and interests of young Lasky quite well.

As Lasky was curious, eager for knowledge, and ambitious from an early age, he was fascinated by books and people alike. His interests were numerous and manifold, ranging from history, politics, and literature to theatre, classical music, and movies as well as various sports. Judging from the diaries that he started to keep in May 1939, Lasky spent a vast amount of time reading through a wide range of both American and European literature. He was extremely driven in his reading; at one point in his diary, for example, he jotted down: "must read like a machine."[1] He also commented on many of the books by way of one to three line mini reviews, where he could be merciless in his criticism or full of praise. In addition to books, he also had the habit of reading various newspapers, sometimes even a German newspaper. Trotskyist-leaning magazines such as the *Socialist Appeal*, *Labor Action*, and the *New International* as well as literary intellectual magazines such as *Partisan Review* and the *New Republic* rounded off his extensive reading. What Lasky liked to do when he was not reading, writing, or going to the movies was meeting people and having intensive discussions. He often attended lectures by intellectuals and academics such as John Dewey, Sidney Hook, and Lionel Trilling. In the subsequent discussions, Lasky would make critical comments and try to meet these renowned people. On occasions like these, but also at numerous parties hosted by his friends, his fellow students, or people associated with the magazine *Partisan Review* like Dwight Macdonald or James T. Farrell, Lasky began to form a network of contacts that he would expand over time and fall back on, especially during his early years living in Berlin. As his own writings and interviews with family members and other contemporary witnesses show, Lasky appears to be a socially active and caring person, hardworking, knowledgeable, keen to debate, outspoken, and of an independent mind. At the same time, he seems to have been very sure of himself, dominating, opinionated, and incredibly ambitious.

While Lasky always wanted to write, review, and thereby participate in intellectual discussions, for a long time he felt torn between the idea of doing this as a historian or as a journalist for an intellectual magazine. Even though he eventually opted for the latter, his deep-rooted interest in history never dwindled. His first experiences as a journalist date back to his time as a student at DeWitt Clinton High School in New York, where he wrote for the school newspaper and, as he later remembered, was "equipped with the elementary journalistic rules of how to write a lead . . . , and where to cut a story" (Lasky 2002, xix). After obtaining his high school diploma in June 1935, he enrolled as a student at the City College of New York, a renowned tuition-free university and very popular among the sons of Jewish immigrants. During his four years as an undergraduate student in the social sciences he continued his

German language training and took quite a few classes in German literature. In addition to his academic studies, he actively participated in heated political discussions and fights that took place between the famous Alcoves One and Two, little niches in the university cafeteria. While the Stalinist students met in Alcove Two, a much smaller number of supporters of anti-Stalinist groups such as the Social Democrats or the Trotskyists that Lasky strongly sympathized with gathered in Alcove One (author's interview with Nathan Glick, 16 March 2009 in Arlington, Virginia and with Daniel Bell, 10 November 2009 in Cambridge, Massachusetts). It was in this atmosphere that Lasky became acquainted with the anti-Stalinist New York intellectuals. Not only was he invited to their parties, but starting in 1938, he also wrote his first reviews and articles for *Partisan Review*, the intellectual organ of the anti-Stalinist left. The social critic, author, and editor Dwight Macdonald, at the time the editor of *Partisan Review*, became a role model and mentor for Lasky, who would write long, emotional, and very personal letters to Macdonald describing his plans for the future as well as his personal experiences as a graduate student and later as a soldier in World War II.

In September 1939, Lasky enrolled in the master's program in American History at the University of Michigan in Ann Arbor and thus left New York and his family for the first time in his life. He continued to be politically active, regularly participated in student discussions, and even displayed a certain missionary zeal in trying to, as he himself put it, "bring them [Stalinist fellow travelers] around" and win them over to the Trotskyist camp.[2] Returning to New York in the summer of 1940, Lasky resumed the immensely dynamic social and intellectual life he had led before he left for Ann Arbor. He started to submit reviews and articles not only to *Partisan Review* but also to magazines such as the *New Republic* and the *American Sociological Review*. Every time a piece was accepted or his name was mentioned anywhere, he enthusiastically noted it in his diary. With a mounting restlessness, he wondered when his career would eventually start. At one point he wrote despairingly: "What's to become of me? My own 'wave of the future' has turned into an 'ebb-tide.'"[3] And a couple of weeks later, when a publisher reacted positively to a book project, he euphorically jotted down: "Can this be it? Is this the 'break'?"[4] With a prospective teaching position at City College and registered as a PhD student at Columbia University, Lasky most likely was aiming at a university career. However, economic circumstances forced him to take up a job as "Junior Historical Archivist" at the Statue of Liberty. Hating the work routine that prevented him from pursuing his own research, writing, and, most of all, fulfilling his dream of publishing his own "cultural review," he was more than delighted when in late 1942 Daniel Bell offered him a job as an editor at the *New Leader*, a Socialist democratic weekly.[5]

It was around this time that Lasky started to break away from Trotskyism, a development that can be traced both in his contemporary and in his later autobiographical writings. The war in Europe, the development of which Lasky followed very closely, had a major influence on his political thinking and beliefs. The dramatic events unfolding in Europe and especially the fate of the Jews eventually led him to gradually abandon his radical beliefs and to give up his adamant opposition to the US's entry into the war in favor of a position of "critical support" of the American government. After the United States actually entered into the war in December 1941, he increasingly distanced himself from his prior Trotskyist sympathies.[6] So when a year later his first and long-awaited career move was imminent, two major turning points in his life coincided, an ideological reorientation and a new professional beginning: "As something of a Social Democrat I joined Danny Bell on *The New Leader*, and never looked back."[7] But as the war had already started and not only his predecessor at the *New Leader* but also many of his friends had already been drafted, he was quite aware that he might not have too much time to learn the ropes of this business.[8]

On 30 November 1943, he was in fact drafted. For over a year he was trained in various US Army camps and prepared for his eventual position as a combat historian in Europe. Starting on the day of his induction, Lasky used a new notebook for his diary entries. Most likely, he did this for pragmatic reasons and not with the intention of marking the beginning of a new period in his life. It is striking, though, how this third diary clearly differs from the two previous ones. While he had very regularly recorded the events in his daily life and his thoughts in short sentences or in note form in the diaries he had kept in New York and Ann Arbor, the entries in his third diary were very irregular and mostly lacked a date. Since the tight schedule at the training camp apparently did not allow for much free time, the entries he eventually composed were much longer and more elaborate. In full sentences, he reflected on and described his daily routine and—with a mixture of indifference, disgust, and amusement—commented on army life. Far away from his family and his usual intellectual circles, he suffered immensely. To escape, in his view, the "endless, unutterable, incomprehensible stupidity," the dehumanization, and what he perceived as a lack of intellectuality in the army, he tried to read as much as he could and next to his recordings of the daily routine also composed little stories about his superiors and his fellow GIs.[9] This diary can be seen as the precursor of the war diary, not only because it covered the period until right before he was sent overseas, but especially due to its content, format, and writing style.

At Camp Lee in Virginia, Lasky managed to qualify for a course at the Quartermaster Corps Officer Candidate School and was subsequently promoted to second lieutenant.[10] Thanks to recommendations by renowned professors, he was then transferred to the Historical Branch, G-2 in the War Department in Washington, DC. Thus, on 27 October 1944, he took up his new assignment as a combat historian in the research department of the Historical Section of the Seventh US Army. Three months later, Lasky was shipped overseas and on 7 February 1945, arrived at the European headquarters of the Seventh Army in Lunéville, a small town thirty kilometers southwest of Nancy. His unit was "attached to the Seventh Army for the purpose of compiling the historical data for the Army and writing the After Action Report of the operation" (Army of the United States 1946, preface). Lasky later described his work assignment as "Historical Officer" as follows: "I was issued a Leica camera and a Smith-Corona portable typewriter ...; and we were instructed to prepare for the final offensive against Hitler which would liberate Strasbourg and therewith the whole of France. The subsequent crossing of the Rhine was to initiate the last offensive against the Nazis' so-called Third Reich and begin the victorious occupation of post-Hitler Germany" (Lasky 2005, 273). To write his own reports, Lasky had to read the combat reports of the various units that had participated in a battle, visit the scenes of combat and, most importantly, interview the troops and officers involved. Because combat historians could move around with more liberty and had to plan and coordinate their work themselves, they had—at least in contrast to the fighting troops—a great measure of freedom in the respective theater of operations (Pogue 2001, 102). This kind of leeway enabled Lasky to explore the area he was based in, to visit neighboring cities, and also to talk to the civilians he would encounter. These little ventures allowed him to pursue his personal interests while at the same time fulfilling his duties as a combat historian. In addition, he apparently also found enough spare time to resume a habit that he had suspended for eight months during his course at the Quartermaster Corps and the subsequent service in the G-2 Historical Branch: the keeping of a diary.

The Diary: "'First Indorsement' Journal of a Conscript"

A few months before Lasky began to keep his war diary, he had already deeply felt the need to put down his thoughts in writing once again to cope with his situation and, most of all, to compensate for the intellectual frustration he felt about being in the army. In a letter to his former mentor, Columbia University professor and historian, Merle Curti, which he mailed just a few days after he had been transferred to Washington, DC, he explained his diary project as follows: "I've done almost no writing ... and only a little notetaking. I feel that I must, out of a slowly growing inner need, write something about the Life of a Conscript some day—but what its form or controlling intention will be I'm yet in no position to say."[11] It was only because of the specific circumstances of Lasky's assignment in Europe that he was able to actually realize this ambitious project. First of all, combat historians could move around and plan their activities comparatively freely. Second, Lasky could plan his official duties in a way that would leave him enough spare time for regularly composing his diary entries. And, third, with the typewriter he had been given for typing his official reports, Lasky was perfectly equipped for his private writing and notetaking. He would regularly send carbon copies of these entries to his family, friends, and intellectual contacts back home in the US. Since he did not always have sufficient time to write individual letters, he—as he explained to Dwight Macdonald in April 1945—considered "the journal [as] my substitute for correspondence."[12]

The first 250 pages of Lasky's journal dating from 26 January 1945 to 19 December 1945, form a diary in a narrow sense. They contain dated and very regular entries of several pages each and at times also drafts of letters and copies of letters that are inserted in chronological order. Some of the single-spaced pages of the typescript include corrections in Lasky's handwriting; in some cases, more than one carbon copy of a particular page has been preserved. After these 250 pages of "real" diary follow ninety-eight pages that include observations and comments on the political, economic, and cultural developments in occupied Germany and other European countries. These were compiled after Lasky had been demobilized in July 1946. The entries after 19 December 1945 were mostly in the form of jotted notes, letters, interview notes, travel reports, drafts, and final versions of articles. Only rarely can a dated diary entry be found. The very last entry is dated 21 November 1946 and was written by Lasky in London where he was waiting for his transatlantic passage back to New York. At this point, he did not know that only a few months later he would come back to Berlin and eventually spend the rest of his life in Europe. Therefore, his journal, i.e., both the diary and the subsequent collection of notes and materials, completely covers—as he himself called it in a letter to Hannah Arendt—the "unbelievable unreal adventure" that he experienced in Europe during the war as well as some time after.[13]

The diary entries during the war follow the movements of his unit in the Seventh Army. After the end of the war, the entries correspond with the respective changes of location that his subsequent job as a combat historian required. On the cover page of the journal, Lasky put down all the major cities and places he had passed through or visited on his way to and while in Europe. These were in the following order: Washington, New York, New Foundland [*sic*], Azores, Scotland, Paris, Lunéville, Alsace, Strasbourg, Nancy, Kaiserslautern, Darmstadt, Frankfurt, Heidelberg, Munich, Salzburg, Innsbruck, Constance, Berne, Geneva, Zurich, Vienna, Rome, Copenhagen, Stockholm, Berlin, and London. Again, his official duty as a combat historian was to write reports that were to be part of the official history of the Seventh US Army. This three-volume history entitled *The Seventh Army in France and Germany 1944–1945: Report of Operations* was published in May 1946. From the start of the occupation, as a historical officer in the United States Forces European Theater Historical Division based in Frankfurt, Lasky was charged with researching and writing a "History of the Occupation."[14] In contrast to his official work assignments, which he viewed very critically and fulfilled unenthusiastically, he put a lot of effort into keeping his private records. In a letter, Lasky summed up his general approach and his journal's contents as follows:

> I have tried to keep a daily journal, and for the last period I've been quite happy about it. It has no "tone," or "style" or "theme" or anything of that character, has nothing in fact except a fantastic variety of impressions and information—everything from American brothels, to battlefield scenes, to university libraries and ancient cathedrals and castles, to a number of rather "delicate" military-political situations, which unfortunately will remain censorable for a long time to come.[15]

His detailed notes provide a very good overview of Lasky's activities and daily life as a soldier and indeed include a great variety of topics. He reports on his work, his fellow GIs, and his superiors. He is often quite critical about the activities of the US Army and later the American occupational authorities. He describes the cities he passes through, the ruins, and the people he meets on the streets. Often, he would talk to civilians about their experiences during and after the war and would try to capture their views and moods. In the devastated city centers, he intuitively would head for the historic sites as well as to libraries and bookstores. By documenting his impressions with the Leica camera that he had been provided with, he essentially created illustrations for his diary entries. These reportage-style entries clearly show Lasky's experience with journalistic writing. They reveal not only his views on the events transpiring around him but also his moods and emotions. He wrote at one point that he sometimes could hardly put down his experiences in writing, and considering what he had seen and experienced raises the question of what effect his war experience might eventually have had on his personal development.

Without discussing the diary's contents in detail, one aspect must be mentioned, because in a way, it can serve as a link between Lasky's interest in German history and culture before he went overseas and his later activities in postwar Germany. In his diary, Lasky not only commented elaborately on the devastated German cities and the general political and economic situation during and after the war, he was also very eager to substantiate his impressions by talking directly to local people. It is striking that as an American Jew who had lost members of his extended family in Łódź during the Holocaust and who had passed through various liberated concentration camps when entering Germany, Lasky had a fundamentally positive and open attitude toward Germans. Despite the strict military order of absolute nonfraternization with the German people, i.e., no shaking of hands and no talking, he had long conversations with Germans of all age groups and social classes, meticulously recording what they told him about their experience during the war and their current situation. How moved he was by these conversations and also how hopeful and optimistic he still felt about Germany's future is documented in a letter to Dwight Macdonald written just a few days before the war ended:

> There was a doctor in Frankfurt who helped me find the old museum at Goethe's birthplace ... ; for an hour on the rubble we talked, and his earnestness and passion (and broken heart) touched me more than perhaps anything I have ever known. But then he was something of a political or developed person. There were two simple fellows in Darmstadt who understood little beyond the outline and substance of the events which had rained in on them; but the events themselves had been instructive and tragic enough. Even they, non-Nazi and petty-bourgeois, left me full of hope—not perhaps for a new Germany or a healthier European order, but for something much more practical and even immediate: a returning sense of the dignity of people, of the independence and honesty and character of a human being.[16]

In addition to Goethe's birthplace and museum, he visited—equipped with a *Baedeker* guide and almost as if on a "Grand Tour"—a multitude of historic and cultural monuments and sites such as the festival theater in Oberammergau, the Fugger houses in Augsburg, and Linderhof Palace. While traveling throughout Germany, Lasky also tried to get in touch and meet with German writers, intellectuals, and other renowned individuals whose works he partly had already read in New York (Jaesrich 1985, 17). These endeavors are proof of Lasky's strong desire to expand the number of contacts he had and thus to grow his personal and intellectual network from the US to Europe. These transatlantic networks formed the basis for Lasky's later activities in the context of the cultural Cold War, at first in Berlin as the founder of the intellectual magazine *Der Monat* and the cofounder of the anti-communist Congress for Cultural Freedom (CCF), and then in London starting in 1958 as editor of the CCF-financed intellectual magazine *Encounter* (Lerg and Roth 2010).

Comments on the War Diary as a Source

Lasky's war diary as a stand-alone source turns out to be a truly fascinating historic document. Due to its mix of both sober descriptions and emotional comments, the reader learns a great deal about the daily life of an American GI, including the work routine of a combat historian and historical officer both during and after World War II. Some of the content, such as the description of conflicts with and between fellow GIs and their superiors, as well as the accounts of encounters and affairs with local women, might be typical for a diary of this genre. But since Lasky—even when he at times sounds quite precocious and schoolmasterly—was a very well-read, curious, critical, and, most of all, eloquent observer, the diary moreover offers very interesting and new insights into German postwar life. His in part harsh criticism of the American and Soviet military governments, the detailed retelling of his conversations with local people of all ages and walks of life, and the description of his meetings with intellectuals such as Karl Jaspers can serve as good examples for the specific approach Lasky took in writing his diary. This approach is one of the main differences between Lasky's diary and that of Forrest Pogue, who also served as a combat historian with the Third US Army and recorded his experiences from his shipment overseas in March 1944 until the end of the war in May 1945. Pogue, born in 1912 and in his civilian life a professor of history at Murray State Teacher College in Kentucky, saw himself primarily as an accurate chronicler of events taking place around him (Pogue 2001). In a very sober style, Pogue wrote about his experiences at or near the front line, which sometimes included combat operations, but mostly detailed the processes and challenges of his work as a combat historian. Even though there was occasionally a personal note to his records, Pogue was clearly focused on chronicling the events in his immediate environment and the direct context of the war (Pogue 2001, 51, 147, 216). Lasky at no point in his diary aimed at being this type of accurate chronicler. While he does write about his work and daily routine, he—diametrically opposed to Pogue—always put forward his personal view and opinion on whatever he saw and experienced. Hence, he seems to have been emotionally affected and involved to a much higher degree.

Another dimension of Lasky's diary grows clear when viewing it not just as a standalone historic document, but when analyzing it in the context of his personal development from before he was sent overseas to his activities in Europe after the end of the war. From this perspective, the diary appears as a kind of hinge that documents the transitional phase between his life in New York and the one in Berlin and in a sense also explains—at least in retrospect—his decision in favor of a transatlantic move. As a combat historian, Lasky was able to combine his interests in history and journalism, interests that he had already pursued long before he was drafted. Even if he eventually opted for a career in journalism, his fundamental interest in history in general as well as his interest in people's specific personal histories can be noticed in all of his notes and publications. The war diary, therefore, is much more than—to quote Lasky once more—a "substitute for correspondence"; it is rather a very extensive exercise in writing or even a raw version of a full-scale manuscript.[17]

Because of the great degree of mobility he was granted for his official research and interviewing, he was able to pursue his private interests along the way. He could satisfy his intellectual curiosity by incessantly establishing contacts with all kinds of people, a habit he had already developed in New York. This way he could gain firsthand insight into the general mood and cultural life in postwar Germany. His basic knowledge of German and his familiarity with German cultural and intellectual history proved to be very helpful in this endeavor. When he, for example, personally explained the current state of the humanities in the US to Karl Jaspers, or in long letters described the situation of cultural life in bombed-out German cities to his friends among the New York intellectuals, he fostered a transatlantic intellectual exchange and acted as an early mediator between the two worlds. To some extent, he was essentially pushed into this role, which can be seen in a letter he wrote to Dwight Macdonald, urgently asking him for help only three months after the end of the war:

> There are no German books, there are no foreign books. What US editions there are over here are all valueless, which means that I spend embarrassing days and nights trying to give overall reviews of the political, literary, philosophical, academic situation in the 30s and 40s, in a stuttering inadequate German.... But the point is, if you can send any materials over whatsoever, they will be very welcome. Old issues of PR [*Partisan Review*] and *Politics*, all kinds of scholarly reviews, what books there may be available. I want of course to write to Meyer Schapiro and/or Sidney Hook and see what organized relations can be set up with respect to the German intelligentsia and American (students) writers.[18]

The war experience represented a very decisive and formative period in Lasky's life on his transatlantic route from New York to Berlin. For Lasky, who already had the habit both of writing and keeping a diary, the war diary became a document of transition. On the one hand it was a vehicle to escape—at least in thought—the intellectually uninspiring military environment, and on the other hand, it served to record his experiences and strong impressions, thus his coming to terms with his emotions. How fundamental and far-reaching these experiences really were is documented in a letter Lasky wrote to Hannah Arendt while recuperating from minor lesions in a Berlin hospital:

Lying in a bed day after day I finally got a glimpse of a perspective of my life this last year. What an unbelievable unreal adventure! I wished so hard I could find powers within me some time to come to terms with my own experience, my own past. And I wondered whether changes in me—really: the way I talk and walk and think and read, the tone of one's ambition, the range of one's confidence and sensitivity—were as deep, as I sometimes, in a fit of autobiographical terror, suspect.[19]

Acknowledgments

Parts of the research for this chapter were graciously supported by the Gerda Henkel Foundation, Düsseldorf.

Maren Roth is Research Associate and Director of the Lasky archive at the Lasky Center for Transatlantic Studies. She has been awarded research fellowships by the Bavarian American Academy as well as the Gerda Henkel Foundation and has taught at the universities of Munich and Augsburg. Publications include *Erziehung zur Demokratie. Amerikanische Demokratisierungshilfe im postsozialistischen Bulgarien* (2005) and *Cold Water Politics. Melvin J. Lasky. New York—Berlin—London* (with Charlotte A. Lerg, 2010). Roth is currently writing a biography of Lasky's early years.

Notes

1. Lasky New York Diary I (8 May 1939–Sept. 1941), 24, Lasky Papers, New York Box 1, Folder 1.
2. Letter from Melvin Lasky to his parents, undated [December 1939?], Lasky Papers, Correspondence before 1945, Samuel and Esther Lasky, Folder 2.
3. Lasky New York Diary I (8 May 1939–Sept. 1941), 73, Lasky Papers, New York Box 1, Folder 1.
4. Lasky New York Diary II (10 October 1941–October 1943), 6, Lasky Papers, New York Box 1, Folder 1.
5. Lasky New York Diary I (8 May 1939–Sept. 1941), 106, Lasky Papers, New York Box 1, Folder 1.
6. Cf. Memo to Michael Allen from Melvin Lasky, 18 May 2004, 16–17, Lasky Papers, Memoirs Box 1, Folder 31.
7. Letter from Melvin Lasky to Alan Wald, 2 December 1982, Lasky Papers, Correspondence Box 10, Folder 20.
8. Lasky New York Diary II (10 October 1941–October 1943), 80, Lasky Papers, New York Box 1, Folder 1.
9. Lasky New York Diary III (30 November 1943–13/14 May 1944), 44, Lasky Papers, New York Box 1, Folder 1.

10. Cf. Diploma of the Quartermaster School at Camp Lee, Virginia for Melvin J. Lasky [undated], Lasky Papers, New York Box 1, Folder 8.

11. Letter from Melvin Lasky to Merle Curti, 31 October 1944, Wisconsin Historical Society, Merle E. Curti Papers, Box 23, Folder 25.

12. Letter from Melvin Lasky to Dwight Macdonald, 8 April 1945, Yale University, Macdonald Papers, MS 730 Box 27, Folder 706.

13. Letter from Melvin Lasky to Hannah Arendt, 30 October 1945, in: Melvin J. Lasky, "'First Indorsement' Journal of a Conscript," 225, Lasky Papers, New York Box 1, Folder 1.

14. Cf. Manuscript dated 11 February 1946 for Lasky's lecture on "Your Sources of Information," held at the "Conference of Historians" of the Historical Division, United States Forces European Theater, 15 February 1946, Lasky Papers, New York Box 1, Folder 11; Letter from Melvin Lasky to Charles A. Pearce, 11 November 1945, in Lasky, "'First Indorsement' Journal of a Conscript." 228.

15. Letter from Melvin Lasky to Dwight Macdonald, 8 April 1945, Yale University, Macdonald Papers, MS 730 Box 27, Folder 706.

16. Letter from Melvin Lasky to Dwight Macdonald, 20 April 1945, in: Melvin J. Lasky, "'First Indorsement' Journal of a Conscript," Lasky Papers, New York Box 1, Folder 1.

17. Letter from Melvin Lasky to Dwight Macdonald, 8 April 1945, Yale University, Macdonald Papers, MS 730 Box 27, Folder 706.

18. Letter from Melvin Lasky to Dwight Macdonald, 31 July 1945, Hannah Arendt Archive, University of Oldenburg (Original in Hannah Arendt Papers, Box 13, Manuscript Division, Library of Congress, Washington, DC). Meyer Shapiro (1904–1996) was a renowned art historian and professor at Columbia University in New York.

19. Letter from Melvin Lasky to Hannah Arendt, 30 October 1945, also part of the diary. See p. 271.

References

Army of the United States. 1946. *The Seventh Army in France and Germany 1944–1945. Report of Operations.* Vol. 1, May 1946. Heidelberg: Aloys Gräf.

Jaesrich, Hellmut. 1985. "Den Großschriftstellern Paroli geboten. Demokrat aus Überzeugung, Berliner aus Leidenschaft—Melvin J. Lasky wird heute 65 Jahre alt." *Die Welt*, 15 January.

Lasky, Melvin J. 2002. *The Language of Journalism. Volume 1: The Newspaper Culture.* New Brunswick: Transaction.

———. 2005. *The Language of Journalism. Volume 3: Media Warfare.* New Brunswick: Transaction.

Lerg, Charlotte A., and Maren Roth, eds. 2010. *Cold War Politics. Melvin J. Lasky. New York—Berlin—London.* Munich: Lasky Center for Transatlantic Studies.

Pogue, Forrest C. 2001. *Pogue's War: Diaries of a WWII Combat Historian.* Lexington: University Press of Kentucky.

Chapter 2

Not a Beginning but an End

Melvin J. Lasky, Diarist

George Blaustein

To bed. Cool night; one blanket.

—Melvin J. Lasky (8 May 1945)

Why read a diary from the past? And why read *this* diary? Maybe we read diaries for their details, the more specific the better. Melvin Lasky's diary of Europe in 1945 abounds with them. "Department and clothing stores had been ransacked of men's suit stock," he notes on 30 March, having recently crossed into Germany. "Empty clothes hangers were everywhere, and German uniforms were found hastily flung all around the rooms." A symbol of retreat? Of defeat? Of guilt? Of how easy it is to change clothes and loyalties? Six weeks earlier, in Strasbourg, there was a "little boy in Münsterplatz, carrying a huge American flag," who "ran along with us and asked for chocolate. I gave him a bar. He took out a small red swastika'd armband and rewarded me with his Hitlerjugend diploma" (18 February). A German boy with American chocolate is a now-familiar image of the American occupation; other details are striking for their incongruity. In the Laufen internment camp near the Austrian border Lasky encounters "'Bobby' Montgomery—a Brooklyn negro entertainer! Captured on tour with his Blackbirds in Copenhagen. Tapdancer [*sic*]. His manager, a Russian, disappeared" (10 May). The war is ending, and Montgomery is "trying to set up shows," working with two "negro boys from Belgium" who, alas, "just ain't got the rhythm, that old Brooklyn bounce!" It turns out that Montgomery had "once put on a show in Hamburg in 1930," Lasky recalls him saying, "me and a Jewish acrobat, and we took over the hall right after a Hitler speech. My dressing room was the one the Führer came out of." These details, whether they vividly confirm our expectations or stand weirdly out, make this diary a rich document for cultural historians.

Or maybe we read diaries to get a feeling of history occurring in real time: historical events we already know, experienced with uncanny newness. "Heard, too, that Mussolini was dead, shot at Como after a trial by partisans, and his body lay in a square in Milan," Lasky writes on 30 April. "So ends Il Duce and his *fascismo*. All the threads of our history seem to be finally rolling themselves on to some spool." Sometimes the revelations come piecemeal, filtered through Lasky's milieu in odd ways. Dachau was liberated on 29 April; the diary first mentions it on 5 May, in passing, when a soldier named Jordan is regaling Lasky with stories: "He was long and eloquent with tales about the tunnels in Nuremberg, and the horrors of Dachau; raiding the Agfa factory for cameras and film equipment; shopping for sardines ... and parachutes; a drunken escapade in Augsburg." Jordan is one of the diary's larger-than-life characters: a Southerner, often drunk, often violent, possibly shellshocked. Lasky finds him entertaining but also fears the damage Jordan will do.

Events unfold in real time as does the language itself. The diary charts changing terms and emerging vocabularies. "Displaced persons" first appears on 30 March, and it is in quotes, like a new phrase. Displaced Persons, capitalized and not in quotes, appears 5 April. By 13 April it is "DPs." Our diarist, wittingly or not, is tracking the fine shifts of a discursive terrain. Survivors are everywhere, but the word "survivor" appears only once, at the end of the year.

I.

To read the diary in those ways is to read it for the raw data of experience, so to speak, before the details have been shaped into a narrative or an argument. Yet Lasky was an intensely self-conscious diarist, fully aware of the diary as an artifact, both historical and literary. Literary allusions are everywhere. Lasky was far from the only American writer to graft T. S. Eliot's *The Waste Land* onto the European wasteland of 1945 (3 April). Noting that one's *Baedeker* travel guide had been rendered obsolete by bombs was also a reasonably common gesture. "As the *Stars and Stripes* correspondent ah so wittily remarked," Lasky notes on 10 March, "no guidebooks will be necessary for GI tourists of Cologne." The photographer Margaret Bourke-White looked down from a small airplane onto German wreckage with a *Baedeker* in her hands (Bourke-White 1946, ch. 10). Edmund Wilson would entitle his postwar "sketches among the ruins" *Europe Without Baedeker* (Wilson 1947). But Lasky's other references and literary encounters are more surprising. On 20 March he asks: "What happens to an Alsatian Tom Sawyer in all this degradation of a world, when there are no fences to paint, but only rubble? I had not thought to imagine Marianne Weber, Max Weber's widow, reading Van Wyck Brooks's *The Flowering of New England* in Karl Jaspers's house, and yet there she is, "with a dictionary to catch so many of the strange phrases" (31 July). Throughout the diary, bookstores and libraries, in various states of dilapidation, are a common haunt. In Heidelberg, a sign says, Sie haben Zeit zum Lesen! and Lasky finds *Babbitt* and *Gone with the Wind* (18 April). At a school library in Darmstadt, he spots an inevitable *Mein Kampf*, but he also notes that "the old liberal culture of Germany could not be entirely liquidated" (27 April). The books one happens to find in the ruins take on new meaning by the mere fact of having been found there.

It is a nice touch that as an Army historian, Lasky was tasked with gathering documents, diaries among them: "I have done a little of everything: tried to collect letters, conversations, diaries, odd items." He says that "historically speaking," such items are "priceless" (12 March); at the same time, he grows quickly suspicious of the history that is being written, and of the history he himself must write. The Historical Division is not spared the bureaucratic chickenshit that defined modern military life, and his frustration is almost immediate: on 13 February, their colonel, the "historian-in-chief," demands Taylorist efficiency: "Let's get the output up! For Christ's sake, if research takes up seventy-five percent of your time, cut research out! Just write, and then everything will be speeding along!"

The diary is distinguished by its manifold antagonism to history, or rather to History with a capital "H." Sometimes it serves as Lasky's draft of a *truer* history that will rival false official histories. Sometimes he laments that no one in the future will really be able to understand what the moment was really like. Perhaps the modern scale and speed of destruction defies historical narration itself: "In the old days when the historic process could take a leisurely pace, catastrophes could be recorded as 'decline' and 'fall,'" he notes on 9 April, contemplating the total destruction of Darmstadt. "Now, disasters are sudden, instantaneous, and complete. The tragedy of this city can only be summed up as—'poof!'" On balance, though, Lasky's diary presumes a posterity that might find meaning in its pages. "Diaries are texts that are written privately but are probably kept for the purpose of rereading," Werner Sollors has noted in his consideration of wartime and postwar diaries; "why else would they be written?" (Sollors 2014).

II.

Step back and regard Lasky's diary as a single text, as a work of literature unto itself, and a powerful narrative architecture does emerge. This was not something Lasky could have engineered, but the pronounced form of the whole is all the more remarkable for being unplanned. This requires an exegesis.

At first, our narrator is a precocious young intellectual, still brimming with his undergraduate education at City College and his master's in history at the University of Michigan. Having returned to New York in 1940, he was eager to keep writing for *Partisan Review*, and to impress New York's literary coterie. Most of the diary's early entries, from January through early May, are well-composed commentaries, miniature travelogues, or vignettes with novelistic characterization and romantic episodes. Many seem written with an eye toward eventual publication. He even seems enamored, at times, of his own writerly facility. At the outset, Lasky bears some resemblance to Julien Sorel in Stendhal's *The Red and the Black*, the hyperliterate yet self-consciously inexperienced peasant who leaves the French provinces for Paris. Both characters feel themselves to be participating in a great historical and intellectual drama. (Lasky himself quotes a particular line from Stendhal in the diary—twice, in fact.)[1] This is not to say that New York was a province, only that for Lasky, *culture* in the fullest sense had a European and transatlantic center of gravity, and he was pulled to it.

But 8 May, VE-Day, brings a dramatic shift in style and shape. The diary moves away from a young man's chronicle of adventures to a much starker confrontation with ruin and holocaust. In counterpoint to the familiar songs of Allied jubilation, Lasky's writing turns clipped, fragmentary, modernist. The entire entry for 8 May could stand as a modernist poem, formed as an unprocessed list of everything seen in a single day. It opens with a road sign—YOU ARE NOW ENTERING AUGSBURG. COURTESY OF THE FIFTEENTH INFANTRY— like a line from one of John Dos Passos's "newsreel" chapters in the *U.S.A.* trilogy. Then: "Warm sunny day. Left 0900." Hard-boiled prose vies with compressed imagism: "The war was over. Convoys of trucks, jammed with prisoners; an old woman, a young girl waving goodbyes; they walked on slowly." The stark and simple catalog of images conveys an enormous historical *happening*, distilled into one line: "Planes strewn along everywhere; the last of the *Luftwaffe*." Haste or shock surely account for some of this change, but the effect is no less literary. "Hitchhikers, wanderers, pilgrims." The last line is a six-word story: "To bed. Cool night; one blanket."

Then for several entries the diary is overtaken by other voices. The Brooklyn tap dancer is among them, but more vivid and poignant are the flashes of concentration camp inmates, wanderers, and marchers, as on 10 May:

> 1600 Jews (seized in the Polish ghetto and elsewhere) left Buchenwald. On the road for thirty days. Many died, others collapsed and were shot. Two hundred arrived here. Spoke to a few. Would never return to Poland—he had a *Zeide* in America! A long name of a city, he couldn't remember. Philadelphia? No, he couldn't remember, but he would find his *Zeide*.

That entry is wholly given over to the life stories of people Lasky has encountered and interviewed. "Maria. Twenty-two. Inmate of the women's prison. Sturdy, healthy girl; pug-nose, might have been Irish." "Elizabeth Kind; husband a Swiss-German. Lived in Berlin since 1932. Tall, thin, blonde; haggard, worried; spoke half in English, half German." The prose shifts seamlessly into *their* first-person narration, without quotation marks. Some lines read as answers to an interviewer, with the questions left out of the text: "Yes, he was a friend of mine." The effect is of a voice speaking directly at the reader: "And I, I am young, but look at me. I am thirty-five and I have gray hair and am already an old lady . . . But then I might have been dead." The next two entries, 14 and 15 May, alternate between modernist fragments and unfiltered life story.

How strange, then, to jump from that narrative mode to Lasky's first lines on 1 June, which feel telegraphed from another world:

> Wonderful, how exhilarating the first free moments on the road are! You are at last alone and rather carefree, and what is most important, unlocatable: imagine, you repeat to yourself, no one in the whole world knows where you are! You drive happily, and chant for hours. This is "freedom," and not the least larger aspect of the liberation is that it is essentially a flight. You have managed an escape from the burdens of routine, respect, and responsibility.

The diary seems to return to its earlier style of coherent narrative and essayistic travelogue. Yet it is not really a return to normal. It cannot be.

III.

If this were the diary of an anonymous conscript, it would be an extraordinarily powerful document: a treasure we were lucky to have collected. (The diary's penultimate entry figures the diarist, ironically, as a "collector" whose collections are doomed.) But knowing that the writer will go on to become a key figure in the cultural cold war makes us read it differently. We want to find what it reveals about culture, ideology, and transatlantic relations in the longer term.

The diary illuminates, in a way that other documents cannot, how the experience of the American occupation and its failures informed the cultural cold war that was to come. Lasky laments "the spectacle of our American hypocrisy" (17 March). His criticisms of American military personnel and American policies are often blistering. The diary offers straightforward accounts of assault and looting by American soldiers—the aforementioned Jordan speaks of his division as "the rootin'-lootinest [*sic*] sons-a-bitches in dee Army" (9 April). In a more diagnostic mode, on 4 June, Lasky writes that European "disaffection from the American occupation already exists," and that "the US representatives are already losing what holds they had previously in European public opinion." In October, he observes that "no one believes in education for Germany, partly because also the educators have no faith in themselves, and rightly." In short, he comes to comprehend the occupation as both a tragedy and a farce. All that he had seen had turned out to be "the data for the story of chaos." (This would be a sobering reminder to readers of later decades, especially when post-1945 occupations were recast as success stories and happy models of military occupation in Afghanistan and Iraq.)

The diary's key epiphany is that the American occupation did not inaugurate a new historical era. Rather, the occupation, together with the war itself, was the hideous conclusion of an era. He realizes he is recording not the beginning of something but the end of something, a historical cycle at least a century long. "How poignant the peace is!" he writes to Dwight Macdonald in October. "What a cataclysmic end for the world of the international middle class, the fine heroes of the nineteenth century!" The early diary had invoked T. S. Eliot's *The Waste Land*, predictably, but the diarist has changed his mind by the end. "This is not a spectacular barrenness of a *wasteland*. This is a deep, organized, systematic, humdrum emptiness," he continues. "This is the twentieth century with its throat cut and looking only slightly pale." Throughout the diary Lasky has sought to define the predicament of his own generation (as distinct from, say, the "lost generation" of the 1920s), and he lands on this sad state of affairs: "This is the world of the new generation, not lost, not to be pitied, only aimless and flat."

But one should not conclude that this total suspicion of, and pessimism about, the possibilities for American occupation is the diary's ultimate message. The revelation of the occupation's failures and cynicisms, its deeper continuity with the past rather than its break from the past, is better seen as the precondition for the postwar transatlantic exchanges in which Lasky would play so prominent a part. We might find an absurd rehearsal for postwar cultural diplomacy in Lasky's encounter with some Russian nurses on 14 May, smack in the middle of the diary's modernist, fragmentary phase:

> Asked me to tell them a little of America. Where to begin. Some gossipy remarks, which pleased them. How about American songs. Folk music. Tried to think of something other than *Old Kentucky Home* and *Dixie*, but pleased by lilt, and I put away my bad tenor. They went on with Russian songs, and we soon had a traveling sing in a jeep. Things became warmer when I swung into the International. All smiles and friends.

A more earnest contemplation comes on 13 June, when Lasky commiserates with the journalist Hans Wallenberg, "a fine, sensitive soul," about "the disaster of the occupation, the emptiness, confusion and corruption of our policies." Lasky's prose betrays some of the pretention and grandiosity of a still-young diarist: "Those whom our War and our Peace has not shattered, it has corrupted and left them only with a terrible mindlessness." The "our" contains America and Europe; the effect of "our Peace" was not to restore, but to shatter again. "So we salute the desert of our future," he says in that day's last line, and one can imagine them raising a glass. Though he could not fully discern it then, that disillusionment would become the premise for his later work as editor and impresario of the cultural cold war: when the failures of state, military, and modern bureaucracy are laid bare, the deeds of the next generation's writers and intellectuals become pivotal. Civilization is dead; long live culture. Propaganda is dead; long live literature.

Maybe this paradox is why we read a diary, and, in certain moments, why we might write one: you can confess your total fatalism, but then by some alchemy of expression, the confession itself is what lets you imagine a future.

George Blaustein is Senior Lecturer of American Studies and History at the University of Amsterdam. He is the author of *Nightmare Envy & Other Stories: American Culture and European Reconstruction* (2018). His essays and reviews have appeared in *n+1*, *The New Yorker*, *The New Republic*, and *De Groene Amsterdammer*, as well as *Amerikastudien/American Studies* and *American Quarterly*. He is also a founder and editor of *The European Review of Books*.

Notes

1. The reference is actually to one of Stendhal's epigraphs in *The Red and the Black*, a quote that is attributed to Antoine Barnave: "*Voilà donc le beau miracle de votre civilisation! De l'amour vous avez fait une affaire ordinaire.*" Describing his last encounter with an American lover before leaving, Lasky writes on 24 January, "I can't help thinking of a line of Stendhal's. Somewhere he remarks: 'Here is the supreme achievement of our civilization—out of love it makes ordinary affairs.'" Later in the diary, Stendhal returns: "Remember that line somewhere from Stendhal—'This is the supreme triumph of your civilization. Out of love it makes ordinary affairs.'" But this time Lasky worries about his sexual encounters being reduced to "the ordinariness and even sordidness of commonplace fornication" (week of 6 July).

References

Bourke-White, Margaret. 1946. *"Dear Fatherland, Rest Quietly": A Report on the Collapse of Hitler's "Thousand Years."* New York: Simon and Schuster.

Brooks, Van Wyck. 1936. *The Flowering of New England, 1815–1865.* New York: Modern Library.

Dos Passos, John. 1996. *U.S.A.* New York: Library of America.

Eliot, T. S. (Thomas Stearns). 1999. *The Waste Land: and Other Poems.* London: Faber and Faber.

Lewis, Sinclair. 2002. *Babbitt.* Amherst, NY: Prometheus Books.

Mitchell, Margaret. 1936. *Gone with the Wind.* New York: Macmillan.

Sollors, Werner. 2014. *The Temptation of Despair: Tales of the 1940s.* Cambridge, MA: Harvard University Press.

Stendhal. 1830. *Le Rouge et le Noir: Chronique du XIXe siècle* (The Red and the Black: Chronicle of the 19th Century). Paris: A. Levasseur.

Wilson, Edmund. 1947. *Europe Without Baedeker: Sketches Among the Ruins of Italy, Greece, & England.* Garden City, NY: Doubleday.

Chapter 3

Between Denazification and Reconstruction
US Occupation Policies and Practice in Germany 1945

Jana Aresin

Following the surrender of Germany in May 1945, the Allied Powers announced in the Berlin declaration that they would "assume supreme authority with respect to Germany, including all the powers possessed by the German Government, the High Command and any state, municipal, or local government or authority" ("Declaration Regarding the Defeat" 1985, 33). The declaration marked the official beginning of the Allied Occupation of Germany. Concrete planning for how Germany should be governed, however, began as early as 1943, once the Allies had agreed that the unconditional surrender of Germany followed by a period of occupation would be the only acceptable way to end the war (Reinisch 2013, 19).

Between 1943 and 1945, the Joint Chiefs of Staff (JCS) and the Civil Affairs Division of the US military produced a number of directives, manuals, and handbooks regarding occupation. General aims and principles of military government were outlined in the JCS directives, whereas more concrete, practical details on how to handle a variety of issues, from the future of political and legal institutions and the economy, to matters of food distribution and public health, were formulated in the regulatory documents of the Operations and Training Division (G-3) and the Civil Affairs Division (G-5). The latter was trained specifically for military government (Gerhardt 2005, 73–74). The prolonged fighting in Germany after the first victories of the US Army meant that eventually the preparatory planning and the actual occupation overlapped. In autumn 1944, US forces entered Germany and the first cities and towns came under occupation while the war was still being waged in other parts of the country. Consequently, in 1944 and 1945, directives and policies regarding the occupation had to be continuously adjusted to fit the changing circumstances (Gerhardt 2005, 77). When Melvin Lasky first entered Germany as a combat historian of the research division of the Seventh US Army in March 1945, German surrender was still more than a month away.

The directives and manuals written between 1943 and 1945 did share some general principles and aims. They highlighted the main objectives of occupation: the demilitarization and denazification of Germany, the decentralization of the political system, and the decartelization of the economy (Gerhardt 2005, 89). The general tenet was not one of liberation, but instead highlighted the punitive nature of the policies whose primary aim was to prevent future German military aggression. The April 1945 directive JCS 1067 stated that "Germany will not be occupied for the purpose of liberation but as a defeated enemy nation" (JCS 1067, reprinted in Friedrich 1948, 384). This position was made clear to the German people in a proclamation distributed in all occupied territories in Germany, which Lasky encountered on 29 March in Kaiserslautern:

> Law Number One abrogated Nazi law. Law Number Two disbanded the Nazi courts. The announcement by General Eisenhower explained that we "come as conquerors but not as oppressors."

The proclamation hints at a central contradiction that characterized most of the initial occupation policies. On the one hand, they made clear their intention to significantly transform German society, economy, and institutions in the name of denazification and demilitarization. On the other hand, they emphasized German responsibility for the war and for coping with its consequences. Originally, only a minimum amount of economic and humanitarian support was planned in order to maintain a degree of law and order. Lasky observes on 7 April that the German people were "expected to 'shift for themselves,'" and adds, "how much starvation and chaos will set in remains to be seen." Similarly, JCS 1067 emphasized that economic assistance should not be allowed to create a higher standard of living for the German people than for its neighboring countries or for the millions of displaced persons (DPs) within the country—mainly former forced laborers, freed concentration camp survivors, and POWs (JCS 1067, in Friedrich 1948, 392; Carruthers 2016, 152). Dealing with the vast number of DPs presented another enormous challenge for the occupation forces. While initially the willingness to support the liberated victims of the Nazi regime clearly outweighed any sympathy for the German population, the difficulties of managing humanitarian aid and repatriation of DPs led to an often anti-Semitic backlash (Carruthers 2016, 170, 187). Lasky himself, though not hostile to the DPs he encounters, also seems more comfortable in his interactions with German people, whom he portrays with a surprising level of sympathy, whereas his descriptions of DPs are often distanced and display his shock at their "bizarre" living conditions and how "unrecognizable" the "thin, unshaven, unkempt" concentration camp survivors seem.

Leaving responsibility to cope with the devastation of World War II to the German people themselves clashed with the goal of denazification and the close control of institutions and administrative structures that it required (Reinisch 2013, 57). This contradiction was aggravated by a general unease among parts of the US government and the general population about fully embracing their role as occupiers. Despite a long history of occupying foreign territories, for example in Central America, the Caribbean, and Asia, the prospect of a prolonged occupation of Germany was not met with enthusiasm in the United States (Carruthers 2018, 28). The opening of the School of Military Government at the University of Virginia in Charlottesville in 1942 was harshly criticized in the media. The idea of giving significant political and administrative power to the military stood in conflict with the United States' self-understanding as a model nation of republican liberty (Carruthers 2018, 27–28). Whereas training at the school followed an approach of minimal interference with local structures and institutions, the overarching Allied plans were based on the assumption that a fundamental change of society was necessary for Germany to ever be able to return to the international order as a peaceful nation. These contradictory positions obstructed consistent and efficient planning and training for occupation (Carruthers 2018, 34–35).

If and how Germany could be rebuilt as a peaceful nation had been up for debate throughout the early 1940s. Scholars turned to the question of what had caused the rise of fascism in Germany and how Nazi ideologies could be dismantled. In 1943, US American psychologist Richard M. Brickner asked "Is Germany Incurable?" in his book of the same title, in which he explained German military aggression and expansionism as a result of collective mental illness (Brickner 1943, 30–31). In the same year, German American psychologist Kurt Lewin published his article "The Special Case of Germany," which emphasized the role of "culture" for political and social change (Lewin 1948, 47–48). The concept of "reeducation" that became an integral part of early democratization efforts referenced these new approaches from social psychology (Tent 1982, 13). The realization that a long-term change of German society would have to include (re)educational reforms stood in opposition to the more radical denazification aims and the initial unwillingness of the US to engage with the reconstruction of German society (Tent 1982, 20–22).

The uncertainties regarding the treatment of the former enemy, how much sympathy and support the war-torn country should be granted, and whether there was hope for a new Germany to emerge, are evident in Lasky's writing in numerous places. At one point at the end of March, he recounts an encounter with refugees who tell him that the majority of Germans were "worthless and mean" and that "'all of them' were 'bad,'" but in his own thoughts Lasky expresses doubts of this assessment:

> But then an opportunist is not a fanatic; his belief and loyalty have a different intensity; and the fact that even a few are now changing sides actively is a revealing light on the myths of blanket Hitler worship and unmitigated allegiance. (30 and 31 March)

Lasky's reluctance to condemn the German population collectively might be connected to the familiarity and appreciation of German culture and language he experienced through his family and educational background (Roth 2018, 138–39). Yet he also clearly recognizes that a fundamental transformation of Germany is necessary and asks: "How could there be a new Germany when the tragedy of the old was not fully deeply understood?" (13 April) This quote sheds light on another assumption underlying the early occupation policies: the need for a transition period before democratization and reconstruction of Germany could begin. The initial plans for occupation proposed the complete suspension of all political, legal, and social institutions, followed by a transition period that would be primarily concerned with "denazification" (Gerhardt 2005, 89–90). This included the dismissal of Nazis from all prominent positions, the conviction of war criminals as well as the dissolution of the National Socialist German Workers' Party (NSDAP) and the abolishment of all laws and decrees based on Nazi ideology (JCS 1067, in Friedrich 1948, 385–86).

The idea of a transition period contains some aspects of what scholars in the 1990s theorized as "transitional justice." This concept recognizes that past violence and abuse of power need to be addressed and reckoned with to restore a new normative basis of justice and shared truth before a society can be rebuilt and conciliated after conflict (Boehling 2018, 64). The Nuremberg Trials of 1945 were one of the first instances of such a "moral use of the law" (Andrieu 2014, 90). This is evident in the occupation policies' acknowledgment that a far-reaching transformation of Germany, subsumed under the directives of denazification and reeducation, would be necessary before democratization could be achieved. It was particularly strong in the US occupation zone, whereas in the British and French zones security concerns and the demilitarization of Germany prevailed over more idealistic goals of rehabilitation (Boehling 2018, 66).

However, this ambitious approach of reeducation was soon met with various difficulties, as it had to face the realities of post-surrender Germany. Firstly, the recognition that a transition period of rigorous denazification was necessary effectively delayed concrete preparation for democratization policies and long-term plans for how postwar Germany should be rebuilt. Regarding this matter, there was tension between advocates of a punitive approach that emphasized the radical dismantling of political and economic structures to eliminate Germany's ability to wage war and those who considered a more constructive reeducation indispensable for ensuring a permanent change of the population's attitudes (Tent 1982, 26, 30; Boehling 1996, 18–19). The absence of a coherent plan for occupation beyond the immediate aftermath of war was apparently felt on the ground as well. In an entry from 28 April 1945, Lasky wonders "what changes on the high-level have been made in international policy, and whether any large program will ever make its way down effectively to the low units of execution."

Secondly, the practice of denazification soon came under criticism for being ineffective. The military government was faced with the problem of how to approach the issue of the collective war guilt of the German people. The initial plan to expel all prominent NSDAP members from public offices and institutions was confronted with practical necessities to keep basic social structures functioning (Boehling 1996, 55–56; Benz 2009, 117). In the fall of 1945, the denazification measures of the military government came under increased criticism, as reports of prominent Nazis walking free, unpunished, and resuming their former positions were published in the US media (Tent 1982, 50–51). Judging the level of guilt and responsibility of individuals naturally proved a difficult process, beginning with changing definitions of who should be considered a "real Nazi." From July 1945 onwards, the US Military Government used questionnaires that were handed out to all German people over eighteen years of age in order to establish their level of involvement with the Nazi regime (Benz 2009, 117). Despite these attempts to hold the entire adult population accountable for the Nazi atrocities, the general focus remained on the removal of Nazi elites and failed to fundamentally question which structures in German society had facilitated widespread Nazi support—and even the removal of elites proved only rarely effective (Boehling 1996, 57–58). As a result of the 1946 *Befreiungsgesetz*[1] and two amnesties in August and December of the same year, the number of people convicted as guilty or dismissed permanently from their positions dropped radically (Benz 2009, 118–19).

Although far from condemning the entire German population and seemingly appalled by some of his fellow soldiers' "lack of moral alarm" when discussing the German people's fate, Lasky expresses strong disillusionment with the way denazification was handled, and how idealistic striving for justice was often quickly replaced with pragmatic approaches to ensure order and stability. He recounts his frustrations with the treatment of the mayor of Heidelberg in an entry from 20 April 1945:

He was a Nazi party member. His explanation was, of course, that it had been required of him in order to continue in office. And the Army accepted him as such. In the by now terribly familiar pattern the basic intention was to remove him, but he would be of service temporarily, for he was "not sufficiently prominent in the Nazi hierarchy to warrant his immediate displacement!"... On these hollow and lazy phrases all purpose is lost. The removal of the Nazis, summarily, unconditionally, could have become the consistent symbol of the end of the old order.

Lasky's early observations about the priority of order and stability over morals and justice seem to anticipate later changes in official policies. In the aforementioned JCS 1067 from 1945, "the elimination of Nazism and militarism in all their forms" is listed as the most important measure to ensure peace in Europe (JCS 1067, in Friedrich 1948, 385). A revised directive from July 1947 replacing JCS 1067, however, states that "peace can be achieved only if conditions of public order and prosperity are created in Europe" and that "a stable and productive Germany" was necessary to reach this (Directive to Commander-in-Chief, in Friedrich 1948, 402–3). This change of emphasis fully institutionalized the previously implicit tendencies to prioritize reconstruction over the uncompromising enforcement of a moral norm.

Other factors that impeded the efficiency of denazification were the increasing pressure to shorten the occupation period and let the soldiers return home as well as rising tensions with the Soviet Union and fears of the spread of communism (Boehling 2018, 76). Soldiers' demoralization set in soon after German surrender and the end of open conflict. Uncertainty about the length and nature of occupation trapped many soldiers in a liminal state between wartime Army routines and return to civilian life at home that produced frustration and boredom (Carruthers 2016, 205). The strict "nonfraternization" order that initially banned all contact with the occupied population and required soldiers to be "just but firm and aloof" intensified this situation (JCS 1067, in Friedrich 1948, 384–85). As Lasky observes, the policy was "not, of course, very popular," and that "it is common knowledge that there are more than a few violations." Its unsustainability is obvious in Lasky's frequent mentioning of the "furtive exchanges of glances between pretty German girls and the GIs" and the accounts of his and his fellow soldiers' numerous affairs with local women. In addition to the policy's inability to prevent soldiers' sexual relations, nonfraternization was accompanied by a more general sense of social isolation. Lasky declares on 13 June 1945 that:

> We both hungered for "life," for a refuge from the poverty of our isolation; we sought everywhere for glimpses of the people and the ordinary course of existence.

The policy was gradually relaxed and lifted in late summer 1945 (Gerhardt 2005, 152). Despite his critique of the nonfraternization rule, Lasky himself seemed to be less concerned about his prolonged stay, probably resulting from his personal and intellectual interest in European history and culture, yet he expresses frustration with the seeming inefficiency of the occupation machinery. When he meets a deputy of the Military Government in Munich who complains that "thousands of civil employees used to work in the administration; now some thirty or forty Americans are supposed to be efficient," Lasky draws the cynical conclusion: "So we do nothing, and call it Occupation. A glorified regime of Do-Nothingness" (20 June).

Notably, as early as 19 July 1945, Lasky draws a connection between the inefficiency of the military government and the possibility of Germany turning toward the Soviet Union and communism, anticipating future concerns of the US government over German allegiance in the Cold War. Lasky predicts:

> The more of a failure America makes of its military achievement the more reconciled the German *Militarismus* and *Kleinbürgertum* become to the prospects of finding some opportunities only under an energetic force of communism.

The contrast between the gradual return of some normality in soldiers' everyday life and the anxieties of the looming Cold War are visible in Lasky's descriptions of the occupation. In a letter to his sister Floria from August 1945, he describes the changes of his mental state throughout his only seven months in Europe "from the wildness of the boredom—to the widening horror at all the destruction, and the corruption and moral emptiness of our world—to the simple delight of receiving new stimulations and impressions."[2] Just four days later, most likely in response to the atomic bombing of Hiroshima and Nagasaki, he proclaims in a somewhat dramatic tone:

> In the shadow of the coming atomic destruction of Europe a nostalgia for this peaceful present begins to grow. How we must learn to cherish this epoch of simple rubble! We may be living our last moments before the fundamental disintegration of the earth. (12 August)

In conclusion, the occupation policies of the United States in Germany, which in retrospect have often been characterized as an unquestionable success story, were in reality fraught with various uncertainties and contradictions. Idealistic and ambitious aims of restoring justice and rebuilding a new democratic society from the rubble of postwar Germany were faced with the initial reluctance of parts of the US government to involve the military any more than necessary in postwar Europe. The practical necessities—food distribution, basic economic reconstruction, health provisions, and transport—needed to ensure a minimum of social stability further complicated the process of occupation and the complex task of denazification. Even though a significant number of directives, regulatory documents, and handbooks were issued to guide the different aspects of occupation, an underestimation of the level of devastation and the fast-changing circumstances in the last months of the war meant that these original plans were often inadequate or had to be readjusted. Quoting T. S. Eliot, Lasky makes an observation regarding "social reconstruction" in Europe: "Between the conception and the execution, as the poet says, falls the shadow" (28 April).

The period of inefficiency and uncertainty described in Lasky's diary entries from 1945 arguably came to an end in the late 1940s when the Soviet Union replaced Germany as the main cause of concern in US foreign policy. Occupation policies shifted from a strong emphasis on demilitarization and denazification to economic recovery and reconstruction of Germany as a democratic, capitalist US ally. The often complicated and protracted task of judging Nazi allegiances was in many cases replaced by an interest in the German people's future compliance with rules and regulations instituted by the US military government. Lasky's concern with the occupation policies' inefficiency in reconstructing society and his simultaneous criticism of the unquestioned retention of former Nazis in office for pragmatic reasons might have motivated his future engagement in Cold War cultural diplomacy. After attending the new rector Karl Heinrich Bauer's speech at Heidelberg University in August 1945, Lasky recounts Bauer's statement that "the wars are over, but the *geistige Kampf*, the war of the spirit, is just beginning" (15 August). This conclusion seems to foreshadow Lasky's later engagement in winning European "hearts and minds" during the Cold War.

Acknowledgments

My work on Lasky's diary has been part of a research project at FAU Erlangen-Nürnberg on "Reeducation Revisited: Transnationale und kulturvergleichende Perspektiven auf die Nachkriegszeit in den USA, Japan und Deutschland," which is funded by the Deutsche Forschungsgemeinschaft (DFG, German Research Foundation)—Project Number: 407542657.

Jana Aresin is a doctoral researcher in American Studies at Friedrich-Alexander University Erlangen-Nürnberg. She researches the cultural and media history of the early Cold War (1945–60) in comparative perspective, with a regional focus on the United States and Japan.

Notes

1. The "Law for Liberation from National Socialism and Militarism" was passed in March 1946 and delegated the responsibility for denazification procedures and tribunals to the German people (Boehling 2018, 71–72).
2. Letter from Melvin Lasky to Floria Lasky, 8 August 1945, Lasky Papers, War Diary Typescript Materials.

References

Andrieu, Kora. 2014. "Political Liberalism after Mass Violence: John Rawls and a 'Theory' of Transitional Justice." In *Transitional Justice Theories*, ed., S. Buckley-Zistel, T. K. Beck, C. Braun, and F. Mieth, 85–104. Abingdon: Routledge.

Benz, Wolfgang. 2009. "Deutschland unter alliierter Besatzung 1945–1949." In *Gebhardt. Handbuch der deutschen Geschichte. Band 22*, 3–221. Stuttgart: Klett-Cotta.

Boehling, Rebecca. 1996. *A Question of Priorities: Democratic Reform and Economic Recovery in Postwar Germany*. Providence: Berghahn Books.

———. 2018. "Transitional Justice? Denazification in the US Zone of Occupied Germany." In *Transforming Occupation in the Western Zones of Germany: Politics, Everyday Life and Social Interactions, 1945–55*, ed. C. Erlichman and C. Knowles, 63–80. London: Bloomsbury Academic.

Brickner, Richard M. 1943. *Is Germany Incurable?* Philadelphia: J. B. Lippincott.

Carruthers, Susan. 2016. *The Good Occupation: American Soldiers and the Hazards of Peace*. Cambridge, MA: Harvard University Press.

———. 2018. "Preoccupied: Wartime Training for Post-War Occupation in the United States, 1940–45." In *Transforming Occupation in the Western Zones of Germany: Politics, Everyday Life and Social Interactions, 1945–55*, ed. C. Erlichman and C. Knowles, 25–42. London: Bloomsbury Academic.

"Declaration Regarding the Defeat of Germany and the Assumption of Supreme Authority by the Allied Powers." 1985. In *Documents on Germany 1944–1985*, United States Department of State, Office of the Historian, 33–38. Washington, DC: Department of State.

Friedrich, Carl J. 1948. *American Experiences in Military Government in World War II*. New York: Rinehart.

Gerhardt, Uta. 2005. *Soziologie der Stunde Null. Zur Gesellschaftskonzeption des amerikanischen Besatzungsregimes in Deutschland 1944–1945/1946*. Frankfurt am Main: Suhrkamp.

Lewin, Kurt. 1948. *Resolving Social Conflicts: Selected Papers on Group Dynamics*. New York: Harper & Row.

Reinisch, Jessica. 2013. *The Perils of Peace: The Public Health Crisis in Occupied Germany*. Oxford: Oxford University Press.

Roth, Maren. 2018. "'What an unbelievable unreal adventure!' Melvin J. Lasky als Akteur im kriegszerstörten Deutschland. In *Feinde, Freunde, Fremde? Deutsche Perspektiven auf die USA*, ed. V. Benkert, 135–58. Baden-Baden: Nomos.

Tent, James F. 1982. *Mission on the Rhine: Reeducation and Denazification in American-Occupied Germany*. Chicago: Chicago University Press.

Chapter 4

"Clio Continues to Serve"
Melvin J. Lasky as Combat Historian
Charlotte A. Lerg

Becoming a Combat Historian

A 1983 article in the newly founded journal the *Army Historian* listed common "traits" of combat historians. Having identified them as generally college educated and/or prone to "voracious reading," the author, a veteran of the trade himself, adds: "Most historians also share a penchant to write, to keep journals, to keep a record of what they and those around them have experienced" (Nye 1983, 6). Lasky was a typecast for the job. He was indeed a more than avid reader and was also in the habit of writing, both privately and for publication. Before he was drafted into the Army, twenty-four-year-old Lasky was already working as a journalist. However, he had also signed up to do a PhD in history at Columbia University in New York under the supervision of Merle Curti, an eminent professor of European and American History. Although his plans to study at Columbia never came to fruition, Private Lasky kept up correspondence with his would-be adviser during army training and visited the Columbia library while on leave in autumn 1944.[1] This visit gave him the opportunity to reach out to Henry Steele Commager, who was also a professor of history at Columbia University and a member of the Army's Historical Advisory Committee that had been established by Assistant Secretary of War John J. McCloy in the summer of 1943 (Conn 1993, 34). Lasky had recently passed the exam for the Quartermaster Corps Officer Candidate School and now, having solicited letters of recommendation from Columbia University historians, including Commager and Curti, received a much hoped for promotion: Lasky was appointed to the Historical Branch with the rank of a second lieutenant. After spending a few short months in Washington, DC, he was finally sent overseas in late January 1945 and began writing this war diary.

We have numerous diaries from World War II. Intriguingly though, there is only one other known diary of a combat historian (Pogue 2001): Forrest C. Pogue was slightly older than Lasky and already held a PhD in history from Clark University when he was commissioned to Europe as a combat historian in the spring of 1944. He was assigned to cover parts of D-Day, making his work one of the most read accounts after the war. Unlike Lasky, Pogue would also remain connected to the army later on, employed as a civilian to conduct research in military history. His published diary, which focuses on events rather than internal reflection, as well as later descriptions of his experiences, serve to complement and contrast what we find in Lasky's war diary.

The Historical Branch

The Historical section itself seems to be the bastard creation of some enterprising military mind, with one hand on Thucydides, one eye on the future and the judgement of posterity, and one foot into the next war.
(12 March)

Combat historian, Second Lieutenant Melvin J. Lasky, thanks to the types of assignments this job entailed, enjoyed an unusual amount of freedom in the army compared to the average conscript, even those of higher rank. However, in his diary, there is little appreciation for this privilege. Instead, he complains about "the confusion and incompetence of the history-recorders" and within a week of arriving in France, he notes in frustration: "I can't seem to be able to find anybody who knows what he is doing. Policies are unclarified, procedures are botched, and the method and theory of the historical section absurd" (13 February). While young Lasky's impatience and impertinence clearly shine through here, his evaluation was probably quite accurate. The Historical Branch had only been officially established in the summer of 1943 and many of the methods, techniques, and organizational processes were being devised on the go (Shulman 1993, 46). In later narratives, World War II became the starting point and ever-prominent touchstone for professional combat history (Arthur 1991; Wright 1985; Clarke 2006), but more than once, Lasky and his colleagues doubted whether what they were doing would really serve a purpose in the long run: "The details are so mean and trivial it pains me to think what some monographer of future years will make of the 'historical program of World War II'—she [*sic*] will no doubt explore patiently all the directives, and all the manuscripts, and come away with a contrived myth of abstracted events" (22 April).

Every so often, the swift organization and smooth running of the historical work was obstructed by conflicting visions and rivaling authorities. There had been what was generally called "historical work" in the US Army before World War II, most notably at the Army War College. Within the purview of this institution fell the teaching of military history—with a particular emphasis on "lessons learned"—but also the preparation of historical studies for the general staff. Collecting, archiving, or in any way arranging material and information on the army's campaigns and operations as they unfolded, however, was initially not part of the tasks when the Army War College was founded in 1901. The lack of systematic documentation was felt bitterly in the aftermath of World War I; a special section of army historians was formed to sort through the somewhat randomly collected material pertaining to this first US military involvement in Europe between 1917 and 1921. Unfortunately, with archival holdings strewn all over the country and the project rather understaffed, they were still lagging behind considerably on the World War I files when the US entered World War II.[2]

Nevertheless, the head of the special section, General Oliver L. Spaulding, in an attempt to apply the lesson learned from World War I, suggested shortly after World War II was declared, that "for the period of the present war," all Army records "of historical value" be brought straight to the Army War College and collected there (Spaulding cited in Conn 1993, 30). Work to that effect began toward the end of the year and was sanctioned a few months later by the War Department after a letter signed 4 March 1943 by President Franklin D. Roosevelt urged all federal agencies to make an effort to preserve "an accurate and objective account of our present war experience" (Conn 1993, 30). For all the major commands, both overseas and on the home front, Washington appointed "historical officers" to prepare basic lists and synopsis of the material that was being collected (Conn 1993, 32).

Soon it became clear, though, that the Army War College was unable or unwilling to carry the growing administrative burden of coordination. Therefore, in late July 1943, Assistant Secretary of War John J. McCloy saw the need to establish a separate agency under the authority of G-2 (military intelligence).[3] Forrest Pogue remembered "a sudden outpouring of money" which made this move possible (Shulman 1993: 32). In their offices on the top floor of the Pentagon building, the roughly twenty-five members of the newly established Historical Branch went to work. Leadership was shared between a military representative, Lieutenant Colonel John Mason Kemper, who had been instrumental in establishing the program, and the civilian Chief Historian Walter Livingston Wright, who had previously been the president of the American Women's College in Istanbul and a historical consultant with the Library of Congress (Conn 1994a, 22); "old Dr. Wright" as Lasky refers to him.

When the Historical Branch was initially conceived, it was meant to simply take over the supervision and coordination of the Army's historical work; however, by the time it was established, it was given "absolute power over all Army historical publications ... superseding the Historical Section of the Army War College" (Conn 1993, 35). This radical redistribution of authority had likely been further stimulated by a disagreement that emerged regarding the timing and the function of writing an official narrative of the ongoing war. Spaulding, of the Army War College, had repeatedly insisted that a proper history could not and should not be written before the war was over and all the relevant material—including that of the enemy—had been viewed and evaluated. While fighting was still going on, it was the time for collection, not for composition (Conn 1993, 35). But in Washington, DC, a different view on the role of military history in wartime had taken hold: Army Chief of Staff George C. Marshall had initiated and commissioned a series of short monographs covering individual battles and operations, which were to be distributed to those wounded and the families of those killed in the respective campaigns (Shulman 1993, 31; Conn 1994a, 23–24). These publications, known as the "Army Force in Action Series" were intended to highlight the relevance and sacrifice of the average soldier.[4] Naturally, this required a certain kind of writing, but also a new, less top-heavy perspective on history, which Lasky also ponders in his diary:

> Now military history has been stood on its head. And what could be more ideologically appropriate in an era when it is for the Common Man that everything is sacrificed and it is in the name of the Little People that history is made.... Not Eisenhower's, or Patton's, or Clark's, or Patch's, it is all the genius of some Joe in his Foxhole ... Joe has his philosophers, his artists, his politicians. Now, in his supreme achievement, he has found his historian. (12 March)

The ironic undertone, a mixture of Lasky's (intellectual) snobbery and his skepticism with regard to the notion of military sacrifice, exposes the propaganda motive behind the new approach. Catering to the public's interest in the war became a new priority in military publishing. In fact, writing a "popular history" had been explicitly named as a key task for the Historical Branch (Conn 1993, 35). In an interview in 1993, Forrest C. Pogue concurred when asked if the historical work during World War II could be considered "the real birth of public history in the army" (Shulman 1993, 40).

In addition to this "popular" rendition of the war, the Historical Branch would also publish a series of source collections, much like the project that the Army War College History Section was working on for World War I. Moreover, a multivolume detailed official narrative was to be written and edited after fighting had ceased, which was a new type of project. It would be based on a combination of the original sources, the short monographs and pamphlets written during the war, and the transcribed interviews conducted with participants; it also included captured German material and narratives prepared by German officers recruited among prisoners of war (Wegner 1995). For this greater purpose, the Historical Branch merged with the Historical Section of the Army War College in November 1945, creating the Historical Division, Special Staff. In 1946, they published the first volume of *The United States Army in World War II* series, commonly referred to as "Green Books" (Conn 1994b, 18).[5] Over the course of the next decades, a total of seventy-eight individual studies appeared, covering all the theaters of the conflict, special studies on individual forces and services, the history of the Department of War, and a Pictorial Record (Adamczyk and MacGregor, iii). Plans for this grand design were extolled as motivation for the combat historians in the field; alas, Lasky's comment on this venture is equally dismissive as his view on the popular history, if not more so: "The dream is of a hundred-volume set, complete, exhaustive, definitive. They can see it on the shelf. Some even can make out the cumulative layers of dust. But that has hardly disconcerted scholars in the past" (12 March). This scorn for history writing more generally, which after all Lasky had previously contemplated to peruse academically, may well have been heightened by the frustration and the strict guidelines on how he was to write his reports.

The Combat Historian in the Field

> Went through division, regimental and battalion records; interviewed all the available key officers and enlisted men involved in the engagement; went over the terrain with commanders who had participated in the action.
>
> (3 March)

Lasky was one of about three hundred men sent overseas in Military History Detachments (MHD) to collect material for the Historical Branch. They served either as members of one of the nine Information and Historical Services (I&HS) units assigned to particular commands or in one of the thirty-six additional units that moved around between them (Case 1948, 320). Each unit was headed by a lieutenant colonel who, as "command historian" coordinated the work of his monograph team (one officer, two "enlisted historians," and a clerk), who were composing the narratives, and a changing number of "contact teams" ("two enlisted and two commissioned historians"), who explored the surroundings and collected the material—army slang called them the "the 'bird-dog' staff" (Wright 1985, 3).

Lasky was part of the MHD 6 placed with the Seventh Army. In the published report he is listed under "researcher," which means he was both writing reports and gathering material (Seventh Army Report). His diary includes long elaborations on the editing process, but he also distinctly remembers "a brief career as a 'bird-dog' . . . scooting from headquarters to command posts to front-line positions and back." He describes his trips to seek historically relevant material, for example from the French Resistance, and his visits to the battlefield, which he finds "strange and exciting" and where he takes pictures. Lasky seemed drawn to going out and exploring for himself, a young man on an adventure: "If I could have my own way I would take off again tomorrow morning for the front" (12 March).

Not uncommon in war diaries, though, the excitement for the authenticity of the battlefield is complemented by the powerful trope of the human cost of war: "these poor unfortunate boys died in forests and fields they would never even know by name" (23 March). Almost in awe, Lasky notes "every tragic detail of the terrain, the trees and bushes along the stream where men took cover in their terror" (3 March). Yet, he also seems concerned or at least torn, lest these kinds of emotions compromise his carefully crafted, intellectually removed persona. After poignantly relating how he found a memento in the Colmar Forest, "a Christmas greeting card to 'Sonny' from 'Mother,'" and vividly describing an affective scene from a recent battlefield, where "floating in a water-filled foxhole, was the cover of the Army edition of Ernie Pyle's *Here is Your War*," he adds apologetically: "I simply report what I found: Am I responsible for the obvious sentimentalism?" (3 March). A mere month and a half later, he appears to show even less patience for "self-tortured sympathy" (22 April).

Arguably, this episode highlights Lasky's ambivalence toward recording and reporting the events—caught between the role of the historian and the journalist. His academic schooling in history, according to the discipline's dominant currents at the time, led him to mock the notion of telling history from the perspective of "Joe in his Foxhole." At the same time, though, he also felt disenchanted with established historical practice and tradition: "Ranke is with us every moment through the vast labors of investigation, but the end-product narratives are invariably 'as Things Never Actually Happened'" (22 April). The stories the soldiers tell seem to Lasky more relevant and more fascinating, they add, as he explains, the invaluable "living context, the flavor, the excitement and passion and nervousness, the vocabulary—in a word, for me the truth" (12 March).

The somewhat postmodern dilemma between actual and emotional truth also affects the writing process of the report Lasky was assigned to produce on a small engagement at a river crossing near Colmar named for the farm house close by *La Maison Rouge*.[6] "I have necessarily to make it a conventional thing," he notes in his diary as he begins in April 1945, "but it still may take on a tone and force of its own." Eventually the established academic practice seems almost superfluous to him. Footnotes and references become a burden and he opines: "the formal apparatus of scholarship in problems of this type of historical composition performs no real function except as a kind of soul-soothing ritual" (3 March). By the time his first draft is ready for submission, Lasky seems so acutely conscious of the gap between professional requirements and his own favored approach that he feels the need to preface the report with his "Credo," which he also copies into his diary:

> In my own manuscript nothing has been invented. Not a fact or detail appears which was not submitted to me in good faith and checked as best as could be done under the circumstances. I have added nothing to the records and testimonies offered me except for the obvious requirements of composition and simple interpretive synopsis. . . . At no point have I indulged in literary or journalistic license. Everything that has been included has its source in critically examined evidence, and of the many omissions of details and events, committed in the ordinary activity of an historian "selecting" his data, none of them would substantially alter the picture drawn. (3 March)

While the majority of this paragraph reads like a professional code of conduct for the traditional historian, the final sentence reminds us that all history writing is essentially predicated on subjective choices and styles. Working as a combat historian, employing unconventional methods for the time such as oral history interviews and on-location research, Lasky had become convinced: "The man of sober fact has rarely been able to see the documentary truth for all the dust on the archives" (12 March).

While clearly prompted by particular circumstances and ulterior motives, namely propaganda and some kind of emotional comfort for the people, the new focus on the average soldier in collecting information allowed for early developments in new methodologies such as oral history (Pogue 2001; Shulman 1993).[7] Three years after the war, the first civilian program for oral history in the US was created at Columbia University, initiated by Alan Nevins, who had also worked in Europe during the war for the US War Department. Incidentally, he had also been the third Columbia professor to write a recommendation for Lasky in 1944. What would later be called history from the "bottom-up" would not make its way into traditional military history, or indeed other fields of history, until two decades later; and then, in the 1960s, the approach was pioneered and advocated particularly by anti-military, left-leaning historians such as Howard Zinn in the US and E. P. Thomson in the UK (Lynd 2015). In retrospect, Pogue remarked: "I don't think it ever occurred to any of the people I was working with in the Second Army that we were making use of a new kind of history" (Pogue cited in Shulman 1993, 31). Methods of data collection through interviews were becoming more common though, certainly in other disciplines than history. For example, the 1930s and 1940s saw the emergence of opinion polling and market research, and New Deal programs had funded large-scale anthropological endeavors. Only months after the war was over, psychologist David P. Boder conducted—and audio recorded—interviews with survivors of concentration camps (Boder 2011). For the combat historians, at least at first, these methods were born out of necessity, not based on theoretical deliberation. They took their pointers from journalism; Pogue recalled reading "several books by newspaper people on interviewing troops" (Pogue cited in Shulman 1993, 45). Pogue had a hierarchical attitude in approaching his interviewees and on the subject of history, explaining, "when I was interviewing infantry men, many of the people we talked to were not thinkers in any sense.... You had to draw out of them what they were talking about and you soon realized—he doesn't know any more than that he did this at some time [sic]" (Pogue cited in Shulman 1993, 34). Usually no stranger to snobbery, here Lasky held a different view. A journalist at heart, the young second lieutenant thrived when it came to interviewing the average soldier. Less interested in the kind of standard information of exact times and locations that could just as well be honed from official files, he almost gleefully sprinkled his reports with colorful direct quotations. Moreover, he was keen and curious to talk to the local population. "It is almost maddening to think that there are thousands of people, in Darmstadt, in Worms, in Kaiserslautern, and no one knows what they are thinking, what they are feeling!" he records in his diary on 9 April, even before the official ending of the war. Naturally, he did not let nonfraternization regulations stop him: "I ventured a few tentative questions." These interviews had no place in the official Army reports, so Lasky consigns them to his diary, which in these instances becomes his field-journal.

Both Lasky and Pogue comment on the thrill of immediacy and access, writing and recording history "as it *happens* to people" or, in Pogue's words, "history while it is hot" (Pogue cited in Shulman 1993, 40). In retrospect, Pogue admitted that he was captured by the potential of this work with an eye on his later career: "We wanted that one book to our credit. We were smart enough to know that we had first access to a great number of documents that would not be open to general historians for years to come" (Pogue cited in Shulman 1993, 40). He then adds a passionate defense of the entire official Army history project that did indeed make his career: "We got to people, and we got to papers, much earlier than the so called [*sic*] regular historian. And we were able to get certain first hand [*sic*] recollections that would have been lost in two or five years" (Pogue cited in Shulman 1993, 42).[8] Lasky, already in his diary, was more skeptical. He does concede that "never before have there been such facilities for thoroughgoing original research and explorations into secret documents, and also into the realities in question"; moreover, he certainly liked the idea to "get into a jeep . . . , and you can check your footnote at the front!" (12 March). Still, even if some of the practices of the Historical Branch may appear ahead of their time, what was being produced was still "official history," proofread and sanctioned by the army with clear objectives and motivations that were only partially academic. Lasky cynically highlights this framework when he is ordered to edit parts of the official report: "The manuscript is now clean, ready for the seal of the General. The outline is orderly, the notes and bibliography complete, the pages neatly typed and doublespaced [*sic*]. Here it is, but the real history lies in the white space between the lines" (12 March). Interestingly, while Pogue believed exclusive and immediate access provided an advantage to the official Army historian over those who came after, Lasky saw it the other way around. Observing the mass of "quartermaster's wooden boxes, each packed with reports, sketches, journals, interviews, plans and orders," he felt hope: "In the future it will at least be *possible* for the people to know the truth." Arguably, this was also how Lasky justified his work as a combat historian regardless of the Army's not-so-hidden agenda: "The History itself may be orthodox, official. But as a combat historian here one really becomes a kind of spy in the interests of civilian civilization" (12 March). He was doing a service to future historians—like the journalist's "first draft of history."

Charlotte A. Lerg, Assistant Professor of American history at Ludwig-Maximilians-University, Munich), is Managing Director of the Lasky Center for Transatlantic Studies. She is a board member of the Bavarian American Academy, has held research fellowships at the Library of Congress as well as at the German Historical Institute (Washington, DC), and has taught at the universities of Münster, Jena, and Bochum. Recent publications include *Universitätsdiplomatie* (2019) and *Campaigning Culture* (2017) edited with Giles Scott-Smith. Lerg is also co-editor of the series *History of Intellectual Culture (HIC): International Yearbook of Knowledge and Society.*

Notes

1. Melvin Lasky to Merle Curti (31 October 1944), Wisconsin Historical Society, Merle E. Curti Papers, Box 23, folder 25. I thank Maren Roth for pointing me to this document.
2. About three-quarters of the staff available was tied down with the World War I project, and indeed, still was by 1945 (Conn 1993, 31).
3. Placing this new branch with G-2 had primarily practical reasons: (generally) secure networks of communication and information collection were already established which made it easier to gather material systematically from all the fronts and all the different levels and branches of the army (Conn 1993, 34–35).
4. Only fourteen of these monographs were completed between early 1945 and 1946 (cf. Wright 1985, 3).
5. In 1950, in the context of federal restructuring, the Division was renamed yet again. It remained the Office of the Chief of Military History (OCMH) until the early 1970s when it became the Center of Military History that still exists today.
6. "Melvin Lasky: La Maison Rouge. The Story of an Engagement" (typescript), Lasky Papers, New York Box 1, Folder 9.
7. Among military historians Pogue is celebrated as a "pioneer" in the field of oral history (Falk 2002; Coffman 2006).
8. Pogue went on to write *Supreme Command* (1954), the Army series's volume on Eisenhower and the Allied command, also based on extensive interviews with those involved, though these were the highest levels of the military echelons, certainly not the average GI.

References

Adamczyk, Richard D., and Morris J. MacGregor, eds. 1992. *The United States Army in World War II Series. Readers Guide*. Washington, DC: Center of Military History/United States Army.
Arthur, Billy. 1991. "Clio in Desert Shield and Desert Storm." *Army History* 18: 13–16.
Boder, David P. 2011. *Die Toten habe ich nicht befragt*. Edited by Julia Faisst et al. Heidelberg: Universitätsverlag Winter.
Case, Lynn M. 1948. "The Military Historian Overseas." *Bulletin of the American Association of University Professors* 34(2): 320–34.
Clarke, Jeffrey. 2006. "Care and Feeding of Contemporary History." *Army History* 62: 35–37.
Coffman, Edward. 2006. "Memoires of Forrest C. Pogue, Oral History Pioneer and One of Kentucky's Greatest Historians." *The Register of the Kentucky Historical Society* 104(3/4): 675–84.
Conn, Stetson. 1993. "Historical Work During World War II (1/3)." *Army History* 28: 30–35.
———. 1994a. "Historical Work During World War II (2/3)." *Army History* 29: 22–27.
———. 1994b. "Historical Work During World War II (3/3)." *Army History* 30: 14–19.
Falk, Stanley. 2002. "'Pogue's War' and the Making of a Military Historian: A Review Essay." *Army History* 55: 26–30.
Lynd, Staughton. 2015. *Doing History from the Bottom Up: On E.P. Thompson, Howard Zinn, and Rebuilding the Labor Movement from Below*. Chicago: Haymarket Books.
Nye, Roger. 1983. "The Army Historians: Who Are They?" *The Army Historian* 1: 6–8.

Pogue, Forrest C. 2001. *Pogue's War: Diaries of a WWII Combat Historian*. Lexington: University Press of Kentucky.

Shulman, Holly C. 1993. "Forrest C. Pogue and the Birth of Public History in the Army." *The Public Historian* 15(1): 26–46.

Wegner, Bernd. 1995. "Erschriebene Siege. Franz Halder, Die 'Historical Division' und die Rekonstruktion des Zweiten Weltkriegs im Geiste des deutschen Generalstabs." In *Politischer Wandel, Organisierte Gewalt und nationale Sicherheit. Beiträge zur neueren Geschichte Deutschlands und Frankreichs*, ed. E. Hansen et al., 287–302. Munich: Oldenbourg.

Wright, Robert K., Jr. 1985. "Clio in Combat: The Evolution of the Military History Detachment." *The Army Historian* 6: 3–6.

Chapter 5
(Military) Masculinity and a Feminized Europe
The Gender Politics of the Lasky Diary
Katharina Gerund

When Melvin Lasky was sent to Europe in 1945 as a combat historian of the Seventh US Army, he was not only an academic historian and a trained soldier with the rank of second lieutenant but also a young man in his mid-twenties searching for his identity with a penchant for adventure. Lasky's diary intricately links the transformational moment in European and transatlantic history of 1945 with the individual, life-changing experiences Lasky had while traversing the continent. His journey thus is not only an endeavor to chronicle the historical events but also a very personal *rite de passage*.[1] As readers of his diary, we follow Lasky on his search for relevant information and for himself and his place within history. We learn as much about Lasky's self-fashioning, thinking, and identity as we do about the situation of the Seventh US Army, the civilian population, and more generally, Europe at the end of World War II. In both regards, his account is highly gendered: 1) a predominantly male US Army conquers and occupies a largely feminized Europe and 2) a combat historian exercises his male privilege, his epistemic power, and his "male gaze" (Mulvey 2004) to describe the land and the women he encounters; in the process, he negotiates his own gendered and sexualized identity vis-à-vis the dominant gender ideologies of his cultural contexts. The diary reveals—sometimes in ambiguous ways—how Lasky's gendered perspective as a young, white American soldier corresponds to discourses of the transatlantic relationship between the US and Germany in the postwar world.

In line with his position as combat historian, Lasky presents himself as an avid reader, an intellectual observer, and a commentator with philosophical inclinations. He goes to great lengths to distinguish himself from the other soldiers and even his fellow historians—especially in his performance of (military) masculinity. Military masculinity can be understood, following

Aaron Belkin, "as a set of beliefs, practices and attributes that can enable individuals—men and women—to claim authority on the basis of affirmative relationships with the military or with military ideals" (Belkin 2012, 3). At first glance, it seems to rely on a clear-cut gender binary, to entail an outright disavowal of everything coded "feminine" or "queer," and to designate "a status that, by definition, indicates the truth about who and what a man is" (Belkin 2012, 10). However, military masculinity is much more complex as it "has been structured by irresolvable contradictions associated with US empire" and has been turned into "a site where irreconcilable political contradictions have been smoothed over" (Belkin 2012, 5). Lasky's reflections on his status as combat historian and "tourist-conqueror" as well as on the politics of the US occupation and its early reeducation efforts reveal the ideal of military masculinity, but at the same time expose its ambivalences on the individual and collective level.

Throughout his diary, Lasky struggles with his (male) role and identity. He tries to set himself apart from other members of the army in the way he details his own thoughts and conduct. His position already distinguishes him from the "poor tearful GIs, pleading for some extra-military influence to get them back home" or those working "all along the highway . . . , their clothes soaked and dirty, their faces raw with cold, and their eyes red with sleeplessness and a deep endless fatigue" (9 and 10 February). Similarly, his description of an officers' club bespeaks his efforts at presenting himself as part of an intellectual elite and thus decidedly *not* as one of the "boys": "These boys, for the greater part, face their own violent ends almost every week. . . . [T]he guests break themselves down in drink and fornication . . . . The women are dull, unattractive, spiritless Alsatian bodies. The men are silly when they are not lustful, and altogether pitiable" (18 February). That he himself then ends up "in bed with a spiritless little thing" already hints at the fact that he participates in some of the same activities and performances of masculinity as the other soldiers and officers. His stories of sexual(ized) encounters with women and the slight changes in their emplotment indicate Lasky's transition into the gendered and sexualized roles of military occupation and his reliance on his position in the military to exercise power. Despite his reflections on the (violently) sexual dimension of conquest and occupation, for instance, when he categorizes a "sign on a Nancy street-level apartment: No women. Please do not Knock" as an epitome of the "'social history' of the American soldier in France" (23 February), he increasingly participates in the sexual exploration and exploitation of women on his grand tour-like travels through war-torn Europe. In the beginning, he is still noting down his attempts to stay in touch with Marion, his romantic interest back home: "Poor Marion! I, of course, can easily go on receiving her warm and touching letters, but can she go on writing them? She can't! and I don't want her to. With every line she reworks emotions and sensitivities until her whole spirit is raw and aching" (25 February). His paternalistic comments on her emotional state are not only in line with the "hegemonic masculinity"[2] of his time but also foreshadow that Marion, the waiting woman on the home front, will not figure prominently in the remainder of his diary. They also attest to the continuities regarding gender hierarchies and patriarchal dynamics from New York's male-dominated intellectual culture with which Lasky previously had been associated and the military culture which he was still adjusting to. In fact, Lasky claims to engage in sexual affairs of different kinds, to fall in love with several women, and, over the course of the months, seems to reflect less and less on their individual significance for him. Especially in the beginning of the diary, there are several affairs that he endows with relevance and even depicts in romanticized terms. In this way, he makes his sexual encounters seem more substantial than for example Davis's and Duncan's "terrain reconnaissance," Jordan's reckless "fraternizing," or Mooney's almost uncontrollable sexual urges. Jeanne, who had worked at a Wehrmacht headquarter in occupied France and was, therefore, interrogated by the police as a "collaborationist" and imprisoned for two months after the liberation of Lunéville, figures not just as a romantic interest but also as an informant and source in Lasky's account. He writes about her:

> I didn't want to make love to her as a casual matter-of-course thing: the convenient affair of the American soldier in a little French village. She would never allow herself a pointless unlovely interlude which involved nothing but necessity. We were both wrong, and it was almost too late. This would be our first and last night. (27 March)

More and more, however, his relationships move from romanticized love affairs to exciting flings to a mere enumeration of his conquests and casual sexual relations: "Aina, Monday," "Helma, Sunday," and "Lydia, Wednesday." The ritualization of short periods of courtship and the serial character of his encounters with women is also evidenced through his choice of words when he refers to "another familiar episode of uncontrollable lust" after his "hallway farewells" to Helma, or when he describes his second date with Inga and Lisl as "the next installment."

Lasky, time and again, stages himself as a Casanova-like hero—in his tales, women are impressed by his appearance, readily at his disposal, and, of course, they wait longingly and patiently for his return. From "*l'affaire Sonia*" (9 March) to "*L'Affaire* Princess Lydichka" (2 June) and from Aina, Helma, and Lydia to Inga, Christy by the Necklar, and Anneliese, Lasky narrates his war experience as a long list of sexual adventures and affairs. In this sense,

Lasky turns out to fit in quite well with the "army of playboys" (10 and 11 September), and his routines turn out to be not much different from other soldiers', like the "GIs from the Eighty-Second Airborne, [whose] conversation bounced between what they called 'daytime jumpin' and 'nighttime humpin', or how to come down from the sky and get yourself a woman for a bar of candy (chocolate) or a couple of cigarettes" (16 to 21 August). This conversation indicates that there was an economic aspect to the transactions between German women and American soldiers. Lasky seems to be quite aware of the fact that women also entered into relationships with Americans out of bare desperation and existential necessity. Toward the end of his diary, he states that "there is no 'market' in women, because the tragic loneliness and terrible frustrations of the bad years have made all of German femininity available" (5 December). When Lasky reflects on his own (sexual) relationships, their power imbalances and their specific sociocultural contexts are frequently and conspicuously absent.

Lasky *does* comment, though, on the politics of nonfraternization, which provided the legal framework for contacts between American soldiers and German civilians, and he chronicles his experiences of the crucial transition from a full-fledged fraternization ban to the first relaxations of this policy. Lasky notes how the thrill of the forbidden added to the overall excitement of his adventures and describes how his task of "gathering material" served as a cover: "We were having our usual boyish sensations of doing something we shouldn't, relived only by a rhetorical formula that after all we were only gathering material for historical reportage" (10 June). Nonfraternization, Lasky agrees with German American journalist and US officer Hans Wallenberg, is "a gross colossal failure, and the only success it was achieving was in the creation of a 'Prohibition' atmosphere" (3 June). And obviously, fraternization happened nonetheless:

> On all sides we could see the furtive exchanges of glances between pretty German girls and the GIs. On side streets they were walking together. In the parks they were lying on the lawn. In a dark alley some soldier would be darting in and out. This was "bootleg" love, "bootleg" sex and "bootleg" social life." (13 June)

Once the "new order of Non-nonfraternization" is in place and the official policies were significantly softened,[3] Lasky sees "social life ... [taking] on a feverish almost riotous pace" (30 June). From the beginning, his war diary paints the landscape of postwar Europe as a highly sexualized environment—perceived through Lasky's "male gaze."[4] The account of his time in Scandinavia explicitly reflects on the overlap of his description of the place and his sexual desires and experiences that blur his perspective and influence his assessment. In October he writes to Dwight Macdonald:

I should really write nothing more about Stockholm for what remains is only romantic interlude, the course of which made me into a partisan of the delights, conveniences, beauties and luxuries of Stockholm. An enchanting city!

He later writes about his "Scandinavian tour" when he "saw nobody, spoke to nobody, learned nothing. I fell in love, spent a fortune, was as happy as I could be" (11 November). To some degree, his male gaze and sexualized depiction of postwar Europe glosses over the quite different political and cultural contexts and shapes Lasky's view of, amongst others, France, Sweden, Finland, and Germany alike. His description of postwar Germany not only highlights the destruction but also shows the ruinous landscape to be full of sexual desires and erotic possibilities—before and after the relaxation of the fraternization ban. Repeatedly, he relates how he and his companions randomly encounter and seek out women on the streets. For example, in one instance, Mooney and Lasky are "racing through Nancy . . . , when suddenly down the avenue the blonde hair and lovely figure of some sweet young thing could be made out. The jeep made a wild turn, careened up and down and over the curbstone, and screeched to a stop directly in her path" (9 March). In another scene, they "continued gaily up past the cathedral and the roving eye caught glimpses of two young girls turning into side streets" (10 June). Of course, in both cases they set up a date with their objects of desire. In Munich, "girls [are] flirting with US soldiers on Nymphenburgerstrasse" and, en route to Deggendorf, "girls and women on the road, lying around on the greensward, at crossroads in villages and cities . . . and the unabashed exchanges of lustful glances" (ellipses in the original). In Berlin, "thousands of blondes, cheap, hopeless little girls [are] walking the streets," and in Frankfurt, "there were GIs and German girls mutually accosting each other, and they lingered under the dim street lights as if to fake a certain sociability to the affair." Lasky takes advantage of the mobility and authority that his US uniform and his position as combat historian afford in order to showcase and reaffirm his manhood. His affairs are, of course, also a means to escape the "boredom" of military life and his everyday duties.[5] The fact that his sexual conquests and numerous affairs need to be reiterated and seem to require constant confirmation even for Lasky himself also signals the instability of his identity construction. It indicates that military masculinity as well as the American neo-imperial military strife it is intimately entangled with are, indeed, ambivalent and full of contradictions.

Lasky's war diary not only reveals the gendered dimension of his personal searches, conquests, and affairs, but also pertains to the transatlantic relationship at large and foreshadows one of the most dominant narratives of its development in the postwar moment. Europe, and especially Germany, is shown as a feminized space, characterized by an absence of men and ready to be conquered by the American soldiers: "I remarked for the first time that there were no men here [Kunheim]. Old women worked with burdens that appeared impossible, and children were ... rendering tireless assistance. No husbands or sons or brothers—all deported or drafted" (22 February). In another scene, girls and mothers take center stage:

> Early today there was a little girl with a huge packed briefcase under her arm. She was waiting impatiently. I threw glances over my shoulder as I walked down the avenue. Soon she met her girl-friend, who was a little late and apparently properly apologetic, for they both went off hand in hand. At noon a group of mothers were gossiping in the square. (1 March)

Women take on an almost symbolic role representing the state of Europe—whether it is the loneliness of Mme. Wernert or the nameless "face of an old woman" on the outskirts of destroyed Darmstadt. "So has the continent of Europe been emasculated," Lasky comments at some point in early June; and his notes prefigure how, with the end of World War II and at the onset of the Cold War, Germany was quickly turned into an exemplary case of American style reeducation and how its image shifted from enemy to victim to friend. Lasky reads the numerous love affairs as a sign of the German acceptance of the US occupiers: "The large picture of US-German relations is not the 'resistance of Germans' but the 'acceptance of the Americans.' They have been taken into their beds" (5 December).[6] While this intimacy was a matter of disdain and concern for many Germans as well as Americans, overall, the couples of American soldiers and German Fräuleins came to paradigmatically represent the amicable transatlantic relationship of the postwar years (Gerund 2018, 147–48), which in itself has sometimes metaphorically been cast as a "love affair" (Willett 1989, 2). Petra Goedde explains that, indeed, "the personal interactions between American soldiers and German civilians bridged the divide that the war had created between the two countries" (Goedde 2003, xxii–xxiii). However, she also points out that this was a maneuver with problematic side effects:

> By casting postwar Germany in feminine terms, Americans and Germans avoided confronting the Nazi past. Postwar Germany shed its aggressive masculine identity and took on a new, if temporary, identity of a feminized, victimized, and most importantly pacific, client state. (Goedde 2003, xxiii)

This posture allowed not only for quickly setting aside a substantial confrontation of Germany's immediate Nazi past but also elided the fact that these relationships were hardly welcomed on both sides of the Atlantic. This was especially true for African American soldiers who experienced an unknown degree of freedom from racism in occupied Germany while facing harsh discrimination as a member of a segregated military within their own ranks (cf. Höhn 2002; Lubin 2005; Schroer 2007). Lasky's notes reveal, though less explicitly, how the relationships between soldiers and civilians were also viewed with contempt. Helma initially hesitates to become involved with Lasky:

> I am a German; you are an American. Then there is the war, and the occupation, and the police, and the neighbors—and most of all there is you and I. It comes down only to that in the end. You will be going away, any day, and I will be alone and hurt again. (3 July)

For others, the question of fraternization is not one "of politics, parties, ideologies," but "a matter of personal pride and dignity" (October 1945). Lasky documents how the Americans continued to propagate nonfraternization and how African American soldiers were particularly targeted. His references to African American soldiers (and Black Frenchmen) expose the investment of (military) masculinity in whiteness as its unmarked norm. The way he situates the affairs of black soldiers with "white German fräuleins" who enjoy the luxuries the soldiers are able to provide in the context of VD checks and raids has a thinly disguised racist subtext that mirrors that "social intimacy not to mention sexual relations with Negroes were normally frowned on" (4 December). Lasky also includes a piece of conversation that reinforces stereotypical images of black masculinity when he reports a black GI saying: "Those fräuleins have sure been good to us. I just love that white meat and I'm gonna look for more of it when I get back to the States." The threat of black male sexuality especially for the white (American) woman, which has been central to racist imagery and arguments in the United States, is clearly evoked here and it is cast in contradistinction to the performance of *white* military manhood. Regarding the Algerian soldiers among the French troops, Lasky addresses structural racism in the military by pointing out that "their complexion, their beards and mustaches, their odd flowing capes, colored turbans, curing knives, and barbarous haircuts ... make them something of the image of riff-raff warriors rather than the portrait of a 'good soldier,'" and, therefore, they do not receive the same respect and reputation as white soldiers (28 February).[7]

Lasky's diary, overall, engages in sexist as well as racist speech acts and it reaffirms white military masculinity. There are, however, also moments in which Lasky critically assesses these discourses and, in some instances, even partially subverts them in his notes and comments. When he interacts with women not as a young soldier driven by sexual desire but as a historian with a genuine interest in documenting the immediate postwar moment in Europe, he regards them not primarily as sexualized objects but more as informants, and he dedicates considerable space to their stories. Jeanne, for example, gets an almost heroic story of her own and as he records her narrative of imprisonment in his diary, he adds his own comments and the romantic encounter with her only in brackets—which, of course, makes them secondary to Jeanne's story. He concludes: "Her account, told with unbelievable subtle modulations and personal power, was so terrible and beautiful. Here was a fine and extraordinary woman" (27 March). That their conversations have "some romantic overtones" and he also has an affair with her proves that the two perspectives—that of the young soldier and that of the "serious" historian—cannot always be neatly distinguished and that, in fact, patriarchal dynamics shape both of these position lines. Lasky, however, also records the stories of other women whom he interviews as witnesses and gives them a voice in his diary (e.g., the story of Elizabeth Kind and her perspective on Germany at the end of war are recounted on a full two pages on 10 May). He chronicles his exchanges with Mrs. Jaspers, Marianne Weber, and Hannah Arendt, which further position him as part of a transatlantic academic elite, but also seem to prove that he is quite comfortable with female intellectuals. When he considers "what some monographer of the future years will make of the 'historical program of World War II,'" it is a "she"—either referring to a female historian or the muse Clio as a personification of History—who "will no doubt explore patiently all the directives, and all the manuscripts, and come away with a contrived myth of abstracted events: precisely as we do in our military research" (22 April).

Reading his diary through a gender studies lens, it becomes evident how Lasky constantly negotiates his manhood and how he juggles his different roles as a young male soldier in search of sexual adventures *and* as an intellectual historian chronicling the postwar moment. Both roles are significant for Lasky's self-fashioning throughout the text, and they are firmly embedded in the hegemonic gender hierarchies that characterize intellectual and military communities of his time. His notes do not simply reflect his own gendered perspective on the people and places he encounters across Europe. They also reveal a broader discourse of the postwar moment that casts the transatlantic relationship in gendered terms, linking masculinity with American military strife and facilitating Germany's transition from enemy to friend. In both cases, the constructions of masculinity and of gender hierarchies constitute ambiguous and complex endeavors—they rely on and affirm patriarchal structures and hegemonic masculinity but also, inadvertently, showcase their contradictions and fragility.

Acknowledgments

My work on Lasky's diary has been part of a research project at FAU Erlangen-Nürnberg on "Reeducation Revisited: Transnationale und kulturvergleichende Perspektiven auf die Nachkriegszeit in den USA, Japan und Deutschland," which is funded by the Deutsche Forschungsgemeinschaft (DFG, German Research Foundation)—Project Number: 407542657.

Katharina Gerund is Senior Lecturer of American Studies at the University of Erlangen-Nürnberg (FAU), Germany. She is the author of *Transatlantic Cultural Exchange: African American Women's Art and Activism in West Germany* (2013) and co-editor of *Die amerikanische Reeducation-Politik nach 1945: Interdisziplinäre Perspektiven auf "America's Germany"* (2015). She is a principal investigator of the DFG-funded research project "Reeducation Revisited: Transnational and Comparative Perspectives on the Post-World War II Period in the US, Japan, and Germany" and currently working on a book project entitled "Happy Home Front Heroines? Military Spouses in the Cultural Imaginary of the US."

Notes

1. In Chapter 1, Maren Roth analyzes Lasky's letters and diaries showing that his war experience was a *caesura* in Lasky's life which vitally impacted his future career.

2. I use the term "hegemonic masculinity" as defined by Raewyn Connell: "Hegemonic masculinity can be defined as the configuration of gender practice which embodies the currently accepted answer to the problem of the legitimacy of patriarchy, which guarantees (or is taken to guarantee) the dominant position of men and the subordination of women" (Connell 1995, 77). Military masculinity then draws on and propels hegemonic masculinity in its claims about manhood as well as its claims to authority.

3. The politics of nonfraternization were slowly retracted following Germany's surrender: "in June, prohibitions against speaking with children were loosened; in July, nonfraternization was amended to allow conversations with adults; and, in September, the policy was dropped entirely, first in Austria and then in Germany" (Biddiscombe 2001, 619). Lasky's entry from 30 July reflects the effects of these new rules, which—at that point—at least allowed for conversations between Americans and Germans.

4. I use Laura Mulvey's term here for two reasons: first, because Lasky describes the presence of women in postwar Europe in quite visual terms and spells out the regimes of looking in this specific context, and second, because it marks the imbalance of power between the active, mobile, and male observer and the passive, sexualized, and female object that is characteristic of Lasky's perspective. Mulvey defines the term as follows: "In a world ordered by sexual imbalance, pleasure in looking has been split between active/male and passive/female. The determining male gaze projects its phantasy on to the female figure which is styled accordingly. In their traditional exhibitionist role, women are simultaneously looked at and displayed, with their appearance

coded for strong visual and erotic impact so that they can be said to connote *to-be-looked-at-ness*" (Mulvey 2004, 841).

5. Already during his training, Lasky had struggled with military routines and everyday life in the military, especially due to its lack of intellectualism (cf. Roth 2018, 141). In the war diary, there are also several comments on his perceived intellectual isolation in the military.

6. In October, in a letter to Dwight Macdonald, Lasky elaborates that the news coverage gets it wrong when it suggests that there is an "infiltration of Nazi ideologies among Americans via fräulein girl friends" and downplays the significance of these relationships when he states that "the relations between Americans and German girls, I daresay, never even skirts the issues of war, peace, and politics."

7. Similarly, when he muses about his two companions, Davis and Hamilton, who represent the Old and the New South to him, he is critical of Hamilton's worldview, that is, the idea that there are "white people and niggers," he but also remarks how "every sentiment, prejudice, theory is couched in charm, and presented with the nice trappings of cultivated dinner or cocktail conversation," and "to be properly outraged," for him, "would be 'inexpedient'" (5 April).

References

Belkin, Aaron. 2012. *Bring Me Men: Military Masculinity and the Benign Façade of American Empire, 1898–2000*. New York: Hurst & Company.

Biddiscombe, Perry. 2001. "Dangerous Liaisons: The Anti-Fraternization Movement in the U.S. Occupation Zones of Germany and Austria, 1945–1948." *Journal of Social History* 34.3: 611–47.

Connell, R. W. 1995. *Masculinities*. Oakland: University of California Press.

Gerund, Katharina. 2018. "Transatlantic Romance(s) of the Postwar Years: Interracial Relationships in *Die PX-Story* (1959) and *Transgression* (2015)." In *German-American Encounters in Bavaria and Beyond, 1945–2015*, ed. Birgit M. Bauridl, Ingrid Gessner, and Udo J. Hebel, 147–70. Frankfurt: Peter Lang.

Goedde, Petra. 2003. *GIs and Germans: Culture, Gender, and Foreign Relations, 1945–1949*. New Haven: Yale University Press.

Höhn, Maria. 2002. *GIs and Fräuleins: The German-American Encounter in 1950s West Germany*. Chapel Hill: University of North Carolina Press.

Lubin, Alex. 2005. *Romance and Rights: The Politics of Interracial Intimacy, 1945–1954*. Jackson: University of Mississippi Press.

Mulvey, Laura. 2004. "Visual Pleasure and Narrative Cinema." In *Film Theory and Criticism*. 6th ed., ed. Leo Braudy and Marshall Cohen, 14–26. Oxford: Oxford University Press.

Roth, Maren. 2018. "'What an unbelievable unreal adventure!' Melvin J. Lasky als Akteur im kriegszerstörten Deutschland." In *Feinde, Freunde, Fremde? Deutsche Perspektiven auf die USA*, ed. Volker Benkert, 135–58. Baden-Baden: Nomos.

Schroer, Timothy. 2007. *Recasting Race after World War II: Germans and African Americans in American-Occupied Germany*. Boulder: University of Colorado Press.

Willett, Ralph. 1989. *The Americanization of Germany, 1945–1949: Studies in Film, Television, and the Media*. London: Routledge.

Chapter 6
Melvin J. Lasky, Chronicler of Europe's Twentieth Century
Michael Kimmage

Melvin Lasky had the biography of a stereotypical New York intellectual. He was born in New York City in 1920. This placed him in the second generation of the New York intellectuals, an intellectual coterie not defined precisely by region of origin, political outlook, or writing style. They were defined by some combination of these three things. Raucous, striving, taste-making New York was the center of twentieth-century American intellectual life. For the self-described New York intellectuals, politics meant first of all the question of socialism, then of the Soviet Union, and then of the proper way to oppose Joseph Stalin's Soviet Union. The writing style in which these questions were debated was erudite but not academic, challenging but not snobbish, ambitious in cultural and political scope but not esoteric. It merged politics, literature, history, and philosophy and upheld the drama, stature, and salience of ideas as such. The first generation had come of age in the 1920s, many of them either the children of Jewish immigrants or immigrants themselves, all of them captivated by the Soviet experiment and its consequences for twentieth-century politics and art.[1]

As Melvin Lasky was becoming a New York intellectual in his teenage years, he absorbed the experiences and the questions of his elders. His point of entry was the City College of New York along with Irving Kristol, Irving Howe, Daniel Bell, and many others, after which Lasky studied history at the University of Michigan and launched a career in intellectual journalism at the *New Leader*. Lasky was briefly a Trotskyist, when Trotskyism was in vogue at *Partisan Review*, the in-house magazine of the New York intellectuals. Exactly in synch with *Partisan Review*, Lasky adopted a position of anti-communism around 1941. Stalin's Soviet Union had amassed too great a record of violence by 1941 for Lasky and his fellow travelers. The avant-garde promise of Soviet culture in the 1920s notwithstanding, Stalinism was by 1941 a byword for doctrinaire mediocrity—at least at *Partisan Review* it was. For Lasky and the previous generation of New York intellectuals, Stalinism violated their treasured cultural ideals of complexity, openness, and high-modernist artistic freedom.

Melvin Lasky would never stray from the main trajectory of the New York intellectuals. Gifted in so many ways, he was in fact among the less creative members of the New York intellectual family. He was not a Lionel Trilling, a Hannah Arendt, an Irving Kristol, or a Daniel Bell. He did not write books that transformed the conversation or that became lasting monuments of twentieth-century intellectual culture. Where the pioneering New York intellectuals went Lasky tended to follow. He traced their path to anti-communism; after World War II he took their path to liberal anti-communism, which is to say the endorsement of the foreign policy and political economy fashioned by Harry Truman and John F. Kennedy; and, finally, he followed the path of some New York intellectuals to neoconservatism, to support for Ronald Reagan and the Republican Party of the 1980s. Until his death in 2004, shortly after the outbreak of the Iraq War, which he supported, Lasky stayed within the parameters of the New York intellectual story.[2]

Melvin Lasky was not entirely stereotypical, however. The New York intellectuals were Europhiles. They devoured European ideas, theories, and books. For the first half of the twentieth century, European politics was far more vivid and meaningful to them than American politics: Franklin Roosevelt could not compete with Hitler and Stalin for their attention. After World War II, a number of the New York intellectuals traveled to Europe, and some spent considerable time there: Irving Kristol and Gertrude Himmelfarb lived in London for several years. It was Lasky alone who moved to Europe and remained there, shipping out as a soldier and settling by geopolitical and personal accident in (West) Berlin in 1947. This meant that Lasky did much of his editing, writing, and public speaking for German and European audiences. He was a diasporic New York intellectual, though far as it was from New York, Berlin was a mere 450 kilometers from the Polish city of Łódź, from which Lasky's family had emigrated to the United States at the turn of the century.

Europe refined Lasky's single greatest skill as an intellectual. It made him into a careful, meticulous observer, and here he diverges from those New York intellectuals whose careers were uninterruptedly American. After World War II, the New York intellectuals in the United States found their way to prominence and in some instances to power. Theirs was a story of social ascendancy that happened to coincide with the foreign-policy ascendancy of the United States. This instilled in such New York intellectuals as Irving Kristol and Norman Podhoretz the desire to act upon the world, to shape the domestic politics and the foreign policies of the United States, and to rotate between the cities of New York and Washington, DC. No doubt Lasky had comparable ambitions, and he was a well-known voice in West Germany, a public figure who wielded some degree of influence. Yet Lasky's real skill was elsewhere. He excelled at registering all of the ways the world acted upon him, at witnessing the startling strangeness of reality. That is what made him an exceptional editor. In the end, it is what made him—from 1945 to 2004, for all the years he spent in Germany and Great Britain—an extraordinary chronicler of Europe in extraordinary times. He found himself in Europe in 1945 with a war to fight and an official job to do, which was to capture the history of a few set-piece battles for the US military. Officially and unofficially, licitly and illicitly, Lasky's eyes were open to everything. He began his European chronicle in January 1945, and he did so by setting aside what spare moments he had for his diary.

Lasky's diary bears the New York intellectuals' stamp. His language is relatively simple and often quite close to vernacular American speech, which he sometimes conveys directly by transcribing the voices of the American soldiers around him. It is the writing style that emerged from an intellectual milieu that lionized the essay and that preferred the medium of intelligent journalism to the scholarly article or the monograph. Not surprisingly for a diary, Lasky writes in his personal voice, but this too was a trademark of New York intellectual prose. In this voice, Lasky explores a range of references in his writing that is very wide-ranging. A not especially innocent abroad in Europe for the first time, Lasky writes with authority about European history, literature, and philosophy, crisscrossing with ease the midcentury Euro-Atlantic republic of letters. In a devastated Frankfurt, he makes a point of visiting Goethe's birthplace, which is essentially a pile of rubble with a rusted pipe sticking out of it. He is there to study the place of Goethe's birth and to contemplate what has become of it during the war. When Lasky visits Karl Jaspers and his wife and starts bringing them food packages (they take to calling him Santa Claus), he is not exactly the equal of Karl Jaspers, but he is not his inferior either. This too was a New York intellectual trait: an at-homeness in the world of ideas, "first to knock, first admitted," as Saul Bellow put in the first sentence of his novel, *The Adventures of Augie March* (Bellow 2006, 1).

Another New York intellectual trait was Lasky's preoccupation with literature. Reading literature was not a leisure activity for him, and it was not a professionalized activity. He writes with no PhD dissertation in sight—without any real vocation in sight, including that of a soldier, which is what Lasky officially was in 1945. Literature is his guide and his teacher. His diary is studded with references to Stendhal, who had been a soldier in Napoleon's armies, traveling some of the same territory Lasky himself traveled some 130 years after the Napoleonic wars. Stendhal matters to Lasky for what he has to say about the ironies of war, the mysteries of great, historic events, and the romantic conception of self. Lasky was of the Napoleonic mode, but he was also dismissive of it in his diary, living as he did in the 1940s and schooled as he was in the horrors of modern warfare. Stendhal is an obvious author for any literate soldier to read. More surprising is Lasky's reckoning with Henry James in his diary, James being one of the beloved authors of the New York intellectuals. Amid the rubble and the tanks, the displaced people wandering the roads and a growing awareness of the Holocaust, Lasky finds himself thinking about Henry James and taste. He appreciated James's elevation of taste to a virtue, even on the battlefields of World War II. Lasky relishes the conundrum of a writer as solipsistic and recondite as James, who is nevertheless relevant to the prospect of civilized life in Europe's astonishing spring of 1945.

After the war, Lasky would serve as a correspondent for the *New Leader* and for *Partisan Review*. *Partisan Review* in particular had cultivated the genre of the letter in the 1930s, which is to say a letter written from outside New York informing the magazine's readers of new developments in the world. This genre was not straight-up reportage. It did not limit itself to tales of high politics or to the latest crisis or to human-interest stories. Nor did the letter genre cover book publications, intellectual controversies, and abstract ideas alone. It wove high politics, crises, and human-interest stories into the ongoing intellectual drama. If this genre still exists in contemporary American journalism, it would be in the blog section of the *New York Review of Books*. Lasky could write in this genre as well as anyone, perhaps because his diary was such excellent preparation for this kind of writing, combining the image-driven documentary style of the 1930s with the highbrow intellectual discourse of the 1940s. In addition, the *Partisan Review* letter was supposed to be thought-provoking, neither polemic nor diatribe, a lucid review of the reigning political confusion and a postcard from "the dark and bloody crossroads where literature and politics meet," in Lionel Trilling's often-cited words (Trilling 2008, 11).

The excellence of Lasky's diary resides in its author's sustained ability to surprise himself. A casual notation is a clue to his mindset: "the story began to unfold slowly today," Lasky writes, "and I couldn't leave the loose ends lie" (29 March). He had to go and unravel the loose ends. The story usually *was* the loose ends, and in not knowing where the story would end up, Lasky gave himself occasion to see, to think, and to write. A good example is from a long diary entry from March 1945. In the middle of this entry, Lasky measures his perceptions of Germans against the more categorical judgments of the displaced people he has encountered:

> Most of the "refugees" or "displaced persons" spoke a fair German, and all of them shook their heads glumly when the matter of the German people came

up. "All of them" were "bad." The Germans had beaten them and treated them like dogs. Did you ever see a good German? Well, possibly ten percent, it was conceded, but the rest of them were worthless and mean. (As a matter of fact I think statistical estimates of Hitlerist fanaticism will be steadily revised as more and more contact with Germans is made. And not that the seizure of German territories is turning up anti-Nazis of noble standing. In Cologne, for example, the good party members were being turned in by citizens in every neighborhood. Up the highway toward Ludwigshafen only last week a family called over some American officers and betrayed the hiding-places of a pair of gestapo agents. This can, of course, be dismissed as "opportunism." But then an opportunist is not a fanatic; his belief and loyalty have a different intensity; and the fact that even a few are now changing sides actively is a revealing light on the myths of blanket Hitler worship and unmitigated allegiance.) (30 and 31 March)

The negative judgments of the displaced people are stated without immediate commentary. They are one data point. Then Lasky jumps in with a question about the evidence ("statistical estimates"), surmising that prolonged contact with Germans will yield a sharper image. Cologne serves as another data point, as does the family in Ludwigshafen that betrays the location of Gestapo agents. Lasky does not rush to exonerate Germans at a time when the war has not even ended. His question—which would prove fundamental to West Germany's political culture—was about degrees of belief and loyalty, which widely prevalent "myths of blanket Hitler worship" were certain to obscure. Lasky does not force an answer to the question of where German loyalties lay in March 1945. He has the patience to give the question its due. He is investigating the nuances behind the question. A GI on the move, Lasky derived the necessary questions from the contradictions in his vicinity, juxtaposing myth against fact and fact against myth.

In one instance at least, Lasky is not surprised enough or surprised in too conventional a manner by the war. In December 1945, he encounters an older Jewish woman in Braunschweig, one of the few remaining members of its Jewish community. She intuits in Lasky an identification with Germany that is a subtle theme of his diary. Lasky was himself Jewish; he was certainly aware of the Holocaust, and he recounts a few meetings with Germans in which he chose to challenge a German sense of wartime victimhood. At the same time, Lasky was enamored of German culture, has trysts with German women, and is too curious not to talk with Germans and in some cases to befriend them. Mostly he writes about Germans without rancor: not for nothing did Lasky stay in Germany after the war. Observing this tacit sympathy, the Jewish woman in Braunschweig sees how horrified Lasky and his fellow GIs are by the devastation of German towns and cities—at what the Allies had wrought on German soil. "'You boys,' the old lady said to me softly, 'are surprised and distressed at the ruins, at all the rubble. For us there is not yet enough.'" Lasky wrote this anecdote down on 16 December 1945, the second to last entry in his diary. By the end of 1945, Lasky had not scratched the surface of the surface of the war. Overwhelmed by his experiences, he was aware of his ignorance, though in this particular case he had to be reminded of it.

On 16 April 1945, Lasky described receiving a shipment of books and magazines from the United States. Among them was a "brochure for *Partisan Review*." It might have been an opportunity for Lasky to catch up with the American scene. Yet instead of happiness Lasky responded with sorrow. He had gone to war with Hemingway-esque fantasies of "what sources of strength there would be in the war experience." After only a few months of the war, he felt enervated, hollowed out, weakened. "Things happen to me but I don't meet them," he writes on 16 April. He does not have the sovereign perspective of a *Partisan Review* author and New York intellectual, armed with sensibility and the latest ideas, and quickly able to comment on the state of the world, to master the heart-of-darkness rhythms of twentieth-century politics. "I have been hurt in so many small terrible ways in the months here," Lasky continued in the same diary entry, "by the casual details of the great tragedy which one only comes to know in its humdrum everyday horror.... I can only plead some strange inner weakness which baffles me, and has effectively stopped me from ordering my own impressions." He could only have been hurt by what he had seen, and tragedy often communicates itself most fully through the casual, humdrum details, of which Lasky's diary is such a meaningful record. Entirely understandable, his "inner weakness" was also an inner strength. He could observe and therefore chronicle the war because his impressions had been so starkly disordered. In his postwar decades of writing and editorial work in Berlin and elsewhere, he would not forget what the disorder the war had imposed upon him.

Michael Kimmage is Professor of History at the Catholic University of America. His most recent book is *The Abandonment of the West: The History of an Idea in American Foreign Policy* (2020).

Notes

1. On the New York intellectuals: Wald 1987.
2. On the New York intellectuals and neoconservatism see Heilbrunn 2008 and Vaisse 2010.

References

Bellow, Saul. 2006. *The Adventures of Augie March*. London: Penguin.
Heilbrunn, Jacob. 2008. *They Knew They Were Right: The Rise of the Neocons*. New York: Doubleday.
Trilling, Lionel. 2008. *The Liberal Imagination*. New York: New York Review of Books.
Vaisse, Justin. 2010. *Neoconservatism. The Biography of a Movement*. Cambridge, MA: Harvard University Press.
Wald, Alan. 1987. *The New York Intellectuals: The Rise and Decline of the Anti-Stalinist Left*. Chapel Hill: University of North Carolina Press.

Figure 1. Second Lieutenant Melvin J. Lasky en route to Germany, © Lasky Center, Munich.

Melvin J. Lasky Diary

22 January 1945, Fort Totten, New York

What do I know? What have I learned? So many volumes, so much carefully contrived experience (even rash exposure to events and "life"), and here I remain, desperately unable to live with myself, incapable of ordering my memories and responses, and shaping my ambitions. I spent the day nervously in the reading room of the library here, I must have fingered with a hopeless and frantic hunger a hundred volumes. But there was nothing for me, not a page I could read, not a sentence I really wanted. There was a Walter Pater miscellany, and I glanced at some phrases on Pascal—"the spectacle of the religious history of the human soul."... No, that is what I do not understand! I looked at McGiffert's study on Christian theology, but "Love" and "God" were empty, without meaning. Oh, if I could only comprehend them, take all the great words seriously, patiently, how deeply convenient it would be!—there would be an end to weakness, faltering heart and mind. "Spirituality," and all the supporting strength of classic historic traditions, could be my sanctuary. I could be strong again ... I turned to a volume on history—"the critical consciousness of civilization about its own past." Yes, yes! But what does all my once precise and finicky awareness of Sumer and Akkad and the Gracchi and Innocent and Peter Waldo and Cromwell mean for me now? Paltry, vague, irrelevant memories... I picked up Gide's *Travels*, Cohen's *Logic*, some things of Maugham, a novel by Wolfe, Melville's *Billy Budd*, a tale by Edna Ferber... I must be mad, or ill. Why am I torturing myself? I am lost and despairing. Is there nowhere a page for me—a paragraph, a word, to teach me to live with myself, with my boredom, with my alienation, with my mediocrity? For the first time in my life, I think, I am alone and bereft. My old formulas are gone and useless. I do now know how to be happy.

24 January 1945, Fort Totten, New York

Finally wrote my letter to M. which I had been postponing day after day. But then it has always been difficult for me to "correspond," except under special conditions. Most frequent circumstance have been some impulse of "spontaneity"; something of the moment which simply had to be said, and so it was written and dispatched. —Usually a perfunctory message or some touching or flirtatious sentimentalism. That I've not been "inspired" to write her will, I know, strike her very personally and even depress her. Poor darling! So eternally uncertain, ever in need of loving reassurance. But in a way the silence is right and sincere, for in part it belongs to a mellowness which I haven't quite known before. I think it is sober to say that our time together left no loose ends, no pleasure unshared, no memory which should ever prove difficult in fond recollections of all those days and nights. It was wonderfully full and complete, and as I indulge myself in reverie I become in a curiously serene way "self-sufficient," for there before me is all the warmth and tenderness and understanding which once could only be summoned up in foolish youthful daydreams. Strangely, too, it will soon become shadowy and unbelievable. We reversed every old pattern. Usually with the passing of time memories feed on little myths and idealizations and soon a legend of a great and beautiful romance becomes easily credible. Certainly that's the way it was, must have been! And so by a trick of self-deceit at least something of a deep personal happiness is known. What difference does it make now, fiction or truth? But if they manage to fool the past, the present knows them for their sweet pitiful lie. They remain restless, full of vague longing, daydreaming on in their old roles of adapted Tristans or Juliets. How often I myself have lied in just this way! Disguising poor, mean affairs, or perhaps crudely accepting their poverty of real feeling as some valuable unprocessed experience... The few months we had were truly rare and wonderful. And more and more now looking back, incredible. Were those nights of passion of ours real? (And those occasional daytime hours of playful lust.) How good it was (and how meager the word is to suggest patient loving goodness!) not to be alone, to have some one sit with you and watch for you through endless exercises with books and manuscripts. The mind's eye (or heart's eye?) image of a woman's faith and affection will for a long time be M. seated on a couch, her legs crossed under her, her head resting lightly against the wall and her face lit up like a miracle by sad, warm, sleepy eyes. I adore her for the picture... and a thousand other indescribable scenes (I, once again, will have to assure her; a few even in the darkness of bed) that illustrate our reminiscence. For once, there is no place for even a touch of adornment, a single fictional invention. The colors were all there, in the original: the delight belonged. In loneliness and longing we can run offprints, and be so much stronger in the knowledge that it all happened, the devotion and the kindness and the love. I can't help thinking of a line of Stendhal's. Somewhere he remarks: "Here is the supreme achievement of our civilization—out of love it makes ordinary affairs." It's a little pat and viciously literary for me now to add that somehow we "beat the game." Out of what might so easily have been an ordinary affair (what did we both ourselves bargain for, that first evening?) we made something fine. We were in fact so many times so overwhelmed and agitated we moved in on the cheap stereotypes of *la grande passion*. But that, too, is part of its secret charm. I am so afraid of the terrible embarrassing clichés! But thinking of years of my life and centuries of reading and dreaming: hang them all! If love is ever to be "a work of art" we must lose our shame of sweet simplicities. And when one is "chosen" or "called" (I allow myself a humble mystical mannerism), doubt and question not with cold sophistication, but be glad in the knowledge that there, perhaps but for the grace of God, go two mythical lovers out of some Lawrencian fantasy of love.

26 January 1945, Fort Totten, New York

In many ways it is good to be in camp again. It is not a genuine feeling of security or usefulness, but this after all is the wheel and the course to which you must always come back and take your turn. I am not really sure whether this constitutes escaping or embracing reality. But that was always a simple and naive formula. Life offers a multitude of realities: we face only those for which we have the courage, the curiosity, or the compelling necessity. Inevitably and unfortunately, this always has its invidious implications. There is a suggestion of rejecting the old pale bookish world for the richer if coarser community of everyday men. That is, I suppose, true, if unfair. Coming home has been each time for me a terrible confusing experience. I must have looked only a little different, and talked much the same. Yet I never said what I most wanted to and needed to, and never put in the appearance that was truly proper. That may be striking it a bit too theatrical, but perhaps I intend it that way. We live every moment alone, and each effort to share the private and inner experience has an aspect of melodramatic gesture. We transmute a lonely reverie or despair into a public affecting mood, and make of the quiet strength of new understanding an arrogant confidence. It may be that only the effective actor or poser can be happy. He finds in his role the means to announce himself. So he clarifies his personal drama, and is freed from speechlessness and turgid self-pity. The return here is at least a return to the stage you already know best. The city you once loved with the romantic civic pride of an adolescent seemed mean and inhospitable. The most elementary routines of traffic and communication were so pointless and really hateful. My books confused me, and my old vision of research and composition in quiet libraries was poignantly foreign and irrelevant. Here is a building you know—not a dim apartment in some flat-faced tenement where you work and hope and sleep and never understand it or even see it—but a barracks, standardized for every post, camp, and station of the mass-mechanical army, and standardizing in turn each routine and human response in the military institution. Here is the latrine, the same four seats on the side and one in the corner, the clouded dull mirrors over stained wash-bowls, the small chilly shower room. You go south, or north, but this remains the same, and always it reminds you warmly and strongly of the first time—sitting on the seats, tense and embarrassed (and constipated); scrubbing the bowls and trough on morning details; listening half in disgust half in fascination at the endless profanity and vulgarity. In the latrine the "new life" began, and symbolically enough amidst nakedness (remember now: how uncomfortable one was during that first collective undressing!) and animal necessities. If one was to learn anything about "men" or "life" one must pick up from basic beginnings. And if I were to be serious about the way we live now here is where I must locate my *novus homo*, on a wooden seat over an unflushed bowl... I remember now too one man singing as he shaved, mildly cursing as he nicked his chin, but gay after a day's details on the garbage truck. "Oh, I'll meet you by a garden," he crooned, reciting carefully verse after verse, "in the valley of the moon..." And suddenly he stopped, put his razor down, and turned around. "Well, goddammit!" he shouted. "Listen to those fuckin' words! Just listen to those fuckin' words!" This I carefully noted—apparently there were special illuminations for soldiers, an illumination on the battlefield perhaps, clearly an illumination in the latrine... More and more, I fancied, men would with surprise and indignation hear and listen to for the first time all our words. (Of course, it was not just a mere matter of words, but truly a deep revolution. Great convenient myths would have to be unmasked. But who could live without the mask or the myth in a life of such meanness and soulless tragedy?) A problem and a difficult situation. But this is a little of what I have come to know and belong to.

7 February 1945, Lunéville

Arrived, reported, and have a few days to "locate myself." Well, Lunéville is a little French village, gray and cold and in its first aspect almost deserted. According to the guide-book, it [Lunéville] had a population (once) of 23,000, and was "built in the midst of a broad, beautiful valley," and perhaps so. For now, it seems to have few people and little enough general interest. Even the rather attractive theory that it took its name from a cult which in the Gallo-Roman period was devoted to Diana (or the Moon) no longer holds. From a local history I learn that the Celtic angle has it that *llunn* means healthful, and *ville* place to live. (At any rate I have a slight cold and am concerned with little else beyond a cleared head.)

[...]

Tanks, trucks, artillery pieces have converted the once-beautiful Promenade des Bosquets into a parking lot. Signal communication wires are laced around the necks and limbs of the odd pseudo-Roman–ruin figures in the garden. [...] Now it lodges a rather unlovely US combat division, and its current picturesque animation derives from clothes-lines of o.d. underwear, kitchen trucks and long lines of clanking mess-gears, crowds of miserably poor and dirty little children yelling their pleas for chocolate and chewing gum from the courtyard beside the statue of General Lasalle.

We live in a dark hopeless billet which was converted, with a minimum of conversion, from an old broken-down house by the railroad tracks which could never be sold; the auction sign, a little faded and peeling, is still up on the wall... *une belle maison*. I strolled through a few of the streets in the center of town. Place Leopold is the central square; about two city blocks long, and half as wide, with a striking array of trees, top branches leveled squarely, which in bloom must make a fine green plaza... The usual street-names, but they still "affect" me—rue Gambetta, rue Carnot, and especially rue René Basset: ERUDIT ORIENTALISTE, 1855–1924. Professor Basset's street—which American small-town would have ever regarded him as anything but a crackpot tinkerer with ancient Chinese laundry tickets?—was small, and like Poet Charles Guérin's avenue, chiefly notable for the succession of *sage-femmes* who have their consultation hours neatly announced on quiet little bulletins beside the door-bell. Fortune-tellers![1] And I thought of home again and all those gypsy affairs with offices in old unrented stores decorated with brightly colored curtains... Here it seems to be a respectable, even formidable, middle-class institution!

Posters on walls and billboards still declare the liberation of Lunéville, in September of 1944 (when the Seventy-Ninth Division, then with the Fifteenth Corps of Patton's Third Army, stormed through) ... Even older declarations still stand. Nazi propaganda about STALINIST TERROR; Army injunctions against LOOSE TALK (Churchill is listening!); and occasional remarks about ANGLO-AMERICANS and JEWISH DEMOCRACY. The latest numbers include official Government posters, gaily tinted but on the whole meaningless: WE SHALL WIN! says de Gaulle. WORK WILL RESTORE FRANCE ... etc. There are a great number of Communist announcements up. [...] Of the political movements only the Front National and the CP [Communist Party] have offices in the town. On the Red Cross building—young French boys were inside and outside drilling, *un, deux, trois, quatre,* waiting for their army call—a still older poster remained. 1942, a simple, black and gray Vichy drawing, with apparently a Pétain stalwart in the center, in beret and shorts (powerful muscular legs), carrying a tommy-gun; above and around, a bevy of ancestral spirits—to the right a *poilu* of World War I, to his left a Napoleonic sentinel in full dress and regalia, above with a half-mystical vagueness the knightly and saintly figure of Jeanne [d'Arc]. The text says only: *Dans l'armée française de l'armistice.*

8 February 1945, Lunéville

Spent only a few minutes in the historical section this morning. Hamilton[2] and a few others were busy trying to ferret out from our records the headquarters and CP [Control Post] in a certain area at a certain time—it seems that on 10 December last, some one did a rather thorough job of looting some little French town. Now for "the mystery of the missing madeleines" the historian would play the detective. I learned later that evening at the Vosges bar that, of the many suspects, one (guilty) division had been weeded out. Crime never pays: scholarship will out...

Our own headquarters are in an historic French army caserne ("Clarenthal") and for more than four years it was the central bureau for the Nazi occupation force. Their handiwork is everywhere in evidence. Carefully printed on the white-washed walls in an old German script are innumerable verses; and some are "tactical," others "strategic."

[...]

Mottos, maxims, proverbs were abundant. *Mit dem Führer zum Sieg. Wer leben will, muss kämpfen, Dem Mutigen gehört die Welt,* [...] And finally one that really touched me: *Wo der deutsche Soldat steht, kommt kein anderer hin...,* and there I stood studiously copying it into my notebook!

In the latrine the German scrawlings had faded, but a few of the names could be made out as well as the variety of the usual contexts of latrine lore, propositions, doggerel, and memorabilia.

9 February 1945, Lunéville

A long and picturesque day with the section. So far, have seen no history Made, and no military history Written, but I have no fears for either the pace, success, or color of any effort, if it but shares in the abundance of fantasy, eccentricity, humor, sourness, cynicism, abroad in the office.

Enter Dyer[3] (as I began my duties by cleaning my rifle)—He had just returned from a vacation in Strasbourg, and came back with stacks of volumes in his barracks bag: histories of German literature, collections of engravings and sketches, a fine painting of the cathedral, studies of Alsatian folk-culture... Yet he was very unhappy. You see: "... the Cathedral begins in Gothic and ends in Byzantine!" God, Dyer! came the protests, "you have no soul, no soul at all..." "No, Strasbourg is a desert! The bookstores have nothing in them. The cathedral is a bastard creation. And I was stopped every fifteen minutes by the MPs. (And you know how long it takes an MP to read a pass!)..." He finally conceded that his own book collection was rather good, and that perhaps the cathedral began in Byzantine and ended in Gothic, but then there was always the military police, and he remained very unhappy... Dyer had come up through Africa and Italy with an engineer battalion. The troops would go out, and when they returned, they had hundreds of volumes for "the professor," whole libraries looted out of mansions and schools. "We just saw them around, professor, and thought you'd like them..." It was mostly trash, and the illegal note disturbed him a little, "yet what a feeling for culture!" "Italy is the only land for me! That's where you find real beauty and great history..." And he intended on going back. He has apparently no ties in the States ("family's all busted up"); speaks Italian and reads Latin; and "after five or ten years of loafing in Rome and Florence I can always get along by going into business for a little while, maybe sell real estate along the Amalfi Drive..." The saga of a Harvard man: he quit his graduate studies abruptly after a conference with Arthur Meier Schlesinger—he had told Schlesinger that he would be uncompromising in his opposition to the Conscription and to the War—and the counsel came Not to Do That At All! for he (Schlesinger) had a bad experience with the last one, and after World War I he had nothing to talk about. "So that's what it came down to!" Dyer says, "a War for Conversation!"

Hamilton: who, too, is unhappy, but in another way. He is simply lonely. But that's not quite accurate, for his loneliness is far from simple: it works itself through a whole complex of attitudes and prejudices usually announced with a curious pseudo-levity. He pines for America (by which he means Mississippi)—"You know! That English-speaking country in the western hemisphere..." He has been overseas for several years now, has a son whom he's never seen, and a fund of versatile resentment. He resents Dear-Willy-Stay-at-Home (whose love for native land keeps him on the safe side of the Atlantic), resents the War Department (whose inefficiency has overlooked his rotation home), resents immigrant-foreigners (for it was their restlessness and intellectual corruption which made for internationalism and world wars), resents Europe (for its tragedy has isolated him from home, from his wife, from His Son Whom He Has Never Seen). It is almost grotesque. North Africa remains a warm, glowing memory: its climate was fine, the culture and historic traditions were rich, the type of war still fought in the old form of classic military contest. (This was the first experience; he had just left home; everything was fresh.) Italy began the decline—Rome was a sewer of the past, the Italians were a decadent people, with possibly only their comic virtues redeeming their futile existence. (His loneliness was deepening. . .) France is hopeless. "When I saw St. Dié, the whole heart of the city burned out in battle, nothing left but ruins and destruction, I was glad, glad that this happened to France! . . . The French deserve it! An unscrupulous, unattractive people. Somewhere along the way they lost their soul, and today have no warmth, no friendliness. The Italians were poor and helpless, but their land at least was interesting. Here the French always look prosperous, and there is nothing, absolutely nothing to see. A nation without character! . . ." So he goes on, historical and philosophical variations on a theme: homesickness. In the end, though the bigotry is discounted by charm and wit, it is all very tasteless and thoughtless for me, full of bogus half-serious attitudinizing, deeply annoying because it teases and toys with serious notions.

(After endless hours the note begins to get overwhelmingly monotonous. The chaplain at dinner has his own special case. He finally succeeds in reconciling himself—even to being kissed on both cheeks by French bishops—when in come the poor tearful GIs, pleading for some extra-military influence to get them back home, extolling the virtues of their family and the States. And then he is depressed again, torn by longing and nostalgia. "If only they wouldn't come to me with their desperately poignant tales . . . !")

For the rest: there is the bitterness against Rear Echelon John. In Washington: against draft-exempt civilians. (In civilian factories: against non-essential workers.) In Paris: "What are they doing back there? Do they think the war's over? Why the hell don't they get off their asses and do some soldiering? . . ." In Army Headquarters: "I hear they wear ties and dress-uniforms back there at ETOUSA! Bet they shine their low-quarter shoes every day before going into 'combat' in the Hotel Majestic! . . ." In Division, Regimental, Battalion CPs: "Don't anybody but us do nothing to get this war done with? What in Christ's name do they think they're doing back there? They ought to come down here some time and take a couple of turns up front and see what the lines are really like! . . ." And on the line itself I suspect that Joe in his forward foxhole is ranting against somebody some ten yards behind him—"Do I have to fight this war all by myself? Haul your ass out of there and get up here with me!"

Everybody thinks everybody else has The Good Deal, and resents it. Everybody shares a deep, ugly sense of guilt, but no one cares to take on the responsibility of conscience. The War and the Army is a fiercely hated thing, but the only way the tragedy is faced is by a strategy of delegating conscience-stricken roles to some supporting cast. The protagonist sedulously absolves himself from responsibility, conscience, guilt, from anything but his own innocent heroic victimization.

10 February 1945

Saturday.

Left early in the morning on another "mission" with Hamilton. Yesterday afternoon we made the first of our mysterious departures and spent a delightful time examining the baroque of the Lunéville St. Jacques Cathedral, and then rambling off into a discussion of historical traditions of defeat in war and the complex of religious and political variants of martyrdom.

We stepped out of the headquarters into the beaten puffed mud of the yard, plowed into a strange surface by the constant grind of vehicles and the seasoning of wind and drizzly rain. A battered old jeep was waiting, and we took off for "the front." The roads in the beginning were fairly good and cut squarely through the country in which the battles had raged. Off on the fields to the right and left were regular distributions of foxholes. The whole series of small rural communities were torn apart: only segments of walls remained with gaping red-brick interiors or hopelessly splintered beams. Streams and rivers had finally shook themselves free, and flowed unbound by bridges and footpasses. The devastation reaches a crescendo in the town. Here the wreckage is intimate and touching in a special way. There is no possible "masquerade" now: this is no inexplicable "act of God." Through the rubble and the defacement of rust you make out a sign—LIBRAIRIE. Over a shattered front there is still the attractive friendly invitation—APERITIFS... St. Dié is worse, for the contrasts are far more dramatic. The complete heart of the town is in ruins. The commercial buildings, the residential quarter, both were deliberately mined and burned by the Nazis in their withdrawals to the Rhine. The barest ribbed outline of the structures remain. Block after block is a terrible square of wreckage. Approaching the fringes of St. Dié you see once again—strangely, this seems "humane" (and certainly natural: after continuous hours of ruins-inspection it is the untouched which is unusual and noteworthy)—the normal toll of the big guns, the aerial bombardment, the house-to-house fighting. And just beyond, on the road to Ste. Marie-aux-Mines, even Nature in her aloofness has been struck. On a far-off hilltop the silhouette of the black forest against the gray sky suddenly breaks. A section of the woods had been blasted off, and the bald spot could be seen for miles around, evidence in the heavens that nothing was immune from the devilment of man.

The ride is rough and gruelling. Every so often the jeep breaks down: the mud becomes too heavy and clogging, or the hastily repaired shell-holes on the road jolt its machinery loose. More likely the radiator had sprung a leak, and canning up some water from some nearby farmyard stream we are soon bouncing by again. Especially striking and depressing: the primitivism of human life in the lonely countryside. The farmhouses are old and poor, the people simple and elemental, the substance and hope of existence mean. This place, you cannot help but feeling, is divorced from the world you know, and is informed by another, a strange history. And then you suddenly see a worn familiar yellow sign—"S-H-E-L-L," you make out, and then you understand anew: this, too, by the smallest and the largest tokens, is part of your land and people, and the whole world's tragedy.

From the Valley up into and through the mountains: striking pictures of arresting beauty, even in the harshness of a drab wintry day. The colors were rich, and in many of the turns luxuriant—the purplish gray of the leafless trees set against the deep green of the firs, the distant blackness of the wooded hills, the discolored earth of marked agricultural strips, the occasional white streaks and patches of snow... And this was my first forest, and perhaps it was only my naiveté which invested it with a real atmosphere of mystery. There was a dark romanticism about the Vosges, and many of its landscapes had a sorcerous loveliness, like something out of *Hansel and Gretel*. In the passages out the war came again. Foxholes and dugouts had been dug alongside the cuts and fills of the road. Huge trees, which only a month or so ago lay as gigantic obstacles to military traffic, had been swept aside; endless lumber casualties. Many of the standing trees were almost completely slit at the trunk, and in the chopped niche the charge still remained, poised to fling a fringe of the forest across the road.

Some brief business at Ribeauvillé, corps headquarters. Lunch on the hilltop hotel, with a long view of the flatland between the Vosges and the Black Mountains. Just above us are remnants of several feudal castles; a meager medieval effort to compete with the modern genius for military construction and destruction. (Problem for the afternoon: how the castles were ever built on the pin-point cliffs, how the feudal forces ever manned them, and finally how they were ever taken by opposing foot-soldiers.)

We are now in Alsace; the architecture has changed, the signs of the way read differently. Licht—Dein Tod! posters everywhere warn, but death, as more devastation wrackage reveals, came anyway. Jeep breaks down again in Sélestat, along the Strassburg-Strasse. (This had been taken by the Allies, then half-lost during the Rundstedt counter-offensive, and now retaken.[4]) Pick up some assistance in a neighboring ordnance office (sign on one of the shelves: Keep your hands off this shit), and on to Strasbourg itself.

Figure 2. Changing the tire on the road to Strasbourg, © Lasky Center, Munich.

The maze of communications wires; old limp concertinas in the meadows; carcasses of horses along the highway (the animals are still handsome: black and stiff like a sculpture of death...) Occasional picture of a peasant puttering in the fields—spreading manure, patching up some shell or fox hole (dug by the Germans all along the road, which the American air force was constantly strafing), making some slow lone effort to turn up some soil. Occasional too: a car or truck, crowded with odd personal belongings and a family or two, moving. In the distance: a magnificent-looking Alsatian castle on a hilltop, brilliantly struck by a burst of sunrays through the clouds. Brown skeletons of tanks: charred and rusted. An old city hall: Liberté, Egalité, Fraternité—and next to the classic French inscription, a still clean-looking Wehrmacht sign—Zum Luftschutzraum. Everywhere: on billboards, around tree trunks, on walls—On les aura! Vive la France!

In the Strasbourg suburb there were some signs of defenses and barricades—some overturned trolley cars and adjacent revetments. But on the whole no great impression of a war-torn center. We cut through the streets rapidly—Hamilton's "mission" was nearing completion—and parked along the Krämer Gasse, or the rue Mercière. On one side was an immense square of rubble—clearly a collecting point rather than the wreckage of buildings. In the center of the square, the great cathedral. As we crossed over to the entrance we heard in the distance the crash of a shell—my first shell. The city was still being struck. The Gothic cathedral had suffered some damage: a huge bomb-hole gaped through the dome, and the rain came pouring through. But the great stone floor was cleared, and we walked easily about making our tour. Most of the celebrated stain glass windows were gone: many had been removed, the other had been blasted and jagged panes remained. The golden and red organ near the rear was almost undamaged: a few pipes were missing. The impression was strangely ungothic. The domes in the center were softened in a kind of Byzantine way, and the light in particular was unconventional. With all the windows out, and most of the cathedral bare, the classic darkness was missing, and the reddish brown and gray stone had new effects. The altar was surrounded by French tricolors.

We left the Place de la Cathedrale (Münsterplatz) and took the long way home. Leaving the city—Quai Fustel de Coulanges! Another street in another Alsatian town, Sarrebourg—Richard Wagner Strasse, and rue Jeanne d'Arc. What a history and political story there is in just that! The skies darkened and dripped as we plowed through the mud of the roads of the Saverne Gap, through which the great counter-offensive of December had rolled. An occasional view of war relics—tank treads in a countryside blacksmith. The jeep needed water again, and we stopped by a stream, and the driver went forward. Suddenly the car started rolling for the bank, apparently unable to control its thirst. We leaped for the break and almost jumped out wildly. It jolted to a stop: just teasing. We strolled about a bit, and inspected a large German antitank ditch some fifty yards off. A little French boy came by, sporting a cane, and inquired casually, *Promenadez?*—*Oui*, I answered, *et regardez...* —*Oh*, he said, tossing a quick look over his shoulder at the water-filled tank ditch, *les Boches...*, and strolled on. As a matter of fact we had come over to relieve ourselves, and although I will not pretend to make any symbolism out of it—it was merely convenient and somewhat appropriate—we made our own little contribution to the flooding of the Nazi defenses...

It was cold, muddy, and drenching. The last miles home were miserable. We didn't know whether to protect our bruised backs against the jolts, clear our faces and eyes from the splatter of the road, or keep our noses dry. But still we were well off. All along the highway and its branching trails, GIs were working, their clothes soaked and dirty, their faces raw with cold, and their eyes red with sleeplessness and a deep endless fatigue. The road had to be made.

Finally arrived. Went home, made a feeble effort to wash. [...], slipped myself into my twisted sleeping bag, and slept the night. Learned the next day that most of the town was awake through the rumble and roar of the Tenth Armored which passed through in the early morning. I heard nothing.

12 February 1945, Lunéville

The village at night is lost in a black and lonely darkness. There are no streets, no population, no life. An occasional ray of a flashlight catches a cone of the drizzly dampness and finds a squishy path. Suddenly, as if from somewhere beyond a hill, a burst of illumination strikes the road ahead. Some vehicle with imperious headlights makes its way through. The glare seizes a front of the street, an angle of trees, a shape of a building, a store, an idle wagon, and composes a fleeting fantastical picture of brilliant beads and streaks of black and light. With a grinding turn, silence and darkness is recovered again. Another street, another corner, and you are almost there. What a mysterious course! A foreign town, unknown by day or night, lonely and afraid and isolated in the war. Its people are hidden, its spirit gone underground. Where there is no light there is no life. Man has become literally afraid of his own shadow. The suns, which in his promethean greatness he created, are without warmth or power. Life has become a coldness and a darkness.

Whoever first created the inflection of betrayal, or employed the tone of resentment, in the well-worn phrase, "vicarious experience," fathered one of the great myths we live by. It is the Myth of the Real Experience, and it sustains itself on the celebration of the transforming virtues of sharing earthy realities. There is the fond illusion of the "broadening of travel," the classic liberal optimism about the trials of mankind and history, the journalistic fetish of the "inside observer," the celebration of autobiographing adventurers, the subtle feeling of shame and guilt on the part of large masses fed on cinema and fiction and standardized daydreams by a mechanical culture.

13 February 1945, Lunéville

If the confusion and incompetence of the history-recorders reflects the actual situation of the history-makers then the chaos of the battlefield is reaching new depths. I can't seem to be able to find anybody who knows what he is doing. Policies are unclarified, procedures are botched, and the method and theory of the historical section absurd. The Colonel took a morning recently to restate functions and objectives. After an hour or so, Mooney[5] asked permission to make a comment. "Sir, that's all very well and good, but—" and he hesitated only a moment, "but frankly—I don't know whether to shit or go blind!"

Which just about sums it up. As someone remarked today, the historian-in-chief is "an insurance salesman... And the only trouble is, we're not selling insurance!" A few minutes later the Colonel came through. He tossed a few hasty glances at the oddly occupied office. "I think some of you people ought to find out the unit of measure around here," he said. "It's hours, not days! Every goddammed thing takes days, days!" And he left. Some time later: "How many pages have you done today?" The number was apparently negligible and inadequate, and he stormed. "Let's get the output up! For Christ's sake, if research takes up seventy-five percent of your time, cut research out! Just write, and then everything will be speeding along!" Mooney, Eggers, and Gottlieb[6] (the current "bird-dog" staff) all tell me they were introduced to their units with—"I don't know anything about this son-of-a-bitch. I don't know who he is, what he can do. But I'm leaving him here, and see that he's kept busy. I don't want him laying around, fucking off!" The poor fate of a combat historian! There they were out in the cold of winter, sleeping with the men in holes and dugouts, worried about the Rundstedt offensive. And then a call would come through. It was the Colonel. "Eggers? Is that you? Come on in! I've been searching all over for you. Come on in... I want to send you out again." Notes are accumulating. Nobody has time to prepare any manuscripts. A bird-dog's life indeed!

"Have you read much of eighteenth-century literature?" Dyer asked this afternoon, turning aside from his records and maps. "Then you know Gibbon, of course. You know the more I go on with all this, the more I find myself writing like Gibbon. I read my own prose, and there it all is, the Ciceronian periods, the great Latin eloquence. Why, this page here—the Sixth Corps assault on Montélimar—why, *mutatis mutandis*, it might be a brilliant purple passage on the vices of some Roman emperor..." He shook his own head in acquiescence and went back to his records and maps.

14 February 1945, Lunéville

A fine sunny afternoon. On the ground the pools of mud have dried into damp soft earth. In the street little pink-cheeked French children are playing, clomping along the cobblestones in their wooden shoes, singing and shouting *un, deux, trois, quatre...* Above, the air is busy with the ceaseless drone of planes. The sun has shown itself, and the land and the people look fair again, and somewhere not far away bombs are tearing apart an enemy.

[...]

15 February 1945

Took off in anxious hurry early in morning. Colonel indignant at delay: you want me to get back after midnight? No one could make out why he was going along in the first place. Most plausible theory: the weather was nice. And so it was. Chill in the early hours made things uncomfortable for a while, but the morning was clear and the whole trip was a series of pictures. Through the Vosges mountains again. Into Colmar suburbs (signs still "fresh" with propaganda and imprecations against *Juden-Demokratie, Angloamerikaner, und Bolschewisten*). Picked up girl on road, going into Barr. Daughter of town "tribunal." Pleasant little home on a hill street. Balzac on table. Father head key to *bibliothéque* which I with my usual gaucherie called a *librairie*, Victor Hugo and things (she proudly said). Studied some English in school (we got along pretty well on my German), and even read a little Shakespeare—passages, but translated versions. By André Gide. Whereupon we got off on an irrelevant discussion on Gide. Sutton commenting that he no doubt was "one of the century's great literary figures ... but a collaborator." It incensed me. But he could not be moved. He heard it from "a very intelligent and cultivated person" at a Paris party recently. That after all was "inside" information. Arrived in Kunheim. Succession of towns east of Colmar wrecked, house after house. Stopped with Fifteenth HQ. Little book stall: several volumes of Goethe. Religious bric-a-brac around. Chickens in barn. Army latrine in backyard next to crammed woodpile. Straw lightly matted over mud. Picking up a little information about Colmar Pocket operations,[7] some stray gossip stories. . . . (passwords-drama in days when "George Patton" was the entrance-exit formula for week after week; the mild weary contempt which the staff spoke of those halcyon days. . .)

Went out into the backyard. The darkness was a black impenetrability. Stumbled over an old wagon against the haystack. Finally found my way, by the expanding light of the brightening moon and stars. In the distance over the Rhine flares were burning intensely, lighting up eerie stretches of flatland, bloody battlefields of only last week. Silently tracers were flying over the Rhine into Germany; soundlessly they flared and burned out. A quaint perspective: the War as seen from a straddle trench. Later on that evening I wandered slowly and alone down the road (to Seventh CP). Suddenly some guns opened up. Things shook ever so slightly, and a moment of fear struck without notice in the palms of my hands and through a small tremor all over. I reassured myself: just an occasional harassing fire from our own mortars or artillery. I wondered how I would feel if the old well-worn "all hell broke loose."

17 February 1945

Moved last night from Kunheim, HQ of Fifteenth Infantry Regiment, to Jebsheim, Third battalion CP. Jeep felt its way almost blindly along thick, wet and cold mist which had dropped over the countryside. Narrowly missed trucks on road, tank parked at crossroad, and teetered for a bit along the bank of a river. Set up in upper bedroom of the old Jebsheim house. Shell had torn huge holes through the wall, and the shelter-half canvas covers hardly kept out the penetrating cold. Slept in all my clothes, jacket, scarf, wool hat, and still froze.

Found in the morning, over in the carefully piled and swept debris, a picture post-card addressed to the Oberlin Family in Jebsheim: a pretty, aerial view of Cannes, with affectionate greetings—dated: *Nice, 12 Aout 1934*... Mme. Oberlin came through a little while later, and we talked. The family had lived in the house for over a century. It had been untouched in 1914–18, and badly hit in 1940, but not destroyed. Once again knocked apart, but still standing. One of the few houses in Jebsheim—evidence: battalion HQ here. Story of the fanatical burgomaster. Children speak French only *un peu*. German schools of last years. Even French phrases were *verboten*—orders against traditional *merci, bonjour, au revoir*—yet townspeople never said: *auf Wiedersehen, guten Morgen, danke schön*. The old woman said: we would see the burgomaster, and we would "greet" him—*bonjour* ... Never saluted *Heil Hitler*. A handful collaborated. One volunteer for Army. Eighty were drafted. Five families were "good Germans." Rest: "always French in heart" (she said in her Alsatian dialect). Now the burgomaster and some assistants across the Rhine. Took off early. Other "German" families still here. Daughter saw them on street yesterday. Flew into rage on sight. Still well off, well clad. She looked down at her own shoes, dress. Not an issue in four years—"they" got all they needed. Daughter about eighteen. Parents tried to hold out against *Hitlerjugend* vainly. Son here beat up (ten years) by leader of the Youth: spite beating, bloody and cruel (Youth leader: seventeen). Complained to burgomaster—letter. Reply: Son *lernt folgen*. Leader now in SS troops. Father of M. Oberlin—burgomaster of Jebsheim for forty years: Michel Buhart....

Working at interviews almost all of day. "K" company stories in corner town house; eighty-eight shell tore hole in wall, tore four men apart—remains splattered against walls and roof; hardened and dried out now. Captain Stuart called for me, and walked warily up the stairs—"How the hell can you guys live here and be happy?" he cried.

Took ride over to Maison Rouge country, made some shots.

Sleeping here another night. Food fine, with some Alsatian special dishes tossed in. Beer plentiful. Company interesting, instructive, pleasant. "Old soldiers" a rich crew.

Wish I could handle whole Maison Rouge story.[8] A great and terrible story of a panic and flight on a battlefield: armor vs. men. But saw Sutton, Friday morning down at Neuf Brisach and said he: "I wouldn't like that at all. In

fact I would hate it..." A well-meaning good-intentioned fellow, but it's a pity goodness can't simply be willed. He lacks warmth and heart, for all his avowed Philosophical Christian sentiments. A streak of coldness always there; in part, crankiness; in part, an old-maidenish concern for all details and his relationship to them; an unattractive dead-seriousness which wetrags his sense of humor.
[...]

19 February 1945

Wandering through Strasbourg ... the dramatic untitled white arrows on walls and gates and doors; mute, but universally understood, guides to Bomb Shelters. Along Goethestrasse to the university. The statue of young Goethe, in proud aristocratic stance (one hand on cane, one behind back). The Place de l'Université is somewhat damaged, but the real shock is in the empty building and unpapered bulletin boards—[...] no notices, no announcements, nothing but barrenness. In the office of the concierge: some Nazi leftovers. *Die Kunst im Dritten Reich*, which he gave me for a few cigarettes; an anthology of Italian poetry dedicated to *Hermann Göring dem Freunde Italiens in Verehrung*; a Tauchnitz edition of George Moore's *Coming of Gabrielle*,[9] with which he ran after me and offered me another "souvenir." The Library building has been hit, but it remains a striking structure, a little reminiscent of South Hall at Columbia with its roster of cultural greats, except here adorned with profiles: Lessing, Goethe, Schiller, Gottfried von Strassburg, and on the left: Molière, Calderón, Dante, Shakespeare. (Later, on the sides: Thomas Aquinas, Melanchthon, Erasmus...)

Managed to stroll by the caretakers, and through the various library chambers. The tables in the reading room are warped, the shelves are bookless, bare except for fragments of broken boards, brick chips. Soaked and dried-out volumes lying around in heaps. *A Manual of the Writings in Middle English, 1050–1400*, John Edwin Wells (Yale U. Press). Stacks of volumes ugly with black-gray dust. Masons are working on some walls. The calendar: unleafed: reading "September 1944." The Librarian appears. Tells me the story of the great Strasbourg library, once one of the finest collections in the world. In 1939: the evacuation of the library. 1941: Vichy submits to the Nazi demand for the return of books from Clermont-Ferrand. A huge blockbuster destroyed thousands. Fire in the depot at Barr, when the war passed through with artillery and street-fighting, ruined tens of thousands of others. What was not burned was soaked by the fire-fighters. This explained the endless stacks behind the reading room of charred, and water-warped volumes. Hundreds stood on end on all the tables of the library, pages spread to dry out, in a small attempt to recoup great losses. The chambers smell uniquely—and certainly no library in the history of culture can have smelled like this. Where is the old musty odor of book-lined academicism? The cold air of February rushed in through huge holes in walls. The burned soaked volumes flavored the atmosphere strangely. For decades perhaps students will study in the sight and smell of war. Now as I fingered volumes the war was here with its outdoorness and its death...We walked out. He touched the stacks and shelves splintered by shrapnel, and said a touching goodbye. He asked me to return—to see the rare book rooms, the great manuscript collections, anything I would like. "Come back soon when things will be better, when life returns to the university..." I promised, but suggested perhaps I would sooner call at the University of Chungking, or Tokyo. He smiled and sighed. (The Library director had married an American student in Paris in the days after the last war.)

To the streets again. Bismarckplatz is now Place de la République. Ludendorffstrasse is the rue de Général Gouraud. Rudolf-Hess-Strasse was shortlived, after the English *hegira* became Hermann-Göring-Strasse—now Avenue de la Liberté. Walked across the river bridge. Startled to see it was L'Ill River. Only yesterday, as I talked to all the men at the panic of Maison Rouge, the Ill was a swift-currented stream which meant terror and death to fleeing, frightened soldiers helpless in the face of the German armored onslaught. Now it flowed pleasantly under a quiet bridge, lit by a warm sun in a Monday afternoon sleepiness... The little children in the park speak only German. *Un peu* French they tell me. A few of them apparently picked it up at home. Most learn it for the first time these months in *Schule*.

18 February 1945

Battalions, regiments, the whole division is moving. I go into "hiding" for a day or two at the "Rest Camp" in Strasbourg, a handsome officer's club for the Third. These boys, for the greater part, face their own violent ends almost every week. A few of them I recognize: constantly on the line bidding for miracles and another few months' grace of life. Hardly of course any opportunity for "rest," as the guests break themselves down in drink and fornication... The women are dull, unattractive, spiritless Alsatian bodies. The men are silly when they are not lustful, and altogether pitiable. This afternoon "Slim," hopelessly drunk, sitting on the floor, lapping up spilled drinks from the low table, his cheeks red with rouge, his black locks pasted over his eyebrow, and the raucous laughter as he mimicked *Heil Hitler*... And "Doc" (from the Fifteenth, and the Third Battalion), coming out in bandana (with tennis balls for breasts), heavy-make up, and slight silky loin-cloth, pairing with the wild Russo-Polish girl for an amazing half-orgiastic half-orgasmic dance: wild, lewd, hilarious. Upstairs: in bed with a spiritless little thing. Suddenly firing breaks out, along the river. You can see through the window huge tracers going out over the Rhine, and the rumble of artillery shakes the pane a little. You glance at the half-stripped woman beside you. Downstairs there is dancing and music and laughter. Strange, always strange: men are now being murdered, soldiers are dying. What one has to learn—men are always dying... The House itself was the Gestapo headquarters in this district of town. A civilian was in this morning, a commissioner of the city—he had been "beaten up," he remarked, in the cellar here. Before that, according to the garbled account I got from one of the chambermaids, this had been the home of the "elders of the church," *padres mit grossen Bärten*. Now it is a kind of pleasant little brothel for American combat troops. The chatter is endless, but no one understands each other. "*Nickts compree...*" runs the constant refrain. *Okay, bebbee?* And all kinds of innocent rib-tickling inquiries—*Qu'est-ce que c'est*—"*horny*"? *Wie süß? Wie Honig?* The table is in guffaws... Blonde tells me story of all the *Heil Hitlers*. To themselves the Alsatians would say as they raised their palms above their heads—*Jusqu'à ici la merde!*

Strasbourg.

The people were out on the streets today, and coasting along the crowded avenues and thronged squares proved something considerably less than dull. A little boy in Münsterplatz, carrying a huge American flag, ran along with us and asked for chocolate. I gave him a bar. He took out a small red swastika'd armband and rewarded me with his *Hitlerjugend* diploma... A guard, marching a host of shabby hard-pressed civilians down a side-street, called out to us, "We're getting them, all right! We'll get all of them, all right!" Collaborationists and German agents left behind... The name of Strasbourg's Park now has also been changed—from *Sechster Juni* to *Vingt-Deux Novembre*, the German and French liberation dates respectively. Business assistant in one of the newspaper offices gives me a back-number file: how curious the Alsatian headlines read, "Wir sind frei," etc. [...]) The Nazis left Strasbourg in great disorder, and a huge intelligence and film library has been taken by the troops. The editorial office itself was once the "Labor Front Bureau," and I expropriated two volumes—a biography of von Moltke, and an anthology of German literature called *Unsterblichkeit* (in rather characteristic National Socialist fashion it opened with Pericles's speech to the Greeks, from Thucydides... great Aryan oratory no doubt.) There is an extraordinarily interesting military and political drama to the Allied taking of Strasbourg, but I daresay nothing official will ever be released. As I piece together the plot and *dramatis personae* from "odd reliable sources." [...]

Spent several hours searching for university professors, but the windows of all the homes were barred. Nobody had remained in the city, after the academic secession to Clermont-Ferrand in the early days of the Occupation.[10]
[...]

20 February 1945

Once again: long, eventless trip west from Strasbourg. The countryside remains picturesque, but then on a pleasant sunlit day what green country is not striking and full of pleasing effects and designs? Has man ever made anything to match the stable quiet wonders of natural beauties? More towns and villages, more ruins and squalor. Children by a farmhouse smiling and waving their hands at your passing car; sometimes one scowls, and one this morning threw rocks (no doubt a subtle political symbol). On the road to Saverne: kids in a town side street playing with a full belt of 50-caliber machine gun cartridges. The war, thus, has already been incorporated into the everyday play and games of the street corner.

Mooney continues on his madcap course. "Look!" he shouted, as the jeep careened speedily down the highway, "I'm driving without hands! Look! Look!" Then he would feel the wheel tenderly, and let up, and caress it again. Now it was "loose reins"—we were, you see, going over the hurdles! And through Sarrebourg, we were racing down "the home-stretch." He whistled, and kissed his lips, and raising himself slightly off the seat, in simulated tension, waved his arm wildly, snapping the whip... And his philosophizing continued in its noisy homely accent. "Shit!" he screamed, as we cut through a farmhouse aroma of fresh manure, "that's France for you! Shit everywhere you go! And the more shit they have the richer they are!" Frequent concentrations of French troops and just as frequent outbursts of explicatives. "Goddamn Frogs! Give them a uniform, and wave some flags and they're happy, they're delirious. Look at those MPs. The Nazi insignia is still on the helmets, and the goddamn paint don't hide those belt buckles. Soldiers! But maybe they are real soldiers. They live this war. We fight it. Real soldiers probably think we're stupid sons-a-bitches! Wanting to finish the war. Then everybody is out of a job... Great people, these Frogs..." (Out in the occupied towns the French troops are indistinguishable from American formations. They wear US uniforms, carry US equipment, carry themselves in identical style, to the blousing of the pants over the leggings and the painted insignia on the helmet liner. "Papa..." so the story runs of the little *babee*, "Papa ... tell me why all ze Ammericans wear the *poilu*'s clothes?")

Stopping over in Lunéville again.

22 February 1945

Anxious and almost sick with worry: nothing was shipped with the regiment, and so everything I own is in some strange, battered house in Alsace hundreds of kilometers from here over a route I hardly remember. Took off for Kunheim early, and made it there by lunch. The French had apparently moved into the old American command post, and there I to my great surprise and relief located everything. I pieced the things together, spying one blanket here, another there, asking the sergeant to remove his sweater (it was mine). An embarrassing job, but there I was fighting for my private property. The camera was intact (except for some fiddling with the film, and what happened to my battlefield shots remains a mystery), and so was all else, except for a dozen packs of cigarettes, and one pair of shorts. Mark those as non-battle casualties.

The town now looked odd and lonely. I remarked for the first time that there were no men here. Old women worked with burdens that appeared impossible, and children were carrying loads or pushing carts and rendering tireless assistance. No husbands or sons or brothers—all deported or drafted. Now that the throng of American youth is gone the emptiness of the village becomes for the first time apparent.

The French style is of course markedly different from our own headquarters. It seems looser, and although more "intimate" for me I must confess less attractive. The commandant invited me for lunch, which was a poor meal, except for the wine and schnapps, and the dubious delight of being waited upon by the French colonials, with their original combination of skin texture, eye slant, and stringy hairy mustaches and beards. Tried to make inquiries about the Army structure, political sentiments, relations with the old FFI elements, but didn't manage to learn very much.

Returned much relieved along side routes, bored as I was with the main highways. We cut through Schirmeck, and there turned back to Natzweiler where the old *Konzentrationslager* of the Germans had been. (Girl on the streets in Strasbourg, I now recall, had mentioned that many of her friends had been sent there for "political" offenses.) We turned into a sunless valley (it seemed very melodramatic) and then wound ourselves up a twisting highway to the mountain top. An old hotel, Struthof, once flourished there, but in recent years had been supplemented by barbed-wire barracks, a gas chamber, a number of torture cells, and a crematorium. I rummaged in abandoned offices, found some SS remnants, some requisitions for chemicals. Engaged one of the young guards in conversation: he hadn't been in the FFI but had worked as a partisan—in Strasbourg. Knew well the "Club," as the old Gestapo headquarters, and had been in there many times! It seems that the partisan lieutenant was a member of the Gestapo, and so his band knew what was going on and could find access to Nazi quarters. He dramatized with the classic finger-cross-the-neck the fate of many of the key personnel; he had participated in many of the "raids."... Struthof now was a French internment camp. The satanic trappings have of course been removed, but the place is still a dismal, dreary hole for all the magnificence of the backdrop of considerable natural beauty. It is as if Nature herself could not bear to live with the camp.

Made Nancy by night, and stayed in a drafty, smoke-choked hotel. Walked along rue St. Jean a few blocks before going to bed: located a handsome bookstore and read titles in the window by flashlight: a fine display of the Glotz and Sagnac series of historical studies. Ferdinand Lot was there on the Roman Empire, and much else.

23 February 1945

Up early, and to Pagny-sur-Moselle. The morning was chilly, although the day was clear and otherwise pleasant. (The Germans did a tremendous demolition job with the huge stone bridge across the Moselle from Nancy...) How much countryside I have already seen—yet I don't seem to grow tired of it. The crystalline frost powdered the fields, glistening now in the sun with a new unearthly green... Finally found my battalion as I turned from Avenue Jean Jaurès into rue Anatole France. The area, in fact practically the entire *arrondissement*, was being bombarded by American music echoing over the hills from great special-service amplifiers. The "boys" wanted music, and the Army was giving it to them. Of course it made no difference that all the troops were out in the field, and nobody had remained to reap the delights of GI jive except the poor unundertsanding Lorraine peasants. But from Pompey through Pont-à-Mousson to Vandières and Pagny the jam session went on. I heard: Fats Waller and Ada Brown in *That Ain't Right*.

Sign on a Nancy street-level apartment: No WOMEN. PLEASE DO NOT KNOCK. There, I suppose, is the "social history" of the American soldier in France.

The new jargon: beaucoup as in "beaucoup armor" and "beaucoup Kraut." Partir as in "so we parteed." *C'est la jerree, comme ci, comme ça*—both extravagantly interspersed into conversation, already punctuated continuously with "rough" and "rough deal" and the whole host of other Army standardized responses.

The unmistakably French picture: the bread-carriers... the long, elongated loaves, and the large rings, plus odd-shaped fragments of breads, all carried under the arms without cover, and only rarely accompanied by any other purchase whatsoever. Mission: for bread...

Left early Saturday morning. Via Nancy to Lunéville. Shower, and shaved. (Mooney used to shout in exultation—"There's nothing like it in all the world! You take a shave, and a shower, and a shit! What a privilege! What a pleasure! That's the real life!") Straightened out things. Went to Balzac movie with some friends (one tells me that now he sees soldiers strolling about, but for four years Germans were only drilling and practicing, with rarely a break!), and to bed early. (Letters from Marion)

25 February 1945

Sunday evening.

Poor Marion! I, of course, can easily go on receiving her warm and touching letters, but can she go on writing them? She can't! and I don't want her to. With every line she reworks emotions and sensitivities until her whole spirit is raw and aching. And nobody can take that sort of thing indefinitely, which is the cruel and needless program she seems to have set for herself. I wonder if the sweet darling will understand me. If only she could stop revelling in reminiscence (what a tender exercise though she makes of it) and organize herself in the present; compose her days and nights and prospects for the future with something of her old normal balance and strength. It hurts me and grieves me to think of her trying to live only with her loneliness and dreams. I am afraid she will take some of my words harshly, yet they are all with real fond concern for her. But we can't go on playing every sentiment and every minute on a high tragic level. How can I resell her on life—there are so many things yet to be seen and experienced, so many events to happen. And I want her to be strong and well, especially in spirit. Nothing else matters ... love, memories, myths, longings. In the end you live alone, only with yourself.

Tried at last tonight to write her these things, but no I'm afraid I haven't said them right. She will misunderstand and be hurt, and I will have reopened wounds. My god, how can one explain to a woman that you care so very much for her to be adjusted and happy!—And I must have said some tasteless things too—"how glad I am, my dear, to be a correspondent of yours!" Which is an extraordinarily gauche way of suggesting the genuine richness of her letters.

25 February 1945

Sunday.

Began making sketches and ordering my notes for the Maison Rouge narrative. I have necessarily to make it a conventional thing, but it still may take on a tone and force of its own. What I want is simple to state if the most difficult creation of art or history: a genuine and subtle evocation and recapture of a tragic and fantastic experience. Here is the battle, and here is its design and inner meaning. But that of course is a little myth of my own. When will I ever be able to achieve either the craft or the wisdom for such a work? Certainly it is impossible now under the pressure of small and mean exigencies.

Spent most of the evening talking with Hamilton; beginning to be ever so little of a bore (James David Tillman Hamilton) but his charm and wit and intelligence are undeniable. We began this evening's conversations on the subject of uniforms. At first it was a "joke": the local efforts to create an individual style on the part of the various military dress-horses; the cheap longing for modishness: the scarf in the open collar; the silver chain of the dog-tags through the epaulet; the swashbuckling leather pistol holsters at the bar and at dinner, etc. And we moved into the problem of the first standardizations of military uniforms. [...] Disputed a little about the uniform of the knight. Clearly that is a somewhat different matter; the prescription there was one of status, civilian status so to speak inasmuch as his armor and insignia belonged

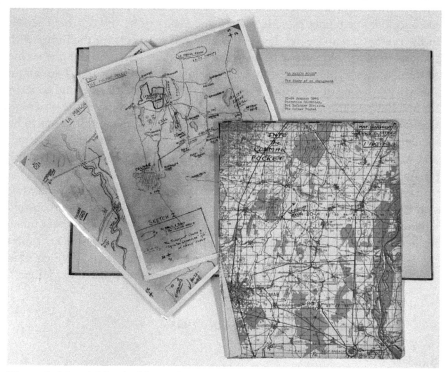

Figure 3. Material for the Maison Rouge report from Lasky's personal papers, © Lasky Center, Munich.

to his role and life in everyday society. After a few gin-and-juices we cut into Americans' attitudes towards uniforms and armies. And I am afraid Hamilton fed himself a little too strongly on the clichés of our national opinion. We are said to despise the army, and yet we worship the military hero. We are supposed to have only contempt for old-world fetish of uniforms, yet from our elevator operators to our mountainside filling stations the uniform prevails. And it is not only the standardizing influence of corporate patterns in economic life. What American small boy is not in his youth taken by the image of the fireman or the policeman and at one stage or another doesn't form a little club which has first on its agenda the purchase of some standardizing jacket (or windbreaker, the garish colors of which would stand out like a parade for blocks around)... Then we reached the point where distinctions and specifications had to be made. Yes, I was talking about metropolitan centers, urban patterns of life. And he was thinking of Mississippi (or the South) where an old cantankerous individualism still prevails. The distinctions grew wider and deeper. Hamilton went on about his family; his birth and boyhood in a world dominated only by relatives (uncles and great aunts, a host of grandparents and great-grandparents, a succession of cousins from the first to the fourth remove); his manhood prescribed for him by generations of ancestors (only certain schools, a classical education, marriage within the circle). In his own career he made certain variations on the Hamilton pattern. But it was most stimulating and disturbing. Here was a man who in a very sincere way felt the contemporaneity of his whole past, who was fed on roots in rich times gone, who lived with a tradition. His manners, his religion, almost the whole course of his life and death, were set, yet at the same time were vitalized by his own deeply-felt renewal of family and regional values. How much of modern lost literature has been a quest for just this kind of an inheritance! And how naive and hopeless all those frantic generations were! For it is not really the root that matters, but the growth. [...]

I couldn't help feeling that if this, after Eliot, were tradition and contemporaneity and the sense of the past then only rootlessness could be a beginning for the great and deep liberation...

26 February 1945

Composed some, wrote a few letters (an angry one home, an earnest one to M.). Read a little: Henry James's really exquisite story, "Madonna of the Future." Once again I am convinced his stories of writers and artists (indeed every line he ever put to paper on the subject of creative life), are a unique contribution to the literature of rich and liberating experience. In many ways his entire life and career was an execution of an art style carried over into ambition and personal destiny. He addressed all his hopes and energies to the fundamental urge of creation and power and understanding in the imaginative life. Not a word he has ever written fails to touch the passionate theme of an artist wrestling with his craft and inspiration.

Listened to Davis reminisce about North Africa. Apparently the real historical story is pretty much as we suspected it in the early days of Darlan. As he saw it in Tunisia and elsewhere, the betrayal was heartbreaking. The underground—"magnificent people who had been ceaselessly hounded by the Gestapo and Vichy"—were prepared to strike their blow. In came the Army, fraternized with the old crowd at dinner parties and on yachts kindly made available for American military personnel, and out went the plebeians. Vichy kept the control; the militants found themselves at last in concentration camps, and on the very days of "liberation" the unofficial US contact man with the underground broke down completely. He was, according to Davis, one of our vice-consuls, and he was taken away mad. Remains today in an asylum. The pressure and the tragedy had been too great. And the mistake was horrible—in terms of military expediency (troop movements were upset, war shipping was sabotaged, prestige and respect and friends were lost).

Much annoyed and disturbed at the impersonalization and casual objectivity one is forced to take of the War in this kind of work. "That's a nice little action," the Colonel remarks easily, glancing over the phase map of the fronts. "Run out and look it over and see if there's a story there for us. . . ." So it has become with the slaughter of men, and hours and nights of terror.

28 February 1945

The flags were out today. Gleaming new tricolors mounted everywhere from windows, trees, and assorted public places. Machine guns were emplaced in the four corners of the town square, and the fête could proceed. The Generals were going to decorate each other.

That, to be sure, is not strictly true. Last week de Lattre did give Devers and Patch the *Croix de Guerre*, and they in turn bestowed some appropriate ribbon or medal on the French.[11] Now it was the turn of the heroes on the line. The list was long, and the citations eloquent. For all the cynicism about awards and certificates of heroism, everybody was a little glad for the fine show. It gave a little color to drab winter days.

"Cynicism" is perhaps not the best word for it. The soldier's attitude is at every point touched with a deep ambiguity, and the ambivalence here too is quite interesting. There is without doubt much genuine respect for the heroes . . .

men decorated with bronze, and silver stars, distinguished service crosses, and other varieties of brilliant ribbonry. Yet what they always succeed in doing is to take themselves in: accept all the conventions about which in the first instance they had no illusions. The farce of manufacturing heroes according to fixed schedules of distribution is well-known from echelon to echelon down the line. At the Army headquarters a phone rings and an inquiry is made, "Who in your section is available for a *Croix de Guerre*?" Well, no one has as yet turned down an invitation for glory, and so some poor unfortunate young man at a desk is suddenly decorated for conspicuous inspiring valor. Along the front the charts are carefully kept, and when one battalion falls too far behind the others in numbers and weight of awards, why then the corrections are promptly made. Some of the commanders never trouble to put in nominations in "bad periods." "Christ!" I was told the other night in Alsace, "we're just crowded with heroes! But Potter's boys feel bad about being at the bottom of the league. So we've got to go through a couple of lean months... Or maybe," he added as an afterthought, "maybe some Joe in regimental or division or army thinks he ought to get decorated. Some GI here has to get riddled with lead, kill a dozen kraut, lay out in his hole for three days, crawl through the mud for a couple of miles, and then if he's lucky he'll get a bronze star... The brass back in the rear piss on some old shoe or something that caught on fire, and they're decorated from shoulder to shoulder!" In the end the farce is subtler and more tragic than they suspect. For in the end, they always accept it, play their roles untroubled by doubt or insincerity, and feel all the more grateful for the bright parade of deceit.

The fine show of international amity similarly disguises the true relations. I know there is no love lost between the GI and the "goddamn Frogs," and I suspect, from the documents, that the contempt is mutual on the high staff level. It is altogether believable that de Gaulle archly inquired of Patch when they first were introduced—"And where is this Guadalcanal? And how large is it?" In their turn, the GIs in the foxholes continuously ask, "And where the hell are the goddamned French?" I don't know the full or real story, but apparently there has been some consistent delays and mishaps in French operations; the armor is late; the infantry take the wrong town; a column runs out of ammunition and is stalled when gasoline tanks have become mysteriously empty. Then too the French soldier walks around in US Government Issue equipment... and walks around in most conspicuous embarrassing ways; I myself see them on the road lounging in gardens, strolling with girls through town streets, standing around on a corner with large oval chunks of French bread munching away as if no other duty in the world awaited them. A French truck never rolls by but the driver has his arm around a woman beside him, or is making conversation with several of them, "stowed away" in the rear. "You see what I mean!" my little agitator screams, "they live this war! We have to fight it, we only want to win it and fast."

The Second *Division Blindée* is a notable exception. Their reputation is that of "fighting fools," and their armor is being called for by every US unit that needs effective assistance. The Ninth Algerians might be similarly respected—their record under Monsabert[12] is an amazing story of real military daring—but for their complexion, their beards and mustaches, their odd flowing capes, colored turbans, curving knives, and barbarous haircuts, which make them something of the image of riff-raff warriors rather than the portrait of a "good soldier." At any rate, there is no warmth, no real friendship or love, no understanding. In the combat zone one emotion dominates—bitterness, resentment. One company resents another; one battalion or regiment despises the next. We dismiss it as "meaningless" because the actual course of significant events never cuts past this abscess. Clearly, the international aspect of this mean temper will not be so fortunate. One World will have to reckon with Damn Frogs.

[...]

I still know only a little about the French Army, its organization and its political or spiritual tendencies. Some of the high-level matters are instructive—de Gaulle's insistence to Wilson[13] that his French divisions be used "in this period only in France;" refusing to countenance any postponement of a French assault on Marseilles; Béthouart's[14] curious apologies about Giraud, and his fast exit (he would still wear the uniform but exercise no command functions, take occasional assignments as events would necessitate, but travel nowhere on official business without express permission);[15] Wilson and Alexander[16] were more than a little miffed that the world knew more (and sooner) about French state and army changes than did the Allied staff; the struggle for prestige and national greatness on the part of the French was apparently a widely-disconcerting factor... As for the politics, the commandant on the Rhine last week told me nothing when I broached the political and FFI issue, and I imagine it is still a tender issue. Since the FFI was disarmed, not without ultimatum bullying by the State, I have discovered no public information about where the lines are drawn. *L'Humanité* did call the other day, however, for a "genuine national army." The editorial, by André Marty as I recall, pointed with pride to the victories of the Glorious Red Army of Stalin, and hinted that de Gaulle might well get around to cleaning up the bad compromises made in his initial taking of power.

1 March 1945

Spent the best part of an afternoon (yesterday) and a morning in the Front National office, and not without profit. The young man—strange I don't know his name yet!—has been rummaging around trying to locate old newspapers and pamphlets for me, and so far the success has been modest but exciting. A series of Vichy pamphlets on the war and the resistance: an obsequious defense of Nazi unification of Europe by Dmitri Petchorine (22 June 1941 is the great turning point of history);[17] a call to the continent to "awake" to the dangers of American attack (Africa was the beginning of *ton espace vital*); a thoroughgoing job on Gaullism by Marcel Déat and André Chaumet... A series of Nazi propaganda publications—the speeches of the good Dr. Friedrich.[18] *Actualités allemands*: wonderful sunlit photos of life and labor in Germany; photostats of new grand editions of Goethe; accounts of the great French historians, Michelet, Thierry, Guizot, their triumphs born of German romantic inspiration, their failure to understand the racial basis of modern historical development; Christmas scenes in Berlin; unparalleled works of Nazi engineering, etc. etc. Most interesting was a volume by a K. I. Albrecht *Le Socialisme Trahi*. Apparently it is a liberal-socialist, uncompromisingly anti-Stalinist account of life in Soviet Russia. It was, however, published with authorization by Vichy in 1943. It has no Nazi or Vichy touches about it, and it would seem only that Albrecht had little care about the imprimatur on his message. The volume is dedicated "to the victims of Bolshevism, to the memory of the unhappy Russian people, to all the true socialists of the world" as "a warning," and is vigorous in pressing its thesis of the urgency of anti-Kremlin struggle. The text has a remarkable series of illustrations with many shots of both Soviet scenes and personages hitherto (in my own experience) unknown or unavailable in America ... pictures of old and new Bolsheviks (including shots of young Stalin and Trotsky, Kamenev, Bukharin, and Wilhelm Pieck now of Free-Germany notoriety), shots of GPU prison camps,[19] photostats of various things including some letters of Clara Zetkin, and much else. In many places it struck me as a serious personal study of social life, although I may be mistaken. I must inquire about it.

The Front National man himself is far from a politically educated militant, but he is a very warm person, and has had quite a time of it during the Occupation. Like many others in this area he was one of the secret "conductors" on the underground railroad for anti-Nazi refugees, made dozens of trips in and out of Germany, sometimes with the Gestapo at his heels. Spent "fourteen days" in one concentration camp, a month or two at a number of others. Speaks German (should by now) fairly well (although he is constantly reversing his numbers so that he last fled from the SS in '34), and is modest and self-effacing about his own exploits.

Yesterday afternoon a gray, drawn woman came in to thank him profusely for a piece he had put in the local papers the other day. She is the wife of one of the leading partisans in Lorraine, the mayor of a little town north of here.

He was deported to Germany last year, and the other day several hired hoodlums (including one ex-FFI youth, which confused me almost endlessly in the narrative of events) broke into the house (which once had been a shelter for hundreds of refugees), beat up the old woman, assaulted the two daughters and cut their hair. "Why" is still a mystery, although "my young man" aided in the hoodlums' apprehension. Clearly, though, it has revenge-politics as the motive at one level or another.

This morning we were visited by a sturdy but sensitive looking man who turned out to be—of course!—the schoolteacher in one of the agricultural suburbs a few kilometers from here. Really a perfect type. He had something of a knapsack on his back, and it was being filled during the course of the day with things for him to read: he would come to the Town only occasionally. These days naturally there is almost nothing for him in the bookstores (nor for anybody else). He did manage to locate some new scientific works on insects and new tendencies in biological research, which made him very happy. He apologized sweetly, aware that the texts themselves were of small interest to me, although he sensed I would be touched by his plight. His current fare were some 1936 copies of *Lorraine*, an old literary weekly (with pieces by Maurois and many well-known others). It was indeed touching, and for me a fine and wholesome interlude.

But then again the whole city seems to be coming to real life. Before the community, if it existed at all, seemed to be devoid of a humanity—I saw only a crowd of shadows at the French cinema one night, and a host of drab young girls at the local club one other evening. But now the Place Leopold has been tidied, which gives a kind of central dignity to the village, and street shops are being set up in its square. In the morning I now see the lines going off to school. Early today there was a little girl with a huge packed briefcase under her arm. She was waiting impatiently. I threw glances over my shoulder as I walked down the avenue. Soon she met her girl-friend, who was a little late and apparently properly apologetic, for they both went off hand in hand. At noon a group of mothers were gossiping in the square. The small children were off to one side noisily pushing each other about, screaming and giggling and overjoyed at their own inane antics. The simple universals of childhood warmed me... At last "humanity" is beginning to show itself. At least I am not alone! A native life is being lived somewhere about us.

Sutton and Mooney returned today, with their sheaves of notes on the Colmar Pocket. Their preliminary reports, as they loaded their cots and bedrolls wearily into the headquarters, were characteristic and certainly for me just about the best things they will probably produce from their "bird-dog" expedition. Said Sutton: "It was very innaresting, it was all really very innaresting for me..." Said Mooney: "Same old fnnattibus and fnnattibi..." As long as

Sutton doesn't run out of things which with earnest appreciation he finds "innaresting," and Mooney keeps a strong hold on his double-talk, I think the Muse History need have no fear of betrayal.

Old Colonel Ganoe[20] is apparently inexhaustible. There is no limit to his beatitude and his sincere (and I am afraid attractive) pomposities. Said he at dinner tonight as we completed our circle around the table, "What would Da Vinci have done if Christ's last supper guests had not all contrived to seat themselves only on one side?" And also: "Somebody once asked me what I thought the world's greatest barbarism was ... (pause) ... and I told him—Civilization."

Clio continues to serve. Today there was an inquiry from somewhere in the army as to whether the Passion play was still being given at Oberammergau. Our documents had no evidence to offer, but there was some recent intelligence in the G-2 German prisoner reports that the Apostle St. John had been captured. I am not quite sure whether that curious bit of information was found useful.

3 March 1945

Completed today, "La Maison Rouge: The Story of an Engagement," and feel at least a little elated that something now at last is done. In the larger narrative and study of military operations—to be sure—this account of one day's battle would constitute only a small footnote to history. It is not the story of the destruction of Hitler's last salient on the western front, nor is it even a complete picture of what happened at that terrible bridge and road junction (through the Third Division's attack, the German counterattack, and the final holding of the river and road line by isolated elements of a few platoons). But it is, after all, my first effort at War Documentary ... and it does sketch in its main outlines and details how "Operation Grandslam" felt its way into the covering flap of the Colmar Pocket.

And it is in itself an historical reconstruction of a military operation. No cheap fictional contrivances, no vulgar cheerleader's propaganda. Went through division, regimental and battalion records; interviewed all the available key officers and enlisted men involved in the engagement; went over the terrain with commanders who had participated in the action.

The actual field of battle was strange and exciting: I knew every tragic detail of the terrain, the trees and bushes along the stream where men took cover in their terror; the river, dangerous and swift-currented, where so many of the panicky men fell exhausted and almost drowned; the bridge, which collapsed under the weight of the tank and left the infantry helpless without armor; the flat fields over which the Jagdpanthers[21] rolled raking the flight of Americans with machine gun and shell fire and mashing into the snow others who were unfortunately behind in their shallow foxholes... Stuart, Vayssie, and I inspected almost every inch of it. At one point, Vayssie stopped, pointed to a little ditch beside the stream running down from the bridge. "And here," he said, with a quiet pensiveness, trying hard to recall, "I saw a GI... no, it was an officer, and he was dead... Yeah, that's right, lying right there. I remember it now, and very well, because you know, Stu, it looked like you. I thought it was you!" For the first time in the weeks I since I have known him Stuart lost his cheer, that curious happy-go-luckiness which alone can carry a soldier through fear, murder, nightmare. He looked pale, and suddenly became serious and grim. "Cut that shit out!" he shouted, "Just cut that shit out!" Vayssie was a little abashed. Maison Rouge had been his first fight, and he was guilty of a contretemps. He looked apologetic, and we all went on. Nothing more was said of it... By the way, I found further north near the Colmar Forest a "souvenir"—a Christmas greeting card to "Sonny" from "Mother." Close by, floating in a water-filled foxhole, was the cover of the Army edition of Ernie Pyle's *Here Is Your War*. I simply report what I found: Am I responsible for the obvious sentimentalism?

And so I am submitting the story of "La Maison Rouge" as an historical narrative composed according to the lights of what is professionally called "critical analysis" and "scientific investigation." I know full well it will be the time of my life to try to convince the mediocrities... No doubt there will be considerable skepticism as to its dramatic tone and details. ("Gee whiz," the typist said, "it reads just like in a story.") But the drama, my argument is running, was "inevitable."—"What happened in the fields east of the Ill River was a panic and a wholesale flight of troops confronted without support by German armor. Every minute of the one-day-and-night action, according to the testimony of the men in the line, was vivid and unforgettable, and many who would have been ordinarily frightened out of their wits knew no fear (they confessed) because it was "so exciting." Certainly it becomes the responsibility of the historian to recapture, in addition to the course and pace of tactical events, something of this drama and excitement without which the narrative would be lifeless and unreal. This is his obligation even at the risk of incurring charges that what he has written is not "the way things actually happened" but only some self-fashioned fictional version.

The whole tone of the "history" is so unorthodox, and the format so drastic a departure from the dull leaden presentations of the previous "bird-dog" research into combat materials, I myself expect a whirlwind campaign of criticism. The text has not been equipped with a point-by-point documentation, and this will probably surprise Colonel Ganoe, and just shock old Dr.

Wright.²² But, first—to cite sources for the endless detail of a reconstructed battle picture would be to clutter the manuscript with footnotes until each page looked as if it had a five-day growth. Second, because on deeper consideration the formal apparatus of scholarship in problems of this type of historical composition performs no real function except as a kind of soul-soothing ritual. A half-truth or exaggeration or lie in the text can always and easily be "substantiated" by a fabrication in finer print at the bottom of the page. More likely than not no reader would ever be the wiser!

I was obliged to profess my Credo, and my introductory statement of it is perhaps a little too pat and eloquent—"In my own manuscript nothing has been invented. Not a fact or detail appears which was not submitted to me in good faith and checked as best as could be done under the circumstances. I have added nothing to the records and testimonies offered me except for the obvious requirements of composition and simple interpretive synopsis. When I note size, shape, color or quality (a "small, creaking staircase," men, "frightened and dazed," "a heavy-footed run through the snow drifts") the description has been extracted from the sources. When I quote orders or conversations directly the remarks in each case have been literally transcribed from oral testimony as to what was actually being said and felt. At no point have I indulged in literary or journalistic license. Everything that has been included has its source in critically examined evidence, and of the many omissions of details and events, committed in the ordinary activity of an historian 'selecting' his data, none of them would substantially alter the picture drawn."

Mutatis mutandis, this would hold for my attitude to history under all conditions of composition.

Both the writing and the reading of History requires at once an act of faith and an act of deep understanding. In the final analysis it is always the self-conscious integrity of the Historian which is in question. And that is best judged by the internal qualities of his work and a review of his method, his assumptions, and his temperament.

4 March 1945

Routinism, that great curse of sedentary life, is setting in again. The sameness of each day, morning after morning and night after night, first confuses you— "My god! Is today really Sunday" is the refrain now—and then depresses. But today was really Sunday! The Colonel rose from his desk in a bustle of papers, grabbed his helmet, and made conspicuously for the door. "Guess I need saving," he explained. Some twenty minutes later he came storming in again, dropped his helmet with a crash on his windowsill, and exploded—"The damned church services don't start till 11:30!" He would have had to wait "out in the cold" for another half-hour. "I don't need religion that bad!" he said and started fussing with his sheaf of notes and memoranda. The religious urge did not come again.

Nor was that the whole story of this Sunday. Mooney received a package from the States. Much sweets and candy which we all eliminated with relish and rapidity. And also a small pocketsize handsome edition of the New Testament. He fingered the fine leather, and scanned the neat print turning hundreds of pages at a time. "Now what the hell is this all about!" he inquired with his characteristic gentleness. He seized the back cover and proceeded to give anxious curious glances at the final pages. "Not even a calendar!" he shouted, more than half-serious. Later the day he penned his sweet thank-you note. "I treasure it greatly," he wrote in his tender final remarks on the Bible, "and I take it with me wherever in the front lines my assignment may carry me. I read it and it has already brought me much comfort. It was wonderful of you to think of me in such a sacred way."

Spent some time in the evening with the "propagandists" of the Psychological Warfare Branch. They are of course relentlessly busy pamphleteering and literally bombarding the Nazi troops with messages, leaflets, booklets, newspapers, a host of ingenious appeals. Their work, they confess with a little sadness, is only of a "tactical" nature. Which is understandable: their disappointment, that is. Propaganda which is not operating within a high strategic framework must inevitably appear to the craftsman as sabotage, a conscientious withdrawal of efficiency. But they are of course more than mere craftsmen. Wallenberg (who curiously enough remained in Germany as an editor until 1937!) knew the political implications of mere tactical propaganda.[23] The Army had nothing to say to the German soldier. The Allies had no real substantial message for him. Whatever the stress on his political credulity (after the overwhelming series of Hitler-Himmler-Goebbels disappointments and even betrayals) they could make no effort to touch, divert, reorient the Weltanschauung. The PWB output is almost solely devoted to the creation of "war prisoners." *Zwei Worte*, the leaflet screams in huge red letters, will save a million lives. They are, namely—"EI SÖRRENDER." Much of the newspapers issued weekly are concerned with the straight factual reporting of the military developments. The truth, so far as I could discover, was not swerved from. There was hardly any reason to: the Allied victories have been almost continuous. Some small problem arose when von Rundstedt broke through last December. But it was correctly decided to tell that straight too, or the entire campaign might well be abandoned. "Trust," as they curiously put it, was growing in German minds: the Americans don't go in for falsehood. Some of the propaganda works the "Distress" theme—*Wo ist meine Familie?* The simple and natural concern about the home front is consistently exploited. *Was wird aus deiner Familie, Landser, wenn der Sturm im Westen losbricht?* And after much to do about "home" and "loved ones" the appeal—*Darum: Schluss mit dem sinnlosen Widerstand! Schluss mit dem Krieg! Fasst Mut und handelt!* The language of surrender is conveniently offered in a little leaflet (mysteriously titled ZG 77 K): "Five Minutes of English." The "blitz-course for German GIs" (I wonder what the German army equivalent for GIs actually is!) features—"Ui ssörenda," followed by an ingenious series of pleas—"Wen ken ai tek a bahs? Wer is ser hot wota? E letta blenk, plies. When das se mehl liew? Gat änising tu ried? Sam mor koffi, plies" and finally: "Senks for se ssiggarets." That, according to the Propaganda theory, should convince them.

I am certainly in no position to know what the real effectiveness of the appeals is. Every now and then German troops begin to "surrender in droves," as the line inevitably goes. The current report is that Allied PW camps are now going into their second million... Almost all are, of course, military prisoners, captured in the course of battle—rather than "morale prisoners," distressed by pessimism, worry, and personal grievances. At any rate, all I have to go on is the PWB statement that their "most effective" work was being done by "US/GB/F-ZG 87–1944," which is an ingeniously printed "*PASSIERSCHEIN.*" The German script is authentic, and the entire make-up is confidence-inspiring. It looks like a huge bank-note, or some high-state form. The text explains the "SAFE CONDUCT": "The German soldier who carries this safe conduct is using it as a sign of his genuine wish to give himself up. He is to be disarmed, to be well looked after, to receive food and medical attention as required and to be removed from the danger zone as soon as possible." It adds: *Gültig für einen oder mehrere Überbringer.* It is printed with official imprints of all kinds (American eagles, French flags and coat of arms, British lions), has a French and English translation. And is signed by Dwight D. Eisenhower, *Oberbefehlshaber der Alliierten Streitkräfte.* If the note was sufficiently reassuring on one side, the other side featuring the bright cheering legalisms of the Hague 1907 Convention might well sell whole battalions the propaganda bill of goods. So far, I suspect the "deserters" have all been the ill-trained, ill-fed recruits, pushed into the Army ranks in the recent military emergencies.

Footnote: was told today of prisoners in the recent Colmar Pocket operation. At Houssen the Americans were energetically calling for surrender: "Hindy ho! ...Hindy ho!" or the Infantryman's version of *Hände hoch!* Surprisingly enough the dialect was caught, and some of the enemy came out. Seeking some further demonstration of their peacefulness—their hands were high over their heads—the Germans shouted, some in perfect English, "Fuck Hitler!" The GIs were convinced. "Them's were our sentiments too..." one of the boys wryly remarked.

9 March 1945

Last night ended, but one can never be too sure in such things, *l'affaire Paulette*, and on my own part *l'affaire Sonia*.

We were racing through Nancy several weeks ago, Mooney and I, when suddenly down the avenue the blonde hair and lovely figure of some sweet young thing could be made out. The jeep made a wild turn, careened up and down and over the curbstone, and screeched to a stop directly in her path. "Here we go again!" Mooney roared. "Ask her where the center of town is." We, of course were on our way to Pagny-sur-Moselle, but such matters were nothing: the Center of Town formula it still remained, and I in faltering French and German made the proper inquiries. "Okay, okay," Mooney cut her short. "We got it the first time, baby ... Now ask her whether she'll go dancing with me tonight. Cloob Offitzeer. Deenehr too!" I tried again, but this time I was cut short. That much she could make out in English. Fine. It was a date. Paulette for Mooney. Sonia, the sister, for me.

So it went. I had little time for Sonia, but Mooney had a great and by now famous romance. He speaks not a word of French or German—except for "beaucoup," "wee," "toodjourz" and "nickts compree"—and she not a word of English except for "me no like" and "hawkay, bootch." She was a beautiful little creature, and her twin sister made it two. I managed to make some conversation go, and doubled as an interpreter for them. But the arrangements were unsatisfactory. Mooney preferred to go along on his own speed, pile up misunderstandings and misinterpretations until she became furious, began to rant ("whot you tink I am, hoor?") for god knows little enough reason, whereupon she would get belted a few times, would cry a bit, and crawl back into his arms. "I don't understand it!" Mooney would shout, through the explosive bursts of his almost constant laughter. "So help me I don't understand it! But it works!" And he would grab her and head for a bedroom.

The girls had been in prison last fall, rather badly off on charges of political untrustworthiness. Apparently a cousin of theirs back in Alsace had deserted the labor corps, killed a member of the Gestapo, and had been known to pass through Nancy. So Paulette and Sonia landed in a concentration camp. In September when the Seventh Army tore through Lorraine, they were "liberated" literally. They now were very fond of American soldiers, although that sounds morally worse than it really is. The girls are very simple and in some petty ways full of a rural rectitude. The German officers were unconscionably *stolz*. Their formalities never deserted them, not even in drink. They couldn't recall one occupation instance of a public spectacle involving a Wehrmacht officer. They glanced up now warmly at the bar, and at the smiling, laughing, noisy, teetering Americans, and from the pleasant fun-loving glance in their eyes we could see what they meant.

Last night we all came to Lunéville. After an hour of bickering as to where to go, and there is no place to go, I remained in the back of the car, and Mooney took off for the apartment. Hours later, trembling with the cold, Sonia was still indignantly inquiring about the whereabouts of her sister. I finally confessed they had taken off in "tryst," or some foreign-language equivalent. She now became furious, and I tried with curiously little success some of the Mooney technique, and then decided to leave her broil in her own anger. I went home to find Mooney and Paulette all dressed again, ready to return. They had been—the poor bedroom was practically wrecked—"happy as pigs in shit," Mooney explained. "It was simply marvelous! Simply marvelous!" he went on, as Paulette on her part broiled. "I stood in the middle of the room naked (as she lay in bed) and holding the pisspot as you instructed, fingers extended and joined, and slightly tilted, I pissed! It was like Niagara! The whole house must have heard me, and I couldn't help roaring with laughter. God! It was like a cavalry battalion of horses over a stream! Marvelous!" That was the end, too much. Something fine in Paulette was bruised. Never again. And so it was.

10 March 1945

The news was a little electrifying—the First Army is definitely across the Rhine. The story, broken down, appears to be a hair-breadth finish: the Germans planned to blow the great Ludendorff bridge at Remagen at 1600. At 1550 Able Company of the Twenty-Seventh Infantry reached the approach. The demolition charges were ready, but one lieutenant rushed across, and the infantrymen swarmed over after him. How long they can remain is still a vague question.[24] The counterattacks will be coming in furiously now... At any rate Cologne is secured; what there is left of it. As the *Stars & Stripes* correspondent ah so wittily remarked, no guide-books will be necessary for GI tourists of Cologne...

The highways and the streets of the town have been crowded with long and heavy movements. At noon today as we came out of the house several huge trucks with gigantic engineer bridging equipment were parked across the way. Said Mooney, breaking the story down in his irrepressible manner: "There's the big stuff! The stuff to cross the Rhine... And there's a kid, with an infantryman's badge, stopping, looking things over, watching the guy lash the beams a little tighter. To us it's just 'big stuff' for a big operation. To him it's a span for his own feet. Maybe next week he'll be moving forward over it.

Look at the way he's watching, checking. Yeah, he knows what it means. Some guy says, 'let's go!' and so the assault begins, and here is Joe getting a preview of what tomorrow is going to be his great stage..." I doubt however whether we here are going to make any Rhine crossings, just yet. Too bad: the "big stuff," and its attendant melodrama, may only be deceptive movements.

Went through some back-number reports, and was startled to find that the Germans sent two raider platoons over into Markolsheim the afternoon I passed through! I saw some rabbits in the fields east of the city going north and was almost tempted to run through a clip with my carbine. I laughed, though, and played with the notion that the rounds would probably fly wild over the Rhine and start some needless engagement over on a quiet sector... Who knows? My bad marksmanship might have wiped out a squad or two blindly, and then what have we here, a hero?

Churchill figured in the Story of the day. (He made his first visit to Germany today on Hodges's[25] First Sector; "What do you think of Aachen?" someone asked; and cracked the Great One, "Was that Aachen?") Said Churchill to Montgomery, before the ruins of a German town on the western front—"There will be no unemployment in this town after the war..." Tacitus—pro-German or no—would once again have been right: they make a desert, and they call it peace. Now they also call it the solution of our social problems...

12 March 1945

Monday.

Rediscovered again this evening in a local copy of Cervantes "the pleasant discourse between Don Quixote, Sancho Panza, and the Batchelor Sampson Carrasco," and the fine exchanges reminded me of how thoughtlessly we proceed in the reconstruction of our Military History, with what unawareness of method and tradition, and how complete the unsophistication! What do all these sedulously precise pages amount to? True: the divisions and armies did move exactly as indicated; these engagements were fought in the following named places; advances and counterattacks occurred as listed; difficulties and problems proved troublesome as suggested. Yet nothing ever happened as it is here recorded! The living context, the flavor, the excitement and passion and nervousness, the vocabulary—in a word, for me the truth—has been lost in the distillation of what is considered the significant course of events. But then, of all the problems of civilization the tragedy of war has always been the least known or understood. It has been universally and immemorially shared, yet either because of political or moral incapacities its real shape and substance has remained inaccessible to literature of all kinds. The man of imagination makes a contrived romance out of it, or an unrelieved horror. The man of sober fact has rarely been able to see the documentary truth for all the dust on the archives.

[...]

My own work here, in its largest aspect, is unfortunately not clear to me nor to the historians who are supposed to organize and edit my assignments. That is by now, of course, an old Army situation. The Historical Section itself seems to be the bastard creation of some enterprising military mind, with one hand on Thucydides, one eye on the future and the judgment of posterity, and one foot into the next war. The tendencies, as I have felt them so far, all reflect this kind of three-way pull.

There is much enthusiasm on the part of many of the historians (Davis, Hamilton, Ellis) that the production of the staff will be (or at least could be) a serious and even a monumental contribution to literature. Never before have there been such facilities for thoroughgoing original research and explorations into secret documents, and also into the realities in question. Get into a jeep and tear through the countryside for an hour, and you can check your footnote at the front! (Only the other day Hamilton discovered the old mayor who had led the American troops through a wild forest to the Moselle sector where a bridgehead could be effectively established.) Stop at a headquarters and you can see and talk to the staff and the men in the line: the dramatis personae of the campaign are still on the stage. (In the end, curiously, only the historian knows truly what transpired: Mooney's narratives have been read by commanders who learned for the first time what actually went on during their campaigns. . .) The dream is of a hundred-volume set, complete, exhaustive, definitive. They can see it on the shelf. Some even can make out the cumulative layers of dust. But that has hardly disconcerted scholars in the past. The value of a preserved recorded past is indisputable. To what greater theme can they dedicate themselves than the War? So the progress of the history goes. The caserne offices here are jammed with the quartermaster's wooden boxes, each packed with reports, sketches, journals, interviews, plans and orders. I can't help feeling, for all the hopelessness of the prospect of someone some day going through thousands of boxes for all the armies of the world, that something substantial is being done. In the future it will at least be possible for the people to know the truth. The History itself may be orthodox, official. But as a combat historian here one really becomes a kind of spy in the interests of civilian civilization.

To be sure, the military bureaucracy will allow nothing to pass that threatens its shining armor. Unfortunately, if you even so much as breathe vigorously you are likely to cloud that sensitive plate. The last few weeks I have been "editing" the manuscript of the Seventh Army's narrative. Quiet, dull, devitalized. All the real issues and problems of the planning (for a single instance) are tenderly knit together, so that all the twists and turns of the invasion and subsequent campaign appear to be masterfully crocheted together by artful strokes. The international intrigue involving American, British, and French prestige; the amazing conflicts of entrenched military bureaucracies on various fronts and centers; the real character and consequences of so-called military science—in a word, everything which an historian of imagination and insight would seize upon has been rendered innocuous... or left in the bottom corner of one of our old boxes. There is no excuse for indignation on this score. That, after all, is what an official history is. It matters not whether the slot takes a dull or a shiny nickel; the machine will play the same tune. I straighten sentences out, and try subtly to suggest something of the great themes of confusion, hypocrisy, and mass-production death. But that is besides the point. The manuscript is now clean, ready for the seal of the General. The outline is orderly, the notes and bibliography complete, the pages neatly typed and double-spaced. Here it is, but the real history lies in the white space between the lines.

Finally, there is the new practical utilitarian school of historical-minded military people. Many of them are intelligent and cultivated, after the manner of the *Infantry Journal* editors. The whole truth of a combat situation needs to be known because only then are effective lessons learned and battlecraft perfected. So the historian, versed in the literature from Herodotus to Clausewitz and the latest field manuals, becomes a tactical observer manqué. In the finer focus of small-unit narratives all the futilities, stupidities, and assorted scandals of an engagement are recorded. The fears and terrors of attacks and withdrawals are caught. Even the mad fantasy of battle responses has been touched. Marshall's *Island Victory* is very far from being a good book, but it has this kind of thing in it, and it is certainly, I think, a unique achievement in war documentaries.

One thing, by the way, strikes me in this connection which is a little irrelevant but nevertheless interesting. The military history which can now be casually dismissed as old-fashioned never departed from its central theme—the Commander, his strategy, his tactics, his genius. Napoleon struck so, and the assault was victorious. The staff hit upon the great plan, and the stroke of annihilation was registered. The Army and the State, through its official leadership, remained the central characters. Now military history has been stood on its head. And what could be more ideologically appropriate in an era when it is for the Common Man that everything is sacrificed and it is in the name of the Little People that history is made. The hero of history is not Foch but the *poilu*, not Pershing but the doughboy. The pamphlets are now being turned out by the dozen. And they record great victories, unexpected and ingenious improvisations on the battle-field, feats of audacity and military daring. Not Eisenhower's, or Patton's, or Clark's, or Patch's. It is all the genius of some Joe in his Foxhole. A sergeant shouts, "God damn those sons-a-bitches! We'll have their asses hanging out in the breeze! Follow me!" And it is to this non-com[bat], far removed from war rooms and high-level field orders, that the historian has turned for his protagonist. The victory belongs to the generalship of the sergeant and the corporal. The brass is left to their own privacy. Joe has his philosophers, his artists, his politicians. Now, in his supreme achievement, he has found his historian. This could, I am sure, only happen to him in our own time. The reasons are complicated, but for one (symbolic) thing he had first to find himself. Joe as such can hardly be said to have existed in the trenches of World War I. When Joe became entitled to his own hole, he became entitled to hagiography.

My own work, as I say, is confused, and so I have done a little of everything: tried to collect letters, conversations, diaries, odd items, which are historically speaking priceless ... made an effort to loosen the official straitjacket of the over-all historical narrative ... and also had a brief career as a "bird-dog" which is the local slang for the field research of a "combat historian" scooting from headquarters to command posts to front-line positions and back (if a stray bullet or mine-field doesn't censor him) in order to reconstruct his story of the battle. If I could have my own way, I would take off again tomorrow morning for the front...

[...]

15 March 1945

The days now have the new wondrous warmth and sunniness of a coming spring. I left early and went out into the country. The scenes in the hills were a real miracle of brightness and shadow. Little children were running playfully up and down the village street, and the smells of the farmhouses, the hay and the animals and the earth itself, were strong and fine. With the night came a new unbelievable sky. You could do nothing but stare at it. And then the theme would dominate your mind exactly as it did since the first sensible view of the stars through baby's eyes. Was it all real? And how did it come to be? And was there any more significant or entrancing pursuit in life than the discovery of the infinite mystery of our heaven... I came out after dinner, and simply sat quietly on a little mound in the field not very far from the station. It was not to be for very long, for soon after—I could record the time to the split second—the skies began to roar. The fighters and bombers were coming out, and they stormed all night for Germany. Inside Hans was preparing a leaflet, *Schluss machen*. In three minutes (it would say) treasures of the decades will be destroyed. In a few minutes' time ten thousand aircraft would add new years of reconstruction to the burdens of the people. Capitulate! In the morning, at ten minutes to eight, the fighters were soaring in noisily to the local landing field. Serene formations of the "liberators,"[26] high in the sky, flew on by.

At last, in the dinner conversation, I discovered the "why" of those wonderful breakfasts in the recent mornings! There is apparently a glutted egg market in Sicily. And some one has been "borrowing" the General's plane and stealing into Palermo. Crates are jammed into the plane, and every week now mysterious shipments of fresh eggs have been available. How bewildered the poor chicken could be at the consumption of its Messina or Agrigento creation in faraway Lorraine...

The bridgehead is still holding out. "Ludendorff" apparently continues to cast his dark defeatist shadow across Germany's fate. A Nazi commentator said today: "The bridgehead was established at a point tactically unfavorable to the enemy, who is now compelled continually to pour fresh troops into it in order to hold his gains. Nevertheless, the bridgehead constitutes a threat to our defenses, and our commanders are paying it all the attention it deserves." The propaganda broadcasts droned on with more of "bestiality, horror, sadism, destruction, brutality, cynicism, and terror." Hans Fritzsche's[27] interesting phrase for the foundation of the Anglo-Saxon Imperial New World is: "machine-made terror."

And in this connection, I should add that Hans tells me that "definitely" there are saboteurs among the German front correspondents and leader writers. The Nazi propaganda on the "Coming Murder" has been savage, and more; and even, to our eyes, to the point of ridicule or absurdity. There seems to be no doubt as to their oppositional tendencies. Prospects are luridly painted, for these are the prospects offered the people by the present leadership! That, I think, explains some of the extreme strident hysteria of the current German response.

The office went postal[28] this noon, and as I prepared a box of documents for shipment everybody wrapped their collections of souvenirs. Said Mooney: "God, I love to do this! It's like wrapping Christmas packages!" He carefully tightened and folded corners, and confessed: "That's my life! Simple things like that! Clearing the snow from my front walk, with my dog bouncing around and kicking up spray... Wrapping and ribboning all my presents... The war is a shame, a real goddamn useless shame."

17 March 1945

Spent a few minutes with Jean Casali at the Front National this morning. He continues his search, and today submitted an additional sheaf of Nazi leaflets and a collection of pamphlets including an anthology of Hitler's speeches in French and some things by Jacques Doriot.[29] He added some photographs which were striking shots of what now he calls "the old days." A magnificent portrait of Rommel and Kesselring, striding across a barren Tunisian road, roaring in laughter, yet stiff and proud in military appearance. A photo against the backdrop of the Coliseum of casual sloppy carefree GIs marching down la Via del Impero surrounded by a formidable guard of inscrutable German MPs. A fine close-up of the extraordinary interiors of the Church at Monte Cassino. This film, like the others, bears its little Nazi propaganda message— *détruite par les Anglo-Américaines.*

Jean tells me that once again he has made efforts, but in vain, to get back to the front. This latest time it was a foolish attempt to crash into the American ranks. I had to smile. He was a lieutenant in the FFI and before that one of the chief Lorraine agents in the underground railroad. When the Maquis were disarmed,[30] his commission was denied him in the regular national French army. After some haggling, he was once again offered his lieutenancy—but only for some bureau post in Nancy or Metz or some other rear area. He refused. He wants, as he says, to go to the front, *zu Deutschland... kaputt machen.* That, for a man of partisan FFI background, is apparently too "dangerous" for the old military bureaucracy. So he remains here, fussing around with propaganda, doing what he can.

My room is now crowded with the literature which accumulates. The press every day is exciting and I can hardly refrain from purchasing every publication in the store. The leading editorials, the special polemics, the occasional chronicles, have all a fine passion, and some even distinction. François Mauriac writes regularly for *Le Figaro*; also Paul Claudel. Paul Éluard has some political verses in *Carrefour*, which also featured André Chamson's first article in four years. But I have so little time to read.

This evening I talked a little with Mme. Wernert, and found myself unable to do anything more but to go to bed and sleep. It never ceases to alarm me, this spectacle of people taking their lives in stride, torn apart as they have been for generations by the tragedies of war. Her first husband was killed in World War I. Five sons are scattered over the European theaters; two are soldiers; two are prisoners; one is missing. The last she heard of any of them was four years ago. All she has left is her daughter. And Jeanne's husband ran away in 1940 from the German labor draft, and has not been seen since. He lived and worked only in Clermont-Ferrand, but never dared visit, and never called for his wife to come. The marriage seems to have been harshly uprooted. Jeanne, or *Jeanne-darme* as we have agreed to call her because of her fanatical insistence on her own privacy and isolation, now lives alone, and works almost all the time. She is pretty and lively, but the years have made her strong and cold in a very special way. Mme. Wernert was still a little distressed about her meat problem. That little saucer-full which is her ration for the week will obviously not keep for seven days, and she is not altogether pleased with the prospect of having to eat all they have early in the week and waiting impatiently for the next dispensation. But the news came that one egg will be on the ration for next month! That has cheered her considerably. She heard too that some Liberty ships were en route from America with food and good things. "So there!" I said. But ah no, that was only for the *Grossköpfe. . . les grandes têtes*, and not for the poor people at all. Perhaps she knew. . . She added to my collection a copy of the *Annales* for 1901—Maurice Maeterlinck on the *triomphe d'automobilisme* and Camille Saint-Saëns on the wondrous beauties of Richard Wagner's new works (first sheet of *Siegfried* appended).

18 March 1945

Jeanne and I spent a long evening together last night; I finally managed an invitation. Her place is a really lovely apartment, carefully kept up during the bad years of the war and occupation with an apparent tender solicitude as if there were nothing else in the world to care for. She was making a fire and I picked up a fragment of a novel in the collection of kindling paper. *L'Amour refleurit* . . . I read it with a studied pensiveness and curiosity, and I did draw her out. She gave a few unmistakable signs of cynicism and contempt. *Schwindel!* was her word for it. I asked a little further. "Well," she conceded, "perhaps it really isn't. . . But for myself I had a pretty bad time of it. No luck, no love. . ." Clearly she didn't want to talk about it. What then? Oh, what you will. . . So we spent some time in small chit-chat and soon she was telling me a rich, genuinely exciting narrative of the years under the Germans.

The ten months she spent in Germany began in November 1943. She was conscripted with so many other French women to work for the Army bureaus along the Rhine headquarters. As an Alsatian she speaks both French and German fluently and so she became the bureau's chief interpreter. She worked faithfully and efficiently. There was nothing else to do. But this was a far cry from "collaboration!" Every moment of the day brought some little conflict, a new declaration of war. Her blouse was a polka-dot affair, white with odd red and blue dots. "So!" the chief would scream (and she does a wonderful comic-serious imitation of his facial and speech mannerisms), "you always have to exhibit your colors! You can't sit here a moment without draping yourself in the flag!" Innocently she would look down over her clothes. "Where? What? I have some things to wear, and what I wear concerns only me!" Daily they fought, and in every little tale Jeanne's simple goodhearted horror (and also contempt) for meanness and officiousness was eloquently displayed. She would not be allowed to warm her hands in the morning. "Work!" he would shout, "we have no time to dilly-dally!" When the planes came over, she would sweep her desk clean and make for the shelter. "What's the matter?" he cried indignantly. "Where are you going?" "What's the matter? Where am I going? Are you out of your mind? The bombers are here! One has to be crazy not to know it's dangerous! *Auf Wiedersehen!*" Finally it grew unbearable. She of course had given fierce refusals to his proferred offer of the privilege of becoming his mistress. And that only added fuel to the hatred... The only recourse was to see the commandant, a general officer. Her account of him seems to be very sympathetic, and apart from the color of the personal situation (he did help her) rather on the objective side. Jeanne and the General apparently had several conferences. And each time she came away impressed: he was an "admirable man." He apparently put the bureau chief in his place; after that there wasn't much violent trouble at least. The General seemed to be unhappy about that, and many other small and large aspects of the occupation and the war. But, as he once told her, "I am a soldier. A soldier remains at his post and does his duty to the last." Which he did. In September the bombing and strafing became massacres. The walls of the office shook all day and night. The windows were smashed, the poor air-raid shelters ruined. Jeanne's last night in Germany was spent at her desk making out passes and official releases and the final payroll for all the French and German workers. The General had given his permission to evacuate the civilians. She and the other French girls would leave before dawn. The German girls cried, and many begged to be taken along. No one had been so unhappy and miserable as the German girls who were also conscripted for work in the military bureaus, and who were treated *wie Soldaten*. They were constantly in tears, and over and over again confessions were made to Jeanne (who alone had nerve enough to stand up to the bureaucrats and the Gestapo) how terrible their plight and fate was, and how much they would give to be *Französin*. Strange, but many of the soldiers among the German garrisoned troops often said the same thing. And even a few of the older officers. (About the women, of course there were many different "strata." The horde of mistresses which the army put up in the best hotels were quite of another sort; but this much is interesting—the Nazis always threw it up to the pretty French girls: their make-up for the lips and cheeks and eyebrows was decadent and corrupt, and real beauty (after the German fashion) was simple and wholesome. Yet in no store could any lipstick, powder, rouge or perfume ever be found. They bought out the stocks wholesale, and either sent it home or furnished it to their local sweethearts. Who wore it, Jeanne says, in the ugliest manner imaginable. Not having, the explanation is, any real hand for it.) At any rate, "the Americans were coming." The Nazis reminded them of this daily and with appropriate bitterness. And then the *Schwarzen* would arrive! And everything would be kaput! Not much attention was paid. The French collaborationists would reinforce the arguments, but nobody was concerned... The air raids grew worse, and then the panicky evacuation broke. The collaborationists were left stranded; the Nazis never trusted them and refused to allow them to withdraw in their own ranks. (The military sections of Vichy, most corrupt and vicious of them all, were summarily shot by the partisans.) Jeanne left before daybreak, and ran for hours through the countryside. The attack grew in intensity, and she scrambled regularly for the ditches and the dive-bombers came in for strafing sorties. Near Avricourt two of her comrades were hit. One took a shell fragment in the shoulder, the other just a few yards behind her was riddled with machine-gun fire. She finally made her mother's house here in Lunéville. Mme. Wernert knew that the "final attack" had begun and had feared the worst. Jeanne—it should not have been a surprise, because if anybody could "beat the war" this wonderful little spitfire could—had come home. She was in bed for weeks with fevers and nervous shock. She would cry, and her mother for a while could not really understand it, every time she heard a noise. If a plane came by she broke down completely. In a month or two she had almost completely recovered. She found some work of her own and tried to recover something of normalcy. (She had a few run-ins with the FFI who, according to her account, became packed with all the worst elements of the community soon as the Americans began to take over; the *partisans* and Maquis of the long resistance struggle were fine and heroic; but the opportunists, who had played with the Germans when they were in power, were now changing horses; and Jeanne had told the SS and Gestapo off and now she would have none of their home-grown variety of officiousness.)

It was after one when I left and stumbled through the dark streets to my own place. She agreed to tell me more soon of the "history of the times."

20 March 1945

Awoke early, in the dark, this morning for the trip to the Rhine, and just a little taken by my sudden recollection of the dream of the night. What an amazing image! There was a great awesome threat of danger, and we grouped together hastily for protection. But the danger, curiously enough, was from an avalanche—the roar was the roar of rocks and boulders coming down. And then with a great dramatic stroke (was there ever such a deus ex machina?) I found myself removed. I was now seated in mid-air in a dark chamber. And the destruction of my comrades was instantaneously framed in a screen. I was safe and now a spectator to the tragedy... How inescapable the movies truly are! We are not even free from them in our dreams. Their cheap terrible (and irrelevant) melodrama dominates the imagination; and their central technique of vicarious safety, or adventure, or joy, becomes our meager apparatus for experiencing life.

The ride was long and cold over roads which I am beginning to know as well as any route on the planet. Baccarat, St. Dié, the Vosges through Ste. Marie-aux-Mines, through to Ribeauvillé, and then in and around the Colmar area (Ostheim, Guémar, Markolsheim, Kunheim, Houssen, Fortschwihr, Holtzwihr, Illhaeusern, La Maison Rouge). The day was devoted almost entirely to walking over the terrain, making some notes and mental corrections, and shooting pictures. The day was quiet, eventless. The Colmar forest did appear a good deal different from my own conception of it, but nothing was too surprising. The scenes of battle there were like the scenes of battle everywhere in the pocket. An old battlefield is a huge junk pile. (Sometimes the Army junk-collectors, the quartermaster salvage teams, do a thorough job, but "restoration" is never possible. Ruins, rubble, and garbage remain.) Here at the Niederwald farmhouse in the middle of the forest, one house was still standing; the other two had been badly devastated. Piles of cans, papers, boxes, old ammunition shells, littered the clearing and the entrances and all the rooms. Over at one edge of the crossroads there were five German graves, marked with black crayon on plain and now warping slats of wood. One American grave (his "body" had apparently been lowered into the hole on a shovel) was marked on the other side. Length: foot-and-a-half... In the farmer's *maison* itself, some old books. The volumes were still soaked and I had difficulty making the delicate operation: the pages tore as I tried to leaf through. The two I could handle easily were ancient things. One struck me as a rather extraordinary edition of St. Augustine's *City of God*; what I could make out of the print and the binding and the plates attractive and fine. The other was a study of Colmar—with wonderful portraits of the suzerainty of feudal times, the nobility and peasantry of earlier centuries, the peacefulness and gaiety of Alsatian countryside scenes, the historic sites illustrating the long rich traditions of the people's religion, industry, politics, folk culture. I pushed—again for a shamelessly sentimental reason—some of the cans and rubbish away, and let the volumes remain. If War itself cared to dramatize its own deviltry with such obvious pathos, my own duty perhaps was only to preserve the image, and forever to pity it.

For the rest there were only, as we photographers never tired of saying, "good shots." A little child hanging onto the back of an enormous hay-cart, dangling her feet, as tanks and trucks passed her by. The steeple of a church jutting upwards, almost with no foundation, in the complete ruin of a little town. The face of the clock stared out into the countryside. The hands were still intact. The hour (the hour of its "ungodly" fate) was half past six. The children in the rubble everywhere, playing their games, but never so absorbed as not to run out to greet us with their universal *shawkalahd?* I wonder what their childhood memories of these times will be; what flavor of reminiscence there will be to their recollection of growing up and playing and making first youthful friends and enemies. (What happens to an Alsatian Tom Sawyer in all this degradation of a world...?)

22 March 1945

The Ludendorff bridge is down, its great spans twisted and crumpled in the Rhine, but perhaps only Goebbels will be sufficiently warmed by the divine mysticism of the sudden stroke to relieve the cold bleak German picture. The retreat is now assuming the proportions of a great disaster. Equipment is being abandoned and destroyed; thousands of troops are surrendering, willingly and even in a sense enthusiastically; the invading forces are being greeted with white flags in town after town. And now with the spring weather set in, the planes roar out every day. Said Hans Fritzsche today in his broadcast: "We possess the key to a true European order. We have found the secret of how to maintain peace in Europe." Perhaps the ruins of Worms, Mainz, Bonn and Cologne are only the hiding-places for their great keys and secrets.
[...]

23 March 1945

Some of the family's letters began to come through this week, and although I am, of course, glad, it is nevertheless distressing to think that my rude angry prompting must have hurt them, and harshly. The long silences did trouble me, but the separation and the loneliness are difficult enough without having smaller complicating irritations. I was brusque only out of love and anxiety for them all, for there isn't a day that I don't think of "home"—of how months and years are passing and changing so many things, of how the girls are growing up and maturing and the folks are becoming old, and of what they have been thinking and doing and hoping. I could only tell them I was "well" and rather "happy," and they, I think, will understand a little beyond the pleasant cliché. Seeing and learning much is only a part of the story. Every moment always brought its sights and lessons. But now I am beginning to feel so much stronger and independent, and in a few respects, I trust, a little wiser and more self-disciplined. It may be a long time before I come home again, but I reminisce about the old days always, and feel constantly warmed by memories of a loving family's affection and loyalty.

Intended to spend part of the afternoon walking around in the fine sunshine, but was lured into a bookstore, and wound up with another dozen volumes. The Halévy in the window attracted me irresistibly—a really interesting critique of the histories of the French Revolution. Then: an edition of the *Chanson de Roland* with an introduction discussing Boissonade, Ferdinand Lot, and others; a biography of Pierre Duhem; an edition of the letters of Degas; Rilke's *Lettres à un jeune poète* (why do I always forget that he wrote in German, and all the French titles are translations?); a fine volume of Montesquieu's *Cahiers* and a study of Machiavellian traditions, which scarcely seems on the subtle side (all the references were obvious) but could never be dull. . .

G. was very upset today. His account of one of the winter battles was returned from division headquarters with a firm stern refusal to approve. Everything was denied. Apparently they would not admit to a word of the terrible tale: what! Such stupidities and callousness on our part? No! These were only the grave mistakes and misinterpretations on the part of the historian. . . Of course: most of G.'s distress is author's wounded pride. But his pretty paragraphs were not just mere editorial niceties. Here was how the callow kids and the simple nobodies from everywhere, who yesterday were standing in the village square ogling the little French girls or in the movie house blowing up and floating condoms when the projector broke down, here is how these poor unfortunate boys died in forests and fields they would never even know by name. It wasn't a style that was turned back. It wasn't that somebody thought "chapters need tightening up" or that certain themes were being "underplayed" or "overwritten." How the whole of writing gets trapped in the technical conventions and problems. A word or a sentence comes to have a substance or body of its own. And we get to think only of its internals, and rarely look to see its face. Here the face was the simple, horrible mask of "murder," the real face of War. And no one—at least officially—recognizes it. . . The other afternoon one of the battalion's S-3s was in from the Third Division, and we made our old round of grim jokes. We laughed about "Iron Mike," and how commanders pray for his relief—"maybe we'll get some guy a little more peaceloving. . ." And laughed about all the butchery. "Don't you ever get conscience-stricken about all the men you've sent to the slaughter—good nice young clean kids—who went in more often than not without a chance? —Sure, it's a great division! But all you have to do is throw enough men into the line and you'll gain your ground—take enough chances and your spectacular stunts will come off. . ." Mooney and I were more than half-serious, but we were all laughing. If they didn't protect themselves with cynicism and selfishness, they could never do what they have to do, they could never survive the nightmare. Wgtmn was concerned only with his own fate: he was still alive and that was what counted. The rest were "eight-balls who couldn't handle themselves," or anyway "it's just too bad, just too damned bad." The head shakes slowly, the eyes glance away filled with sadness for a moment, and then the war goes on.

24 March 1945

Call came in this morning from the general hospital (at Nancy). Shocked and surprised to learn it was Wgtmn. The Division, he reported, had been badly cut up in the Siegfried line, and he burned the wires for several minutes with curses for the G-2. Apparently they had been told that only one out of every five or ten pillboxes would be manned. "Well," he cracks (even anger can hardly be sustained for more than a brief moment), "the krauts must have been firing by remote control..." Mortar fragments chopped into him at a half a dozen places, and he still wasn't certain he wouldn't lose an eye. But: *c'est la guerre*...—the ubiquitous substitution for any kind of personal or original response. *C'est la guerre*. Most of his whole battalion was destroyed. Eight-balls. Eight-balls like himself! "That's what I get for hanging around the rear echelon!" He had been at his battalion headquarters. "I should have been up there in some goddamn foxhole. Woulda been as safe as the Virgin Mary there." Every morning the General was curt but eloquent in the briefing session. "Keep pushing forward!" was the burden of his daily directive. "There isn't an organized squad between you and the Rhine. Keep pushing forward!" That was all. "These are thrilling times!" he might add sometimes as an historical afterthought, "these are thrilling times, gentlemen!" And the division would push on...

The pressure against the German forces must almost be unbearably severe by now. The news today: Field Marshal Kesselring for von Rundstedt as a chief of the Armies.[31] And General Dittmar[32] hit a new theme in his survey of the Nazi military situation. He actually paid tribute to the ability of the enemy (American) command to put to good use the "superabundant" means at its disposal. It reminds one, he added (amazing!) in more than one respect "of the German offensive abilities in the first years of the great struggle." But he came back with: after five and a half years, the Wehrmacht's tenacious resistance evidences (at least) the "great moral strength" of Hitler's new order. He warned against the "peace of the graveyard."

Have long been bored with the literary conversation here, but now I find it really difficult to control explosive anger. Never is there a word, a touch which might suggest that the commercialization and vulgarization of intellectual things were not complete and terrible. The writer is the man who sells (to the slick magazines, to Hollywood), who is gossiped about, who succeeds... The naive awe in which a "name" is held, the yearning envious respect for his reputation and rewards, almost sickens me. Wasn't there once a time in America when literature was a thing of the spirit, when a writer's career embraced a great personal ideal, informed and inspired by tradition and some force of prophetic hope? So much has passed away. There will be no end to mourning for the death of the heart and the death of the mind when once we awake to the great poverty of our world. We have been robbed of our deepest achievements, and what is there left even to remind us or suggest a sense of our profound loss?

Even good talk is dead. The conversation is doughy, limp, lifeless. Not a remark which isn't obvious and at the same time wrong (because it is always arrogant or uncritical or stereotyped). When I tried to suggest, merely in passing, that "a generation" is not at all the mathematical thing it once was (three or five or eight years), but now can almost be said to be defined by the age limits of the universal conscription laws, I proved to be only bewildering and very silly! What was I saying but that "a generation's experience" was now completely dominated by the tone of war which touched the younger and the older men alike. Small matter now that the college classes were a decade apart, or that the depression came "too soon" for some. The War was the thing which caught the careers of all mankind equally. The tragedy belongs to one crowded international generation. But apparently there was something zany about all that... And something even madder to my playful notion—we had been talking about how popular songs catch on—that a fortune awaited the man who could exploit the region between boredom and pain. When a song is heard for the first time no one is interested. When it is repeated for the thousandth time (the song-plug machinery is now functioning smoothly), it is no longer a casual unnoticeable thing in our life, for it has become a creature of positive boredom. The radio plays it constantly, no band overlooks it, everybody is humming it, singing it, whistling it. The lyrics become pulpy in our mouth and the overwhelming tune crowds every last phrase of music out of our memory. Soon the boredom becomes painful, and the song fades. But what a glorious career! I insisted: find a place to stand between Boredom and Pain and you can move the world!—Zany? What on earth was I talking about? I am not hurt very much, but it is depressing, and I am becoming so lonely, so anxious to make a friend, if I don't find an opportunity to renew some old theme of thought or spirit I will soon, I am afraid, break down or at least lose myself in some ruinous or insipid routine of inanity.

25 and 26 March 1945

The atmosphere seems almost electrical with news and expectations. The local secret is out: it was the Twelfth Armored which had moved through recently and which has been running wild in the Rhine pocket rounding up droves of prisoners among whom, so it claims, are SS troopers, at which all eyebrows are being lifted. But nothing appears to be in the way of the push, and the roads are being ground up by an army rushing forward. Men were coming back from the front black with dust and dirt telling their tales of the unbelievable traffic moving to the river. The Third was assembling a few thousand yards west of the Rhine, Sutton just reported, and there was no doubt that the time had come. As he sat there somebody barged into the CP. "We've got a couple companies of DUKWs for you," battalion Commander was told. "Son-of-a-bitch!" he said. The time had come. And when Wgtmn called again from the hospital in the afternoon he gossiped: "You know we're going over tonight!" "Sh-h-h!" came the frantic admonition. "Oh Christ, everybody knows about it!" Since the pillboxes at the Siegfried line the Germans have been offering nothing. Hundreds are surrendering, and marching back to assembly areas practically unguarded. Division, corps, regimental CPs are packing up to move again before they're settled. One of the Signal "refugees" who were crowding the village last night remarked that one evening he darted around buildings and street corners trying to string wire in the face of sniper fire. The next morning, he was in "rear echelon." Artillery pieces would set up, fire a couple of rounds, and displace again. But still the country was barren, littered with the wreckage of destroyed towns. And what was left standing was soon to be mopped up. In one ruin only a church remained, and a "long tom"[33] was zeroing in on that. "Funny," the lieutenant said, "how we used to talk about Nazis bombing out churches... Well, I guess in war you have to do what's necessary, and sometimes play all the rules of the game. But we don't always have to say it's right and pure..." The church, he insisted, was lone and isolated; functioned in no military way, no artillery observers, no snipers. But down it went, crumpling into the rest of the devastation. This, I know, will "surprise" many some day. But even shock, amazement, bewilderment, are too mild. Wgtmn is bouncing around Nancy again, having fled the hospital in his anxiety to "look up a few pieces I heard about..." Tried checking a few points with him, especially about the shooting of wounded prisoners. "Sure," he said, "sure, we shot them. Hell, we were only twenty men in the patrol. We couldn't fool with goddamn krauts. Anyway, what we used to say about the Indians, goes for these fuckers too. Only good German is a dead German..." And of course it was not only necessary, and proper, but also fun. "Shit!" he went on, "if the bastard wouldn't answer questions fast enough we'd plug him. You've got your goddamn pistol right up against his chest, all you have to do is pull the trigger. And then you can watch him explode, he coughs and staggers with his hands up in the air. Not bad!" N.B. The captain is a very pleasant guy, clean-cut, straightforward, and personable. He is the Portrait of the Barbarian as a Great American Boy. And in war he plays all the rules of the game, and never questions, never argues. "Hell!" is his only regret, "when the krauts in the Siegfried zeroed in on me, I was just jumping off to take a whole town all by myself. You know, I might have gotten a silver star for that! But they must've known I was coming..." The barrage came over, and Wgtmn dived into a doorway. The roof and the floors broke the plunge of the shell fire and only scattered fragments tore into him. Still, a few inches either way and he would have remained in the shattered passageway, dead in a strange house in a nameless town. But that is not the real shape of the tragedy. The mystery of death in war interests nobody, neither its stupidity or fantasy or horror. Dying becomes "just too bad," an inconvenient impractical thing because now, as one can plainly see, there would be no more medals, no more girls, and not even an opportunity to ransack the house for souvenirs. Taking life, war, love, history, mankind, thoughtlessly and soullessly, death too can be accepted without curiosity or pathos. Just another casualty, and no mind or spirit need be troubled...

Cast a cold eye
On life, on death.
Horseman, pass by!
[William Butler Yeats, "Under Ben Bulben"]

27 March 1945

Jeanne was very pretty last night, and very gay; and pressing the point a little, if with some romantic overtones, we were sitting up again, long after the very proper hours which she is almost fanatical these days about keeping, going through "the burdens of war."

One or two of the concluding details of my "first installment" the other evening was a little misleading. "The day of liberation" had come to Lunéville when Jeanne finally reached home. The story, I took it, was quite over. And that perhaps is why I didn't understand much of her bitterness and contempt. She wasn't home for more than a few hours when the police came and arrested her. The FFI was rounding up "collaborationists," and the prison cells were crowded with men and women of all sorts. She was held there for a week. She refused to eat and refused to talk. They would beat her every day—"stupid, cruel boys of seventeen and eighteen"—and then they cut her hair. (It suddenly struck me.

Of course. Her hair had been cut! That was it all the time! She had burned all her old photos, and nothing but the memory of fond golden locks remained. She was still very embarrassed about it. I was so moved and confused that I laughed. And she became hurt: it was no joke, and it wasn't right for me to make fun of her. I apologized sincerely, distressed that my helpless little laugh should misrepresent my feelings. I ran my fingers gently, fumblingly, affectionately through her cropped hair, which in the candle-light of her apartment, was becoming for me a lovely affecting thing. She smiled and I kissed her, and all was well and understood...) The gangs would come in and push her and slap her, and when she wouldn't give signs of pain or cry out they'd go at it a little more intensely. "I wouldn't permit myself to cry. They weren't worth tears, and I told them so." She was French, and now, after all the years of the Gestapo, to be put to death by Frenchmen would be an ironic fate. In the same cell was an old friend of hers who during four years of occupation had been the chief Allied liaison agent for underground intelligence. She, too, had been arrested on "collaborationist" charges. Jeanne was known to have worked in a Wehrmacht headquarters, and so the charge was obvious. The old woman (who remained in prison for six weeks, until confirmation could be had from London from secret sources) had a large house in the town suburb and did regular entertaining for the German staff. That was clear enough indictment for her. She was released after almost two months: that's all Jeanne could tell me of her story. Jeanne herself was transferred to "solitary confinement" after the third day. "If you're innocent," they argued, "then who are the traitors?" They prompted her with names, many of which she knew as German agents, or at least as friends of the Reich. But she said nothing. "Who were these people to set themselves up as the Law? To make mass arrests and conduct their own Nazi torture chambers? We would reckon with the enemies of France when the courts are re-established and real hearings could be held. To these self-appointed tribunes I had nothing to say! Oh, my Lord, what becomes of us when with a word or two over a horrible bargain-counter I can sell other people's lives to save my own..." At the end of the week some measures of internal control were taking place within the resistance forces. The FFI began to discipline its own ranks, and with the appearance of an old captain of the partisan bands of the region she was "identified" and released.

The poor girl was almost broken, and for weeks and months nothing could shake her disconsolate bitterness. Her mother wept when she saw her bald head, and her father was mad and roaring: "What have they done to my little one!" Jeanne recovered, and kept to herself more than ever. On the street she still sees the police people who had mistreated her, the men and women whose angry mean words had her labeled as a traitor, and so many others, "solid citizens of the community," who worked and profited with the German occu-

pation, and whose daughters entertained and slept with the Nazis. "For now there is nothing for me to say or to do. I am afraid there will still be a bloody reckoning when some of the troops return, and when the army of prisoners comes home. Those will be terrible days again! But then I will clear my name. I will tell my own story, and then leave this mean angry (*böse*) village... No. I am French, but these are not my people. They have no heart and no spirit. They don't know how to be happy nor how to be strong... Nor even grateful." She looked up sadly. There have already been threats to recut her hair—for associating with the Americans! An embittered twisted patriotism, but an indication of the explosive uncertainty and turbulence of the tortured national spirit. "And what can I do now, or where can I go? To America? So far and so strange. To Paris? Without friends and in loneliness... And I will soon be all alone. My mother and father won't live long. They've aged so in these last years! They too were practically ostracized. We were Alsatians and therefore strangers. And we were uncompromising and therefore even more alien. The little things we all went without, because what was 'necessity' for the people was (*doch falsch*) for us still wrong. The Germans would dispense beer, all your thirst would demand, in exchange for copper. And so candlesticks, ash-trays, cups, and what not, found their way into the Nazi supply, and Lorraine could drink again with its meals! All but not my mother. My father, you know, has no small thirst. But she'd rather see his tongue hanging out dry than give them one metal splinter. Oh! what was is now gone! And I can't afford to depress myself again. My luck has been all bad, and perhaps my own stupidity is part of the blame. One has one's own notion of how one must live, of what is proper and what personal dignity is. And then come what may, there is your fate. I had to be what I was, and do what I did. And so my marriage was destroyed, and the war, which so many learned to live with, became an eternal hell (*ewige Hölle*) for me. I will probably be alone from now on. And that's the way I want it to be! Because there is nothing else that can save you from the meanness and the angriness... The captain has offered me jobs regularly, but no. He is amazed that I can be 'happy' or 'satisfied' washing clothes—and I am not! But it makes me independent and free. I can walk down the street and I have all the pride I want. Let them say what they will! They are not my people..."

I cried at many points in the night's long story. I think she understood why. I could not control my tears. Her account, told with unbelievable subtle modulations and personal power, was so terrible and beautiful. Here was a fine and extraordinary woman. I looked at the snips of her blonde locks returning, her blue eyes which could change so mercurially from merriness to sadness to anger, her slim small body which was never still for a moment. For all her nervous intensity and energy she had managed some serenity of the spirit. I don't know France and I don't know the War. The "people" are still foreigners to me, and all the death and suffering remain yet intellectual, if moving, abstractions. But there was one soul which had survived the degradation of society and civilization. And the real deep tragedy was that she remained poor and lost with all her love and dignity and understanding for which our world had no use. So much through my blurred eyes I could see, and so much I can at last say I have learned...

27 March 1945, Lunéville

Tuesday evening.

The family was at dinner as I came home this evening. Another thin meal, filled out somewhat with my small contributions of beer, cigarettes, and C-ration candy. We exchanged as usual the news of the day, I with my now familiar story of paper-work at the caserne, and they with the everyday details of the "New France." This morning the city depot burned down, and now the poor old man guards only ashes. He left on schedule for his first night-watch tour at eight o'clock, but still we made our parting jokes. If his bed and clothes and little guard room had been burned, then the infesting rats had perished too, and no longer would his good *amerikanische shawkahlahd* be looted behind his back: "That, surely, was true..." Mme. Wernert rationed him another Hershey bar, and gave him the regular stern warning to husband it at all costs: it was priceless! He smiled, shrugged his shoulders at me (Ah! These Women!) and left.

I made my announcement: tonight was my last night. Tomorrow early the whole Army would move. We were all a little saddened, but packing was a busy time. Nobody allowed me to touch a thing. First, all the pants were pressed and folded away neatly. Then my pyjamas were washed and promised dry and clean for early in the morning. Then all the socks and underwear were collected and deposited systematically in my dufflebag and valpack. The occasion had its obvious sentiment, but it was being made into a kind, warmhearted thing. Finally all was done, and nothing but the bed remained. We sat around the table, relighting the candles as the electric power went off and on. I cursed to myself as the radio went dead in the middle of movements of the *Beethoven Sixth*. What a luxury even the simple recording of a symphony had become! Jeanne at the old, fixed time made signs to go. It was nine o'clock and she was tired. She fumbled with her coat and I reached casually for my jacket. She stood up and sat down again. I picked up my pipe and pocketed my matches. She muttered a few oh wells and I said wait a minute and reached for my flashlight. I would walk her home. We walked through the dark street, crossed her corner (where rue Castara becomes her rue de la République) and came to the house. She opened it quickly and we went through the hall. I had said goodbye to her here last week in a silly and somewhat embarassing awkwardness, kissing her but uncertain as to whether to make love to her, hesitating and stuttering, and finally shaking her hand goodnight. Upstairs now perhaps she would make coffee again and we would talk. But nothing went per schedule. She put the stove on and I put it off. She turned for the cups and I turned her about again, kissed her and sat her down. She kissed me and we lay on the couch. Not a dozen words had been exchanged. I said now, with a note of helplessness and shyness, that the buttons on her blouse were *très compliqué* and she with a look of sweet pouting disbelief opened them. I said now, with a new note of hopelessness and desperation that the couch was small, inconvenient, impossible! We put out the lights and went into the bedroom. We undressed, kissed each other at the awkwardest moments, left a small light burning in the kitchen. The bed was large and soft and the sheets were crisp in their clean-whiteness. Jeanne held me and kissed me and touched me and began whispering.

I knew what had happened. We had grown very fond of each other, but out of a peculiar respectful uncertainty each of us hesitated. I didn't want to make love to her as a casual matter-of-course thing: the convenient affair of the American soldier in a little French village. She would never allow herself a pointless unlovely interlude which involved nothing but necessity. We were both wrong, and it was almost too late. This would be our first and last night. She held my face in her hands and cried a little. She was stupid and had always been stupid. Her whole life had been cut out of stupidity. She had always missed her opportunities, tried to salvage a little happiness when it was too late.

She was sorry, she was miserable, she would never forgive herself. I caressed her and upset her hair and kissed her to stop her self-recrimination. She held me fiercely and we made love and went to sleep holding each other softly and awoke and smiled and upset each other again. I kissed her a hundred times before I left early that morning. She was still lying in the bed sprawled under the cover when I waved goodbye. Yes I would not forget to write, and yes perhaps we could, really we could, see each other some time, in Nancy or in Paris or after the war. No, I would not forget her, no I didn't think badly of her, you stupid little wonderful little thing. I went back again and kissed her nose and her eyes and her lips and her hair. She brushed her hand across her forehead as if to sweep away locks which might have been falling across her face but were only suggesting little curls in a golden crop. I waved goodbye again from the door, my arm felt heavy and clumsy, and I left. I had already missed breakfast and was late for the convoy. I repeated to myself her name, Jeanne, Jeanne, Jeanne, and thought how beautiful it might have been, how beautiful it had been.... I was happy, but somewhere a little sick with sadness and the beginnings of longing.

29 March 1945, Kaiserslautern

The whole Army is now in Germany. "Forward" moved to Sarreguemines earlier in the week, and moved again to catch up with the divisions racing across the Rhine. "Rear" is now in Kaiserslautern, set up in an elaborate German caserne, and with equipment close to the exits for another displacement any moment.

GERMANY STRAIGHT AHEAD the improvised GI signs along the road read as we sped towards Sarreguemines and the Saar Basin. The offensive had rolled through this area a scant two weeks ago and all the devastation was new. Still the people were coming back and trying to set up their communities in the rubble. Farmers were hoeing their fields around the waste heaps of old ammunition dumps and over the heavy dug-in tracks of the tanks which had roared through tearing up the earth. Little remnants told poignant tales. Gasthaus zur Post by a shattered front of a café. FEIND HÖRT MIT on broken walls of buildings which once warned against street-corner gossip. And then in the heart of newly liberated towns the French signs—now no longer the simple bands of *On les aura!* which one saw before in Lorraine and Alsace, but large, rich, professional posters, with bright colors and much art-work orchestrating the old cry. The trucks were setting a fierce pace. Children were still around waving at the convoy going by, but this time there was no response. Were we still in France? Wasn't this German territory? No one would risk a gesture of fraternization, and the new coldness was a little bewildering. Sandbags were stacked against windows and doorways and a few elements of a town managed to survive. In the suburbs, lines of clean wash were strung from battered beams of farmhouses close to pillboxes and trenches. Town after town, nothing but destruction! And my worst fear was that it would become "monotonous"— what if one becomes callous or adjusted to this terrible wasteland? I fancied that every house had suffered a little differently, had its own pattern or design in ruin and rubble. Each hearth perhaps had its own private death. At least so the sense of tragedy could be held through the endless view of walls, windows, shuttered foundations, stone and wood and fields, strewn over a devastated country. Every barn was a wreck, every store was smashed, only occasionally was a church found standing. After each village you think perhaps now the resistance had been broken and something had been saved. But no! The next town is worse. In Wittersheim the sun broke through the gray drab skies, spotlighting the relentlessness of the war's fury: here was something more!

To HOMBURG the road-signs read. We moved out of the hills and in the distance in a valley a whole village seemed to be standing. Touched by the rays of the sun (and then there is always the inordinate sentimentalism about a valley) Blieskastel appeared lovely. As we went through it we saw, however, that nothing had escaped. The fighting had simply been confused house-to-house ambushes, with little artillery or mortars possible. So the red roofs were vouchsafed for the long view, but not a window or a wall was really intact. The war would not even allow the ancient tricks of nature to maintain a deception about the realness of all this horror. Two of its streets were missing—Platz der Deutschen Front and Bismarckstrasse, both kaput. German air-raid warnings everywhere. Also many *Strengstens Verboten-s* It goes on and on. A river, and the bridge is blown. A town, and continuous blasted squares. The countryside again, and chopped fields, squashed barns and farmhouses, stiff dead horses... A little village and miracle of miracles it is whole and untouched. We ride through its only street—Schillerstrasse! Perhaps the subtle mysterious rewards of culture... The Siegfried line was behind us, but where the border was I never managed to learn. Vans of prisoners in their deep green Wehrmacht uniforms rolled by, and perhaps they would spot it: for them, I suspect, it would have more significance. People are thronging cross-sections in the city for glimpses of the American convoys coming in, the Nazi convoys going out. In a village a woman waves goodbye to a crowded truck of Germans speeding back to France. Frantic signs and messages on stone fences—*Volk steht auf!* And—in clean whitewashed scrawl—"Onward Slaves of Moscow!" On route to Kaiserslautern we strike the first German town. Flags are hanging on every avenue—sheets and pillowcases from flagpoles and windowsills, fluttering in a ghastly unbelievable whiteness! The railroad yards: smashed, and beyond it a two-mile collection of freight cars, and locomotives. This was apparently the graveyard. At the end, a huge pile of coal. And over the road for five minutes nothing but men, women and children hurrying their little carts along to pick up fuel. Front-yard scene: a German soldier sitting quietly on a chair in front of a house, his head and arms swathed in white bandages, watching the traffic... (Curious.) More white sheets, hanging from "forts," obelisk-pillbox-like affairs. Kaiserslautern: mangled industrial works; modern apartment houses on Ludendorffstrasse razed. Finally the caserne, or now: *Kaserne*. We move into what was once a three-room apartment. Haul the baby-carriage out of the bedrooms and drop it out of the window. Sweep out all the dirt, including sheafs of picture postcards from Italy and Yugoslavia. I set my things up in a little office in the headquarters, and rummage a bit in the scrapheap, coming up with three volumes of a set of the Collected Works of Goethe (Five, Seven and Ten, or *Dichtung und Wahrheit, Sorrows of Young Werther*, and some verse and plays). We go back to the "apartment" to sleep. Across the street are Ger-

man families, a group of mothers talking out of the windows, the children running around the front steps. We glance quickly at them, make sure that all our smiles and laughs have pointed internal references. Only the other day a piece of Hershey's chocolate was found in some little boy's hand and court-martials were threatened. We are a little more careful about blackout. I creep back into my bedroll on my cot, apprehensive about the cold night and the old discomfort after so many wonderful weeks of a soft warm French bed. But this is Germany... "the sacred soil" as the day's jest went, or as Mooney said in his preliminary summing up, "what a fuckin' eight-ball country!"
[...]

29 March 1945

Thursday evening.

We are, nominally speaking, settled in Germany, but curiosity held the upper hand all day and practically no work was done. The rummage expedition in the scrap of the Kaiserslautern *Kaserne* yielded two more volumes of Goethe (poems and plays), some handsome portraits which I have mounted on my office walls to everybody's horror (Bismarck and Frederick the Great), and some other little odds and ends. Jordan[34] arrived last night in a new German-model coupe, which he "captured" in a Nazi motor pool further forward in the Rhine sector. (He strode into the garage, spotted the flashy little "auto-union," fingered his revolver, and demanded: "Gib mir zer key!" Somebody ran out and came back; the car was started, and Jordan had a vehicle.) Mooney went out with him this morning, and after another profitable expedition the section now has a convertible Sedan. (Mooney is very happy and is almost sold on the great German race. "Gee!" he explained, "the roof slides back smoothly, and on nice sunny days I'm really going to have myself a pleasure cruise... Almost like home!" Of course at home "with the top of the car," he carefully pointed out, "all you have to do is press a button and race the motor and off she goes." A minor inconvenience.) The vehicle was cannibalized from the wreckage of the fields. Wheels from one smashed chassis, battery from another. The body of this one had a Red Star and "USSR" painted on; obviously it was used by liberated Russian prisoners who were running around last week (and who were involved in a pitched battle with German prisoners which raged all night, until a couple companies of American tank-destroyers quieted things down).

I took a brief run into the city itself, and paused for a few minutes on Hindenburgstrasse to read the bulletins. Law Number One abrogated Nazi law. Law Number Two disbanded the Nazi courts. The announcement by General Eisenhower explained that we "come as conquerors but not as oppressors"

(*Wir kommen als Eroberer, jedoch nicht als Unterdrücker*). Law Number Five dissolved the Nazi party and some fifty-two varieties of Hitler front organizations—"in order to end the regime of lawlessness, terror, and inhumanity." Other bulletins concerned details of milk for babies; the value of currency (Law Number Fifty-One); threats of penalties for espionage, sniping, plunder, looting, killing, and any other kind of sabotage of allied occupation; blackout regulations; and the city curfew (7 to 9 am, 3 to 6 pm, and citizens will be shot on sight who venture outside their dwellings and make any attempt to hide or escape). I scribbled a few notes on the back of my roadmap of France, and slowly behind me the crowd began to gather like spectators at a steam shovel excavation. I felt just a little bit uneasy and all kinds of cheap melodrama unfolded itself luridly in my imagination. Half-playfully I checked behind me (a huge Hitlerjugend headquarters, with GIs lounging over the windowsills) and up and down the avenue. I decided it would be a little less "nervewracking" to get all the civil affairs data from G-5 itself, and made it back to the *Kaserne*.

The real discoveries of the day, however, were at home. Last night the crib really interested me. A baby must have been here, but the name on the mailbox and over the doorbell read plainly, "Fräulein Emma Susanne Sauer." We tossed the crib out; it was in the way, and it was an ugly thing to boot, built intricately with fine mesh wire as if the prison-house slavery of the German began in his very infancy. The story began to unfold slowly today, and I couldn't leave the loose ends lie. Simply to move into the apartment without a thought for its previous career struck me as a kind of special barbarism, or at least a stranger-coldness which easily made for dullness and boredom. My romantical claim was that "unseen presences" were living here with us, and it was imperative, no less, that we identify them and so conquer and make real our occupation. The boys went to work. Every drawer and closet and corner was systematically searched. And one by one the documents revealed the fräulein's story. Exhibit A was an amazing form-letter which made an urgent inquiry as to the fatherhood of Harald Sauer, born 5 September 1944. Child Harald was an *uneheliches Kind* (N.B. The Nazis left the stigmatic word in usage! Rather poor semantical strategy to say the least—and a cultural lag in National Socialist vocabulary which will have to stand.) and the *Reichsgesetz für Jugendwohlfahrt* wanted to know immediately its *Erzeuger* and some other details of living conditions. The communication was a mimeographed letter and apparently did regular service gathering vital statistics on the bastards of the New Order. Exhibit B was a certificate testifying that the fatherhood of Rosemarie Sauer, born 13 July 1938, had been acknowledged by "*Mechaniker* Otto Theobald." That brought the score up to two. What Emma busied herself with in the long cold years between '38 and '44 was not quite clear. This evening several more exhibits were added to the dossier. A Kaiserslautern

Gutschein recorded the birth of Friedrich Sauer on 23 June 1943, and that accounted for one more year. That Otto was still around, and perhaps further involved in the schedule of illegitimacy, was established by an envelope to "Emmchen" mailed from an army post by *Unteroffizier* Theobald. Clearly his fine steady work for the Reich was not going unrewarded. Finally we learned a little more about our hostess herself from an old diploma which for some curious reason was hiding in the frigidaire. Emma Sauer, born 21 April 1921, in Kaiserslautern, completed eight years at the *Volkshauptschule*, with *lobenswertem Fleiss* and *hervorragendem Betragen*. (Exemplary deportment indeed!) Her work in *Religion, Zeichnen,* and *Hausarbeit* was satisfactory (*entsprechend*). In *Deutsche Sprache, Geschichte, Naturkunde, Hauswirtschaft, Rechnen,* she was *lobenswert*, praiseworthy. But significantly her *Singen* was *ungenügend*—"since Beethoven," one of the boys offered, "there's been no real music in the Teutonic soul!"—and in *Turnen* she was (this explained everything!) *mangelhaft*. Failing in spirit of song and sport she could go on only to a career of endless prostitution which fascist society served to make legal and profitable for her. More than a little intrigued by the lustiness of our "unseen presence" we could now live and occupy our apartment. We understood the baby crib! We knew little about the walls of 110 Henlingerstrasse, and the life it had held here. Now we stared at the rooms in wondrous enlightenment. Yesterday we had hit our cots as tired soldiers. Tonight, as we clipped our documents together, we could retire as invaders with historic personalities. So in wild exercises of fantasy do we create a tradition for ourselves, and manufacture "usable pasts" out of dramatized, sentimentalized souvenirs.

30 March 1945

No one knows exactly where the forward troops are, and the mystery is exciting. Patton is said to be reaching Czechoslovakia, and soon all the news sources will be leaking rumors of capitulation, surrender, armistice. Down the main highway, Ludwigshafen west of the Rhine is clear, but the battle for Mannheim is still raging. However, both Patch and the Third Army are deep in the east-Rhine sector to the north and south.

"Behind the lines" data on the recent period is more plentiful and reliable. The Hitlerjugend schools, operatives are reporting, are going through a new phase, and the current orientation is instructing recruits to leave Germany immediately upon defeat. They are told that large financial reserves are ready for them in foreign countries! The military crisis is also intensifying political espionage, and the activities of the so-called *V-Männer*, or informers, now involves high-ranking officers in every branch: commandos, labor battalions, armaments-industry inspectors. The Commandant of the Mannheim Motor Pool, the information runs, was found to be "politically unsatisfactory" and the recommendation was for his expulsion from the Wehrmacht. The respect for German Intelligence operations is not, significantly enough, dwindling with the military collapse of the forward defense lines. A recently captured Order of Battle Chart actually broke down all the American groups into armies, corps, divisions and cavalry units. G-3 testified that the maps were "almost entirely accurate" as to names of units, and approximately ninety-percent accurate as to command posts of units. Details went so far as to give rear-area and operational reserves! Similarly, the abilities of the prisoner-of-war interrogators seem to be able to break down the carefully cultivated American security habits. In the estimate of recently captured German interrogators about fifty percent of Americans taken prisoner give only name, rank, and serial number. How many times that theme has been drummed in training sessions! But the other fifty percent "talk." Sometimes it is stupidity or foolishness. More often what is involved is battle-shock plus very shrewd psychologizing by the Nazis. A cigarette, some hot coffee, a few simple soft-spoken questions in casual correct English, and a whole picture of a sector of the front can be put together. Evidence of less subtle but so far rather effective German operations was found in Cologne. Department and clothing stores had been ransacked of men's suit stock. Empty clothes hangers were everywhere, and German uniforms were found hastily flung all around the rooms. The return at last of the "German civilian..." What suprises me is that the enemy prisoner-of-war interrogators whose greatest achievement is the breakdown of well-trained security-minded troops apparently succumb themselves to the blandishments of American G-2. Now they themselves talk and tell all! Adepts at the "soft" method the Germans seemed to have built up little or no special resistance on their own part. They went on to report that only a few (about ten percent) of the Americans refused to talk altogether. "Generally those who forgot their security regulations were prompted either by a desire to brag about the power and prowess of their units and weapons, or were lured into traps by adroit questioning."

[...]

Education of a Hitler Youth—Second Lieutenant Klaus Dietrich Polz, captured 11 March: August 1934—entered the Junior Hitler Youth, *Jungvolk*, nine years of age. Schooling and various organizational positions until October '43 when drafted. A Hitler Youth *Gefolgschafsführer*, and a *Disziplinarstellenleiter* (crime investigator), etc. Sent to OCS at Haguenau (Alsace), because of Hitler Youth background. "Germany is going to win this war, if not immediately and glamorously, at least in the long run, you may rest assured. The Allies may succeed in occupying all of Germany north of Württemberg, Bavaria and Moravia. The Russians and the Anglo-Americans may join at the

Elbe River. We shall then entrench ourselves in the uncontrollable mountains and forest of Southern Germany and Austria, and hold whatever can be held of Italy. As a matter of fact, the war in Italy can go on for several years. But whatever stretches of land you may occupy in Germany you will never conquer or defeat the German nation. As long as there is a German alive he will fight you. In the occupied parts of Germany we shall fight a partisan war of nerves against you. No Allied soldier will ever feel safe on German soil. There will be no traitors, no collaborationists. Although outwardly we may smile and bend under the Allied yoke, we shall resort relentlessly to ambushes and tricks of guerilla warfare until in the end every inch of sacred German soil is freed from the hated invader. A master race born to govern cannot be held down eternally. Do not underestimate us Germans. We have learned to hate a world of nations that is denying us living space. Great deeds inspired by this immortal and sacred hatred have been performed in the past. New war ruses will be born and new methods of fighting. Soldierdom and domination are the two avocations of Germany, and we Germans shall not rest until we fulfill Germany's mission. In his last speech the Führer said: 'God Almighty may pardon me the last moments of this war.' We may even follow the example of our national hero Arminius (Hermann), the Germanic prince, who posing as a friend of the Romans, went through the Roman educational institutions and war academy to acquire the military knowledge and leadership which, in the end, enabled him to ambush the Roman Legions of Varus in the Teutoburg Forest in 9 AD to free his enslaved tribe from the Roman yoke. One man and the spirit he created will always be the guide of our youth: our Führer. Stronger than any clearly defined philosophy, our national socialism has the power of myth. It does not appeal to cold reasoning. It appeals to the warm depth of our feelings and emotions, it overwhelms us by its twilight effects. We do not think. We feel, we believe, we act. We have faith."

Product of the Langemarck *Lehrgang*,[35] preparatory school for Nazi fanatics. Eighteen months program for *Gymnasium* diploma (nine years high school). Condensed secondary education dominated mostly by Indoctrination and Physical Conditioning.

30 and 31 March 1945

We see no newspapers, hear no radio reports, know nothing. We meet no people and observe little else than the green black masses of the Sickingen hills in the distance. Mooney burst in this morning—"My god! It's like prison! F' Chris' sake, let's bust out of here!" He settled down in a moment to a wild frenzy and would bargain for "anything, any rumors, new or old, anything about Patton, true or unfounded..." Here we were sitting in army headquarters, and we were probably the most ill-informed body of people in the world. I did hear that Mannheim surrendered yesterday afternoon, and that we were entering Heidelberg; and that along the Main River, the Seventh had a twelve-mile front. But nothing more. It is only the first few days, and our isolation remains more a source of amusement than a real psychological or social difficulty. "Same faces all the time, all the time!" Mooney protests, "Same food! No women! No movies!" In really trying moments we have an uneasy time watching him writhe and squirm and almost take off for some passing girl. "Some one, god knows, has got to break the ice!" Or so his argument runs. "The war isn't over yet. The occupation is still ahead. Oh, Lord! How are we ever going to get home? You know they're never going to build a bridge!" When all the strange qualities of our loneliness are exhausted then there will be opportunity enough for seriousness. "I'm going to go nuts! They're fencing me in! And we're the 'Conquerors'! It's like the foreigners in China—Germany is swallowing us up... and your goddamn Bismarck and Freddy the Great One look down and watch it."

Which was not strictly true. This afternoon we went out into the fields here and cannibalized a few old German vehicles. Some children were playing around the smashed chassis, and as we approached the eldest, a boy of about six or seven, came to attention. He stiffened and clicked his heels three times as each of us approached to tinker for spare parts. Yesterday another boy, somewhat older, asked for permission to remove something from the junkpile. A can of C-rations had been dropped out of a truck and mashed around by the traffic on the road. The hungry boy had found it, but dared not touch it or claim it for himself until he got some official approval. Under Hitler apparently there wasn't even the freedom to scavenge.

In Kaiserslautern itself the picture is dismal. The wreckage has been considerable, and how the remnants of the civilian population manage with combat curfew restrictions is something I don't know. G-5 here is not "civil affairs" for a liberated country, but "military government" for a conquered one. There are lines in front of shops, and so I suspect that a real food crisis has not yet set in. We ride through, and stroll about, and only occasionally does anyone ever glance at us. One old man, with gray hair and black mustache and the characteristic battered cap, smiled at me on one street corner as I laughed at some inane remark somebody had just made. I had to stare past him.

In an old building, "Barbarossa-Schule" we located a Russian camp, housing liberated war-prisoners and civilian labor conscripts. They did odd jobs for the military in the area, and were in turn fed by army rations until transportation could be arranged for them. The courtyard, the halls, and the chambers themselves, were all bizarre. Men were sleeping on bundles of cloth, boys and girls were playing and riding bicycles and a few were making love. They were dressed in everything from old peasants' garb to Nazi uniforms. Many were sleeping or cooking something, a great many were drinking, and the schnapps had made more than a few merry; groups were staggering around arm in arm, others were singing Russian tunes. I had time to speak to only three or four. One, a boy who had just reached his eighteenth birthday, had worked in Germany for some three years; his most recent assignments were in the great defenses of the Maginot and Siegfried lines, building and reinforcing bunkers. Others were prisoners or conscripts from Kiev, the Urals, Moscow (an obvious "slicker" from the big city who now with the license of drunkenness made comic efforts to impress us and all the rest with his cosmopolitanism).

[...]

Most of the "refugees" or "displaced persons" spoke a fair German, and all of them shook their heads glumly when the matter of the German people came up. "All of them" were "bad." The Germans had beaten them and had treated them like dogs. Did you never see a good German? Well, possibly ten percent, it was conceded, but the rest of them were worthless and mean. (As a matter of fact I think statistical estimates of Hitlerist fanaticism will be steadily revised as more and more contact with Germans is made. And not that the seizure of German territories is turning up anti-Nazis of noble standing. In Cologne, for example, the good party members were being turned in by citizens in every neighborhood. Up the highway toward Ludwigshafen only last week a family called over some American officers and betrayed the hiding-places of a pair of Gestapo agents. This can, of course, be dismissed as "opportunism." But then an opportunist is not a fanatic; his belief and loyalty have a different intensity; and the fact that even a few are now changing sides actively is a revealing light on the myths of blanket Hitler worship and unmitigated allegiance.)

For their own part, some of the Russians are "turning in" SS terrorists who have been left behind in occupied territories. This morning one of the ex-prisoners trapped a trooper in a cellar, and practically strangled him before depositing him with the police. He showed me his mayor's pass which allowed him to wander the streets at his own whims and suspicions. The army apparently is using him (among others) as a kind of bloodhound or counterintelligence.

Now the singing began to grow, as tune after tune was taken up. We declined the Moscow boy's ersatz vodka, but no one else did. An accordion which someone brought up gave a traditional flavor to the folk. They sat around in a musty dirty chamber, adorned only by old religious portraits on the wall, eating and drinking and sleeping and singing (and a few went a little berserk, for one of the guards told me he had hit somebody that morning with the brass knuckles). I told them I really didn't know when they would be able to get home to Russia, "but perhaps soon..." That bit of a promise from an American officer seemed to be all they needed, and the chorus and the merriness swelled. I mumbled my goodbyes and fumbled for the door. Somebody brushed against me, pushed me aside, and reached for the knob; then he stood there at attention and held the door wide for me to pass. Courtesy even if it kills you. I left, and could hear noise and song and odd Russian shouts and cries as I walked through the courtyard.

31 March 1945

Mannheim surrendered. Entered Heidelberg. Army to the Main River. Goebbels in *Das Reich*—"History As our Teacher" [...]

1 April 1945

[...]
    Officers captured; unimpressed by hopelessness of military situation; fighting to the last; Older officer tells of two camps, young and old: "Military leadership in the German army is clearly divided into two camps of men in the older and younger generation. The majority of the younger officers in the German Army are brought up totally under influence of Nazi ideology and know of no other form of reasoning. One cannot condemn all these young men as criminals. They firmly believe to be in the right in carrying out the Führer's orders and are willing to fight unselfishly to the end."
    I have been pretty well these months, and unless my capacity for self-delusion has expanded, I think I have been learning a little and growing stronger in special ways (where to be "weak" was for me terrible). What I have managed to see, to be physically present at, these last weeks, outruns most of my old foolish romantical expectations. I haven't been in a fire-fight battle ("just yet"), but all the discomfort, dirt, dysentery; and boredom, weariness, futility, exasperation; and also inanities, stupidities, and horror (moral)—have all been worth it, for it is all the soundest kind of investment in an immunity and insurance against the most Monstrous Kind of Bullshit about the War, soon playing.

2 April 1945

The upsetting news at supper was that General Patch was very angry. Apparently he had been out on reconnaissance and was watching a huge convoy making its way over the Rhine bridgehead when something broke down and brought all traffic to a standstill. The General fussed and fumed and discovered it was a little captured German vehicle. "Get that goddammed thing over the bridge!" he shouted, "and I don't want to see another one of them in my Army!"

We were distressed, because after three days of tinkering and scavenging for parts and cannibalization of every vehicle in our sector we had two DKWs running in fairly good order. Closer to the front, of course, the German autos had been picked up in far better running condition, and whole battalions and regiments were moving forward in deluxe transportation. Which was not exactly the best combat formation, nor did it leave the gasoline supply at any level G-4 would be particularly happy about. So it looked like the end of a good thing, and we decided to make our last run in the little duck. (It did almost prove to be that in more respects than simply our sentimental farewell to an ex-Nazi sedan.)

We raced off for Kaiserslautern and roamed up and down the deserted streets. Military police stared at us—we had not yet painted any insignia on the chassis or roof—but on we went. Here were factories completely demolished, and magnificent castles on the hills just beyond the plant torn apart by concussions and direct hits. Here was a huge skyway bridge of the great local autobahn network twisted as if some destructive giant had become dissatisfied with a plaything. Here was a charred, rusting Panther, a Mark VI with its 88 pointing straight down the highway from France—and this proved to be our undoing. We stopped, and clambered around the turrets and the treads. After a few minutes of useless snooping, we returned to the duck. But it was cold. It refused to start. We shook it and pushed it and threatened it. It would roll down the hill along the sidestreet, but the engine was kaput. Gottlieb's theory was that "it was just a simple matter of fraternization—even the goddamn Nazi vehicles stick together—a kaputt tank, and now a kaputt *Auto...*" We were a little dubious about that but at least it was more substantial than Mooney's plaintive, "I think there's something wrong with it, fellas, I think there's something wrong." We pushed it up and down hills in frenetic bursts of energy until we were almost out of town. Night was falling, and on the outskirts of town a few of the Germans were wandering around from house to house. None of us had either a rifle or a pistol, and we knew the city was full of SS terrorists and snipers. A man would watch us, and one of us would watch him as we tried to leave that block rapidly behind us. In the distance we could hear occasional firing. Once in a while our little motor would sputter and then backfire and all of us would jump a few feet. We pushed it on. To the right suddenly a great explosion went off. Time-bombs. We smiled at each other, and laughed at our nervousness. At a crossroads near the underpass exit we paused for a few moments. Suddenly shutters on several sides were opened and heads popped out of windows. We all whirled and grimaced at the houses. The heads popped back in and the shutters were closed. The wheels reeled a little faster now through the underpass. Finally a truck came along and offered to push us. It made no difference where he was going; so long as he was leaving the city. So off we went on a small winding road, and after about twenty or thirty minutes he halted at a road junction. He was taking a left for Mainz, and we could take a right for Worms. Oh, my god! How did we get out here? Several MPs came out of the darkness with flashlights and we felt much better; they had M-1s and full rifle belts. "Some of the firing, I guess," their explanation ran, "is infantry night problems up yonder on the hill [*sic*] . . ." We could see the tracers flaring off in the blackness and were not completely reassured. One of us blocked the road trying to flag a push, a tow or a hitch: the other two alternated at sleeping on the seats in the duck which had also decided to break down this evening. The grinding gears of a truck pulling to a halt alongside awoke us. Was he going to Army headquarters? Well, he didn't know exactly, but he did want to get to some office the name of which we couldn't quite make out. But oh we knew precisely where that was, we would show just how to get there, he wouldn't have to worry about routes or directions at all, in fact we were going to the very same place! So he hauled us back down the hills, through the same smashed railroad yards and cleared road obstacles and finally through Kaiserslautern and to the main highway. We pulled into headquarters, dumped our little vehicle in the backyard, and thanked our truck driver profusely. "Now where did you want to go?" (Some special message center.) "Well," said Mooney, "we don't know exactly where that is, but if you'll drive back in that general direction you'll find an MP. Stop there and ask him. He'll help you. He's supposed to know those things." The driver took off, more than a little nonplussed. We turned off the switch of the duck, locked the doors, and threw the key off into the darkness in the general direction of the Franz von Sickingen hills. Our last, sentimental tour was over.

3 April 1945

How helpless I remain in the face of personal tragedy! Saw, quite by accident, the small obituary notice in the *Paris Tribune* of Sam Sloan's death. I was shocked and hurt and couldn't help crying. When and how will I ever become reconciled to this great unhappy loss? I of course did not know him long or really well, but I remember with warmth and fondness all our meetings, and it is a rare acquaintanceship that has so affectionate a quality. He was truly a sweet and warmhearted person, and like Cap meant a great deal to me in a very special way.[36] He expected things of me, had hopes for my work. He was an abiding source of encouragement and criticism, and his friendship (his very voice and greeting) took some edge from the uncertain frightening aloneness in which one dreams of ambition. He is dead now at forty-five. And for a long time, I suspect, I will wonder in sadness (and in awe of the casual finalities of fate) how I might have fared and what I might have done, if . . .

Everything has depressed me today. I walked along the streets at noon and forced some more cold stares at children playing and men and women passing by. I read a little of the early days of the Führer and was dispirited—how could these common (if brilliant) gangsters have taken power, and held power, and constructed so gigantic and effective a machine? And now as I thought of this ravaged devastated country it was almost inconceivable that Hitlerism has failed, that its cause is now frantic and hopeless, with the whole once-powerful Nazi clique facing oblivion.

Oh, if only a new Germany could be born! A country again of culture and civilized fraternities. . . But what a simple naive hope. Overheard this evening: "Yeah, it was something to see! And you should have seen it, quite a beautiful sight, all those goddamned Heinies, bodies strewn everywhere. . . Then we have to come back here, and see too many of them still walking around." One loses in time one's capacity for moral alarm. The barbarism is deep and everywhere, and no one any longer is able to recognize it. What a terrible wasteland this new war, more than anything else before, has uncovered. And how literal have Eliot's lines become:

> What are the roots that clutch, what branches grow
> Out of this stony rubbish? Son of man,
> You cannot say, or guess, for you know only
> A heap of broken images, where the sun beats,
> And the dead tree gives no shelter, the cricket no relief,
> And the dry stone no sound of water.
> [T. S. Eliot, *The Waste Land Section I: The Burial of the Dead*]

Will there ever be a time again for great heart-born hope? Not the stiff formal constructions that calculating intellects can make from political or ideological optimism. Nor the mindless expansiveness that so many varieties of social energy can manage. But a great hope made out of a great free passion, out of tradition and sensitive intelligence, out of a large earnest tender spirituality.

And it is not History that we must doubt, but our own selves. For it is not a nostalgia for the simplicities of the past that affects us. Sophistication is our curse and our cross, and we are compelled to live with it and bear it until we discover and conquer its own special and transcendental strength. [. . .]

The spiritual devastation of our own *Wasteland* time may only be a "transvaluation of values." Simplicity has become the death of goodness. Naivete is hopeless. Our sophistication is now our wound and our weapon: our suffering can be the means of our salvation. For it is a new deeper sophistication that we need. Not despair or nostalgia—but a joyously disciplined heart, a cultivated liberated mind.

5 April 1945

The trucks had been sitting in the field since early morning, but it was some hours after noon when a grand deep roar came up from beyond the outer edge of the caserne buildings and a crowd of men and women (in the standard army classification phrase, "a motley crew") rushed over and scrambled in. Home-made tricolors were flying and the standards were soon fastened on to the tailgate, the cab, their caps, or simply waved furiously in the air for all to see. Some of the girls were very young; most of the men were youthful, all apparently ex-soldiers. Their clothes were what used to be known as old and shabby but what we now see only as the usual European garb, the uniform of the poor. These were the Displaced Persons, and they were going home. War prisoners had been here for four and five years, conscripted working women for two and three. One of the men was wearing a large white lacy spring bonnet, and another was making his way comically through the van of the truck sampling the lens of all the spectacles in a rather frenetic attempt to have his sight restored with his freedom. I went out into the field and watched the final loading, took a few snapshots. They posed for me, and waved to me, and finally sent up a huge cheer as the trucks began to pull out . . . for France. We stood around and returned the greetings, feeling more than a little awkward and conspicuous as deliberate spectators, but warmed and happy and not a bit ashamed. One Frenchman remained behind, and almost one by one (then later in a chorus) his comrades called out his name in farewell. American soldiers were milling about and he seemed somewhat embarrassed for the tears in his eyes and, in his turn, for the conspicuousness of his position. We stared wonderingly at the column as it made the turn for the Kaiserslautern Road. There were curious sad half-hearted smiles on our faces as if nobody was certain about an appropriate emotion or mood for the scene. "There they go . . . poor bastards," someone said. "Yeah, going home. . ." the inevitable nostalgia came, and with an afterthought: "I guess that's what we're fighting for. . ." One GI was still waving to a group of girls in the last truck. "Never can tell," he explained, "when you're likely to run into 'em in a whore-house in Marseilles or someplace." I closed my camera and walked back across the now empty field.

It occurs to me now that the real great difference between Davis (of Alabama) and Hamilton (of Mississippi), whom I once took to be so alike in their striking regional manner for fine pleasantries, is the difference between the New and the Old South. Both are of course personable, able, and academicians. But Davis is almost a Henry Grady disciple on the campus, or in the military bureau. He is shrewd, adaptable, enterprising, devious, cosmopolitan. Hamilton remains moody, refractory, provincial, unhappy, and maladjusted in many special disturbing ways. With Davis there is only the touch of his speaking voice and accent, and occasional uniquely local references. Hamilton has refused to be uprooted, and even in the long years of his overseas service (Africa, Sicily, Italy, France, Germany) continues to be "nourished" (as he would put it) by "the Mississippi soil," and lives more and more in the shadow of a tradition long since robbed of its finest spirit by poisonous inner growths. The lines of old fanatical exclusivism remain. There are the white people and the niggers, Americans and European foreigners, Jewish universities in New York, crude city-bred Yankees... Nothing, to be sure, is ever offered meanly as such; every sentiment, prejudice, theory is couched in charm, and presented with the nice trappings of cultivated dinner or cocktail conversation. So he manages to be honest and direct without ever being insulting, and for all the endless viciousness the worst that at any moment can be charged against him is monotony. Perhaps I only allow myself boredom; to be properly outraged (there are times when anger and indignation is almost explosive and uncontrollable) would be "inexpedient." At any rate our table-talk farce goes on. We listen politely, and I remain stirred by the spectacle of decadence. The resentment diminishes, but the horror mounts, at the perfumed decay of a mind, the dark hardness of a heart.

L'Affaire Marshall: The visit of the chief of staff.

General Haislip[37] provided lunch (Won't you have some of these cookies, George? I baked them myself...), after which a trip forward in jeeps because of road conditions and proximity to the front. The road passed 105 mm and 155 mm Howitzer battery positions and General Marshall stopped for brief conversation with enlisted men. When a section commander was asked how much ammunition he had on hand, instead of consulting records he answered at once from memory, "Six round of this, eight of that, five of the other" and so on going through the various types of shell and fuses. Types were many but the quantity was very small, so General Haislip asked for the total number of rounds fired in action by his gun to date ("Now tell me, young man, do you happen to know...?") ("Like you told me yesterday, sir—") "Two thousand one hundred and eighty-five rounds, Sir," came the answer without an hesitant's hesitation... ("Now, General Marshall's going to be here tomorrow, and you bastards better not fuck up! Equipment clean, know those goddamned general orders, and be on the ball!")

Meanwhile during General Marshall's absence from Lunéville that town was the target of heavy shelling by various caliber up to 150 mm, and members of the party who had remained there had to put into practice their best technique of taking cover. When General Haislip learned of this, there could be detected in his bearing a certain anxiety and concern. As host he was reluctant to show his distinguished guest the door, and yet he was very insistent that the cars and all else be in readiness so that as soon as General Marshall was ready to leave, no instant of delay could be chargeable to XV corps arrangements. Fortunately, the entire party moved out toward Nancy shortly before the next bombardment hit Lunéville.

Sixth Army Group had provided a helmet for the use of the Chief of Staff. It had four stars neatly painted across the front but Colonel McCarthy,[38] habitual travelling companion of General Marshall, shook his head dubiously saying, "I've never seen him wear one of these things yet." The General was in fact reluctant, but when General Truscott[39] said he would feel much better if he would wear it in the forward zone, he gave it a trial and presently remarked that it was the first helmet he had ever put on his head that was anywhere near a fit. When General Devers and his party left Nancy, General Marshall made a point of keeping the helmet. It is not known whether this unprecedented action was because of the four stars, the perfect fit, or the well-known and invariable practice of General George S. Patton, Jr. to collect a fine of fifty dollars from any officer who ventured inside the Third Army area without a helmet.

[...]

7 April 1945

I finally took the jeep out last night for the Landstuhl expedition. It was just dusk when we reached the town and searched for a glimpse of the von Sickingen castle and the memorial erected at his grave. I stopped a heavy-set portly middle-aged German walking down the street. He smiled and said "of course" he knew where they were. "The castle itself," he continued volubly, "was on the nearby hill," and we coasted to the corner to catch the view to the summit. Its red stone walls were still standing, although he explained, "the castle is really in ruins." Destroyed in the wars of Louis XIV, 1689. It remained the historic shrine of the "last Knight in Europe," but the community was never wealthy enough to make any kind of restoration or even to establish a museum: an interesting footnote to so-called Teutonic traditionalism. The rectory of the Catholic church was closed, but the *Grabdenkmal*, with "its striking Renaissance style was something we really ought to see..." The old man talked on, with growing friendly enthusiasm. No, he wasn't a teacher, but had made a study of the regional traditions and in his own library he had a collection of volumes in and around the subject. "All in German, none in English, unfortunately..." I said, "no matter," and declined (with I am afraid a rather strident tone of archness) his offer to show me around soon. We cut up the narrow side streets past the ancient church, and then decided to return. The way up the hill did not look too difficult, but we would risk it another time. We had not learned much more than the merest visual supplement to the brief paragraph in Carpenter's guide-book. Yet it was the event for the day—we had inspected a national tradition, and had made conversation (to be sure: a non-fraternal exchange of words) with a native.

This region does not appear to have suffered as much severe war damage as the frontier areas. There only a small percentage of the population was left behind, and military government consisted of the posting of proclamations on the few remaining civic buildings in an empty town. Problems were few. Some food and cattle supplies would be located; a search would be made for some sacks of flour. In a day or so a few citizens came out of their cellars and hiding-places. In centers where thousands had lived a hundred or so would be uncovered. In none of these rear areas does there seem to be any native tendencies or activity. Some "underworld" (not underground) agents remain, and each day there are a few gun-fights. Some looting also continues. But on the whole there is peace—a desert has been made, and now there is peace.

The roads themselves are in fair condition and local traffic is extraordinarily light. All movement has of course been frozen, and for obvious reasons of traffic control and intelligence-security. Mayors and secretaries have been appointed in urban centers, and some re-establishment of governmental functions has been made. Soldiers are billeted, *laissez-passer* (in France) controlled, communications set up (for official messages), and some attention paid to agriculture, supply, finance, public utilities and public health. The morale of the French population, according to G-5, has been good—and "there has been no evidence of failure on the part of Germans to cooperate with Military Government." This is as of the middle of March.

Some special cases do come up of course: juvenile delinquencies for the most part, minors concealing firearms, making false reports, providing civilian clothing to fleeing soldiers. But most of the administration becomes routine. Holdings of Reichsmarks are declared, and an exchange rate set up (now fifteen francs a mark, although curiously the Army pay rate is only five francs). Stockpiles of food are accumulated to relieve critical shortages (loaves of bread, canned food). In some of the vacated towns, cellars were crammed with food, and livestock were running free. The industrial picture is blank and hopeless. Principal manufacturing plants have all been destroyed; power-less mines will need half-a-year for repairs before the resumption of operation.

On the German side of the frontier what few prospects open for the French communities do not of course exist. They are expected to "shift for themselves," and how much starvation and chaos will set in remains to be seen. Across the border some beginnings of normalcy are being made. Farmers have started plowing and planting; seed supplies for truck gardening are made available and there is a distribution of items like gasoline, horses, fertilizer. Schools are being opened again, and although I am curious as to how Curricula and Texts are being handled no one seems to know whether an organized educational policy is in effect. Public health is rather closely and conscientiously guarded, and for obvious military reasons. Last month an epidemic of diphtheria was checked in several towns by local doctors supplied with Army serum and anti-toxin; when case after case was reported hundreds of children were immediately evacuated; the schools closed again. The physical condition of the civilian population, it is hardly necessary to add, is poor. Sick and injured in a city like Bitche, under siege for so many months, are everywhere. Ubiquitous, too, are droves of "displaced persons," including Poles, Russians, Frenchmen, and Dutch. Once in a while a "story" breaks—a few weeks ago there was the discovery of a cache in Forbach. The "Monuments and Fine Arts" section[40] was excited: So much damage to buildings and churches (of artistic and historic value), at least one cave-full of old armor and weapons and many well-known paintings was accidentally salvaged.

What else is there to this dreary, funereal chronicle of "reconstruction"? Oh: some insulin for diabetics. A floating reserve of gendarmes for town security. A labor pool for odd jobs of repair on roads, buildings, and cemeteries. (The war is over, and the dead will be properly buried. The undertaker was the occupational luxury of almost forgotten peace-time. Now once again: new proper earth covers the corpse, and with the gravestone Europe's brave new world begins.)

9 April 1945

Army headquarters moved again today; Kaiserslautern across the Rhine to Darmstadt. All the records were repacked, the trucks reloaded, and off we went... The trip was for the most part dull. The route was over one of Germany's great autobahns, and a skyway is pretty much the same the world over. The surface was smooth and we speeded along, the view of the countryside's plains and hills, lit up (at last) by a brilliant warm sun, attractive all the way. But there was nothing more than that. After the driver remarked for the tenth time, that "it was just like at home," and made believe that he was on US 1, or 12, or the Pulaski Skyway, I dozed off. He woke me at the Rhine, and I peeked out long enough to see the swift current racing over the demolished stone remnants of the great Worms bridge. Just on the other side of the river were series of tank obstacles, sitting like isolated curiosities in the vast expanses of field... Across the road a small boy was playing with a huge balsa-wood model airplane. On the side he had painted the German cross, and this was the last token of Wehrmacht and Luftwaffe power: a child zooming and dive-bombing with a miniature in his hand, winning endless plaything victories... The roads now were rougher, and the noise disturbing and amusing. Van after van roared by us, careening wildly on the bumps as the German prisoners shouted protests. We slowed down, for the bomb and shell craters had been very poorly filled. The PWs passed us, having a very uncomfortable time of their last miles. On the left: wires twisted, branches splintered, telephone poles and trees lying sick in a faint across the railroad tracks.

Evening: the city of Darmstadt is beyond belief. Every day you are told of a town that is "sure beat up," and you make some satisfactory mental reconstruction of war damage; or you see a series of photographs, and like good disciples of *Life* magazine we are quite convinced that here are reasonable facsimiles of reality. But the mere visual truth constitutes only a fragment of the picture. Mooney and I took the jeep up and down the avenues and the streets and the alleys, we took a right and then a left, and then another turn, or two, and continued on—nowhere was there a house standing! Every structure had been hit, and there were whole square blocks where everything had been razed. We must have gone miles, and it was hard to believe our eyes. An entire city was missing. We hungered for a glimpse of an interior wall, perhaps with some wall paper, or a picture hanging. But there was nothing but rubble, piles of brick and stone. Each house had been reduced to its ribbed fundamentals—never even a splinter of a piece of furniture or a closet or any odds-and-ends which might suggest that human animals once lived here. Clay and rock had been returned to the earth, and there was nothing more.

Merely to see it was not enough. Night was falling, and we made our way forward in terrible wonder and with an expanding sense of horror. (Could anyone in the history of our world be exempted from the guilt of savagery?) On the fringes of the city a cottage here and there had been missed. And staring out of the window was the face of an old woman. We looked at her and rode by. Had she heard us and come to take a glance? Or had she been sitting there at the sill all the time, a daily disbelieving spectator to the devastation of a whole city... A few military government proclamations were up, usually pasted over old Volkssturm billboards. *Darmstadt bleibt treu*, white-wash on fences read, and on a few someone had disputed the argument with additional coats of white paint (it must have been a German dissent, for we almost never deface that kind of propaganda).

Figure 4. Darmstadt reduced to rubble, © Lasky Center, Munich.

On the steps of the burgomaster's quarters sat two citizens, and I learned a little about the end of Darmstadt. (In the old days when the historic process could take a leisurely pace, catastrophes could be recorded as "decline" and "fall." Now, disasters are sudden, instantaneous, and complete. The tragedy of this city can only be summed up as—"poof!" It was here and gone within one single hour of a late summer night.) Once a city of one hundred ten thousand; an industrial center (machines, foundries); and home of well-known artistic circles. The damage as of last year was only slight; a few buildings hit, several hundred casualties. On the night of 11–12 September 1944, the bombers came. Thousands. The raid lasted forty minutes. The city was now a thing of the past. Great fires raged in every section, and the streets, crowded with fleeing people, became mass fire-traps when strong winds came up to fan the flames. Bodies were found charred and shriveled on street-corners and sidewalks. Some fifteen thousand people died. I was surprised to hear that more than thirty thousand civilians still remained in Darmstadt. Where they lived, and how they could sustain themselves was beyond me, but the two citizens stated the statistic as a fact, and I won't deny it. They admitted that there is not enough for even a fraction of that number to live, and guessed that most of them were lodged in cellars. They would never, of course, forget that last night, although from what I could hear from those two, there was no note of bitterness in their voice. "The Americans," one of them remarked, "were working efficiently that night..." It is almost maddening to think that here are thousands of people, in Darmstadt, in Worms, in Kaiserslautern, and no one knows what they are thinking, what they are feeling! I ventured a few tentative questions. One of the men said—"Not all were to blame for Hitler, but all must now suffer alike... But what's to be?" The other man simply said—"Hunger..."

Jordan returned late this evening and his jeep came past the caserne's great white-stone monument to Ernst Ludwig bulging with bags and boxes. "What in hell do I send you out for?" the Colonel exploded, "to get information or to collect salvage?" "Good Lawd, Cuhnel," Jordan drawled, "dis is what dee Wah is all aboot!" He'd been with the Third Division for almost two weeks now, "the rootin'-lootinest sons-a-bitches in dee Army," and although he almost always moved into homes, castles, offices, warehouses, just a little late, he managed to come away with a substantial private collection. My own quick inventory of what he had, as of midnight—a German police dog, four Luger pistols, one hunting rifle, five Nazi banners, a Bavarian fur vest and leather shorts, two Army sabers, a great set of mechanic's tools, two chromium-plated alarm clocks ("some goddamn thing is wrong with them, but I ain't seen nothing yet I couldn't fix!"), eleven knives and bayonets, various trinkets and jewelry including rings, bracelets, and rosary beads ("that convent sure was a beayootiful place..."), and a new shiny silk top hat ("always wanted to have one of these fuckers!" he explained gleefully, as he slapped it on his wrist, opening it and collapsing it). For me he had brought back a special haul of books. "I tried to find those *Dootsche Gechickteh* things! But I don't know whether I did much good... You know I can't tell a fuckin' good book from a fuckin' bad one!" He did succeed in making some lucky hits. Three comprehensive historical narratives of German history, all written in the early years of the Nazi regime (when the theoretical and intellectual bent was at its strongest); and a fine large sheaf of art prints including a lovely series of Michelangelos. The rest was trash. It was now late, and we had him finally unloaded and set up on a cot. But he had something more to own up to. "I gotta confess..." he confined to me. "I did some fraternizing... Yeah, there I was, drunk as a bastard on somebody's goddamn wine-cellar, and this French liaison officer and me comes across this interesting-looking building. That must be a castle I said. And he said sure. And I said let's look around. So we go up a couple of floors all empty, and run into an apartment with two women. A mother and her daughter. Here's her picture. (Very pretty.) We explained things all around and when finally nobody understood nothing, we said shit let's have a few drinks. Which we did, see, and then we talked some more. Sure, I can't speak German, but there's always the Language of Love! But I didn't trust them. When the old lady rolls out of bed I didn't take no chances—*Commen zee heah!* I told her, and she stayed put. I got a little leery when the French liaison officer had to leave and report to the CP. There I was all alone! So I took out my pistol, put it at the table next to the bed, and let it sit there cocked within very easy reach! But then I had to take a piss. So I raced out, told them not to leave the room or even the bed! On the way upstairs again I ran into some GI, grabbed him, and put him back in bed with the old lady. I felt a little better then... In the morning I almost got into a little trouble. I was saying goodbye, to the gal, see, and going through her pictures for a remembrance. She's a model and really beayootiful (!) and there was one shot there with just some filmy vague things around her shoulders or hips or something, anyway it was a picture of her tits with nipples and everything, and I was about to grab that when I heard someone coming up the stairs. Shit, I was sober enough then to take off like a ruptured duck! So I raced down, and all the floors were taken up by troops. Funny, they must have moved in during the night, and I didn't hear a fuckin' thing!" I looked at the picture again, agreed that she was really beautiful, and everybody went to bed. He talked on in the darkness about the breasts. "You shoulda seen them! So big and so soft. You put your hands over them and they spill through your fingers! And run right down your arms!" He sighed, and turned wildly, embracing his own chest and shoulders. He murmured something more for a few minutes, and then went to sleep.

11 April 1945, Frankfurt

Frankfurt am Main fell almost two weeks ago, on the afternoon of the 29 March. There was some house-to-house fighting, and then the troops cut through the city to the east. But the destruction is all old. The twisted beams and girders of the great Main bridges binding *faubourg* Sachsenhausen to the city were discolored by ugly rust, and moss was spotting the dustless heaps of debris and rubble. Frankfurt had fallen, Frankfurt had died, a long time ago. The river was still, almost motionless. Nothing in the city was moving (occasionally a prime mover hauling a tank, and every once in a while one of General Patton's guards saluting with praetorian readiness). We stopped the car and listened. The silence was overwhelming. Not a sound. In Darmstadt there were chattering, singing birds. Along the highway there was a strange lovely fragrance of spring blossoms. In Frankfurt there was only a deep lingering resonant silence. Here was the corpse of another great city, broken, burnt and shriveled.

The white-wash was a little different. The most popular slogan appeared to be, *Lieber tot als Sklave! Führer befiehl! Wir folgen!*, which was scrawled across the Gothic facades of the Römerberg, was another frequent message. (According to the confessions of prisoners, current front-line slogan among Hit-

Figure 5. Nazi graffiti "scrawled across the Gothic facades of the Römerberg" in Frankfurt, © Lasky Center, Munich.

ler troops has been—*Führer befiehl! Wir tragen die Folgen!* Führer command! We suffer the consequences...) And how these consequences must have been suffered through! Only this morning I happened across the diary items of a German soldier for last November and December—"I had to get to Darmstadt on the following day to apply for an extension of my furlough to the local commandant. I was given an additional two days. Darmstadt was a heap of rubble. I picked up my ration tickets, and was about to leave when the air-raid alarm was sounded. The planes were overhead instantly, blasting the northern part of the town (the only part which had remained comparatively unscathed so far). The raid lasted forty-five minutes. When it was over the city was a sea of flame and smoke... I passed through Darmstadt again on my way to Frankfurt am Main. The big chemical factory Merck was completely demolished in the morning raid. Some fifteen fire engines were fighting the flames. There were so many bomb craters on Frankfurter Strasse that I had to carry my bicycle for three hundred meters past the plant. Many houses in the neighborhood were destroyed. 'Walls may break, but our hearts never will!' was scrawled on one wall. A woman pushing some belongings in a pram said: 'He must have smeared that on during the night. During the day we would have hanged him.'"

We searched for Goethe's birthplace, but in vain as we came full circle around for the third time to Lessing's statue in front of the unearthly white ruin of the classical city library. I spotted a doctor (white arm-band with red cross) bicycling down the road and called to him. He offered to guide us there, and we followed. Finally we all had to dismount: there was no cleared way for his own wheels much less for our vehicle. We stepped over the bricks and shattered stone. The street was choked with rubble and we leaned up against a lone standing wall. The doctor pointed to one pile. That was No. 23 Hirschgraben where Goethe had been born. A fragment of a cornerstone remained, with a piece of rusty pipe jutting out from behind it. The rest of the historic house lay before us in debris. Part of its museum collection (he explained) had been moved out earlier. But most of the manuscript exhibits, and most of everything else, had been destroyed. "Yes, it is to this that our Führer has led us..."

He made a move to retrieve his bicycle, but my leading questions stopped him. "No," he insisted, "not all of the German people! Believe me, only a small part of the German people. There were great lies told, and the deception and the betrayal have been greater. But from the beginning there were many, oh very many, who never believed and who never were taken in. We were powerless. To say a word was to risk death before a wall. The smallest dissent and you were among the missing. But, believe me, our hearts were broken... We were not blind to the evil, and to that most evil of all the Nazi inhumanities (*ach, so schlimm und unmenschlich*), the murder of the Jews... But Hitler was all-powerful. The youth was at his disposal, and he taught them, gave them faith, made them fanatics. How could they know better when they had never been taught to think or to doubt? And the masses—who are always either being led or being misled—came out of the terrible days of the early thirties prepared to accept everything. But now too they have learned the bitter lesson. *Wir alle sind belogen und betrogen worden.*"

I stood with him on the rubble heap and offered quiet dissents, challenges, promptings. He spoke earnestly and with dignity, and more and more with a passion which moved me greatly. Not a word was news as such—but yet here were all our old hopes! Here was a German, a citizen of the Third Reich, who understood the tragedy, who knew the betrayals and the deceit, who would fight the corruption. "No, you would be mistaken to believe that reasonable thinking people disappeared from our life. They still live, and many will be among the new leadership. I suppose politics will take a sharp leftward turn, but I hope a free Germany can be reborn..." He inquired about Russia, about my own "inner" feelings. I could hardly be expected to make clear my own position on "the Russian question" in a few words of bad German. I mumbled something which I doubt he understood, but he went on to say: "Apart now from all of Herr Goebbels's propaganda, many of us are a little uneasy about the Soviet influence, and the coming of the Cheka..."[41] After the end of the Gestapo we want no more secret police! If only America and England would befriend the small growing democratic groups! We must show ourselves and we must be allowed to show ourselves. If we don't, even what little is left of Germany will, I am afraid, be destroyed and leveled too! There are paths before us. We don't have many choices now—we have had so few for so very long! But we cannot afford to go wrong. Our land and our people have made only enemies. Now we have an opportunity to make friends. Friends of a new free Germany..." His face and voice were grave and sincere, and he held his hand out to me a little uncertainly, and tentatively. I grasped it, shook it, and said goodbye. He carried his bicycle off to the makeshift path and rode away. I stumbled over the bricks back to the jeep. The horn had been honking and everybody was impatient to leave. "You don't believe all that stuff, do you?" "I suppose he's sorry. They're all sorry now!" "You know, those are Nazi orders—fraternize and propagandize!" I refused to be drawn into the argument. Perhaps. —Cities have died, peoples have been crushed, our whole world has been lost. At what point, when can one begin to believe again? Who is so strong as to deny all hope, and so coldly omniscient as not to have a need to trust? Will there never be an end to deceit and suspicion? How will men ever be able to find each other? I could decide to doubt or to believe. I would believe: He was in earnest. Let this be a beginning.

[handwritten notes]
Hannover has fallen (Ninth Army).
Bremen is burning and is encircled by the British.
Patton is in the Thuringian Forest east of Gotha.
Russians have taken half of Vienna.
Thousands of planes over Berlin and Munich.
Prisoners mount—someone cracked: "We must have more German troops than Kesselring has!"
[...]

[typescript continues]
Counterintelligence—Japanese agents in France and Germany; nationals circulating, carrying Chinese passports, operating as Nazi secret agents. There are many Chinese in Germany, most of whom have never been molested in any way; of late however stripped of their papers in order to equip Japs for trip into France and espionage work. German idea is that neither the French, Americans nor English know the difference between Japs and Chinese in appearance; therefore easy for Jap to pass as Chinese; neither language, hardly anyone, spoken in France.

PW (demoted from Lieutenant to Private, for expressing his opinion of Nazi party) stated that if all the officers in the German army were to express their thoughts about the Nazi party there would be enough privates to form a division.

Morale and the regime—the people are tired of the war which now (October '44) appears useless and lost; more and more fed up with controls of fanatical power holders; the frenzied propaganda campaign's effect, not to encourage the people, but to convince them that the war is lost; for several weeks now many Germans are trying to prove to their friends that they are not and never have been Nazis. Newspaper articles are so vague and enigmatic that no one can follow the course of military operations. Harshness of the Gestapo, insolence of the SS, doctored communiqués. . . everything creates little by little "an attitude of apathy which is perhaps harder for the Nazis to handle than would be open revolt."

12 April 1945, Ernst Ludwig Caserne, Darmstadt

A footnote to the Jordan affair:

I came in from Frankfurt rather late, and noted all the lights on and the disarray of the room. On Jordan's bed were knives, guns, silk hats, bottles of cognac. I wondered for a moment what the adventure for the night was, put out the lights, and crawled into the sleeping bag. A few minutes later I heard a commotion down the hall. The drawl was deeper and slower than ever. Jordan was coming home, escorted by two MPs who had all they could handle to keep him on his feet. He staggered over and propped himself up in the doorway. "No!" he was shouting. "I won't go in! I want my goddamn pistol! Who's got my fuckin' Luger?" I hopped out of bed, and no sooner did I identify him when the guards took off. And there I was. "It's all right, Jordie, it's me, your friend, it's me, Lasky. . ." My tones were hopeful and dripping in sugar. "I reckonize you, Lasky, I reckonize you!" he roared. "But who the fuck's got my pistol? It was heah, and it ain't heah now." His holster was empty. "I know where it is, Jordie. Please come in and be quiet. I know where it is, boy, and I'll get it for you. . ." "No, Lasky, they're trying to get me, and I won't go without my pistol!" I pleaded and implored some more, but all in vain. Finally I went to the bed, rummaged through the assorted junk and found the Luger. It was, as is Jordan's wont, loaded with full clip, and I quickly, shielded from his sight by my back, dropped the rounds out. There was probably one in the chamber, but before I could get to it, he began roaring again and stumbling toward me. I whirled with the pistol in my hand, and he lurched toward me. I caught him, helped him to his feet again, and resumed sweetly, "Now, Jordie, everything's all right, here's your pistol"—he already had a grip on the muzzle and I wasn't going to wrestle with him for it—"and now everybody can go to sleep..." "So there's the fuckin' thing! I knew they stole it, I knew they tried to get me, they're all trying to get me..." "C'mon now, boy, I'm your friend, and so let's take it easy, and get to bed..." I sat him down on the foot of my own cot and cleared the knives, flags, swords and what-not from his blankets. He slipped of my cot with a crash, pistol still in his hand pointing to the ceiling. I set him down on his bed, rolled him over and up and finally tugged a cover around him. He began breathing heavily in a doze, and thoughtlessly I reached for his pistol which was now back in his holster, and removed it. Strange, I had no notion of "danger," but simply thought it would be uncomfortable for him! He awoke with a roar. Now he was "mean" and "ugly" in the standard drunken fury. He grabbed the pistol from me fiercely, and pushed me to the floor. "So you're against me too! They're all against me! The whole goddamn regiment!" I opened with a new softer, sweeter tone, but he wouldn't listen, only ranted on. "I'll get you all! Every last fuckin' guy! Trying to trap me, that's what they're trying to do! Get back there!" I tried to pick myself up, but the wave of the Luger muzzle sat me right down again. I knew now that he was uncontrollable, completely wild, and might just as likely as not squeeze that trigger off just to see whether the gun was operational. And there might be a round in the chamber... I was more than a little nervous. I wasn't frantic yet, though I might well have been. My voice began trembling a little, and I wondered whether anybody had been awakened by the noise. (As a matter of fact half the hall was up and listening, and had decided "very sanely" that this was my problem, and they wouldn't budge from their protective corner of darkness.) I could barely make anything out, there was only the light from the flashlight which I had put down on the duffle bag to help us find our way in the very beginning. I reached slowly for the flash, although God knows what difference that would make. Anything, rather than sit still as a life-size bull's eye for the Luger sights. "Goddamn it, don't move! Or I'll get you all, so help me good great God, I'll get you all..." The pistol was waving around wildly in the air, traversing from the left side of my face to the right. I pulled my hand back but upset the light and the duffle bag. The flash rolled a little, and the beam shifted directly to his face. He began squinting and grimacing and yelled, "Get that fuckin' light outa my eyes! Get it out, get it out, d'ya hear me!" I leaped for the bag and switched the light out. Everything was blacked out. There was a silence for a moment. "Now you're making sense!" he said in a somewhat more subdued tone. "Light's outa my eyes, light's outa my eyes..." And he fell. Knives, swords, and alarm clocks jangled out. The pistol slid away across the stone floor. He began mumbling incoherently, and crawled and felt around for it. Then it was still again. No noise, no movement. I sat on my cot almost paralyzed. Every time I tried inching under the blankets the cot began creaking and I froze. Why didn't everybody turn over in their own beds—the accumulated squeaks might cover my own movement. Suddenly Jordan was up again and fell again toward me. He sprawled out half on my duffle bag and lay quietly. I slipped into the sleeping bag and played possum for several hours. Occasionally he would turn. About three he slipped off the bag and grabbed the leg of his cot and pulled it over. At about five he was on his own bed, and I fell asleep.

Shortly before noon the next day I returned to wake him. He remembered nothing. I gave him a brief resumé of the events of the night before. Everything was a blank. I felt worse now than I did when I was facing the muzzle of the pistol: here was a man with a mean finger on the trigger without a single faculty under control. He twisted out of bed, sighing and groaning, and I reached under the blankets and found the Luger. It was empty. No round in the chamber. There were spots of rust on the metal parts, corroded by urine. Jordan's pants were dirty and wet and there were still little pools on the floor. I helped him on to his feet again, insisted he change clothes, guided him to the showers. Now he was curious. "Tell me, Lasky! Don't keep secrets from me! What did I do? Where did the MPs find me? Was it an awful mess? I did shuah make a fool of myself..." I told him as much as I could without acting through the entire melodrama. "I don't remember a thing, I just don't remember a thing!" He kicked off his damp clothes and swallowed three aspirins. "I shuah do appreciate this, boy, let me tell you I'm really thankin' you..." I left him at noon, but it was several hours before he showed up. He put in his appearance with an embarrassed smile, new dress-green clothes, and blood-shot eyes.

I now understood what happened the other night at Bad Kissingen. Jordan must have stormed into the German home and made love at the command of the wildly brandished pistol. What a night of terror that must have been!

13 April 1945, Darmstadt

I found my Two Citizens of Darmstadt again this evening in the old Lagerhausstrasse schoolhouse. They were just beginning their night tour of guard, and we stood outside the *Oberbürgermeister* office and talked for a while. Here were simple fellows, two ordinary Germans, with no great sophistication or special training, who had survived the hard days without ever having shared either in its extremes of fanaticism or despair. In manner, language, and intelligence, how different from the doctor of Frankfurt! Yet their story—hardly a story at all, but rather a sketchy narrative with odd high-points of gossip, reminiscence, sentiment, and history—was in its simple-minded mediocre directness effective, and even moving.

For them Nazism was dead, a thing of the past. "The last Nazi here died the day our city fell... He cut his wrists as the troops were coming down Heidelberger Strasse. It was old Dr. Schilling,[42] Hitler's Kreisleiter, and he knew it was the end ... some others of course fled, like Jakob Sprenger of Frankfurt—he was the Party *Gauleiter* for Hessen.[43] And they still remain fanatical enough to fight on. The total war was theirs, and the total destruction will be theirs, too. Please don't believe all that nonsense about 'Werewolves.' It's bluff! More Goebbels propaganda, and its only function is to make the Americans uncertain and uneasy. He wants us to fight on behind the lines, to conduct partisan warfare. As if there aren't dead and ruins enough! The Nazis would like to see us all dead and everything leveled. They are doomed, and they want to drag everything into the grave with them! Do you think there is anybody stupid enough here to become a Werewolf and to resume the misery? The fanatics can rave on; they only want company in hell."

These two were far from being anti-Nazis or even political people of any shade. They were simply non-Nazis. They had no great understanding of fascism—except that it had something to do with the pattern of German economic life. ("Germany is an industrial nation," they patiently explained to me, "which has always needed international trade to live...") They had no large picture of European events nor any renewed deep national hope. Perhaps they could find a little place for themselves in the years of peace and reconstruction, recover some of their belongings, set up business again, try to live quietly. They were "little people" and in a way there was a blurred class loyalty of the petty-bourgeois in their defense of various institutions and developments of German history. The notion of Germany's place in the sun remained. And the German Army was to be distinguished, they insisted, from the SS and the Gestapo. I had been rather sharp and strong on the issue of military terror, and they were quick to protest. "The party, yes! The secret police, yes again! These were the Nazis, the fanatics, the voluntary willing followers of Hitler. But the Army? The Army was the little men, *und was kann der kleine Mann tun?* I am drafted and you are my officer and what you command I can only follow. And when the Party commanded we could only follow. We dared say nothing ... but *Heil Hitler*. We dared do nothing but stand on the avenue and raise our hands and cheer as the Führer came by. For thirteen years I was the head of a sports club here in the city. When Hitler came the *Turnerschaft* was banned. If we would play we would play Nazi games, with Nazi arm-bands. If we would hold a meeting we would gather as Hitlerists, with Party banners. That was the end of our sports club! Then they took me away from my business and drafted me into the police, and here I remain. That's the way it was."

First one would talk, and then the other. I would interrupt and then both would come back at me together. There was much that they avoided or perhaps could not comprehend. How could there be a new Germany when the tragedy of the old was not fully deeply understood? How could there be a free and peaceful land unless there was a real overwhelming love and devotion to the ideal of freedom and a more substantial hatred of war than derives from mere war-weariness? Was there faith and hope and strength enough to build from the ruins? For new life Germany would need new and revolutionary politics, a new and vitalizing morality, a new and liberating culture. Could anything less than this salvage a people from out of their rubble-choked cellars? They would find their way to new foundations or perish among their own ruins.

A sermon was my very last intention, but in turn I was given something of a peroration, which was eloquent and touching, even if it did possess only the rather cheap and easy dignity of self-pity. It was eloquent because it was sad and sincere, and it touched me for here, after all, was the simplest, most elementary aspect of the national tragedy.

"Listen to me, *bitte*, for only a moment," he began. "You are a young man, an American of perhaps twenty-five. You have been a soldier perhaps for three or four years and perhaps have gone through much. But know this: there is no unhappier soul, no more hopeless and unfortunate human being, in all the world than the German. I was a young boy when the war broke out in 1914. My life was just beginning. During those four years I lost my father and I lost a brother. After the war the inflation wiped out what was left of my family. We lost our money and our home. I grew up in a war and tried to make my way in the hard years of a depression. Then came political crises and one lived in uncertainty and tension, and then more and more in fear. For a while under Hitler material things became a little better. But we were trapped in a dictatorship. Our hands and feet were shackled, our mouth was sealed. And then another war came. My little business was gone. My wife died in the bombings, from anxiety and broken nerves. And now in this ghost of a city I live and work and hope again for a few years of peace... What has become of my life? I am now almost fifty, almost an old man! All my days have fled, and when have I known even an hour of calm and happiness? It is almost too late for anything but to finish up... This is what has become of our lives. And this is the story of our Germany too."

13 April 1945, Darmstadt

Its strangeness is a little evasive, but the note of irony or paradox grows stronger: Henry James himself was so far removed from the vulgarities and routinism of life as it is lived by the mass of men, how curious it is that it should be a sentence of his which illuminates (and tempers) my own predicament in the "howling desert." I have become less and less convinced of the "consolation and encouragement" of art which was his passion and his sustaining faith. His notion that art is the only "intense life," which in one formula or another has dominated our intellectual traditions, begins to strike me as the occupational fetish of the ego-ridden talent. Yet one great sentence of James has remained with me, and I am deeply grateful for it. "There is simply no limit," he wrote, "no limit to the misfortune of being tasteless."

By tastelessness he meant, not some uncritical departure from precious standards, but a tastelessness about life, an insensitivity to its variety and adventure, a blindness to its subtle forms and meanings. And the misfortune, similarly, was not a mere private black tag for dereliction from his personal syllabus. The misfortune is part of the deep waste of our time. James sensed the "darkness" of the spirit which has deadened the imagination and paralyzed the moral will of our world. "Be generous and delicate," he once counseled, "and pursue the prize." But where is there generosity or delicacy? And who is there with imaginative energy and ambition enough to conceive the pursuit of a prize or an ideal?

(Think now of M[ooney] here. For all his enthusiasm, his fine restlessness, his fantastical feeling for "the color of life itself," for all the possessed drama in which he has set his years, what does it all come to? True to American type it is the commercial imperative which drives him on. He has had to come to the European fronts, to "see the war," to "live with Joe in his hole," and now he is going to take off for the Pacific, to "discover what Joe is thinking, feeling, how he's fighting and cursing and dreaming in a jungle." He knows something of James's immensity that has to be learned, and he is equipped with vigor and freshness. And on he goes—to build up his stock-pile of lore, insight, mannerisms... in order to sell Joe the postwar world! Society's trial is the advertising-man's field-day, a unique opportunity for mass research. The battlefield is just a vast show-window, and the troops so many potential customers. The war becomes a rich indispensable prelude to bigger and better coast-to-coast ad campaigns! What a gross terrible waste! And how "tasteless.")

So today has been especially depressing. In the morning the news came through of Roosevelt's death. Perfunctory regrets were expressed at breakfast; papers and files were straightened out as a mild discussion of Truman's virtues was carried on in the offices; then *Stars & Stripes* arrived and everybody proceeded to read to each other details of the stroke and the funeral and odd bits of constitutional procedure. "Life," as someone finally said (Life: humdrum, dull, dead), "life goes on..." In the afternoon I assisted in the investigation of a "war crime," and was appalled. The inspector-general, cold and casual, sat at the table with me interviewing witnesses, exhibiting about as much—this, certainly, is the least one could ask—intelligent curiosity as a corpse in a mausoleum. In the evening, the military governors of Darmstadt were hardly more inspiring. Is there something wrong with me? Am I demanding a quality to everyday existence which would be impossible short of theatricalism or hysteria? (But then, anything to relieve the unmitigated boredom!) Is it simply that people don't understand, or that they don't care? Here, then, is another formula for the "real," the "deep" Revolution of Our Times—a Revolution of Taste.

The "war crime" case had both its exasperating and its instructive moments. In the prisoner-of-war hospital at Heppenheim (down the highway between Darmstadt and Heidelberg) a *Stars & Stripes* correspondent found "grotesque living skeletons of American soldiers where their infected wounds leaked into sheets." His dispatch was a lurid account of the German doctor's sadism and the brutalities of the "horror hospital." American newspapers picked up the story. Some time after breakfast the next morning Congress read the various accounts and demanded investigations. The War Department heard from the State Department. The Army began to look into the matter. Breaking it down all the way, I was called in by the IG (who never handles such matters in the first place) to assist in the interviewing of German witnesses. Well, we spent most of the day in the burgomaster's office, asking questions, going through the documents. What was the food situation in Hessen? What were the legal bases for civilian rationing in the Heppenheim district? Who prescribes for prisoners of war? For sick prisoners of war? Did you ever receive any complaints from the Heppenheim bureau about shortages? Hour after hour we tried to piece together a story. But it came to something which bewildered the poor old IG—and left me only with the small satisfaction of another "lesson learned." In modern war there are crimes but no criminals. In modern society there is evil but there is no devil. Murder has been mechanized and rendered impersonal. The foul deed of bloody hands belongs to a bygone era when man could commit his own sins. Now innocence or guilt is a problem beyond the scope of court and legal decision. Here in the Heppenheim case the guilt belonged to the machine. Somewhere in the apparatus of bureaucracy, memoranda, and clean efficient directives, a crime had been committed. Men died in a hospital, of starvation, of medical neglect. But the witnesses were very "unsatisfactory"—who was responsible the IG would never discover. What was responsible could, I think, be established, and convicted, but I am afraid the old man is searching for a "suspect" he can sit down in the witness chair and ply with the routine of cross-examination. The chair will remain empty, and the crimes will go on.

[...]

16 April 1945, Darmstadt

Books and magazines arrived today: letters of Byron, stories of James, some collections of poetry, Dwight Macdonald's *Politics*, a brochure for *Partisan Review*, Willa Cather's *My Antonia* (which proved an interminable bore), a mystery story (Dorothy Hughes's *Fallen Sparrow*, in which I lost myself for an hour madly), some sober works on reconstruction and European affairs. But I have read nothing carefully, and nothing completely, and although I could use the excuse of time and distractions, I suspect it's something more serious. In a way I hope won't be thought weak I have been, I admit, afraid and reluctant to read. Afraid to think or make a sustained effort to understand what has been happening (from any earnest perspective at all). It has been months now since I finished a book or even an article. There were a few pages of Keats (in a volume somebody looted from the Keats-Shelley memorial in Italy); a story of Mann (*Disorder and Early Sorrow*, which still seemed interesting but now curiously wrong); some Pacifica of Melville (pleasant, but so empty). Yet it frightens me to recall all the volumes and opportunities I deliberately let slip by. Perhaps I've lost some courage or nerve. I used to fancy, in my old romantical but at least strong-minded way, of what sources of strength there would be in the war experience. What an illusion! Whoever first created the inflection of betrayal—or employed the tone of resentment—in the well-worn phrase, "vicarious experience," fathered one of the great myths we live by, the myth of the real experience, feeding itself on the celebration of the virtues of sharing earthy realities. For all I have seen and heard and written, for this notebook is crammed, and I am really terrified to think that I have really learned nothing. I have tried again and again to pass a day by striking an attitude or holding on to some note or theme, but to no effect. Something has gone wrong and awry. I can't seem to be able to face my own mind. Things happen to me but I don't meet them. A deadening has set in somewhere, and how can I convey my distress? I have been hurt in so many small terrible ways in the months here, by the casual details of the great tragedy which one only comes to know in its humdrum everyday horror, I am sick to think that the real wound is my own inability to grow. It bewilders me—I refuse to read or write!—I've killed off every personal hope or ambition... and God knows I have been practically wrestling with my soul and conscience to remain here with this page. I can only plead some strange inner weakness which baffles me, and has effectively stopped me from ordering my own impressions. I feel lost and isolated, and cut off even from myself. The first shock lingers—"the largest events of the world have been for so long essentially intellectual and imaginative matters, so much dramas and fables of the mind, it is not easy suddenly to assimilate them to one's personal course of sight and hearing." So I neatly explained to myself in this journal months ago. But I fear seriously that I will continue to waste my days. Where is there a point of strength in the world at which I can stand, when I can't even manage the spirit to face my own self?

18 April 1945, Darmstadt and Heidelberg

The cycle of enthusiasm (or even simple interest) grows shorter and shorter. A day now of stale flaccid documents, pieced together for no point, with the last turns of the War coming through only through the late and invariably foolish and vulgar correspondence of *Stars & Stripes*—and I am left bored almost to the point of desperation. Desperate, indeed, was the attempt to make Heidelberg the other evening; but we did manage to get to the outskirts of the city, *faubourg* Neuenheim on the north side of the river, and despite two flat tires and an empty gasoline tank.

It was after eight, possibly an hour before night, when we cut off the autobahn running south to Karlsruhe and moved into the Neckar Valley. The hills and slopes in the dusk took on a really weird beauty as if we were suddenly lost in the deep romantic tones of a phantasmal German painting. Above Heiligenberg the lines of plotted fields and the blue-gray of blossoming foliage in the distance gave the countryside a curious distinction of age and ancient wisdom. We wound around the hills, and broken eyes of old Carolingian fortresses blinked at us at every turn.

I made the trip again the next day (most of which, unfortunately, was spent with the records of Sixth Army Group). This time, we came through about noon, and the people were out. Men were moving bundles and carts, and women were shopping. Children in all the villages en route were playing games on the street and highway but we raced through and I couldn't catch any of the shrill cries. Here and there small groups were working in the fields, ploughing, and almost always they were old women (faces beaten and wrinkled, kerchief-covered heads, bent over as if they would never straighten up again).

On the road I could make out only friendliness. The old people smiled at you and always volunteered information eagerly. At crossroads directions were given with warm endless detail. The young ones waved at us and a few called out for "chocolate." (So the last dignity of Nazi fanaticism passes away—the vaunted loyalty of the Hitlerjugend! lost for the pangs of a sweet tooth...) In Lützel-Sachsen I stopped at a fence along a field and asked the family group what was being grown. (I was particularly curious about what we had been calling "the host of golden daffodils.") *Löwenzahnen*, the father said. *Ach, ja!* the children shouted, *die gelben Blumen... Löwenzahnen!* (No we were not referring to the dandelions, but for now we would have to be content with that intelligence.) I drove off, and felt a little put out when I saw the father come back to the fence with a handful of *gelbe Blumen* for me. We had left too soon.

Neuenheim was strange and affecting. The streets were clean, houses and windows were intact. Handsome show-windows along Brückenstrasse glistened in the noon sun. There were flowers blooming in the garden. We waited for the traffic to clear over the pontoon bridge, and in those few minutes I recovered a bit. Here was a city which had survived, and it was untoward and upsetting. For the first time I felt that I didn't belong—what was I doing here?—why and how had I come? For a few moments the continent had an aspect of peace. This was old Europe. I perhaps was a tourist as of earlier days (a tourist! in Heidelberg, visiting the university, living with a family). But in a moment, we were at the Neckar. Slumped in the water were the broken bridges, the Hindenburg Brücke, the Friedrich Brücke, Karl-Theodor Brücke, the current breaking and rushing past the shattered stone. The river flowed free and wild again, and the earth was no longer a world: there were only hateful islands, and each island had become a redoubt of a terrible separatism. We crossed the Neckar and the smell of its deep clear green water was strong and surprising as if in the destruction of the land the sea itself had recovered its own secret strength.

In Heidelberg proper, undamaged as it was, a touch of the Tour returned, but we would be tourist-conquerors as the proclamations on every billboard never ceased reminding us. Little crowds of people were still accumulating to read "No. 1" announcing the end of the Nazi regime, although Heidelberg "fell" almost a month ago. (After the devastation of Mannheim, "just a long tom's distance away," the mayor called up Army headquarters and surrendered by telephone.) I suspect not a few of the citizens were learning basic English from the double texts of the proclamation and translation. Hauptstrasse was a busy thoroughfare, but once again "non-fraternization" enforced coldness. We walked and stared past each other. The policy is not, of course, very popular, and only in a very few cases is its political or military necessity recognized. I was much amused and interested to note a huge marker outside of Army Group headquarters (which are in the university buildings)—PRO STATION THIS WAY.[44] A block down on Seminarstrasse an MP stood guard. Through the wire entanglements of the roadblock, you could see the people pass. A pretty girl strolled by. The MP smiled at me self-consciously, and murmured, "Boy, I sure could use some of that fraternization!" Now that the availability of prophylaxis has been made public and conspicuous, I suppose it is common knowledge that there are more than a few violations. However, the isolationism—physical as it is in most cases (no one is allowed to wander beyond our own caserne

Figure 6. American Pro Station in Frankfurt, © Lasky Center, Munich.

walls!)—has not been too difficult to maintain; and only rarely is there any extremism. (When Waters and Blumenson[45] passed through several weeks ago, they failed to get around to the university, because they couldn't locate it and were afraid to make inquiries among the Germans!) There is little if any real unfriendliness or hostility, but a coolness is kept.

American touches in Heidelberg: the anti-aircraft radio on the Grande Terrasse of the Castle hill blaring *Ramona*. In the garden at Peterskirche (fifteenth- and sixteenth-century Gothic) a thundering orchestration of *And Her Tears Flowed Like Wine*. In a local window, Sinclair Lewis's *Babbitt*, and A. J. Cronin's *Die Sterne blicken herab*.

The city itself is a little dim and disappointing. Yes, the university was founded in 1386 on the great medieval style of Paris—and the Romans established the city as a gesture to the *cult de Mithra-Mercure*—and all the historical campaigns of the Western tradition from the conversion of Clovis through Barbarossa, from the Reformation and its series of political and religious wars (1622 Tilly, marshal of the Catholic league, devastated Heidelberg) through Louis XIV and the treaty of Lunéville reshuffling frontier-lines and sowing the seeds of nationalist enmities—all were here somewhere. But Heidelberg and its celebrated tradition must really be a spirit, a tone, a *Gemütlichkeit*, which has to be lived and shared. To see it, to search for it as a sight on a tour, is wrong-minded and insensitive. I took a last glance at the century-old tombs in the Peterskirche garden (was the jive coming from the cathedral itself?) and decided to leave.

Two stops: A large bookstore front, featuring Goethe, Hutten, Fichte. A sign read: SIE HABEN ZEIT ZUM LESEN! One of the windows had apparently been dedicated to English literature. Eighteenth-century prints and engravings hung over the exhibition which told something either of taste, scholarship, or the availability of editions. I noted: half-a-dozen plays of Shakespeare, Milton's *Das verlorene Paradies*, Macduff's *Sunsets on the Hebrew* (sic!) *Mountains*, *A Memoir of Paul Vinogradoff* by H. A. L. Fisher, poems of N. P. Willis (with a frontispiece sketch of Concord!), Owen Wister's *The Virginian*, Frank Moore's *The Civil War in Song and Story*, and finally a work on theology by Henry Churchill King. Two Germans, young men, were window-shopping. One poked the other and pointed. "Look!" he whispered. "Churchill..." I heard nothing else.

And across the street: a lending library, its own window-display bright with gaudy dust jackets. I went in, and my entrance caused a little flurry among the afternoon clientele of women. On the shelves: Philip Gibbs, Louis Bromfield's *Der grosse Regen*, Max Brand, Zane Grey, A. J. Cronin, Pearl Buck's *Die Mutter* and *Das geteilte Haus* (which a nun picked off the shelf over my shoulder), and *Vom Winde verweht* by Margaret Mitchell. The Mitchell, the little bookseller reassured me, was "very beloved, very popular, and now more than ever!" Since the war, naturally, American, English, Russian literature had been under ban. "*Ach! Das war sehr schlimm!* The police, the Gestapo, were always here to examine and to censor...Yes, there were a few of our books that were allowed. Here is one..." He picked a volume from the stacks and showed it to me— *Babbitt*, "bei Sinclair Louis [*sic*]..." I laughed. Cronin, too, was omitted from the index for his *Stars Look Down*. I smiled again. The bookseller had hidden the old volumes in the cellar, and last month ("at last!") he dug them out again. He was quite happy about their restoration to circulation: the shelves were filling up. The real crime, he carefully explained, was that the police came in, expropriated the "refractory" volumes, and never replaced them with anything! "*Ach*, it wouldn't have been so bad if they had given me some substitute! Soon my whole bookstore was bare!" He scurried about, proudly showing me the new stock. *Ach ja!* I thought, Culture is now Free. A liberated bookseller now redeems his frozen capital. Private property in shelf-space has again been restored, is sacred as in earlier fine prosperous days. But my distress is foolish. Worlds are not saved by great heroic strokes of a devotion to liberty. We will be fortunate enough to find our way as we can—even on the mean strength of small occupational grievances of shopkeepers, anxious only to please the customer, and do business as usual.

19 April 1945, Darmstadt

At least there is one thing to be thankful for: boredom can be exasperating for only so long before something bursts. Well, we have been sitting for weeks now, staring out at the country through the window of a *Kaserne*, creating new anxieties each day to give some interest and tension to life. The war that is no war... And the compound formula for the varieties of our boredom consists now partly of hysteria and partly of fantasy.

Fragments of the day. Carter:[46] "Did I ever tell you about my invasion of Normandy—on D plus 110... That was rough, rough as a cob!... There we were, coming in from LCIs, and we hit the beaches with both barracks bags! ... Rough, that's what it was. We carried them three miles and then we took a break for chow.... A memorable assault!" Maske:[47] "I guess I'm what they used to call the forgotten man. An o.d. collar worker that nobody knows. I don't figure in nothing. I just don't rate in the Army—don't rate for demobilization or rotation or reeducation or fraternization... C-ration that's were I come in!" Mooney: "You know what the best thing that ever happened to me was? The best goddamn thing that ever happened to me! ... I was born! ... I mean it! I was born! ... I became! Me! Mooney! ... And now the whole world's before me. I can't lose! Everything's before me—endless possibilities, opportunities, everything! ... Whatever happens I got it beat. Goddamn it, what can I lose? Not a thing! Because what did I invest? Nothing! ... Every little moment is marvellous, simply marvellous. The good with the bad, the dull with the exciting, the pain with the pleasures... I was born. What a break! From that moment on I had it beat! ... No matter how you play the hand, no matter what cards turn up, you wind up with blue chips. You were born—and you can't lose! ..." Dyer: "They say I'm bucking for cardinal, and perhaps I am. But there are evil forces working against me. I hear Carlo Malo has turned thumbs down on me. It's very distressing. The odds are now shifting. It is being reported that I may make a bishopric in Patagonia. But never the big-time for me. I am sorely distressed. Sweet ineffable Jesus! ..." Sutton: "I've got it! The perfect title for my memoirs of the war: 'WE Won Anyway'... Pretty *bon*, isn't it. Bony day when you can think up a good title." Carter: "*Trayz interssantai, trayz interessantai*, but you never read Chapter Three of my great war novel. It's called 'In the Shadow of the Buzz Bomb.' The place is London, last year, and the whole atmosphere is rich with the strange carnival carpe diem spirit of those days. What a time that was! It wasn't worth four years in the Army maybe, but it was quite an experience. Terrific! That was war too, but not a foxhole with lousy coffee and hash cans. *Beaucoup* liquor and *beaucoup* women! Eisenhower was worried those days about the GIs and international niceties. The brass thought we were having a good time. And we were! And all—

In-the-Shadow-of-the-Buzz-Bomb!..." Lasky: "We can make our second act long, very long! The first is normal, see, running about fifty minutes. The second act runs three or four hours. We can bore them, bewilder them, drive them mad. The first two scenes will be set in practical darkness. Joe sitting in a room, a desk, a chair, a few papers. Regular clatter of door, opening and closing. No, no mail. No, no *Stars & Stripes*. No, no nothing... This will be the Real War. And we'll have our casualties. Booby-traps in the aisles for elements of the foolish retreating audience. Roadblocks on Broadway and Shubert Alley. Collecting stations can be set up in the lobby. This will at least have some bloody truth about it." Carter: "The climax is wrong, all wrong. Mail, mail, what's so special about mail? Look at me, I'm sweating out a package..." Maske: "You know what I always say. Let's give the Jap his co-prosperity sphere. It won't work but what the hell! Do I want to save Borneo for Dutch-Shell? All together now—'To Hell with Dutch-Shell!'" Mooney: "Do you know what this means? No matter what happens, I can't lose, I got it beat! Christ, I'm so far ahead of the game it's staggering!" Weinstein:[48] "You're in men, don't worry about it, you're in! We've been hurtin' up to now, hurtin' bad, but we're all in. Oh, take it from there!"

20 April 1945

Friday.

Some fragmentary details of the push across the Rhine from Ludwigshafen seemed to me especially interesting, and at least a momentary flight from the routine fantasies of military gossip and political prejudice. Mannheim was in ruins, and the roads to Heidelberg from the river area and south from Karlsruhe were frantic refugee escape-lines. The city of Heidelberg itself was almost bulging. Peace-time population of eighty-six thousand; and now it held more than one hundred ten thousand. Heidelberg had become the sanctuary of the Rhine. (There were only about two thousand displaced persons, mostly French.) The people, according to all early observers, appeared to be well-fed, and the town was in all respects normal. The shops and the banks were open, the university was intact (guarded now to protect against looters), and except for the railroad yards the whole city with its historic buildings was undamaged. The Neckar was quiet, and some communications had been established, for little rowboats were coming over and back from shore to shore. Several hundred bodies were still lying around, soldiers and civilians killed in the street-fighting of several days before. The burgomaster, and this was a point I had missed in my own rather hasty "reconnaissance," had been in office since 1929.[49]

He was a Nazi party member. His explanation was, of course, that it had been required of him in order to continue in office. And the Army accepted him as such. In the by now terribly familiar pattern the basic intention was to remove him, but he would be of service temporarily, for he was "not sufficiently prominent in the Nazi hierarchy to warrant his immediate displacement!" To be sure, he had refused to submit lists of prominent Nazis and locations of Nazi property. But he could help keep "order" and "administration" for the time being. On these hollow and lazy phrases all purpose is lost. The removal of the Nazis, summarily, unconditionally, could have become the consistent symbol of the end of the old order. In each town, village, county, everything but the memory of Party power could have been eradicated. Instead, spurious reasons of military and official expediency dictate compromises, blurring and distorting the clean break which would have proved constructive and vivifying. Once again victors and victims alike are prisoners of the machinery of evil. And our real deep helplessness suggests itself at least to me in every detail of the conquest and the occupation. Each report is a conspicuous unwitting exercise in the tragic ironies and paradoxes of the War. "All churches were required, under the Nazi regime, to submit copies of sermons to be delivered. Pastors and priests are continuing this practice." "The local prison was almost destroyed. However, one cell block, containing about eighty cells, has been cleaned up. It is considerably damaged and without windowglass, but it will serve to accommodate about 150 persons." "Concentration-camp situation reports were made out and the individual inmates' questionnaires were left to be filled out by the inmates. The camp was being administered by three of the inmates who had imprisoned the German guards and taken over the management when the camp fell into Allied hands. The three were an Englishman, a Frenchman, and a Belgian. The prison was running so smoothly that it was determined not to make any changes..." The Imitation of Art by Life is no idle intellectual fancy, but is literal and terrifying: the whole war begins to unfold as an ingenious adaptation of Franz Kafka!

Discussions of the evening. Carter on the partition of Germany: "Partition her? Why, we're going to rent her out! This country is going to be one vast To-Let sign! Or maybe, after all the bombings are over, she'll be a deep enough crater simply to allow the sea to rush in. Then we'll all take occupation furloughs and go fishing. Every now and then something'll bite and up we come with a Heidelberger, nice and fat and Aryan, or a Frankfurter... Looks as if we're in for one good deal after another! Imagine! Nothing to do but fish and swim in *Mare Nostrum*..." And Mooney, once again, on Bates Fabrics, bedroom furnishings, and problems of advertising and merchandising ladies-ready-to-wear.

21 April 1945, Darmstadt

Am nominally occupied with the autumn phase of the History—the slowing down of the Dragoon offensive,[50] the preparations for the winter offensive against Strasbourg, the Maginot and Siegfried lines. The records are impossible: sketchy, dull, and useful only for formal reference; with the result that every maneuver becomes a bore. This may be a variety of military narrative, but it certainly isn't history. For a brief time, the character of the fighting in the Forest of Parroy was arresting: a vicious tangle of brush and woods which held up the Army for weeks.[51] Notable: no return at all to peek-a-boo Indian fighting! Forward observers hopped about from tree to dugout (many old World War I trenches) and brought down lethal artillery tree-bursts, as new armored maneuvers sent tanks through clearings and firebreaks. Alas, there is no avoiding the mechanization of war! Even in the forest, home of the classic hunter and warrior, the spirit of contest is gone.

Little more to report about the death of Roosevelt, except that the details of the nation-wide grief in the States have been coming through in letters and clippings, and there is only surprise. Here not a tear was shed, not a soul was touched or moved. Casualty lists have made death too much of a commonplace to make any passing anything more than a casual emotional experience. The regret is perfunctory and the loss momentary. So many friends have been killed, so many intimate names forgotten, that few important distinctions remain unblurred: nothing is historic, everything is ordinary. There were some reports about "memorial services" but so far as I know the Army routine went on uninterrupted. Conversations have returned to their old themes, and in a week I have heard a total of three significant references to Roosevelt or Truman. (One: An idle speculation of the Great White Father's role in the Great Beyond—a New Deal for sinners and saints alike? Priming the pump for the resurrection? Two: A burlesque of Truman's foolishness—so everything will be over on July Fourth? Just in time to plant firecrackers under Hitler's mustache? Three: A quip that international power-politics now consists of the Big Two-and-a-Half.) Nor, I suspect, is the deep and universal cynicism only a matter of spiritual and emotional callousness. There is a devious element of social powerlessness and futility, a sense of political nihilism, involved in our coldness. It is true that our lives, every day and night, are people-dominated routines. Never were the issues of personality, competence, individuality, so vital and overwhelming. Yet "good man" or "eight-ball," nobody in the end prompts or draws anything but indifference and insensitivity. "Fate" in the Army and in the War has taken on a vast impersonal massiveness. From the beginning when GI careers were picked and dispatched by the efficient steel rods of the International Business Machine the course of events became a mechanical thing. Continents may shake and giants may fall, but the historic process remains something final and beyond us all. What matters is the next inevitable moment. That is all we need to master. So it is that Franklin Roosevelt died—"FDR," who dominated American lives, whose very voice touched and upset the national career—without an appropriate remark, response, or gesture.

As for myself: I must confess that he never stimulated in me love or loyalty or admiration, nor anything indeed but the great and serious sentiment appropriate to the critical spectator of an overpowering international personality. Now that he is gone I think the whole face of America has changed, the very way the states seem to fit together. The strength of his own ambition and political power and idealist direction gave a special unifying color to the national aspect. Things have suddenly become paler and looser. The *Stars & Stripes* headline is tacked on the *Kaserne* wall before me. "Roosevelt Dead." It is true, and it leaves me with no hurtful sense of loss, yet still there is some curious disbelief. His shadow was a commonplace of our lives. It dominated (and frustrated) the political development (and in a real way the intellectual and moral progress) of my whole generation. His "affectionate warmth" for Liberalism and Democracy, and his "pity" for the People, caught up so many young minds and spirits in a deadening cant! Roosevelt was an idol of millions and for many serious intellectuals an intense personal symbol. I can only say that for me his was a greatness without distinction, a devotion that wanted the strength of love, a power that was cheapened by patroonish mannerism. He was History, I know, but I can't think of him as world-historic. There was a personal smallness to his stature, and in the large profound perspective, a meanness to his role in terrible times of mass misery and murder that is for me inescapable.

I wouldn't want the element of mere political disagreement to be exaggerated. Franklin Roosevelt (I know this is an inadequate way of putting it, but it represents an indictment deeper and more serious than the superficiality of the phrase) lacked personal culture. He possessed magnetism and charm, but they were promiscuous, indiscriminate things. The Great White Father of the New Deal never could rise above the table of great shrewd plays and hands. He was a great shuffler and a steady uncanny winner. He was a giant among boys in the back room. Much was decided there, much was won and lost that changed our lives and destinies. But stacks of blue chips, for all their security and convenience, are far from being the appropriate counters in the reckoning of the whole tragedy of our time.

22 April 1945, Darmstadt

Von Papen has been captured in the Ruhr; Nürnberg has fallen (liberated to the tune of *Der Führer's Face*[52] which had apparently become the official anthem of the liberation); Leipzig has been taken (troops surrounded the city, and when the Nazis held out over the protests of the Mayor, and the Police Chief, and the Military Commander, they smashed the way through to the center and the University strongholds); Goebbels, in his birthday-eve speech for Hitler, is sober but helpless (offering nothing but vague phraseological hope for survival and ultimate peace and reconstruction). But I still remain dismayed by the unreality of it all, and no one, I must confess, appears to be more than nominally excited or curious about these last historic days of Hitlerism. "Non-fraternization" has made us all a little cold; and it has not been an easy thing to live with. For most of the troops it means first, no source for souvenirs and street-life, for everything German (a whole nation!) is off-limits; second, no women, and in every outfit but a combat-line-company most of the day is devoted to hopes, reminiscences, jokes, plans, doggerel, art-work, and assorted folk-lore of fornication; and third, a rather uncomfortable personal feeling, staring past passers-by on an avenue, rudely ignoring occasional smiles of old folk and the playful greetings of children waving at the columns going by. For a few it would seem to be a properly harsh uncompromising personal attitude toward barbarians (they did use rubber hoses and flush them with hot water until your bowels burst!). For a very few others it is politically futile and wrong-headed—the new burgomaster is powerless and without prestige, and the people (like the Germans who have been stopping me and inquiring eagerly about newspapers: Army or civilian, in English or German, but something!) survive in a national vacuum—and morally, it is part of the deep and enervating emptiness of the whole war.

Enervating, too, in its smaller but more immediate way, has been the dreadful farce in which our so-called Historical Section has been engaged. The details are so mean and trivial it pains me to think what some monographer of future years will make of the "historical program of World War II"—she will no doubt explore patiently all the directives, and all the manuscripts, and come away with a contrived myth of abstracted events: precisely as we do in our own military research. Ranke is with us every moment through the vast labors of investigation, but the end-product narratives are invariably "as Things Never Actually Happened." History has disjointed our times, and it is neither being made nor written "properly."

A headquarters full of historians, and who would believe what goes on? The Colonel and his Grand Vizier have gone to Paris. Goddard is, of course, a fool, an honest, hard-working, ill-equipped, ignorant man. (The other day he was editing the manuscripts of the recent period and insisted on a half-a-dozen changes—"this battalion could not possibly have taken this route of advance: we'll move them through the woods"—"you can't have both companies attacking at the same time, and I don't care whether they did or not, the chief of staff will simply think we're dumb! Space them twenty minutes apart..." It was absurd and unbelievable.) Duncan is neither a fool nor honest, and he has managed to work himself into authority. He busies himself most of the week with his romances and sight-seeing, and [he] pauses long enough at his desk to issue an innumerable number of pompous memoranda designed only to cut everybody's efficiency in half. (And he has had a notable success.) Davis continues to look impressive and indispensable as the chief historian. He goes through a file of the *Beachhead News* to make up his phase outline, and then departs for a "terrain reconnaissance," which means, as usual, Lunéville and "fraternization." In literal chaos and confusion the researchers await his return, and then get no clarity but only further injunctions on the necessity of meeting the "target date" for all chapters. (Unless the narrative is finished, you see, the General will not "rotate" him home!) So Sutton wastes a few weeks doing research which Dyer has already completed; everyone competes for the same G-2 and G-3 documents, for every chapter runs on to every other. Dyer, who for all his eccentricities, is able and intelligent, has long ago ceased trying. ("When the Major tore the heart out of his Rhône Valley parallel-pursuit analysis," Carter explains, "he just about quit trying to write military history! Old Charlie changes a verb, puts in a comma and two quotation marks, and his job is done.") This morning Davis was a little concerned about the meaning of "subsequent." "Dyer, it means 'before,' doesn't it?" Dyer snapped: "Sweet Jesus, no! It means 'after'!" (The Sergeant is leaving soon anyway, returning to his "water point," which will probably take him back to Italy.) Gottlieb diddles with his notes, chewing on his gum furiously, fingering the dictionary for every other sentence. Eggers and Jordan are in the field roaming about the front with no earthly notion of what they are supposed to do. Waters has just returned; mission was accomplished: he brought back a radio. Weinstein frankly admits that his labors for the week were fourteen air-mails, sixteen V-Mails, and two cablegrams. Mooney fondles his latest "bird-dog" story, reading and rereading it, pleased as punch with its bulk and typography and sheer lovely completedness. He reads back sentences to me (which I wrote for him) and asks me what I think of it huh; and then puts on exhibition the table of contents and captions, and proceeds to brush off my criticisms (comments on my very own work!): "You forget that what I'm trying to do is . . ." —But those are small things. What strikes me more forcefully is that he continues to miss his own points—he feels so much, but understands nothing, and embraces so much of life without seriously digesting a single experience. Last night he left our burlesque themes and went off on the deep end of "Joe in the Foxhole" again. "What do we know of the War? Only he's fighting it, suffering and miserable and dirty! We sit here in rear echelon and appreciate nothing of what he's going through. . ." etc. etc. I have had enough of that kind of thing, and I think I shut him up. We have made an effective joke and a vaudeville routine of all the foolish, pulpy, grandiloquent, hypocritical and empty-souled pieties of the War. But every once in a while discipline breaks, and someone succumbs to what only that fine American expletive can sum up: "bullshit." It is so far from being a genuinely sincere return to seriousness and values, or to humility and a shaking tragic sense of the war, that it could only leave me dejected and angry. The war, or rather the miserable campaign, with its endless engagements and pushing forward, day after night of assembling and jumping off and digging in and assaulting and patrolling, has indeed made for suffering. And we have shared very little if any of it. But all the self-tortured sympathy, all the wracked expressions of self-recrimination, serve only to disguise the weakness and anxiety of our overwrought conscience. The great problem of personal guilt, which shapes every aspect of character and personality, is neither solved nor even faced. What is involved in the self-deprecation is the simple formula of masochism. The mechanism is unsubtle: the wounds of breast-beating and flagellation induct us into the blood-brotherhood of battle. We, too, have endured the dark days! We contrive a convenient verbal unhappiness, and by virtue of nervous eloquence legitimate it as suffering. Once again pity has become vulgarized and corrupted into a deceit for self-love.

The evening fled at a hectic pace. Hamilton had returned from Worms with several cases of fine wine, "Liebfraumilch," and bottles were being merrily emptied. (Hamilton, by the way, is doing nothing these days, waiting only for the hour when the whole History will explode in our faces. I find him reading Froude and Livy and *Readers' Digest* and H. G. Wells, and occasionally he would make a suggestion, "At this point in the narrative, I think, we ought to include a half-dozen blank sheets, and our legend should read: 'During this period operations were so horribly dull that nothing of interest need be noted.'") Disputes of all kinds were raging in every office, and if I couldn't make out the points at issue, it has after all become so easy to identify themes. As always the conversation was dominated by Cynicism and Boredom. Special vocabularies have been devised to express the range of sentiments and prejudices. For months now we have lived with each other and worked with the same problems and shared the same grievances. We can't, as a matter of fact, bear to hear each other talk, and what is there really to say? And so every remark is littered with the rich collection of stylized circumlocutions picked up in the run from Marseilles and Cherbourg to the Rhine. At least the clichés are fairly fresh and relatively original—there is "beaucoup" (usually "bo-koo" and sometimes "bo-koops"), "tray beans," "trayz interessantai," and "ah wee"; nobody leaves but he "partees," and in the end everything comes down to *c'est la guerre* (sometimes "say la jerry"). Linguistic devices are frantically improvised to impart some flashing new color to everyday speech. Patter about the weather revolves closely around "bony day" and chit-chat about women turns sedulously on "cooshay aveck" and "combyen" and "sharee." The jargon is more than a mere new vulgate of slang, for here among us it is employed with a knowing desperation. It is almost as if the very structure of language has become feverish and hysterical! Nothing is immune from the sickness of war. We have been dispossessed from life, will, ambition, dignity, and even from tragedy. We have been robbed, had our souls and hearts cut, left lost and helpless. And in the end there are not even words.

I myself was caught up in the controversy of the Carpenter case, and as usual Carter was pressing the argument for Freud, and Dyer for sainted Thomas Aquinas and the great Immanuel Kant. Carter was eloquent. "Now, look! It's really very simple. Carpenter jumped off with everything set against him. His personal, his psychological T/O called for homosexuality.[53] And all his life he has been waging a great campaign! He has refused consistently to give ground! He could retreat or surrender and go out searching for a nice young boy, or a clean old man... But no! The repression of society's ways, and his own subconscious discipline, have held him to the line. And so while he's never slept with a woman, or even kissed one—he told me so himself!—his sexual deficiencies have never broken him nor diverted him from normalcy. He's won his battle, but what a casualty! He flutters and waves his hands and squeaks, and diddles and daddles and piddles with some stamp collection of Gustavus Adolphus, or a hunk of baroque from Frederick Barbarossa, or maybe a ruin which suggests to his ultra-sensitive antiquarianism the influence of Mosque stylisms on Roman architecture via the Levantine trade of the Pistoia merchants. Or something... Carpenter is the portrait of the frustrated homosexual as historian. Mind you, he is not really aware of any of this! After all, how many people have either the intelligence—let me say training—or the courage to know or to face their inner psychic life. No, he is probably very happy pursuing what he knows as a pleasant and interesting hobby! But the line of departure was homosexuality! And his current phase line is a ridiculous frenetic aestheticism. His unconscious drives have taken him from the 'corn-hole,' so to speak, to the 'cubby-hole'..." "Sweet Jesus!" said Dyer. "Sweet Jesus! *Nec scire fas est omnia* (it is not permitted to know all things)—and yet you make your pronouncements as if god-like wisdom were yours. Ab initio I should say you are derelict in your theory. After the *Summa* and the *Critique of Pure Reason* how any intellectually trained mind can speak of the free will and the unconscious and the enslavement of the soul by ids and egos surprises me! [...] I can destroy your argument on this one single issue! Sin is public, corruption is conspicuous. If Carpenter is as you have made him out to be, and he has failed to make the grade, as you put it, failed to face the crisis of his own sexuality, and has lived his entire life in ignorance of the dark maneuvers of his soul, then you have lost the entire world! Then we all live and work and fail in darkness. Then none of us has hope for salvation, for none of us can ever know our terrible ungodly predicament. Who can face his sins when displacement and sublimation and the subconscious rule the universe?"

Dyer was a little wide off the mark all evening. Carter pressed him wildly, and Maske sat in the corner keeping score. Occasionally Dyer would win a point or two for "effective counter-battery fire," or "withdrawing to more favorable positions according to plan." But on the whole Carter's rebuttals were penetrating his positions almost at will. Maske insisted that Dyer might conceivably have reserves, and so it was ruled that only a phase of the argument had come to a close. "Dyer has been temporarily repulsed with heavy losses," Maske's After-Action report read. But according to my account, the Worms Liebfraumilch had cut all lines of communications some hours before.

[...]

25 April 1945, Darmstadt

A morning of stories and characters. Ferguson returned from Romilly, and is now a master of the techniques and formulas of military government: "You're the boss, see, and what you say goes, see! You move into this little town, down there at the school they call's it a *Gemeinde*, and you sets yourself up! Move into a castle or something like that, live pretty good, see, and run things! It might get a little lonely—but, hell! If she's pretty she's a DP! They got me slated for Property Control. And you don't have to know German. I picked up pronunciation down at Romilly, but Jesus! you don't have to know the language to get along. There was a little gal at Troyes, and we got along swell, see. I says, *vooz avvy mari*—you married—and she says, *wee, prisonnier*—a PW in Germany—and then I says, too bad, *dommage, dommage*—and you're all shacked up. It's a good deal, a real good deal! Anyway, we got this little detachment and Christ there's a lotta rules but I think it's the old baloney. When I was down there there was a lot of fuss and feathers over requisitioning property and taking over German equipment and that kind of thing."

[...]

K. returned from a brief visit to one of the prison camps, now jammed with whole Nazi regiments and divisions. Stopped and spoke to one of the soldiers. He was a member of the *Schnelltruppen*. "*Schnelltruppen?*" That was a new one. "What are those?" *Schnelltruppen*—"We were conscripted two days ago—committed to the line yesterday—and we surrendered today... *Schnelltruppen!*" And Mooney returned from the hospital. One sidelight was rather striking. Most of the tents of the "evacuation" detachment were taken by sick prisoners, Germans. And one afternoon in the shower, the surgeon ranted. "God! Do I get sick of this! Out here in the middle of nowhere, with nothing to do, nobody to speak to, nobody but these goddamn krauts, who don't deserve to live in the first place... One of these days I'll just kill them all and be well rid of the whole filthy lot!" You see, you see, Mooney went on, "you see how easy it would be to make a mistake and fabricate a tale of atrocity! Why here's the foundation for a Horror Hospital and a Mad Sadistic Butcher of a chief doctor!" The point should have been very well taken. The press has been full of nothing but grisly lurid tales of unique art-work made of the tattooed skin of a Nazi victim, and torture chambers with mechanized medieval wracks with the echoes of screaming still ringing through the dungeons, and so forth literally. It would appear that there is quite a concerted campaign to prevent any sober civil political thoughts on the German question. I don't suggest at all that the evidence of the genuine Nazi barbarities be overlooked. But nothing is ever offered to be understood. The outrages appear in the conventional context of a sensational headline with a few loose monstrous details. And this constitutes "orientation" for the troops, orientation indeed for the melodrama of America in European affairs, Act Two. Strings draw our puppet heroes and villains across the stage—Patton the Terrible and Eisenhower the Cool, Fat Stuff Goering and Loud Mouth Goebbels and the rest of the Murderous Beasts—and we sit conveniently as an audience trained in our cues for hisses, applause, anger, sentiment, and knightly noble hauteur. Why not face it? How should the profound issues of War have dignity and seriousness when nothing in the discipline of our society makes for intellectual equipment and responsibility? What is there in our culture, commercialized and vulgarized as it is, to fortify a sense of moral integrity and idealism and an earnest impulse towards some large generous personal duty? Our caesars are triumphant, and upon the meat which they have fed the whole poor world will be nourished.

27 April 1945, Darmstadt

The man's name was D'Hooghe and somewhere in a Darmstadt cellar he had managed to salvage a magnificent library.[54] Or so Frau Greulich told me, in her own clipped British accent. D' Hooghe was an Englishman by birth and education, lived in an ancestral Belgian village, and found himself under the Nazi regime in Berlin something of a favored bookseller. How he had gotten to Darmstadt, or as a matter of fact where and why he was hiding, was more than a little mysterious. Except for the fact that I couldn't squeeze a single element of melodrama out of the situation the whole affair might have shaped up as an adventure. As it was our search was futile and I remained content with a representative local collection in a battered room of the Lagerhausstrasse schoolhouse to which Frau Greulich led me.

What surprised me about the school library was its haphazard Nazification! There were to be sure all manner of Hitlerist literature about—Führer-approved histories, and anthologies of poetry, and political picture-books, and a formidable series of the official texts: Rosenberg's *Mythus des 20. Jahrhunderts*, *Mein Kampf*, and innumerable other swastika-stamped texts. Yet apparently the old liberal culture of Germany could not be entirely liquidated. On every shelf something remained which stood in tacit defiance of the totalitarian state of mind. I browsed in wonder and excitement, and spent long hours of several evenings reading and leafing through the books.

I was first startled by an anthology called *Der deutsche Genius*, which had been edited in 1926 by Hanns Martin Elster—and the introduction was written by Thomas Mann! And the collection of writings was far from being a safe and sober schoolbook. Hegel was there—critical, dialectical Hegel, who had "died," Nazi intellectuals insisted, when National Socialism triumphed! [...] Hutten was there [...] Naturally, von Treitschke was represented, with Bismarck and Richard Wagner, and others who were conveniently used or twisted for ideological purposes. But what is significant is that a rather fair and representative collection of German national literature sat unmolested in a Nazi schoolhouse. Even the black efficiency of the Reichskulturkammer[55] could not fashion a complete pure Gestapo culture! There is something about the inertia of a book on a shelf which can withstand the movements of even the most powerful barbarian reaction. Perhaps a few curious, eager students found strange and dangerous ideas in these pages of Goethe and Freytag and Schiller and Kant. (Also: Schleiermacher, Meister Eckhart, Luther, Jakob Böhme, Paul de Lagarde. *Der deutsche Glaube und die Menschheit*. Beethoven, Grillparzer, Franz Schubert, Jean Paul, Schopenhauer, Novalis [*Die blaue Blume*], Ludwig Tieck. *Von deutscher Kunst*, and *Das deutsche Wesen*. Ernst Moritz Arndt, Mörike, Theodor Storm, Friedrich Ratzel, and of course Karl der Grosse. I was touched by a selection under *Deutsche Freiheit*—it was the Grimm brothers' *Wilhelm Tell*!)

[...]

In the section on literary criticism I found a volume of Wilhelm Dilthey's, *Von deutscher Dichtung und Musik*. "Feurig, rein, tiefsinnig, gütig," Hugo von Hofmannsthal wrote in his introductory memoir, "welch ein Mann"... And, I thought, reading his pages on *Die ritterliche Dichtung und das nationale Epos*

(Hartmann von Aue, Wolfram von Eschenbach, *Tristan und Isolde, Das Nibelungenlied*, etc.)—on eighteenth-century music (Bach, Haydn, Handel, Mozart, Beethoven)—and finally notes on Klopstock, Schiller, Jean Paul—I though indeed, what a breath of culture and scholarship and sensitivity!
[...]
Further along: the Gestapo contingent. *Das Schicksalsbuch des deutschen Volkes. Von Hermann dem Cherusker bis Adolf Hitler,* Hans Grote, 1933. Erich Czech-Jochberg's *Deutsche Geschichte. Nazionalsozialistisch gesehen.* This, too, was published in '33, and from my hasty inspection both seemed to be more opportunist in character than a real ideological effort to reinterpret history. The tone is nationalist, but not fascist in Hitler's special way. I read for example the chapters on Luther and Franz von Sickingen and Ulrich von Hutten, and there were no striking departures from familiar theses about the Reformation and the peasants' revolt and the "communism" of Thomas Müntzer. Significantly enough a 1935 study was already thoroughly Nazi! [...]

What pathos and historic drama there were in the quiet and mustiness of this bombed-out library!

We made some promises, Frau Greulich and I, that we must have known were only warm verbal exchanges. She was reading an old biography of Lord Byron for which curiously enough she made apologies. I said I would bring her some English books to read. She suggested that I return some day when we could talk again under somewhat more favorable circumstances. She gave me a present—a combined English-German edition of *Hamlet*, which quite overwhelmed me. I couldn't help fingering the text in bed, propping my flashlight up against the cot and wall and reading by its beam.
[...]

28 April 1945, Darmstadt

The old academic questions of "the future of Germany "and "what to do" are now almost an immediate embarrassing reality. I wonder what changes on the high-level have been made in international policy, and whether any large program will ever make its way down effectively to the low units of execution. From what I have seen of the actualities of military science and military government would leave no one too sanguine about the substance of any of the great Allied rhetoric. The "real war" has been something far different from the formal arrangements of the general staffs. The face of battle and conquest, truly seen, is unrecognizable in the mask created by plan and propaganda. I hardly believe the programs for European punishment and social reconstruction need engage any one's faith as cruelly as once the naive and misled hopes for peace, war, liberation, caught up our mass enthusiasms. Between the conception and the execution, as the poet [T. S. Eliot] says, falls the shadow. The truth and tragedy of our time lies there, under the shadow of our terrible historic inadequacy.

Nothing is so difficult these days as to discover "what is happening." I simply record now a few scattered notes which may give something of the local Hessen picture. The burgomasters and the military governors are functioning and busy. In some cases the "reliability" of the civilian officials has been re-checked and Nazi backgrounds revealed. In a few others party connections were sufficient grounds for removal. On the whole, however, the politics of conquest is not quite the politics of anti-fascism. Yet there is little real administrative trouble. Civil administration becomes more and more effective and everybody appears to be cooperative. Here in Hessen, I was told, "civilian cooperation has been good. Officials have obeyed orders, and the people have been quiet." As for the western areas further back—"In general, the attitude of the people of Westmark[56] may be characterized by saying that they are obedient and docile, for the most part, with an underlying stunned indifference to the occupation. Outwards the German public has been silent and guarded in its attitude regarding the occupation. Public officials appointed have been cooperative, but this does not indicate that the German people welcome the occupation in any way. They have been so regimented for years that they are well-disciplined and respond to orders even though they do not like the orders nor the people issuing them." Or so the military governors report. In the Rhine cities apparently the pressure of the "vacuum" grows. In Homburg, I hear, the burgomaster requested that a newspaper be permitted in his town. I know little more than that, there is as yet no German press anywhere, and what was done there was merely to post mimeographed copies of BBC news in conspicuous places. Elsewhere loud-speakers were improvised to supplement town criers. The number of disturbances and crimes are significantly low. Most of the high responsible Nazis fled. In Neustadt when a huge collection of Party documents were seized many hung themselves. Occasionally a Gestapo man is picked up. What difficulties there are are minor—clashes among the Displaced Persons, looting by DPs and civilians, circulation violations. And the "Youth problem" varies. Here in Darmstadt, I know, two boys are being held for raiding an American warehouse. Not far away three children were injured while playing with US hand-grenades. So the occupation goes. . . I only wish I had more opportunities to get away and look into things a little more deeply. Last night I heard something about Polish and Russian liaison officers working in the area, but nothing really much. The Russian "visited centers throughout the *Gau* during the week and aided materially in effecting internal camp administrations within the Russian groups." How I should have liked to ask a few questions about that! As for the social situation the Crisis as yet consists only of apparently small petty difficulties. Few, if any, of the German courts are operating. There is little financial business, but banks are preparing to open; of those not destroyed, most have considerable cash on hand, "are financially stable and will be operative as soon as the tactical situation permits." A touch of gossip about hoarding—the frantic great withdrawals of last November, which almost crashed the banking structure until the Rundstedt breakthrough stabilized things, and then the continued private accumulations of cash from late January on. There seems to be an adequate food production at least for this area. The estimate is that the one hundred thousand or so "displaced persons" will be supported on a two-thousand-calorie diet, and the "enemy civilian population" on one thousand to one thousand five hundred. Here there is a shortage of wheat and seed potatoes for spring planting; whole crops will be lost, and what with Bavarian and Prussian supplies "missing," the civilian bread ration will probably be cut to zero. Which means more AMG firmness—"displaced persons should be fed before the civilian population can be considered." Sizeable supplies are being uncovered regularly—typewriters in Rimbach, Kotex in Winterhausen, millions of cigarettes in Bronnbach. Sergeants every now and then come up with a fortune in *Reichsmarken*. Farming is being resumed but not on a large-scale or organized plan. G-5 calls it a "return-to-the-farm" movement, and the "return" is the main agricultural activity. Machinery is plentiful, but no fuel (diesel) oil; population of beef and dairy cattle almost normal, but only available labor consists of children and old women. Small fields and truck gardens are cultivated, which makes the farm situation just a little brighter than the industrial picture with factories smashed, electric power disrupted, water systems broken, and all communications at a standstill. (All undistributed mail has been impounded, and only yesterday the woman at the Laundry in Darmstadt asked me to mail a letter for her—to relatives in Philadelphia!) Archives are being established in castles (off-limits) and the museums are protected. There have been many reports of valuable pieces missing—collected by the troops passing through. The Twelfth Armored, I know, has a great gallery of paintings, and GIs have made personal trophies of the priceless Cologne Museum and Strasbourg University items which have been scattered in caches in this area. Which just about exhausts all my little scribblings of the past few weeks. One more fragment: in Würzburg, as it was being stormed by the Forty-Second Division, the CG declared—all civilians in houses not bearing a white flag would be shot. Sound trucks made the announcement and the people were given some time to comply. I imagine the sheets, table-cloths, pillow-cases fluttered from every window-sill. But I wonder if anything "untoward" happened. There is a slight suggestion of another O'Daniel-Strasbourg affaire here.

30 April 1945, Gmünd

Moving day again, and the morning was cold and threatening. There was talk that troops had reached München as the convoys left—and we remained behind to wait in Darmstadt... for the laundry. There was still some *bügeln* to do so we spent an hour looking in vain for the Russische Kapelle which the last Czar built for his wife, the former Princess of Hessen-Darmstadt. We found the shattered museum building, and the library (with Jakob Grimm and Justus Liebig looking down at us), and then returned for our bundles. From Darmstadt across the Rhine to Worms. The river was green and the city was rubble. The driving rain had stopped and the sun finally made an appearance. I picked up another official German newspaper, this number featuring a huge portrait of Harry Truman, and then spent the better part of three hours hunting down a wine-cellar for Hamilton. He was determined not to leave Worms without several cases of Liebfraumilch. I took a quick glance at the *Lutherdenkmal* and then picked up five bottles of burgundy. We raced past the Lutherkirche (EIN FESTE BURG IST UNSER GOTT on a frieze over partially broken columns, and a bombed out dome), and finally found Fritz Clemens and two cases. We, of course, paid for the wine, and the wine-dealer was warm and accommodating as per international occupational convention.

It rained in the Neckar valley and foothills and further south there was hail and snow. Hour after hour in a wintry countryside and crowded single-lane traffic and we were quite insensitive to the landscape, the route, the people. Weinstein was miserable and frozen, "I'm hurtin', hurtin' like mad, I really am!" and mumbled threats to every civilian on the road or street; long-legged German boys (or perhaps it was only that they wore abbreviated shorts) stared at us during the crossroad jams, and he would shout, "Kick 'em in the ass, somebody! Kick 'em in the ass!" It wasn't apparently a matter of war-guilt, but unhappy as we all were there must have been a crime somewhere and this perhaps would be a fitting punishment. "Get away from there!" The poor lads must have jumped ten feet from the fender they would touch very uncertainly. "Get away before I boot you from here to Berchtesgaden!" Hamilton's drawling contributions, all of which are difficult to make out, and most of which I am glad I missed with the bumps of the jeep's rear, were at a minimum. In Heilbronn—a broken, deathly city—he remarked only, "revenge is sweet." A few minutes later he went on to expound some theory of German history—"Germany's greatest mistake was its national withdrawal from the eighteenth-century princely governments. What these people need is a wise, benevolent despot! Then they could find both peace and good government..." etc. etc. Heilbronn was almost hideous in its desolation. The formations of stone and brick fragments already looked old and commonplace. The city must have had a population of about one hundred thousand, and I suspect practically no war industry. But this, after all, was a key center on the road to the so-called Bavarian Redoubt, and the SS was ordered to hold. The Hundredth Division fought for days.[57] When Heilbronn fell, just about two weeks ago (14–15 April), the artillery and the air force had leveled another city ... And the ruins stood, monuments to no nostalgic grandeur or glory, but only to the murderous riot of a world. On the trails through valleys and mountains—magnificent slopes with wide-sweeping sculptured greenery—mysterious mounts which rose imperiously to a sharp peak from quiet plains of flatland—tilled, discolored hills which looked like old gray patched worn overcoats.

Late: in Gmünd (Schwäbisch Gmünd), and I learn that we were to be in Stuttgart but the French have refused SHAEF's order to move out! Heard, too, that Mussolini was dead, shot at Como after a trial by partisans, and his body lay in a square in Milan. So ends Il Duce and his *fascismo*. All the threads of our history seem to be finally rolling themselves on to some spool. I hardly know what to say, how to look. Mussolini condemned and eliminated by antifascists! Why, my first "historic memory," I can recall, was a newsreel image of Il Duce on a Roman balcony before a roaring cheering mob! These are days when all the chapters in the history of what we like to call our times are being written to a close. "Our Times" indeed! Is all this barbarism and tragedy really ours? And can this chaotic melodrama, this cheap miserable performance, be a time, an era, a truly historic epoch? Surely we, and our records, deserve something better...

5 May 1945, Gmünd

With Augsburg and Munich fallen, and the troops feeling their way about on the Austrian, Czechoslovakian, and Italian borders, our "Seventh Army Rear Echelon" moves again. Which prompted some one: Now that SHAEF Forward has been set up in Frankfurt, the American staff is very embarrassed—it is being said, that Louis XIV housed both ends of his horses in the Versailles wing; Eisenhower keeps only his Rear... At any rate, we packed again and lugged our boxes again.

At almost the last moment Jordan showed up again and with another fabulous haul. He had been with the Third Division throughout the push into the Bavarian Redoubt, and had moved in with the Fifteenth Regiment in Augsburg and Nuremberg. He was long and eloquent with tales about the tunnels in Nuremberg, and the horrors of Dachau; raiding the Agfa factory for cameras and film equipment; shopping for sardines (the Colonel loved them) and parachutes (excellent material for scarves); a drunken escapade in Augsburg

(This he confided to me alone, for the information he hinted might be dangerous; he can't remember what happened, whether he slept with the girl who had been with him "when I captured me a house... God Almighty, I coulda gotten killed. I waked up in the mohnin, with a hellava hangover and my .45 sittin' there all by itself on the table!" Nor does he quite remember exactly how he smashed up the jeep). He made a haul of books for me, "in gratitude," and came up mostly with Vandervelde on love and marriage!

The casualties are mounting: Sutton[58] was rammed by a weapons-carrier on Thursday, as he was returning from Heidelberg. He was tossed out of the jeep and onto the road, unhurt. Damage: one wheel. Mooney was almost killed when a huge truck-and-trailer broke off a limb of a tree which crashed down onto his vehicle. The roof collapsed and the windshield was shattered. The Colonel was a little upset, but that was all.

The trip to Augsburg. German girls on the road, smoking what was obviously American cigarettes. The driver smiled knowingly, remarked: "A pack a throw..." Familiar scenes: van after van of Wehrmacht prisoners passing us. In one small village, an old lady waving goodbye from the sidewalk. Faded roadside signs: TRINKT COCA COLA—HIER STETS EISKALT. Traffic jams in Ulm. The old Imperial city where Bonaparte defeated the Austrians 140 years ago. We cut off the crowded highway to Münsterplatz and took two or three quick glances at the great fourteenth-century Gothic cathedral. The road through the town was still difficult. Our truck crawled along. The town was ruins. Like all the others, like all the dozens, hundreds of others. My god! A whole continent of rubble! On crumbled walls, chalk scrawlings with messages, obituary and change of address. "*FAM. HACKER. Nicht tot. Bergerweg 7.*" Pontoon bridge over the Danube: a little deep-green stream... Beyond Neu-Ulm (Mussolini-Strasse) on to the autobahn. Rough ride, lanes pitted with holes; German demolition. Skeletons of Luftwaffe fighter-planes in the woods along the highway: the autobahn must have been used as a runway.

Another *Kaserne.* Up went the boxes, the luggage. In came the rumors: moving again in a few days. Peace might break out tomorrow morning at eleven—the story is Patch has signed some kind of peace treaty. Or so the dinner conversation went. Jordan walked through with an armful of fish. And where in hell did the fish come from? "Where do you think they came from? The Danube! Where else would fish around here come from?" Lord, Jordan went fishing in the Danube! But no, he confessed, they were given to him. A bunch of Russians stood around the banks grenading schools of fish with German ammunition. The cook, he said, was very glad to have them. To bed. Oh, he had something more for me. A map which had hung in a *Kommandant*'s office. He pointed out infantry and artillery positions of Murat's forces in his assault of Wertingen, 8 October 1805. "The campaign against Austria," he carefully explained to me, "Napoleon. . ." I took the map, mumbled thanks, and dropped to sleep.

6 May 1945, Augsburg

Spent most of the day waiting for the Colonel to come to a decision. Now that I could go out for a week or so the issue was where. Normally of course it would be an important consideration to discover why I was going out, or where some field research would be most valuable. I myself would care to go out to the Third Division, which took Nuremberg and fought in Munich; or the Forty-Second, which hit the concentration camp at Dachau with the Forty-Fifth. I learn too that the Fifteenth Regiment came into Augsburg the day of the local revolution which ousted the Wehrmacht and the Gestapo and the *Volkssturm*. ("My old" Third battalion found the bridges and roads all secured by townsfolk who surrendered the city to the first patrols.) At any rate, there are at least half-a-dozen stories which need to be gotten now, or they are quite gone forever. But another day went by. Duncan and Davis were out, and I had to wait. They were gone, of course, on another "terrain reconnaissance" which has for a long time now been a standing joke of the section. Their current tour took them to Dachau and when Davis came back this evening he was positively gurgling, "they let us in, they let us! We saw it all, we saw it all!" Duncan in his own turn summed up the day in his sober pontifical way, "it was, gentlemen, a most enjoyable trip, a most enjoyable afternoon. . ." And then he reconsidered. "Of course, it was horrible. The sight was a terrible one. So many bodies, rotting away, being cremated. What a house of horror that was! No, I don't mean 'enjoyable.' Let me say it was 'instructive' or 'profitable.'" I suppose now I will leave in a day or two. But Dachau has now been off-limits mainly for medical reasons: typhus. And many of the units may be beginning to move out of the Munich area.

The war in Europe is now only a matter of days. Two more German armies capitulated yesterday, which just about concludes organized opposition to the forces on the Seventh Army front. The whole Nazi fortress has been cut and destroyed. The news this evening is that Daladier, Reynaud, Weygand, Gamelin, and some others, are "next door" at Forward.[59] [. . .] Salzburg and Innsbruck in southernmost Germany have been taken and Patch has linked with Clark in Italy. Nothing remains. Berchtesgaden is gone. Hans Fritzsche now reports that Hitler and Goebbels were suicides in Berlin. The German broadcast for today was simply—that because of communication difficulties the latest communiques were not available! Mooney drove several Nazi generals back from München yesterday morning, and when he remarked that

Kesselring was at that moment surrendering all the forces to General Devers, they muttered: "Thank *Gott!*"

Took a brief run this evening into Augsburg. The first sizeable city with whole sections untouched by the destruction. Many squares, to be sure, were little else but heaps of ruins. But by and large the city stands. We drove down Fuggerstrasse, and finally turned in towards the great ancient cathedral, called simply I believe *Der Dom*. The caretaker showed himself behind one of the doors and we were admitted. It was a magnificent structure. To the left as we came in was the obviously older and original section—built, so we were told, in the eighth century. (Augsburg itself, the Augusta Vindelicorum of the Romans, was founded by a colony sent out by Augustus, 12 BC, after the conquest of the Vindelici.) On the right were the various additional sections, kept more or less in style except for smaller more Gothic details. The cathedral as it stands today was completed some time early in the fifteenth century. Early in the sixteenth Luther attended here, but the church remained Catholic and was a key point in the Conference at Augsburg in 1530. Or so I piece together the history. 15 February 1944. The night of the big bombing. He knew that day the way he must know his birthdate. A huge bomb landed just beyond the cathedral and destroyed part of the garden. Incendiaries started a blaze in the towers and they were some twenty-five hours in putting out the fire. Little damage, however, was evident, except of course for the stained-glass windows, all of which, with the exception of but a handful of panes, had been shattered. St. Anna Kirche, a far smaller Protestant church, was "off-limits." All gates were locked and each door had the ubiquitous *Zutritt verboten*. Next door I noted the book-displays in the window, and a series of Langenscheidt dictionaries caught my eye: I must come back and see what I can pick up for my coming long years in Occupied Germany.

Parting remark at the cathedral: said the caretaker, as we looked back at the rubble in the garden and the crushed wing, *Grüsse von Amerika...* I flared up for a moment. No, no. Greeting not from America nor from Americans—but from *dem Führer selbst!* This and the ruined cathedrals in Cologne and Frankfurt and Speyer and Aachen and Nuremberg are all gifts to religion and art from Adolf Hitler and his National Socialism! Somebody remarked behind us, "He understood what you said..." I went on with some other details of an argument. The caretaker had a small half-embarrassed smile on his face as he nodded acquiescence, agreement. I went off and drove away, wondering whether I should have been angered at all. Down Maximilianstrasse: as always, faces staring out of the windows. Do they window-gaze all day long? Or did they hear us coming? They seemed as curious and unbelieving as we, but in many houses young girls smiled broadly at us, and in several even beckoned to us. We returned via Holbeinstrasse and I wished we could make the Fugger Museum before we move again.

8 May 1945, Augsburg

You are now entering Augsburg. Courtesy of the Fifteenth Infantry.
Warm sunny day. Left 0900.
The war was over.
Convoys of trucks, jammed with prisoners; an old woman, a young girl waving goodbyes; they walked on slowly.
Children playing in dugouts, in dismantled hulks of anti-aircraft equipment.
Third Division road-signs.
Dachau, monstrous growth of modern society—off-limits.
Patch order. Boxcars cleaned, empty.
Typhus danger. DDT powder sprayer at entrance.
Old woman outside. Scribbling a note to her two boarders, two Yugoslavians, who were still alive she had learned. Curious attachment.
Gay painted signs and figures introducing the Camp.
Road to Munich. Concentration camp Allach.
Untouched: Standard Oil filling-station; which tickled me. Only last night: Dyer's theory—Heidelberg untouched, Woolworth had five and dime there; you never see Standard or Shell in ruins, do you?
Munich still stood—but nothing was untouched; the courthouse structure was there, damaged, dirty, struck and ruined in a dozen places. The *Justizpalast*, a civilian identified it for me. *Haus des Rechts*, she explained. *Haus des Unrechts*, I cracked. *Ja, ja*, and she laughed with a note of agreeable bitterness. Magnificent old buildings; now only ugly ruins.
Crossed Isar for third time searching for the Beer Hall, the Brown House.[60]
Girls flirting with US soldiers on Nymphenburgerstrasse.
Lunched at Forty-Fifth Division. Meal upset by brass band playing, and entrance of Jeff. Caffery[61] and other notables.
More ruins. Siegestor. Theater, Cathedral, Museum, *Regierungsgebäude*.
B.'s main concern for the day: his "horniness," the women, the pieces of ass, the "nookie."
Flatlands out of Munich.
First glimpse of the Alps. Vague, black, snow-peaked in the distance, like the back of a quiet sleeping monster.
Planes strewn along everywhere; the last of the Luftwaffe.
Bombers, fighters, rockets for miles—noses and propellers twisted and staring blankly into the sky; others dewheeled, flatbellied on the green fields.
Hitchhikers, wanderers, pilgrims.
Convoys of small vehicles: Nazis driving!
Girls and women on the road, lying around on the greensward, at crossroads in villages and cities... and the unabashed exchanges of lustful glances.
Deggendorf and the Alps foothills.

Corps G-2 documents; the collapse of the German army; the demoralization, desertion; the revolt in Munich; capture of leaders; von Rundstedt; Frick; etc.

To bed. Cool night; one blanket.

Figure 7. Posing in front of the Feldherrnhalle in Munich, once a central location of the 1923 Beer Hall Putsch, © Lasky Center, Munich.

9 May 1945

Morning—no war outside and the strong countryside smells came in strangely. Breakfast, and on the road.

Gasoline station on the autobahn: a Czech DP, Rudolph Hort: war prisoner taken in France, kept in Bernau camp. Worked in nearby war industries. Marched two hours to, and two hours from the plant. Ate carrots. Had soup made from potato peelings. Last days local government gave out small arms to help defend area! Prisoners took off and looted nearby towns, food, clothes, wine, etc. SS moved in, and slaughtered them in square. Four hundred killed.

On to Palling, and Forty-Second Division.

Little quiet village. High steeple of church flying surrender flag—white sheet, fluttering from belfry like a kite, pole plus crossstick. The inn is the officer's mess. Photo shop window: girls in white communion dresses; the old folk; the young local boys in Nazi uniforms, some grim, some smiling, all proud, all children.

More on revolts, disintegration of army.

Check on Jewish concentration camp at Laufen.

Gasoline in tank turned out to be Diesel oil or something. Jeep in a bad way.

Movie for the night—Olsen and Johnson.

Painted scenes on city hall; banners repainted, from Nazi insignia to Rainbow.

Brass band swinging it, moving into medley of British, Irish airs; calculated to defy the hills and the very atmosphere hanging in the valley.

Thursday, 10 May 1945

Anniversary of the Blitz on France. Five years since the strike at the lowlands. The conquerors have been swallowed up and destroyed in their victory.

Left Palling in the lazy warm sunlit morning; dirt roads, dusty, no activity in farmland. To Laufen.

Laufen internment camp. Hostages of Channel Islands; civilians; ex-soldiers; taken after Dieppe raid; aristocracy: Churchill's nephew, son of Princess Mary, King's sister; General Alexander's son; General "Bór" (Komorowski), leader of Polish insurrection! Just missed them. Recently evacuated to Army rear.

Concentration camp improvised by SS at Lebenau, the women's prison. Emergency holding point for political criminals, racial victims, hostages, etc.

Simple collection of barracks. Thin barefooted men in makeshift pajamas walking barefoot along trails. Girls in tight-fitting and short dresses barely meeting their stockings, strolling around (with playful eyes). Shaved heads. Recovering from starvation soup-and-bread rations.

1600 Jews (seized in the Polish ghetto and elsewhere) left Buchenwald. On the road for thirty days. Many died, others collapsed and were shot. Two hundred arrived here. Spoke to a few. Would never return to Poland—he had a *Zeide* in America! A long name of a city, he couldn't remember. Philadelphia? No, he couldn't remember, but he would find his *Zeide*. Spoke to a man from Łódź.

No, no Łódźers left. You'll find them all in the crematorium. He escaped before the ghetto was closed. Found some refuge in a work camp. Mothers paid thousands of *złoty* for men to do away with their children—anything than have them slaughtered by bayonets or thrown into sewer-pipes before their eyes.

The barbarities committed by Ukrainians in the German army.

Another: a worker in the crematorium. The trains came in with their cargo of Jews. Moved into wagons; almost half usually were dead. Gold teeth removed. (Constant interruptions; always reproved with that good-natured Jewish sternness—"Look. I worked there. I'll tell the story.") Preparations for the bath. Gas emitted from shower outlets. Screaming, howling, crying. Children lasted longer. Then all to the crematorium.

In Zamość and Łabunie. Mass executions. A great grave dug. First man shot—by the Gestapo team of three men: Langkampfer, Mazurik, Kolb—and placed in one corner. Next victim lies down, places head between corpse's legs— ("I'll show you, I'll show you," correcting my misunderstanding; demonstrates; the second and subsequent victims were alive!)—and then is shot. Completing the death list for the day, and filling every inch of available burial space.

Apparently healthy students from internment camp helping rehabilitation. Feeding: getting requisitions for food filled. Delousing and medical attention. Baths. Clothes. Doing everything they can.

A brotherhood of persecution. They carried men on backs for weeks; to drop him was to murder him; the SS permitted no stragglers. A couple of potatoes a day. The weak dropped. Hundreds and hundreds lost.

Yet, as one of them remarked—"It's not only their bodies which have suffered and been broken. Their spirits and character too. They're mean and spiteful; they'll steal. Lying has become a habit. They can't be straightforward or honest any more..."

And they were unrecognizable. One of the young boys heard his name called out by a broken wreck of a stranger. Ran up and embraced him and kissed him. It was his best friend—had gone to school for ten years together... A stranger.

The troops came. The SS had fled. Two old guards remained. The sick tortured Jews rose up, clasped hands with GIs, kissed them, cheered them, cried and waved to them. Twentieth Armored passing through. Was told of camp off the road. Celebrations.

Still local difficulties. "Stronger beating the weak. Minor difficulties, but they're hangover from the dark days. . ."

Maria.

Twenty-two. Inmate of the women's prison. Sturdy, healthy girl; pug-nose, might have been Irish. Had been away from home for eight years, working in Kassel war-industry plant. Finally took off on a trip for home. Seized, arrested, tried, sentenced. Eighteen months to serve. But has been "in" three years, working in grenade factory. And would serve to end of war. Father was a *Politischer*. Seized as "communistic tendencies" agitator; shot in 1940. Everything was forced. Compulsion. We had to *heil*. Or else. Up here and in here, we did different. But we were like prisoners always. The whole country was a prison house. So many arrests. Sometimes we thought everybody. You'll find more German prisoners in Nazi camps than were ever taken by you on the battlefield. When will we go home? Can we write, post letters?

Small group of Jews in their odd underwear, and some striped concentration-camp uniforms, singing, marching. Thin, unshaven, unkempt. "We're the last dirty ones!" They were going to the shower. DDT powder for delousing. The beginning perhaps of a new life, or just: life.

Elizabeth Kind; husband a Swiss-German. Lived in Berlin since 1932. Tall, thin, blonde; haggard, worried; spoke half in English, half German.

"Arrested 8 September 1943. Like so many of the arrests with no charges. They thought you were 'dangerous.' The clever people were enemies. The intelligent people. I was a lawyer, and therefore a potential agent against them. With me: the arrest of an architect, a doctor, and an engineer: oppositionists. Accusations came: member of the Berlin underground. And so they were.

Dr. Groscurth, a wonderful man, a wonderful doctor; executed a few months later.[62]

Yes, he was a friend of mine. All of them were wonderful, fine people. All died in our pitiful attempts to fight them back.

They used to print some leaflets, and some brochures for our propaganda. I say our though I didn't belong. It was however my cause. . . But we could do so little.

The Gestapo always penetrated. The triangular system was used. Only one man knew more than two others. Groups of three alone could be trapped if somebody broke down.

Many of our old Jewish friends were in hiding in our community.

But we were alone and isolated. The SS broke our hands; the people broke our hearts." (The phrase she uses: "the real Germans"!)

"Next month we'll be in London my mother once said. My husband (1940) simply said 'Ridiculous!' Maybe Hitler would be, but we couldn't believe it. We had to hope. We were outlawed from our family.

Prof. Weinbaum's daughter (Carnegie Institute) was hiding in my house; that was all I could hope to do. I had three small children! And how could I practice my profession? What nonsense, what criminality the Law had become! Why, if a German girl had anything to do with a French prisoner of war, and they worked on farms together for years; she would be sentenced to thirty-six to forty-eight months! And I would stand before the bar and—? Never.

We knew of the atrocities. Not all of them. But the German people knew of the Jews. And what did they do.

Every day became a trial, a task. We were desperate, beside ourselves to do something. Illegal work, but how and with what? The temptation for me as a housewife was somewhat less. But the men! Believe me, they were frantic to do something.

Like Groscurth we believed that we could fight and win only with the military defeat of Germany, of the Nazi army. Big sabotage was beyond our powers. But the doctor kept our people out of the conscription, got many out of the army with medical tricks. We got a few friends out of concentration camps by bribery.

But still as the years went on, we were more and more alone. Our best people were killed, spirited away. Others forgot, and went along with the regime.

Everything was in their power. Why if you picked up a short-hand book, the lessons said—transcribe: the SS is a fine and good and constructive force... The Nazi nonsense was poisoning the whole country.

And the poison remains. The slave habit is part of their make-up. Here in prison—among our own political prisoners—you can see it work. When the Colonel came and asked me to do some things for the others, nobody would accept my leadership. It had to take the old form. Official announcement. Orders up and down the line. What a tragedy. The Nazi routine has won out.

I have no hope for Germany. A little hope for the new generation, the children who will grow up. But new 'human beings' have to be created.

My own mother! She used to be so proud and glad of her Luftwaffe! Her Luftwaffe and how great it was, and how efficient, and how it used to bomb all the cities! My own mother!

There were good Germans. They are gone now.

I wouldn't trust any one, any institution. My own children will go abroad. Their schooling will be in Switzerland or in England.

We have universities but they have been deeply corrupted. And our religion. Christianity! But for year after year where was their Christianity? They knew what was happening to the Jews, but they stood by. The madmen murdered innocents, helpless; tortured fanatical minds. Step over somebody and you assume some kind of superiority. They trampled others down to build themselves up.

(She began to cry.) Prof. Weinbaum's daughter. Where can I find her now? And her children? Are they alive? How can I begin? Everything is in ruins, everything is lost. And my husband? He has been in flight. But no one can live with him! They have destroyed him! He is a broken man, out of his mind with grief and helplessness... And I, I am young, but look at me. I am thirty-five and I have gray hair and am already an old lady... But then I might have been dead.

The Gestapo called for a death sentence. But I think the court had some professional sympathy with me. Strange. I was a lawyer. Had stood in this courtroom many times. They let me go with a lighter sentence. And now? My sentence is over, but we will never be freed. We are slaves of our tragedy. Germany is our prison..."

Regina Kastenbauer: Arrested 14 November 1938; some time after Hitler invasion (13 March 1938).

Worked with central committee of Austrian CP.

A party stalwart. But then I am not sure. At end of conversation she tried to make sure that I was a Russian officer—which were her impressions of me throughout. So almost all she had to say should be discounted.

At first there was no disagreement with Stalin-Hitler. Then she confessed there was much distress. Dictatorship of proletariat talk. Strong character. Little sense of human wreckage. The struggle, always the struggle.

In Laufen: "Bobby" Montgomery—a Brooklyn negro entertainer!

Captured on tour with his Blackbirds in Copenhagen. Tap-dancer. His manager, a Russian, disappeared. Other boys missing.

"No morality left in Germany." We noted some girls passing. "No morality left in country. Nice decent girl has to be under five years old. Man, some of these women haven't seen a man in years. Boy, the nights sure are rough round here."

Trying to set up shows. Teaching some two new Blackbirds, negro boys from Belgium. "But they ain't got the rhythm, and it's tough, they just ain't got the rhythm, that old Brooklyn bounce!"

"But boy were we sure glad to see you! We were just at the bottom of the league. All of Germany liberated—everybody free—except some little teenweeny portion of Bavaria—and goddamn it, that would be us!"

"Sure I know this country. I toured it for twenty years. In fact I once put on a show in Hamburg in 1930, me and a Jewish acrobat, and we took over the hall right after a Hitler speech. My dressing room was the one the Führer came out of... Yeah, I know Germany backwards. And that's the only way you can get to know this country."

Crossed Salzach River into Austria.

In the distance again the Alps. The white and dark of the snow-banked mountain peaks hung over the horizon like a vast magnificent backdrop, overwhelming and a bit artificial.

On poles and housetops: the white sheets were gone. In the villages flags were hanging, once again, flying red and white Austrian banners.

Battered house of Joseph Weiser in outskirts of Salzburg. WENN DIESES HAUS SO LANGE STEHT, BIS ALLER HASS UND NEID VERGEHT / SO WIRD DIES HAUS SO LANGE STEHN, BIS DIE WELT WIRD UNTERGEHN. House bombed seven times: "Americans?" "No, no, it makes no difference! Destroy it seventy times, but *Nationalsozialismus* goes with it! Better dead from American bombardment than live with them. There was never such misery in the world as those people brought. They made a cell out of Austria."

His flag (his wife tells me) went up before the troops came. SS came and at point of revolver threatened to shoot him; tore down the flag. But it soon went up again.

"What beastliness, what terror those *Banditen* and murderers brought. Seven years with those cutthroats. Never again! If I have to strangle a whole movement with my own bare hands."

The old man was waving his cane, his red face livid, agitated and explosive.

In Salzburg: crossing the bridge. Nazi officer walking alone in uniform, frequent sight, but now spots some others riding in auto by. Salutes... Mozart Museum. Gramophone found. Old recordings: Jeritza, Galli-Curci arias; also Caruso; sextet from *Lucia*; Mozart's *Zauberflöte*; Puccini.

Sunday, 14 May 1945

Ebersburg hospital. Breakfast outside the door. Sunlight streaming in from the countryside. En route to München.

Children waving on the road. Bicyclists out everywhere.

To military government in old town hall.

Confusion, hub-bub; no decision awaiting regional and higher-level military government.

Inquiries about the Munich revolt. Captain Gerngross, Number One man. Suspicions everywhere.

Overground headquarters without permission. CIC hints very dangerous. Physically I asked fingering my pistol—yes. Politically—also.

In Mauerkircherstrasse. MP comes in with a prisoner. Unshaven, dirty, red-eyed. Guard carrying handful of tools. Caught cutting wires a few towns up. German wearing Bavarian shorts, white underwear creeping down and hanging out. A miserable looking man and his explanation was he thought the wires were German. A stupid foolish formula, and the MP-CIC man almost swung at him with the wire-snippers. At least one case, thus, of sabotage.

To Schackstrasse near the ruin of the Siegestor. Gerngross' headquarters. Sign on house—neatly printed: FAB
FREIHEITS-U. AUFBAU-AKTION BAYERN
FREEDOM ACTION IN BAVARIA

Meetings going on. Dr. Gerngross. Dr. Leiling.[63]

Gerngross himself. Tall, handsome; speaks English with attractive British accent. Tweed suit. Mustache. Unfair, but looks like "matinee type..."

[...]

Spent 1936/7 in Britain, London School of Economics, two terms. Studied with Harold Laski! Various problems of law and administration. No particular note of Laski's Marxism or labor politics. Main interest in learning legal language, etc. In 1941 he passed examinations for degree in economics.

The maintenance of political contacts and groups. Intention: more than Platonic opposition. Impossible to estimate numbers because of precautions taken against Gestapo infiltration and discovery. And very few in the years were caught. Word-of-mouth propaganda only. Nothing ever written, put on paper.

Slips meant destruction. Knew the students, Schmorell, Scholl.[64] Prepared leaflets in University uprising of 1943. Shot. What good did it do? Apparently a "practical" revolutionist. None of this idealist demonstration. Wait for the right moment. Don't sacrifice strength, forces.

Everybody, of course, can claim all martyrs and heroes. But actually there were no movements or organizations.

1938. Received commission as reserve officer. 1939, called up, and served in Polish campaign. Hospitalization, minor wounds, and committed to reserve Army in München. Organization of army groups. Difficulties for men were always being moved out to the tactical forces, and thus links were always missing.

Preparation of revolts and disturbances. Had much cooperation and tacit support in high places. Minister Sperr, Bavarian delegate. He was shot after 20 July.[65]

Help also from Division Adjutants, Major Schubert, 467th Wehrmacht, etc. Many others executed after 20 July.

We knew something of the attempt on Hitler, but this was something other than our own program. We were not working for an officers' revolt. Our blow would be a political one, and that is precisely why it really failed. They had no liaison with the people, and their efforts found no popular answer. Anyway, I think Nazism was rooted too deeply in the North.

South Germany is another thing. Liberal-minded. And make no mistake (I hinted: Catholic Bavaria?) it has nothing to do with religion. The people know the failure of the church. What did they do? Where was their leadership? They were passive, the priests did nothing. And now so many wonder when the AMG devotes so much respectful attention to Catholic advice and Catholic leadership. Bavaria was non-Nazi. Matter of tradition, even "landscape"! History of free peasantry. Not dominated by great landowners, or caught in machinery of an industrial proletariat.

Munich was far from being the "capital of the movement"—*Hauptstadt der Bewegung*—the common phrase was, *Hauptstadt der Gegenbewegung*.

The organization of "terrorist groups" and factory centers, and also a collection of "Ranger reliables."

What concrete achievements? Little if any, to be frank. We had to bide our time. There was the SS from the outside, and the Gestapo from the inside. One slip and we were all lost. And of course we were small. It took the great Allied military power some five years to destroy Hitler's machine. Could we alone do anything at all?

The last month. April. German officers sent through to Army for liaison. A French agent (Miremont) and American flier (Lieutenant McMara). Contact with French underground movement among French PWs and conscripted laborers, which has probably disappeared now with the evacuation of displaced persons.

We used their wireless transmission. Notified Allies of SS concentrations, positions.

Locally I was known as a "non-Nazi," but I played their military game. Strict and correct. My company was a model company. No deserters, no trouble. *Dolmetscherkompanie* Wehrkreis VII. Later changed to *Lehr-* and *Ausbildungskompanie*, so that I could keep more key men.

Pheasant hunt—the word. *Fasanenjagd*.[66]

28 April, 0200. Zero Hour.

For operations see other reports, Third Army CIC. Major McGettigan has report.

Was discharged from German Army in Third Army HQ. CIC permission to return to München to continue work.

Tribute from Eisenhower, with personal mention, for cooperation.

Much opposition and suspicion now from local AMG. They want numbers and names and strength and everything on paper. But we could never work that way! To keep a list was to invite disaster. You know the purge after 20 July. The fools had notebooks kept in Berlin safes. The SS caught the whole record, and even innocent people who happened to be mentioned in the course of some document were chopped down.

Publicity. Correspondents. Not overeager about sensational publicity. And indecent question—Christian name of my wife, etc.

The Nazis remain in powerful local positions. Walk around, and nothing can be done about it.

Difficulties of the FAB. No free movement for organizational work. Communists are growing. Nationalkomitee Freies Deutschland.[67] Vast supply of funds. Money coming in from Switzerland, also Swiss passports. Now if I were a Swiss National what trouble do you think I would have moving around?

Denies personal ambitions, no Führer. Personally I want to return to my profession.

We have no money, no food…

München is a paralyzed city. Immediate problem: get the people to work, begin reconstruction. The railroads, I think, can be put in order in two days. Labor can be busy again in a short time. We are formulating a report to indicate these kind of industrial possibilities.

We want to help, and our credentials surely should be considered good. Ours was the only revolt. Not even in Vienna with all the propaganda and support and radio instructions.[68] Munich demonstrated to the world, I hope, that there were anti-Nazi Germans willing to risk themselves.

Our organization is weak. We have typists, but what can we pay them? We have no vehicles, no newspaper, no facilities of any kind.

(Among CIC suspicions: I would find a military-like organization, run by an ex-Army man, in old German fashion. With Gerngross lieutenants saluting him etc. Found as a matter of fact nothing of the sort. But a movement in birth, and the HQ were not unlike many committees at home struggling to get set…)

In minor difficulties because of one unfortunate incident. Pass issued, and then misused because some one wanted to see his girl, and the whole party in our only vehicle was arrested by CIC… Deplorable.

Gerngross on communists. CP independent. A sense of rivalry. Refers to program as vague and usual camouflage. Insists though on national front aspect of his FAB. Communists included, but references to ex-Communists, social democrats, conservatives, etc.

Returned later in the afternoon Sunday. Office closed. Found German also trying to get in. A new member. Heard of the revolt, wanted to join up. Soldier on the Alsace front; fought in Hagenau, Rittershoffen! (Small world). Lawyer.

Cut off Nymphenburgerstrasse. Sight-seeing the ruins. Rummaging in rubble. Found portrait of the Führer. Some girls laughed. Nurses in white. Tear it up they cried. I raised an eyebrow and asked, *Sind sie nicht deutsch?* No, they were Russians, working in the nearby hospital. I tore the portrait. Rode on and engaged some conversation.

Nina and Lida. Robust Russian type with their somewhat "heavy-set beauty." Fragments of remarks. The unhappiness of the Germans in Bavaria. Feared the SS. Hated the regime. Hitler was always being privately cursed. Later crack: der Führer had more things said against him than Stalin!

Picked it up from there. The girls were young, but they heard of oppositionists. Told me of the trials. Had heard of Trotsky. In good graces until the death of Lenin. Knew at least a bit of history. How about concentration camps. Lida knew nothing. Blank. Nina; of course, for politics. Why of course, why *natürlich*. Is it *natürlich* for political ideas to be a crime? A little too deep… They were students, and were happy with the regime. Many opportunities, etc. And now they were terribly lonely for the homeland, anxious to return. Had a half-way critical sense of the Stalinist power, its control, its dictatorship, the GPU. Took tolerantly and with no offense my explanation of some basis for universal German fear of the Russians. The GPU. The dictatorship. The "half-bad" aspect of the Russian regime. No fear of Russians. Peoples everywhere more or less the same, thesis agreed to; but governments differ in good and evil qualities. Agreement. Surprised me…

On tour of the city. Which they knew well. In the gardens and parks. Asked me to tell them a little of America. Where to begin. Some gossipy remarks, which pleased them. How about American songs. Folk music. Tried to think of something other than *Old Kentucky Home* and *Dixie*, but pleased by lilt, and I put away my bad tenor. They went on with Russian songs, and we soon had a travelling sing in a jeep. Things became warmer when I swung into the International. All smiles and friends. Returned them to hospital.

Originally: Yugoslavian boy with them; laborer for two years; now free, and hopes to go to America. Will start soon as pass comes through. Had no idea of how to get the local pass, no idea of how to get to America, where, why, and when. Distrusted Europe. Feared Russians also; the Russian regime, he explained to the girls. Stalin, *hat er nicht gern*. In America at least there would be a job to work, some pay, and then—*Freiheit*. That was very important…

Returned to Excelsior hotel.

Bombs had destroyed only half, and the army had taken it over.

Elevator man. Old man, perhaps sixty. Worked in hotel and elsewhere around for twenty-six years. Talked at length with him on fourth floor. He had no calls and could remain. Not easy to see hotel and city in which whole life spent destroyed. But nothing could be done. And at least the Gang is gotten rid of. What a foul bunch they were… Correspondents were here the other day, and for a few minutes it was like the old days. One of them was an old-timer, and we recognized each other.

No, Bavaria was not Hitlerist. Many Bavarians were Nazis of course. And they're still here. He began to whisper, very close to my face. This hotel, he said, was owned by a Jew, Josephson. Party took care of his property, and he fled to Canada. Herr Leisel (downstairs) was a party member, and got the hotel through his party connections. But we all know the story and they will not get away with anything anymore. The American government knows the history and we know it, and wait till the SS tries to get back. They'll want jobs, and try to make the best of things. But we know them, every one of them! If Josephson comes back—and maybe he won't: Canada might have been good to him, settled down with new business—Leisel will go. And the others will have accounts settled too.

Knew of the revolt and the radio signal. Had relatives in Wasserburg who rose up with the call. Many of them were shot in the suppression. Knew Gerngross and liked him from the old days...

Afterthought on FAB. Interview a little formal. Obviously who could trust who? He was friendly. But clearly I was an outsider and a stranger, and we were sparring subtly most of the time. On the whole the Army seems to be "opposed" to civilian German movements, and he would naturally have to walk on eggs at every moment...

15 May 1945

The conflicts over Gerngross and Bavarian politics continue.

McGettigan (Major, T-Force CI) calls him "opportunist." "He organizes a demonstration when all is lost. Why didn't these boys get busy six months ago or a year ago—and not forty-eight hours before! And now they want a headquarters with vehicles and clothes... They give us no intelligence information, and if they were what they said they were they'd have blueprints of the Nazi organization. Who is this Gerngross anyway? A mediocre lawyer with a small practice. Mixed up with all kinds of people, running from Nazis to royalty. After all Munich was notorious as being the center of movements. The university was a hot-bed. We have to watch out. They only mean trouble. And if they had done something! If they had broken supply lines and contributed to the shortening of the war it would be another story. The whole affair has been much overrated. All these little outcroppings, an industrial movement, a communist movement, this FAB—are all young and small and immature. And anybody who thinks they'll get into power in Bavaria is mistaken. For now we've just got a policy of expediency, waiting for the Commission and Robert Murphy[69] to arrive..."

At FAB headquarters again.

Not a party, not a movement, but a collection of old anti-Nazis: argument. Denied that any Nazis belonged. Denounced lie that Gerngross was NSDAP. Many of the people around were factory workers. FAB became such since 20 July. Before that a number of secret groups existed separated; for example, the Scholl brothers were known, but another sector.

Wolfgang Hartwig, joined *Dolmetscher* company in May 1943, Feldwebel. He had been a former member of the Catholic Action in the Rhineland, *Neues Deutschland* in 1934. "No organized action in recent years. Deserter problems: hiding them in his house, sending them on. . . Had many political talks with Gerngross but was always careful and suspicious. You never knew who was with the Gestapo. When we held our conversations it was always under four eyes. He always inquired, even cross-examined, sounding out for true opinions. When these were discovered either one of two things happened. You remained in the company to work in the movement. Or the adjutant transferred you out to the front." So the *Dolmetscher* company was to become the armed cadre of a Munich revolt against the Nazis.

Talk of the growing Communist organization.

Freies Deutschland committee at 20 Wittelsbacherstrasse. Approaches to FAB membership have been made. Emile Fritz: offered money and passport to go to Switzerland and take up propaganda work.

Internal factionalism.

Riedenauer's split, "strong-willed and impulsive."[70] Quit claiming personal ill-health. He wants to go fishing—and in times like these!

Gerngross: Unhappy, tired, dejected. Movement meeting rebuffs, in particular from Army investigators. We're treated like "swine." Frankly admits he has no idea of the strength of the movement. Separatism (Bavaria) may be springing up. Nazis may be taking over. No controlled organization. "You German swine" is the way we were referred to this morning, by an American officer whose accent indicated he was a German refugee. Mentioned Werewolf threat. The hopelessness of the situation: on the one side distrust, on the other vengeance. Nazis walking around, and they are now better off than others who showed their hand against the party! Essence of the movement, he says (whether he always said so is another matter).

Reconstruction to avert complete disaster; assistance in the struggle against hunger and disorder.

"My natural contacts, through my family and profession, are with the middle and upper classes, but Labor is our orientation."

Denied again Nazis in movement. Later perhaps Nazis, *Zwangnazis*, who were drafted in the party, will be admitted; but for now one has to remain pure.

We have no program. Programs have to be "carried out," and we surely are in no position to carry out anything. We do have however principles. As

I was told this very morning, we are a defeated nation, and there need be no suggestions from us. Treated like a criminal. Refugee as interpreter; mangled my remarks. Much personal bitterness—As Late As We Were! Imagine, he flees the country, and then berates us for taking so long to make a revolution.

(Assistant: Ottheinz [sic] Leiling. Civil Government committee on Railroads, food supply. Eco expert, Dr. Hans Jakobsen.[71] Franz Schneider;[72] Lothar Roda [sic].[73])

(Faces of Nazis: "Walk the street and you can see them. History has done something to their faces." Incident in the mountains with Newsome; spotting a Gestapo; pistol removed; uncomfortable; went on.)

On: Ritter von Epp:[74] "My god! Our member? Why, he was our prisoner. We made plans to seize him and take him with us. As *Reichsstatthalter*, he could surrender Bavaria when we had put the other Army and Party leaders out of the way. He was a weak bloke and could serve our ends."

Again, the sense of isolation.

We had no promises, no propaganda, no messages, nothing. Yet nowhere—not even in Austria, in Red Vienna—was there the rebellion that was made here.

[. . .]

Communist Party: Asked to join the uprising; refused; apparently to save their forces; we lost forty men in the first action. They had a plan to revolt in Dachau, and wanted to borrow some men and guns. Otherwise they were for sitting back and waiting. (And if I sat back and waited I might be a nice PW now, comfortable, eating good US rations.)

As for the "Militarist" rumors. "After all I was a soldier. Does anybody expect me to be in a position to help that?"

Claims large measure of old socialist, social-democrat support.

Submitting lists, rasters of leading Nazis. (First CIC complaint: too long!)

First contact with CIC—the old Gestapo show; we were walked around; a shot in the cellar; some one just committed suicide; ugh! [. . .]

Werwolf Leaflet [. . .]

At Feldherrnhalle—where the first Nazis fell in 1923 and which with Hitler's power became a Party shrine: "*Heil Hitler!*"

Scrawled in large white paint: *K.Z. DACHAU—VELDEN—BUCHENWALD*

Ich schäme mich, dass ich ein Deutscher bin. P. Höpl.

Possibly written by *Freies Deutschland*—no other propagandists around seem to be capable of this kind of sensationalism.

The major's clothes. Also part of the record: a scout car searching throughout Munich for my jeep and the laundry missing.

At *Freies Deutschland*—Gerngross was heard over the radio. The revolt had begun. Men flocked out into the streets. These two went down to the river.

Soldiers were guarding the Cornelius Brücke and the Thalkirchener Brücke. Unarmed persuasion. Soldiers consented. Mines and bombs and demolition preparations tossed into the river. Others raided the *Panzerfaust*[75] supplies. Others brought out white flags.

When troops came down Lindwurmstrasse—*begrüsst*, greetings, cheers, girls with flowers. GIs tossed cigarettes into the crowd. People were very happy. Liberation... "Maybe the Americans don't understand really how oppressed we were. How we couldn't do anything but wait and hope. Bavaria was not Nazi..."

Street-incident: Jakob Lütz, captured in hideaway, Munich cellar. Marched through the streets with revolver in his back, and a great sign: *Lütz, ein Henkersknecht aus Dachau*. Taken to the police from 2nd floor, Muhlerstrasse.[76]

Meeting with Curt Riess[77] and Klaus Mann.[78] Mann up to Munich for a visit to old home; with Mediterranean *Stars & Stripes*. Riess sending dispatches for Scripps-Howard, and current RCA message back on Gerngross revolt, an outrageous and scandalous piece of journalism, full of hearsay, rumor, unchecked gossip, slander, and a really vicious partisanship. Claims Riedenauer and Prince Arenberg told him all; nevertheless his own reportage was at almost every point irresponsible.

Returned late to Excelsior Hotel.

Spoke again to elevator man—Fritz Jahrers. Tells me that Gerngross lived in Room 113 for several years. Never used greeting of *Heil Hitler*, which was always on the Nazi lips. Known as a disciplinarian, but was well-liked. Heard his broadcast on 28 April. Knew the time had come. Relatives in Wasserburg started local revolt. Bridge over Inn River saved. Acted independently and with his own political ideas. Simply took signal from Gerngross. Relatives seized by Nazis. Everywhere people were acting... And when Hitler died— people here said *Gott sei Dank! Die Leute waren froh*... And the American occupation *war unsere Rettung*. Oberstleutnant Nicholas Puhl,[79] assisted in revolution.

14 May 1945, Munich

Rudolph Wiegel, twenty-four.

With Nineteenth Battalion in Munich before the revolt.

"You must understand this. It was very terrifying and dangerous. People are false. They are with you one moment, and the next thing you know you have been trapped by the Gestapo. I was at the Russian front and fought there. But the things I saw made me sick at heart. The way people were treated, especially the Jews. It was unbelievable. Things we never knew about, believe me. Mass executions and mass burials, such atrocities and cruelties! I had to do something. Such things had to be stopped somehow... From 1943 on I became an oppositionist. But they held all the power, all the force. Where was one to begin? One wrong move, or even one wrong word, and you were dead. It was easier working in Bavaria. Northern Germany, particularly Westphalia, was so terribly loyal. I met Gustav Bücker in 1943. And I helped him in the underground until he was caught and hanged. Easter last year. He told me about Dachau and how the barbarism was systematic, a natural part of the regime of *Nationalsozialismus*. It was hard to believe, but when one did it was easy to understand Bücker's fanaticism. Everything that smacked of Nazism had to be destroyed, wiped out! Especially the original criminals, the cadres of 1933–35. They built the foundations... We used to print leaflets on an old machine which he had. Sometimes we would print news for the people, the truth about what was happening. Sometimes we would make calls for the Germans to organize into an opposition. Always we tried to expose the Nazi corruption, in the party and in the government, and the huge profits. In 1943 we had a special campaign and the *Aktivisten* everywhere took it up. That was the time of the Black-Shadow epidemic. You know, these signs up on walls and doors, of the *Pst* and *Feind-hört-mit* variety. We said: this was the Symbol of the Regime—black and shadowy, without hope and without a body. And the question-mark was the question-mark of Hitler himself—neither he nor his war had any future. Bücker was arrested by the Gestapo, betrayed by his girl out of a jealousy for some other woman. She, by the way, got a good job out of it, working in the offices of the *Geheime Staatspolizei*. I went to visit him one morning and I found the police there. They arrested me and took me to HQ—*Brienner Strasse fünfzig, zweiter Stock, Zimmer sechsundsiebzig*." (He recited the address with a precision of unforgettable memory.) "I told them I was making a business call. But they didn't believe me. I lied. But believe me it was a matter of my head! I had to lie and deceive." (He apologized now as if the most ordinary untruth were an enormity unforgivable.) "Bücker identified me. Oh yes, he said, I know him. He's always bothering me about some radio he brought to my place for me to fix. I have it somewhere in a corner. Never found the time to do any repairs. That saved me. They released me, but watched me from that time on. In the Army they wanted to have me go to Officer's school, the report on me said that I didn't have the National Socialist faith and couldn't provide necessary ideological leadership. So I remained with the troops in Munich. On the morning of the 28th I heard the radio program. Everybody was bewildered. In the confusion and desperation people started to take off for home. Discharges were being written in every orderly room. Not hundreds, thousands were going home. They took clothes and ration boxes from the supply places and left the military service forever. I had been discharged myself two days before! It was a great terrible mix-up. I heard General Huebner[80] myself in headquarters shouting over the phone that he would hang every officer who issued a discharge! But I don't think that helped. Some time during that morning I was at the railroad station, and a huge train arrived. One shipment had six hundred reinforcements. The word spread like fire that the revolution had come. I knew that no more than fifty men finally reported to the *Adolf-Hitler-Kaserne*. Everybody heard of the rebellions, and knew it was all over with the Nazis and the war. Here, I show you something. A document written by my friends. They were veterans, wounded four and five times many of them, and they were sent to Dachau on charges of "defeatism." They were treated miserably, but here they say how bad it was, how they were starved and beaten, and how at the last minute the commandant explained that all would be forgiven if they took up arms and fought against the Americans. Here are all the names. 158 signers! It was hard to believe all the terrible things that were going on. And not everybody who saw them and came to believe they truly existed became an oppositionist. On the Russian front there were many atrocities on the other side too. I have seen my comrades lying naked in the snow, their bodies beaten and stabbed and robbed and mutilated. Comrades who were with me in the action only a few hours before... But believe me we could never do that! The SS, they were trained for that kind of war. But not the soldiers (the Wehrmacht). We would take prisoners and treated them the way we would want to be treated. They had wives and families and children and were people... These were dark black years. I have to rub my eyes and repeat to myself again and again that a new, different day has come."

Leiling: Riedenauer, half-Italian, with a strong Italian temperament; a member of the propaganda group; and he felt in the last days that he was not sufficiently appreciated. Formed something of a faction, and then tried to do everything on its behalf. Wanted very much to get passports on behalf of the men, to go home. But it was quite impossible, and only caused a stir. We were against it, and he quit... withdrew from the movement, a little sulkingly.

Arenberg, young prince, twenty-five, aristocratic manner in politics. More concerned with his little brother's promotions. Wasn't around during the uprising. Had quarrels with Gerngross. Cheeky young man. Ambitious and playing with politics.

Riess. His main interest when we met him seemed to be first to interview, Slezak, the singer you know, and to get some souvenirs from the Amann collection.

[...]

Sergeant Bruno Riedenauer: Met Gerngross in September 1943 and worked together in political activity from April 1944. Not a serious political person, though obviously a sincere anti-Nazi. Really wanted transfer to Italian front—so he could desert to his mother in Rome.

Participated and played a leading role in revolt. Captured small Freimann [radio] station at 0200. When the SS closed in on them felt that the radio ought to be destroyed or at least the engineers killed or captured. Gerngross did not approve and was not to be seen around too often. "I have no doubt he was an anti-Nazi, but he was very ambitious. . . . I, I have no ambitions. I am sick and need a rest. What I want to do is to go fishing, some good trout fishing."

Riedenauer used to spot the Nazis among the men in the company—and Gerngross would have them transferred out. So the outfit was kept pure.

R.'s position: no plans for future, no politics, no party. He had a copy of the FAB program at Freimann, but refused to read it; didn't like the idea of a program.

And it was R. who first contacted the prince; thought his name and influence might help get passes for the men.

Curt Riess interviewed him for about five or ten minutes. The correspondent was very much in a hurry.

The Sperr case. The Minister was not really in the underground, but worked in his own way against the Nazis. After 20 July he was mixed up in the Revolt, and he was hanged. Everybody here was very anxious about their own heads, so worried that many said terrible things—like better Mme. Sperr should have been hanged too. That was terrible. But Gerngross and others said it. I felt bad, and didn't like them after that. Also G. claimed Minister Sperr for the FAB, and the old lady didn't like that so she's mad.

28 April—it was really a general strike. No street-cars were running, no workers out, all stores closed. The [Bavarian] flags were out, our old *weiss-blau*. That should have been the end of it. The riot. No more.

Royalty, in the *Staatsbibliothek*, 5 Mandelstrasse.

The youngest Prince, Stefan, nineteen.

Feels the putsch came a little too early. A day later and it might have held power. The troops were called out to patrol the streets, and thus the preparations for defense and resistance were upset. It also showed that the Nazis were on their way out. The regime was cracking. The population as a whole was not active but the word spread everywhere. As for Gerngross my impression was always that he was very "NS" (Nazi version of GI).

Johann-Engelbert: blond, slim, handsome, aristocratic in manner.

Gerngross as a Nazi. Claims two of his best friends saw the Party lists. Which doesn't mean he was a believer. Possibly he had to join. But NSDAP formally. Very vague about charges of his being a "terrible militarist." The prince was not in the Army. Certainly a Wehrmacht captain would strike him on the militaristic side. His impression was that the whole company was Nazi and militaristic. Which might only prove that Gerngross's Theater was quite effective.

Is convinced that the FAB is a very dangerous movement. Confiscating houses for headquarters. Exaggerated role: helped US but not British prisoners across the lines. Gave orders to arrest people. Threatened shopkeepers to join. Why, we might as well have the Gestapo back again! Real danger to public security. (See Colonel Seisser, police president).[81]

(Also: Srbik, Austrian historian,[82] at Ohmstrasse 16, second floor).

Activities like these compromise the Allied occupation. Our main duty is loyalty and cooperation. This is no time for politics, but only for reconstruction, and a new sincere beginning with the world.

G. as an opportunist. Threatened old Bayerische Volkspartei (Cardinal's Catholic Center group); "go with the Reds," unless opposition to him abates. As for his monarchism he thought that was a bit unfounded. His monarchism is probably me... Anyway, I am set against him. Imagine, this man was almost Mayor of Munich. Why then make me Emperor of Germany! He laughed. And *Regierungsrat* Leiling, he was a party member, though once again not a Nazi. G. never contacted me, until he needed me: certainly proof of his character and intentions.

I have frankly a great fear of his kind of adventurist politics. Claiming himself as the only officially recognized group... This will be the return of the old intrigue and corruption. I've fought this cursed Gerngross movement for a fortnight, and if it has really collapsed I will take part of the credit and I am glad.

My own picture of the situation is in part altered by the prince's remarks. He seems honest and serious and able. His evidence may not always be without error, but he is intelligent and appears to mean well.

1 June 1945, Augsburg and Landsberg

Wonderful, how exhilarating the first free moments on the road are! You are at last alone and rather carefree, and what is most important, unlocatable: imagine, you repeat to yourself, no one in the whole world knows where you are! You drive happily, and chant for hours. This is "freedom," and not the least, larger aspect of the liberation is that it is essentially a flight. You have managed an escape from the burdens of routine, respect, and responsibility.

The morning was clear but cold. In Landsberg I twisted off the road and found my way to the prison. *Die Hitlerstube* was here. *Festungsstube 7*—A. Hitler. *Festungsstube 5*—R. Hess. It was in this little cell, with its barred win-

Figure 8. Posing in the "Führerstube" in Landsberg, © Lasky Center, Munich.

dows, old simple table-top desk, and narrow spring bed, that *Mein Kampf* was written. Next door—the rooms all opened off a central dining room in apartment-like fashion—was Hess, and in the other rooms a number of early heroes who never amounted to much. (6—Maurice; 5 (later)—Robert Wagner; 8—Kriebel; 9—Dr. Friedrich Weber).[83] The frame was skeletonized; the Führer's portrait was missing. The inscriptions had been removed (paragraphs from *Mein Kampf*). The large bronze plaque had been appropriated by the first GIs of the Tenth Armored which raced through. Souvenirs were no more, but it had clearly become an American shrine. There were hundreds of signatures, dates, and hometowns scribbled on the walls. "Adolf Hitler, I'm here! Where are you?" "I'm here, Adolph!" "Me too!" "Better Luck, Next Time!" "Tough luck, Adolph!" "You Shoulda Stood in Bed!" From the window at which the Führer so often posed in reminiscence during his reign of power, there is a pleasant peaceful view of greensward and rolling fields. There was a small walking path stretching away and chickens in the farmyard.

Out front there was another generation of political prisoners. German victims of the Nazi regime. Some had listened to Radio London, others had been involved in the black market, one had been a deputy in the Reichstag from Berlin, others had been guilty of sabotage or *Wehrkraftzersetzung*. *Vorladung des Angeklagten: Rundfunkverbrechen*... they read, and everybody laughed. It now seemed so trivial and foolish. Think of it: a six-year sentence for turning on a station. Altogether there must have been some 1,500 in the Landsberg jail, and these included Greeks, Austrians, Poles, truly an international penal colony. They were sitting around, hundreds of them, in front of the entrance, waiting for the trucks and buses to arrive. This was "demobilization" day. But, as someone remarked, "the cells weren't growing cold... The Nazis were now being crowded in." The political prisoners had worked in local labors, gardening, shoe-making, tailoring, etc. There was a small library, but the books were either "old—or the Nazi stuff." As for escape, there were smiles at the melodramatic suggestion, but it had been impossible. Schmitt, the Berlin Communist deputy, added some details. He had been sentenced to fifteen years. If the sentence had been lighter, ironically enough, he would have been dead. With the expiration of the term the prisoner is sent to Dachau or Buchenwald for "discharge." And it was the old terrible story—they came in through the front door and went out through the chimney. "That was our release... Fortunately I still had some five years to serve, and so I am alive now." [...]

On the road again moving south to Schongau, and cut right to Altenstadt for the Michaelkirche. Perhaps the classic model of a small sleepy village: the sun was strong and no one was about. I found the priest of the church and we talked for a while. My *Baedeker* was wrong, he carefully pointed out. The dates of the church were: 1170–1220. "And one other thing Herr Baedeker missed—he was so preoccupied in recent years with Party matters!—the church was reconstructed in 1826 and again in 1938, and then we found old Roman frescoes on the walls! Three are still preserved, and for hundreds of years nobody knew of their existence! Here is St. Michael and the *Seelenwaage ... Johannes der Apostel und der Täufer, zwei Bischöfe, Mariä Verkündigung...* etc." The columns were Roman-Byzantine, and each was different in design, ten in all. The critique of Baedeker went on—this was the first architectural effort at a large arched span for church roofing. And then he modestly disclaimed the encomiums to the interior decorations—"Kitsch!" We went on to talk of other things. The black years of the Nazis. The terror. How little anybody could do. He was a large portly man with a simple good face and when he smiled everything seemed to light up. He was glad and hopeful now. And he even called my attention to the fact that Columbia University—in the Teacher's College—had found the printing plates of the old German schoolbooks. Now perhaps education could begin again. In the church, too, was a young man, a former German art student and soldier. More gossip, and exchange of bitter historical recollections. But the nightmare was over. And the future? Some idle words about American occupation. What was Radio Berlin saying? Well, I hadn't heard it, but the summaries I got were exceedingly interesting—a full, rich, organized propaganda campaign to win over the German people (who, after all, Ilya Ehrenburg to the contrary notwithstanding, were always to be distinguished from the Nazi state). The people were to be treated well. The ration was to be the biggest available. Cultural programs were beginning, music, opera, lectures. There seemed to be no doubt in the young man's mind: "The Germans are and have been anti-Russian—in part, because of Goebbels's propaganda, in part because of legitimate political differences with communist dictatorship. But I know what high-powered propaganda can do. I can remember the huge Berlin demonstrations moving me, bringing tears to my eyes, and thousands upon thousands of voices sang out in old patriotic songs. We couldn't help but feeling, this was the people's voice, this was our home, our happiness. This the Nazi machine could do, and Stalin's machine can work the same maneuver. The people will be sold!"

By: Oberammergau, Schloss Linderhof, to the hilltop at Reith, and down into the Inn Valley. Innsbruck. The 103rd Division on the mountain at Hungerburg. Sonnenberghof Hotel on the other hill at south end—on Brenner pass road... In the evening with Capt Frey, a CIC man to medics and division. Evening of characters. Especially Mike Mahaolikas, wrestler, diver, photographer, philosopher.

2 June 1945, Innsbruck

The view is classic. From Sonnenberghof into the valley still beclouded by the vapors of early morning, and up into the Alpine ranges covered by snow whose whiteness is almost fierce against its contexts of blue sky and green and gray mountainsides. The sun clears the valley, and the city of Innsbruck lies in the pocket of the hills like a loose free dusty jewel. You stare at it, and then agree to say nothing. Poets have been busy here for centuries. There are no words or phrases left to catch the breathtaking note of a beautiful vista.

To the division. Hungerburg I learn means literally that. At one time a tower was devoted to solitary confinement, and bread and water. Thus, the name.

G-5, and the dejection of Captain Weeks. A touching and profound session, for he was disappointed and hurt. Symbol of it all: at the telephone calling up all regiments, etc.—the Austrian flag will come down. It had been up for ten days, the flag of liberation. Now the order had been changed. The *rot-weiss*, like the German flag and the National-Socialist banners, will not be exhibited—until further notice. The people were bitter about it, and the military governors were confused. But so it goes. Asininity crowned with authority. It was not that mistakes were being made. But that they were being made by people who would never learn anything by an earlier error, and who in the first place could hardly help themselves from botching the job. Men without competence, understanding, real responsibility. Their every personal wish is taken care of. They have the best of lodgings, food, services. But in turn they submit very little. Phone call: General at Sixth Corps wants an electrician to fix the lights in his billet. You see what I mean... That's why I want to go home. After the campaign, with so many of mine (and yours) friends killed, to come to this peace! That's too much. More details of the work. The friction with the Russians on the movements of displaced persons. Convoys back to Italy. Cases of rape (no political motive to charges; only time conviction is in case of sex maniac, and one was recently sentenced to be hung). Problem of the whorehouses; legal, city-checked. Close them down? And drive the girls into the side-streets? Or let them go and at least be able to spot them when something turns up... The problem of civilian health. But routine check. Much goiter in the valley. The mountain water needs minerals, iodinization. For the price of a half-hour's artillery range practice we could eliminate all the goiter in the Inn valley. But that of course is not what we are here for. The brass and non-fraternization. No appreciation of the problem, its realities, consequences.

Up the cable car to the permanent snow line. The god-like perspective. The little uniformed conductor (blue serge), reading his newspaper, carefully folded, en route. (A US news-sheet; headline: "Thomas Mann on the Guilt of Germany.") Through rain and snow to the peak. Later with Colonel Molloy, chief of staff. The rain again, and the series of rainbows arching down over the valley in a spectrum extravaganza.

Into the city, up and down the streets. The *Baedeker*. Where is Maria-Theresien-Strasse? And die Triumphpforte, and das Goldene Dachl. Well, she wasn't a native of Innsbruck—she was Russian—but she knew the town and ventured suggestions. She was going to headquarters. I would drive her, and then we could tour. So it went. This was the beginning of *L'Affaire* Princess Lydichka. She was not really a princess I suppose but there was some talk about a royal Georgian lineage, and then she had such a commanding way. A great promoter, and had promoted herself a house, several boys and girls who were practically her servants, and now to be sure an American officer. We drove and talked and became friends. Before nightfall it appeared as if we really had known each other a long time; at any rate we behaved like shy lovers. She insisted on sleeping alone at home. I acquiesced. But tomorrow night, she said, and smiled sweetly, and bent over and kissed me, as I swerved to keep the car on the road. I turned and kissed her, and then she began frantic warnings to take care, the highway was dangerous. I gave her some playful stern glances, and we both went on happily. I brought her home in a downpour. A Nazi convoy was coming down from the hills from somewhere to somewhere but who would stop and check up. One little auto she spotted and insisted that the man was one of her jailors in Dachau. She had been a "political prisoner" for swatting a few of the local Nazis. Temperament too was a crime. But in the rain one could only be indifferent. Some other time Lyditchtka.

3 June 1945

Sunday was a fine morning, and the princess slept late. I drove out into the country and lay in the sun. The children came by in their church finery and waved to me. I waved back, and turned my face to watch them and still catch some of the rays. They came over, and soon we were talking. They had been to church—I had caught the great Corpus Christi procession in Hungerburg—and they had been singing. Would they sing for me? They were reluctant. But I promised them sweets, chewing gum and chocolate, and so one by one they began and the chorus soon swelled. *Das schönste auf der Welt*, Andreas announced. And they sang—[...]

They went through it for me, verse after verse, with appropriate choruses and yodels. And I asked for more. *S' Ländle meine Heimat*, Andreas announced again, and I am afraid I didn't quite catch it.

[...] All of which had been *verboten* during the years of the Nazi regime, but the children had learned the songs at home.... *und rot und weiß weht es durch die Luft, O Vorarlberg...*

Figure 9. Children along the road near Hungerburg, © Lasky Center, Munich.

The *Horst Wessel*? Oh, they didn't know that any more. It was hard to remember. No, please, they couldn't really do that. Finally they consented. They used to sing it every morning and evening in school, beginning the day and just before dismissal. And it was curious to hear little children chanting "*Rotfront und Reaktion erschossen*" and the baby, little Troudy, squeaking out a "*Pfahnehoch.*"

I went back after noon, and Lyditchtka was ready. We would go to Brenner. The ride was pleasant, although the stares and whistling and catcalls became a little annoying. At the pass met poor Halpern from Camp Lee Sixth Regiment; he hardly knew me. We drove back, and stopped at the hotel. Lydia was "preparing" herself. She went through my picture collection. Fortunately found no snapshots of anybody who would prompt further her sudden burst of jealousy. She refused to believe my denials. She shouted I was lying, that I didn't love her, that I only wanted to sleep with her, that she didn't want to have anything to do with me, and slapped me. I slapped her back, twice, and twice as hard, and she put her hands to her face and cheeks, and looked hurt and shocked. She turned fiercely away and stared coldly out through the window. I restrained myself from making apologies. Said nothing for a long time. Looked blankly at the walls. Finally she asked timidly whether I was still angry, and wanted to kiss me. I consented only reluctantly, and she became very tender. We made love.

I called for her again at her house in the evening. She had everybody running around pinning up draperies, tacking down rugs and carpets, straightening out white linen for her bed, She was giving her imperial orders. It was late before we were quite ready to go out. We drove back through the town and up the hill to the hotel. It was dark and quiet and no one for the first time was about. We went upstairs to my room, and happily I was still the only occupant. She undressed and went to bed and I fussed about for a while and joined her, awkwardly stepping on her legs in order to get over on the right side of the bed. She reproved me but refused to let me take it as an insult by wrapping her arms and her legs around me, kissing me and squeezing me and peppering me with questions, *liebst du mi', liebst du mi', wie viel...* She was sweet and loving (if a little tight). Her conversation was wonderful, from her rich dreams of the two of us together like this forever to her inimitable, *Wo hast du das gelernt, Paris?*

4 June 1945, Innsbruck

Wandering around military and civilian offices to see what the Occupation is like.

The French are in Vorarlberg, and the tip of Tirol. The US is in Tirol, Salzburg, Oberdonau to Linz. The Russians hold the rest of Austria. There is no liaison, no collaboration. The US Group Control Commission had been frozen in Italy, and only came up through the Pass Saturday night. They were still busy "planning." Obviously the Russians moving in and holding on to Vienna was a little upsetting. In fact everything was upset. Many Austrians apparently were trying to move into new occupied areas—and the Russians last week had to blow bridges to keep the columns from struggling through.

At the Party headquarters of the Social-Democrats.

Young men waiting around. Ex-Dachau political prisoners, jailed since 1938, some of them had gone underground as youth leaders in 1934 when the party was first banned. They wanted to know many things, and they cut back to 1938, the beginning of the story. The truth about appeasement, about the war guilt of Daladier, and Reynaud, and Chamberlain. They told me about the concentration camp, the special rewards for corpses given to the SS; the foreign commissions which came through in 1938 (Great Britain) and later the various Italian and Axis groups... the same farce. Everything was cleaned up. No one was allowed out. And the visitors were shown the specially prepared barracks. They sat around and gossiped. Like a GI session, except the memories here were of the other face of the war. The excitement of the last days. One of them left the camp as the men were getting to the *Unterführer*, a Böttger, whose hair had already been cut to prison style and was wearing the inmate's stripes. "*Ich bin ein Nazischwein! Ich habe neununddreißig russische Soldaten erschossen, und bei tausend anderen Morden habe ich mitgeholfen. Mein geliebter Führer, Adolf Hitler, Sieg Heil!*" This text he repeated again and again, as the men laughed and jeered and threw stones at him. Occasionally some new improvisation would be substituted, and he would repeat that a hundred times. How long did it go on? Probably till he dropped and some one struck him down. He didn't wait to see. He and some other Innsbruck comrades left, and returned home.

What he found at home several days after the liberation, and for the weeks after, was dispiriting. He and all the others were convinced that "the Nazi organization remains. A few of the big fish have been caught. But the little ones, and the vicious ones, still walk around. And do you think that after all the schooling and training they've had they don't know how to organize an underground? Believe me they've read enough books and been given enough lessons to keep their movement alive! I wouldn't have you believe that we're after revenge, that we would want to shoot them all. (It would be a pity for the bullets—*es wäre Schade um die Kugel*), but put them to work, or at least put the finger on them. In some places the old regime even flourishes. In Vorarlberg the old SS crowd of women, the Nazi whores, have now moved in with the French army!" The secretary put in: "And the women here, they were the first to make 'friends'.... For the others we see them every day. Some of them are still in the offices of the government, a secretary or an interpreter, but important enough to accomplish little jobs! Maybe you people (she concluded with not a little bitterness) don't know really what National Socialism is! You have to live through it, and to have seen millions, so many friends and families, die through it, to know what the Terror truly was! Naturally we can't do anything, but this is the way we feel."

The Dachau man continued: "You are right in worrying about the return of totalitarianism. The mistake was made once. The Nazis seized power. It may happen again. But only this I can tell you. So far as I am concerned there is one man who will be devoted to stopping them, from the streets and the rooftops and the mountains. They got me once, and they will never get me again. Not as long as I can draw a breath to fight those damned bandits! The other side of the picture isn't too bright, either. What are we now? We go to the local administration and we're treated like *Lumpen*. And you wait and see... When the old crowd gets a little stronger—already they've stopped trembling—and they make their first moves, who will be blamed? Some American soldiers will be hurt by snipers, or maybe killed and then the pronouncement will come— The Austrian population has proved itself unwilling to uproot fascism... Just watch!"

Perhaps there was much rumor and exaggeration here. But it is significant that this disaffection from the American occupation already exists, and that the US representatives are already losing what holds they had previously in European public opinion. Of course, these are not the simple folk, but the independent politically minded citizens, who in no respect conform to the requirements of our variety of Quisling,[84] fawning constantly in his gratefulness for freedom at the point of the American rifle. Nevertheless, this is the data for the story of chaos.

And there wasn't very much they could do. "If we talk too much, or try to turn in Nazis—why, we're labeled by CIC as troublemakers!" Reasonable enough. And then there was the flag story, which Weeks had been so troubled about. "*Bis auf weiteres*," no Austrian, German, or NS flags. "Tomorrow, perhaps," the girl said cynically, "tomorrow we will be allowed to fly our *rot-weiss* and our Nazi flags again!" The grievances were endless, and from what I know of the military government personnel and policy, apparently quite legitimate. On the issues of food, quarters, passes, transportation, we worked efficiently, but in no direction which would really organize popular support and guarantee the beginnings of free organizations. The damned system works with old civil-service fuddy-duddies dominated by some social-worker complex of politics and government. Hundreds of political prisoners returned to Innsbruck and found no help till the party was located. Then they were outfitted. The party fed them, clad them, found them a place to stay. There was a world of possibilities. In Austria, street committees or neighborhood committees, run by American control officers, could have cleaned up the town politically in a month. But there is no organization and no understanding. Only the looting and the new personal privileges go on. One old man told a touching tale. The French First Army moved in, and radios were appropriated. One radio happened to be an old "anti-fascist" set; this was the underground radio; we had listened to London here; many had been arrested; some had been shot, here by this dial. No one asked. The radio went.

"Let me say something to you frankly and openly. It will be only a few weeks now before many of us will be asking—who are these people? For what were we liberated? We went to KZ for political beliefs, for a faith in a free liberal social order. What do we return to? Please do not misunderstand me. I don't want a governmental job, and none of us want murderous revenge. If we were to succumb to our passion and hatred and shoot all the Nazis we would become fascists ourselves. We want not revenge but justice. And a chance again to work for justice and for liberty. But this is a nothingness. It is not the old time, and it is not the new time. The past is over, but no one looks to the future or seems to care about it. You are an historian and you perhaps know this better than I. A free people is born in history only through a self-liberating revolution! You know the story of modern events in America and France and England. You have destroyed the military power of Nazism; but the military power was not their whole strength. They were a political regime, with political loyalties and ideals. That politics must be eliminated—as a machine, and as a population. But no one knows how to strike the political blows. And even if you could do it yourself—if you know how, and you yourself admit you do not—it would not be sufficient. The people themselves must do it. Their passion and hatred must be utilized. They themselves must be involved in the making of their own new Austria. It would give them strength again and recover their lost dignity. What was this war after all? A war against fascism or against the peoples of Europe?"

In the Communist party offices, my suspicions were justified. I was told the Moscow Renner government is the symbol of the "people's power against fascism... this is necessary in addition to the Allied military power." Once again the Kremlin had acted quickly and uncannily and moved brilliantly into a political vacuum. There is a longing for newspapers, meetings, leaflets, for the beginnings of democratic life.[85]

The party posters were ordered removed. They were simple crudely drawn cartoons of little special political meaning. A view of concentration-camp brutality—they did not believe in the "greatest statesman" of all times! (victims dead and bloody) .... So they were taught better. Drawing of NS torture chamber—*Das war die Nazikultur!*

Item on the *Widerstandsbewegung*. The SDs were pulling out of the national-front underground. The CP was still apparently holding on. The old *Staatspartei* was coming back, with remnants even of the old Heimwehr (under Hradetsky, now petitioning for AMG approval).[86] As yet no political power or following, but great influence among the old state employees who were always a curse of German government. So the 1934–38 dictatorship is itself returning in the time of national liberation. Here too there is an impatience with the tempo. No radio, no press—why they are even willing to reprint the *Stars & Stripes* and the *Beachhead News*, but they can't get copies! Action was fact to the 3 May, but something has soured since. Six million soldiers for the military effort, a handful for the peace. Names: Harry Damron (talked English), and chief of Tirolean CP—Josef Ronczay.

5 and 6 June 1945

Last hours with the princess.

The stillness and quiet going in. The next morning: everybody was up and around and available as a spectator. We walked down and out. The officers and clerks were milling about. All the chambermaids were out in the hall. The door was locked and we had to wait to make the exit. In a word the affair was conspicuous. I was slightly embarrassed, Lydia was vastly amused. I winced as her high heels rapped out in the hallways, she simply delighted in her proud confident stalk. Details. The high heels. The red dress. The upsweep hair-do. *Liebling* and *Liebchen* and *liebst du mich?* (& *Hast du das in Paris gelernt?*). The last hours. Saying goodbye. Milytchka wanting to go to bed. The princess being stern and throwing her out of the room. The poor sleepy girl calling from the keyhole at the other side. The princess being ruthless and brutal, reviling her, and sweetly proceeding to make love to me. A strange girl, full of violence and tenderness, coarseness and the greatest delicacy. We had both been tired, but if this was the last night, why then—!

And if she was a little pressed merely to go through the motions by the unfavorable circumstances at the moment (Milly was wailing, "No! No! We're not going to bed, we only want to talk and be together for a little while, so shut up and for goodness' sake be patient!") she was still affectionate and even passionate. There was a fine striking assurance to her sexual appetite which was peculiarly her own. She was very simple and direct about love, which in a real sense is the great mark of sophistication.

In the house. Talking with the Russians. Gossip about the GPU, the acknowledgment that it worked pretty much like the Gestapo, that there could be no freedom or genuine security until secret police terrors were eliminated. The skepticism about socialism. The awareness of the great economic differences, the marvelous living conditions for the Party, the hovels of the poor people only a few kilometers away. The extensive black-market corruption. The sentimentality of the old people for Lenin, rarely a word for Stalin. The industrial inefficiency. The mysterious story of the death of Lenin—murdered. Died as a consequence some years later of wounds inflicted by a Jewish woman! Everybody knew it. Each Russian there said oh yes, an accepted historical fact. No one could explain why it was specified that she was Jewish, when the official policy is to label no one by religious titles but only by geography (Russian, Ukrainian, Georgian, etc.). The German engineer: arrested by SS for having married and raised a Russian family; wife and children arrested by NKVD for German father and husband. The unbelievable personal chaos of his situation. How was he ever to put the pieces of his life together? So has the continent of Europe been emasculated.

The trip north. The ascent out of the Inn valley in Reith on the mountain top. Through Oberammergau again, with a detour for the Schloss Linderhof, which is something out of the wildest dreams of Metro-Goldwyn-Mayer, with its gold and silver embroidery, marble columns, porcelain vases, endless mirrors and silk, inexhaustible luxury. The tapestries, the richly carved and gilded ornaments, the green velvet canopies, the coronation gowns, the Italian, English and French gardens, the rosewood furniture.

The by-pass to Nuremberg, and here was the "War" again, destruction, wreckage, a city that was missing, dead. This was in its way the worst I had seen. The churches were rubble like the rest of the structures; the magnificent Frauenkirche, the St. Lorenz, and the others. The old city and its walls. And there was the ineluctable pathos of the rubble; children playing in the ruins, a GI sitting in the skeleton of a bombed-out building, sitting in an improvised easy chair, reading a novel. The people in the street, friendly, and quick to help with directions and odd bits of tourist information. The stadia were dull; weedy fields, chipped white stonework, nothing more. Nuremberg was the worst. Darmstadt after all was like a classic ruin, clean and ghostly. Frankfurt was austere even, in a sullen kind of way. Heilbronn was broken, shattered, little else. But this city was twisted, dirty, ugly, utterly hopeless. It was so gray and terrible one could not even pity it, only turn away in disgust.

Home again. The posters for the new Era. War Guilt items—*Wessen Schuld?* with pictures of Buchenwald. *Diese Schandtaten: Eure Schuld* with pictures of Dachau. Non-fraternization items—"Hello Sucker" with cries of rape from cartoons illustrating the moral of sleeping with a German girl. *Dummkopf* with montage of arms *heiling* Hitler giving meaning to extended German hand for friendly hand-shake. "Still her Dearest Possession," another badly drawn poster with German girl wheeling a baby carriage around affectionately, crowded with Nazi souvenirs and a portrait of the Führer.

Figure 10. Poster in Nuremberg proclaiming the city to be "guilty," © Lasky Center, Munich.

The road back. Dull long views of the countryside. A little wild we create our own adventure. Waving to every civilian, bicycling on the roads, working in the fields, hiking along through the towns. Call it a footnote to history. For if a German Volkswagen rode through the French provinces in say 1942 or 43 what would the similar responses have been? Here we can report that no one failed to wave back at us or in some way express a friendly greeting. Some waved their handkerchief, one girl waved the flowers in her hand and capsized the bicycle and her driver. Almost everybody smiled and were fraternal. There wasn't a harsh uncivil word or gesture all day. From the woman who told us the central square in Nuremberg was no longer Adolf-Hitler-Platz, but Hauptmarkt again—to the pretty girls sitting around in the fields who flirted with us. This is the item. Let it footnote what text there is.

10 June 1945, Augsburg

I have returned again to Henry Adams's *Education*, and now for the first time I find it relevant; indeed, gripping. I turned to the chapter on Germany and then on Rome, and the whole tone struck me with a deep personalness. Perhaps the problem of an American's education in Europe is a fundamental one. And there is no better time than now for me to be reminded of it. I read and hear of all the large pronouncements made on the end of the War, on the German people, on guilt and barbarism, and I am literally bewildered. How do they manage to speak with such loudness and confidence; how can they contrive all that pretense to authoritative intimacy with a situation which defies me day after day... as I talk to the people and wander the streets and impulsively, desperately fashion little adventures? As Adams wrote—"One begins at last to see that a great many impressions were needed to make a very little education, but how many could be crowded into one day without making any education at all."

On Maximilianstrasse. An old Bavarian was sitting in front of an intact house, the rest of the block was hollow, and he was almost a caricature of the folk, with his Alpine hat and feather-brush, his leather Bavarian shorts, the curious vestlet, the long pipe. We were taken by the pipe. And we hunted up a *Drechslermeister* to see whether we couldn't find ourselves one. Joseph Lele: Yes, he repaired them, but why don't you go to Philipp Ruf, he must have some for sale, and give him a *schönen Gruss* from me. We passed on the greeting and after a few friendly words of banter, we sported two long magnificent Bavarian pipes. We stuffed boxes of tobacco into the huge bowl and rolled down the avenue in clouds of smoke.

The sign said ice cream, and with almost childish delight we charged into the store. It was something of a soda parlor, manufacturing cream for the American troops, and for a few cigarettes we inherited several huge platters of what must have been pineapple custard. The afternoon was becoming memorable.

We continued gaily up past the cathedral and the roving eye caught glimpses of two young girls turning into sidestreets. We moved in behind them, and suddenly began inquiring about a host of sites in the city. The Dom? The theater? Did they really show *Faust*? And Mozart was often played? Oh, we should like very much to see it all! Our German suddenly became very halting and stuttering—it seemed, or so our strategy had it, so very much more charming to try to make communication in broken sentences and badly spoken phrases. Why they could hardly help us apart from directions—for after all it was *verboten* to go with German girls. They were almost playful and coquettish about the legal reminder. We pooh-poohed it, and found some reassurance in our nervous smiles at each other, and said we would call that evening. They waved goodbye to us (no, none of us would forget), and we were to see Helma and Regina that evening.

Schwedenweg is a little lonely street in the valley of the town, and we were to all intents and purposes lost when we called there almost at dark. The auto almost tiptoed through the streets. We were having our usual boyish sensations of doing something we shouldn't, relieved only by a rhetorical formula that after all we were only gathering material for historical reportage. (That would have been persuasive had we not been quite aware after all our fine times together that we never really indulged experience for the record, but always for the wonder and richness of the present itself! We had sworn hoarsely so many times that we could not afford to postpone life interminably, put off living to some more appropriate occasion in the eternally sanguine future. The moment was now. With an endowment of wit and energy and imagination every moment "could be made an adventure." We laughed at the memory of the Thurber cartoon, its keen touch of our modern frustration, and its real relevance to our own somewhat gauche—but yet gallant, I am sure—attempts to "Live!," to have vital deeply felt things happen.)

The girls were bright and gay, the parents were friendly and accommodating. We poured the cognac and the benedictine, and later we had tea and cookies. Helma kept insisting I drink and eat ("What will you have? *Fisch, Sterne, Herzen?*" I looked at her fondly, and picked up another heart-shaped cookie.) We mixed songs, gossip, and politics all evening. The girls sang *Rosamunde*, and the combination of new lyrics and a foreign tonal quality made it quite endearing. We broke into the *Lorelei* and *O Tannenbaum*. The father spoke quietly of the bad days, the Gestapo, the Hitler madness. Regina moaned that English was so difficult to learn! Why didn't they write it and speak it the same—as in German! Helma ridiculed her. Why everybody thinks their mother tongue is written and spoken properly? Tell me are you not certain, convinced that only English is perfect in spelling and pronunciation—and that German is a grammarian's horror? I grinned acquiescence; for some strange reason I was very proud of her. And when in a few minutes she went into her burlesque of the German Army equivalents of Mooney's and my rank (*Hauptmann* and *Oberleutnant*), I was genuinely stirred. She exaggerated the saluting and the nervous sense of discipline and the foolishness of the whole militaristic act. Helma (Wilhelmina) was becoming more than a little high, and proportionately brilliant. She told tales and went through the entire feminine vaudeville (pouting and flirting, posing anger and melting away in warmth and sweetness). Her story of the first meeting with Americans was striking. The opening period of the Occupation. Augsburg had fallen. The loud knocks on the door; five American soldiers, quite drunk, with drawn pistols. They were the military police. She knew, of course, that they weren't; or had learned that much since. They threatened to shoot her, and proceeded to search the house; they took her trinkets, her wrist-watch, what little jewelry there was around. Possibly they made a few advances to her, but this went unmentioned. The whole family was terrified. So these were the conquerors! And a few nights later: similar story; pounding on the door; the demand for cognac and schnapps; we don't have any; they shouted and threatened; we have none; finally they offered a fistful of marks for anything to drink; the same answer: there is none here; finally they left, but several of them remained in the house, sleeping on the steps in the hallways. We said nothing to the story. It didn't need verification. We knew of too many other stories. Only the other day in Munich: the minister had been told by the people of all the American looting; and he told them what a German soldier had said, "Why the Americans are pikers—you should have seen us in France..." This was another face of the barbarism. Murder and violence (legal or illegal) creates gangsters, and the world will be fortunate if it is not soon swallowed up in the banditry it created in order to save law and order.

I excused myself from the room, and was guided out by Helma. Where do you want to go? What do you want? I mumbled something. You're incoherent, what is it? I put my hands on her face. She moved in close to me, her soft wonderful body a comfort to my flushed unsteadiness. We kissed each other unbelievingly and then fiercely and then were unable to break away. A call went up for more tea. And we went our separate ways. For the rest of the evening, we two at least said almost nothing but gaped at each other passionately. We left long after midnight. Hallway farewells, and another familiar episode in uncontrollable lust.

11 June 1945, Augsburg

Lesson of The War Number One: the historical account of the battle of the Maison Rouge, which Sutton and I worked on this winter, was returned today from the Third Division. It was strongly urged that the original account not be incorporated into the official record. Objections were numerous and fundamental. A revised draft was submitted. It is useless to go through all the details. Where we knew the men wanted to attack because they were freezing on the other side of the river, the official report now has them "eager for combat and the assault." Where we knew the troops were frightened and hysterical, the story is only of "temporary disorganization and withdrawal." [...]

This is but a small symptom of the kind of truth which has devastated every element of a free spirit in the world, which has bureaucratized and corrupted speech, instinct, and conscience. This is our truth, which makes no one free, and enslaves no one so much as our poor selves.

In Augsburg, to the Dom: Sunday was cool and a little late in the awakening. We missed the services in the morning, but made sure we broke away in the afternoon. The very existence of the cathedral is almost a matter of deep sentiment. It might so easily have been the rubble of so many hundreds of other great European churches. The cathedral is quite untouched, except for some missing stained-glass windows, and the light streams in and strikes the whitish columns airily. There was a lean Gothic austerity to the choral music and of course to the ceremony, but there was no medieval dimness here, but an openness as if the prayerful mournfulness belongs not to the private churchly institution but to the whole world, in the sight of the sun and all eyes. The service had an overwhelming tragic simplicity. Old people, sometimes with little children, came in and kneeled and crossed themselves and made their way to their places. The chanted monotone echoed delicately throughout. In far-off corners and balconies priestly functionaries were quietly occupied. I watched from the very rear, and it seemed as if I could look over the heights of the cathedral into all the centuries of the Catholic religion, into two thousand years of Christian feeling. I forgot for more than a moment the disciplined historical knowledge of the Church and Popery and Vatican power. I could see only the endless funds of emotion which have been devoted to the worship of this God, Jesus Christ, the simple sentiment, the dark and deep emotions, the mysterious love and even fanaticism, and I could see too the genius, the magnificent creativeness of art and music and poetry, and also a unique personal achievement in the way of a devotional purity. Odd reminiscences blurred my mind. I thought of Palestrina and Bach, of Michelangelo and then curiously of Ralph Adams Cram, of Innocent III and Martin Luther and then again of Henry Adams and T. S. Eliot. Mooney interrupted me. "What showmanship!"

he murmured. "This is really the greatest show on earth," he whispered further. "Yes," I agreed, "it's had the longest run in history..." "Come with me," he said, "I'll say a prayer for you and you can see the altar in close-up." We moved forward together, and at the altar he knelt (with a striking grace and dignity, by the way) and I stood quietly by. The procession had just passed, and the atmosphere was strong with the tang of the incense. The music was swelling in conclusion, and the organ notes were majestic and chilling. There were moments then as during the whole service when I could not control my trembling.

We traveled out from the city into the countryside, and the loveliness, somewhat muted now by the threatening sky, reminded me that the natural beauties of the German scene represented the one and only triumph over the American sense of superiority; provincialism's only setback! The landscapes are seductive beyond resistance, and no one has failed to be charmed by the picture-book magnificence of German hills, valleys, rivers, mountains. Possibly its charm has a heightened note of urgency in this peculiar condition of tourist inspection—our real need to lose ourselves from the images of rubble and a devastated civilization. There is a transcendent consolation in the serenity of the natural aspect. The rolls of the hills lie, untouched, quietly, as though they had been sculptured softly by the sensitive palm of a godlike artistic hand and left sleeping. The varieties of color and perspective are an endless revelation.

13 June 1945, Augsburg

Hans (Wallenberg)[87] came in to see me, and we walked and talked most of the evening: a fine, sensitive soul, and there were moments of conversation and moments of silence in which we almost recovered some sense of dignity and even of moral purpose. We strolled through the streets of the city; the evening was cool but pedestrians were everywhere and we could see more and more young people. There were couples sitting on benches in the park squares and there were merry noises of small chatter and by-play. We both turned our steps around in the very same circle, reluctant to leave the street-scenes which for their very simple vitality had in a few minutes come to mean so much. We both hungered for "life," for a refuge from the poverty of our isolation; we sought everywhere for glimpses of the people and the ordinary course of existence; window-spectators watched us from windows. A German soldier, still in uniform, swaggered by and quickly saluted me; before I quite realized I had mechanically returned his greeting. Children on a corner were playing with a wagon but were suddenly distracted by the traffic (burst of) on the avenue—they shouted their shrill identifications of the various elements of the motorized American column (*Panzerwagen! Panzerjäger!*). I learned from them that the competition for American cigarettes was fierce, but that each was averaging about ten a day, and the oldest boy remarked proudly that most of his butts (salvaged), which were turned over to his father, were picked up while they were still burning. We made some facial sign of appreciation for the alertness and speed, and walked on.

We talked on about the disaster of the occupation, the emptiness, confusion, and corruption of our policies, and in one respect the discourse was almost illustrated. About non-fraternization Hans felt pretty much as I did. For him it was a gross colossal failure, and the only success it was achieving was in the creation of a "Prohibition" atmosphere. And that was precisely it, "Prohibitionism" returneth. On all sides we could see the furtive exchanges of glances between pretty German girls and the GIs. On side streets they were walking together. In the parks they were lying on the lawn. In a dark alley some soldier would be darting in and out. This was "bootleg" love, "bootleg" sex, and "bootleg" social life. Hans was even more passionate on the issue than I suspected would be likely. He was after all a refugee from Hitlerism, having fled Berlin in 1933; and he had, I know, received an immense personal satisfaction in witnessing the destruction of Nazism on his native soil. It was he in fact who interrogated all the leading party and army personalities captured in the last months, and many times he became more of a prosecutor than a simple questioner. (One general, according to the transcript, broke down and wept, when the accusation came again and again—this was your crime, your greatest crime, your ignorance, your irresponsibility, your helpless participation and collaboration in the illegality and barbarism of the Hitler government!) Still, the theory of collective guilt, for nothing less than that is the theoretical basis for non-fraternization with the German people at this point, is a monstrous thing. The posters on the circular billboards screamed out the indictment—*Diese Schandtaten: Eure Schuld!* and then a montage of Dachau and Buchenwald photos. People in various sections stood about and read it. I wondered what they made of it. Hans had previously conducted an investigation, and his conclusion had been that its only real effect was the stimulation of additional looting by the foreign element. Polish, French, Russian DPs among others took it as a license and a direct call in fact to conduct reprisals against the common people. And the average German—for the most part he was unable to understand how he too was guilty: in his bluff simplicity he knew himself only as a victim, and one of the regime's first victims—and the only lesson was the hopelessness and unmitigated blackness of the future which held only hatred and punishment for him and the whole people. For Hans this was the Nürnberg laws on the other side of the fence. No, it was not merely a matter of making national ghettoes of the American and German populations here. Repeal Non-fraternization, and GI Joe will get his girl. Fine. But there are greater, historic issues involved. The real wrong of the Nürnberg laws—real wrong, in the present context of expedient practical state policy—was its argument that the happiness and welfare of seventy-five million could be based on the unhappiness, the tragedy of five hundred thousand others. It proved its terrible failure. Just so will our argument that the well-being of a world order can be based on the alienation, frustration, political, and moral destruction of the German people, prove to be the undoing of World War II. For the second time in the lifetime of one generation modern society has declared its bankruptcy.

The extent of our disorientation and inadequacy is unbelievable. Mistakes are made, but no one holds a brief against that natural type of failing. But certain mistakes are inexcusable—mistakes born of the sheerest incompetency, mistakes committed by men who have no equipment whatsoever to learn from them, mistakes which are accounted in the twisted reckoning of our conqueror-complex as virtues for they are after all another form of punishment. It was characteristic for Hans to have refused a high job in the Economic Bureau of the Occupation. He was to have ninety-nine percent of the responsibility, ninety-nine percent of the freedom and authority—I could see the wonderful mansion, the Mercedes, the servants, the prestige. He refused. There were so many experts in the field available! He refused to have it on his own conscience that some thoughtless untrained directive of his was responsible for millions of Germans starving some winter. That the post should have been so freely offered about is characteristic too.

Where does the trouble lie? I am so close to the disease perhaps I am unable to see the real virus for the flushes of fever and the ugliness of the symptoms. Is it American capitalism? American naiveté and ignorance? American political or imperialist reactionaries? Is it postwar ennui? The eternal tragedy of history? The moral atheism of our modern world? Truly now: who here has the integrity and idealism to fulfill his role as his brother's keeper? Who here or anywhere has had sufficient resources of heart and mind to keep himself, to preserve an image of enlightened civilized soul in the deep private realm of his own inner life?

And then there remains only the spectacle of our American hypocrisy. Who are these outraged accusers? They grab the poor citizen by the back of the neck and shake him apoplectically: it was this spineless swine who did nothing against the Nazis, and brought the misery of a world on! But I think I know the accusers for what they are. They know no Germans; they have spoken to no Germans; they know no German history, make no pretense to understanding politics. And as for anti-fascism, why, for some it is meaningless and for others quite without existence. What did they ever do or say or sacrifice in the struggle against reaction and on behalf of a moral libertarian ideal? They consented to their conscription and their commitment to the battle. Nothing more. They are men without love, without seriousness, without humility.

If the glimpses of the devastation of this whole land was not enough, the poor helpless confessions of a folk which has been murderously victimized by the machine of modern history almost drives one to distraction. One always hopes, needs desperately to hope, but more and more the hope becomes mechanical and foolish. There remains precious little of culture or civilization in our great society, and the virtue of character is fast becoming an historic vestige. Humankind no longer has an inner light by which it could possibly have guided itself. In the time of the breaking of nations, broken too is the very spirit of men. Those whom our War and our Peace has not shattered, it has corrupted and left them only with a terrible mindlessness. So we salute the desert of our future.

20 June 1945

To Munich, again, alone, a free day.

The smells of the fields and whole countryside, overpowering almost, and for a moment you feel as if you too were part of the strength and serenity of the earth.

Munich in the sunshine of early morning... Cleaner than ever—shovel formations of ex-German soldiers marching by. The Hotel Excelsior restaurant is open now, but behind the clerk's counter was still the old mouse-like face of the proprietor, the Nazi, still holding on.

The despair of Military Government. Spoke to Deputy MGO (a Captain Laughlin), and he moaned for half an hour. Understaffed, hardly enough personnel to handle a metropolis this size; thousands of civil employees used to work in the administration; now some thirty or forty Americans are supposed to be efficient. The constant interruptions. Friends and relations, Senators, Robert Murphy (who ran through the city in half an hour), etc. And the governors themselves—"They only want to know: 'When's the next PX?'" So we do nothing, and call it Occupation. A glorified regime of Do-Nothingness.

Along Ludwigstrasse to the University. A ruin. In the distance the Frauenkirche: her fractured battered towers: sick, dying, tubercular image.

University bookshop. Found Franz Oppenheimer's *Der Staat*, a collection of Max Weber, Werner Sombart on the bourgeois, some fine Italian prints of Dürer and Botticelli, Mommsen on Caesar, a biography of Rainer Maria Rilke, among other things. What wonderful hours I spent browsing! A good deal of NS stuff around—*Hegel for Our Times*, and Nietzsche's *Message to Us*, and *What We Learn from Goethe*, and similar poison. Also, to my delight, shock, surprise, and amusement—an immense collection of Bouck White's *Book of Daniel Drew*! Here, to be sure, the Nazis found their Typical American Capitalist, with all the lessons of Hypocrisy, Greed, and Social Typology magnificently outlined for them.

Visited the Arenbergs in the afternoon, found Prince Johann-Engelbert at home, and spent the rest of the day with him.

His optimism about the American occupation is fast dwindling. The incompetency is becoming clear. The failure to get the city out of its paralysis. The trams run, but on a limited basis. The factories, the mines, and a host of other industrial institutions are stalled, mostly by bureaucratic red tape. Insists that the reconstruction is simple, that the Germans available could handle the whole thing themselves, if the detachments didn't get in their own and everybody else's way. The Arenbergs have organized a Munich Relief Committee, but tonight the MG stickers on the truck expire, and that means another delay. And what incompetency! The police officer who comes in at eleven, signs four passes, and takes off. He still remains naive about the American personality, so pleasant, so attractive, but good-will, I had to argue again and again, will not solve social problems. His mother's surprise. I thought the Americans were so energetic! And look the weeks go by and so little is done... The general feeling: the Nazis must be laughing; why even under the air-raids and in all the desperation, the Nazis had the city functioning, factories, labor, communications, everything! More and more people say: *Ach*, the old Nazi energy... No nostalgia, no regrets, but it is obvious that something is lacking in the American occupation. Several engineers the Prince knew have gone over to Russian occupation—they can find work there and achieve things. Results... The prince pokes fun at the German civil official—whose life is in his bureau, knows nothing above it, only work. They could really put Bavaria back on its feet.

Met Dr. F. Schäffer, prime minister, an elderly sober soft-spoken German official.[88] A frank talk about Bavarian problems and the American supervision. Quiet confidence, conservative, but intelligent. Little Nazis flood key offices—his statistical-finance branch has many. But can't be removed until replacements with technical training are found. However—big Nazis! The finance minister is an old well-known Nazi! Remains in office. The various provincial posts were cleared and the replacements in very few instances are better. The problem of creating a democratic public opinion, with a German press; question of making new loyalties and confidence—overlooked completely. Rumors spread. When soldiers died in the boxcars at the Munich railroad station there was talk of the "Dachau of indifference." The Dachau of criminality had boxcars full of corpses at the concentration camp. Now the "crime" is of a somewhat different shading, only.

So the day went.

Supper with the Arenbergs, in the evening (on French cognac, what a relief from our old supply), out to garage and locating Nazi vehicles which might possibly be of use to someone.

To bed, and in the morning the race back to Augsburg.

25 and 26 June 1945

Left at five, and rather hurriedly to beat the new memorandum to the door—officers forbidden to drive jeeps alone. Hit the autobahn and the old route, Dasing, Odelzhausen, etc., was a reassurance. Found the Adlerwerke for the Triomphe-Junior key but had no model number so gave it up, and headed for Mandelstrasse.

The prince was at home, father, too, and we had dinner again. Delight of fresh eggs, butter, fruits. Had bowl full of cherries from Rimsting garden, and then the old German superstition: no water after fruit at penalty of death! The old man, however, had a strategy: wine serves to cushion the blow; the rarity of fresh fruit in soldier's digestive life may be too much of a surprise. I finished the wine. Felt no better, no worse, simply fine. Reminiscences of America—naval student in 1910–11 at Pensacola, New York with its varieties of ice cream and sodas, the endless appetite, the wonder at the bars with thousands of different cocktail specials, the horse-leavings in the street (is New York still so dirty?—Why, no, horses have completely disappeared—of course!).

Went out for a little ride, visited Nellie B. House intact, although wings bombed. Had been born in Alaska, lived on West Coast, studied art in Germany, married German. A Nazi. Had two children. Managed divorce, and has now picked up her babies who had been deposited in Ravensburg and Heidelberg. A charming, slender blonde, with pleasant far-western accent and thorough American-accented German (fluent, but every syllable was our pronunciation as of German classes in college). The prejudices of society. The talk of the "mob" and the "masses." The strong hatred of Maquis-French violence and vulgarity. Here is the "terrible people" of the French revolution again. (Although I have a fair understanding of what they find repugnant.) The prevailing image of France is a terrible, corrupted people, footloose and violent. Of Russia, of the Brutal Horde. German girl's insistence: why people can die! (drinking water after cherries), we laughed, but tried not to be offensive. Nellie's plans: to remain in Germany, return to her painting. Portrait of Constantine (young Prince of Bavaria, who gave me Declaration-of-War-on-Russia copy of *Völkischer Beobachter*). Story of his marriage. What is she like? Pretty? Intelligent? "Oh... well... well, she is elegant!" Glimpses of the old tradition of nobility's marriages. The Prince (Johnny) seemed more independent and mundane, and had to smile at the royal past crowding in on the present. Touch of old Munich social life returning; hopes for future. Invitation.

Early next morning, off for the Chiemsee. The prince has nothing to do. He had been removed from his position as assistant to the governor (Schäffer), and is now unemployed. No reason given for removal. New personnel, new *Fragebogen*, new suspicions. How AMG functions—waves of distrust and suspicion; Nazis still around; but questioning old choices (a little hysterical), out go the few anti-Nazis who had managed to be called up. The old route east; this was main route before Hitler's autobahn; mark one improvement down for Nazism. Rimsting. The Arenberg house. The long view of the lake and the whole Chiemsee valley. The special delight was not in the loveliness of the landscape, but simply in its being there! The beauty of this whole countryside has strange, upsetting effects. One has to struggle against taking it all for granted. It might have been a prosaic nothingness, but it wasn't—it was a wide glistening lake, dotted with islands, and the black masses of the fore-Alps dominating the horizon. The wonder was not so much in the natural spectacle, but in the role of spectator... The return of the family. The daughter, a quiet shy not very pretty girl (sixteen); the son (Willie), a tall sunburned handsome boy who had been in the Luftwaffe; and the mother, the Princess Eberhard von Arenberg, who was a distinguished and charming woman.

Notes on the family. The Belgian tradition of the mother. The Hohenzollern suggestion for a place in Germany. The castle in the Rhineland. Caught in World War I and remained German, although the children were born in the Lowlands. Their isolation in the Nazi era. Refused to collaborate. Challenged as "Jews" when no Nazi swastika emblem was on their cars. Cut themselves off from society because of political differences. Accusations against sons as "cowards" for non-participating in battle. "I refused to have them serve, and when finally we could hold out no longer, I did everything to keep them from the front. It was not at all a matter of personal safety for them. This was a Nazi war, and we were not fighting for a cause or a country but only for these Party madmen. I would not have my children fire a single shot on their behalf. It was an unjust war, which we started and which I hoped we would lose. I can't tell you how the boys felt when they were to be called up for the invasion of Holland and Belgium. It was a terrible time for them and all of us." Conversation interrupted by visitors. Young man and girl. Princess very curt, failed to introduce us until the last moment, extended no invitation to join us. The girl had been a leader of the *Deutsche Mädel* group, a real fanatic. The whole family (Count M. of Bavaria) capitalized on the Nazi war machine. Now of course there were efforts at rapprochement, but it was not to be. Efforts during war. Doctor, old man, who had been married to Jewess for thirty years, now to be sent to the mines to work (sixty-three years old!). Attempt to intervene with *Gauleiter* Giesler[89] in old man's behalf. Party personnel always in their bunkers. Finally, an interview. Ranting for half an hour. These people have to be destroyed! A fat red-faced vulgar madman, who recited the *Völkischer Beobachter*. No hope. "Saw Hitler only once. At the theater (Polish ballet) in Munich. A very nervous fearful unhappy man: impression. Constantly gesticulating with hands. Seemed to be afraid of the crowd. Surrounded by SS-men. He never could have had a moment of happiness. I wonder often whether he was not one of the great mediocrities of history or whether he was really a great dynamic personality. When the show was over, he and entourage rushed out. The crowd was pushed aside, and the Führer disappeared. A very strange and for me profound performance. This was the barbarian who would bring all of Europe to this irremediable mess. . ." Other themes. German girls marrying in China; unhappiness; matriarchate. . . Her career in photography. International exhibitions and awards of special camera art. The house crowded with documents and archives of the Staatsbibliothek. Impressions of the occupation: run-in with local officers ("we don't want any of these soft guys around here," said one MG captain); the paralysis. The loss of American prestige with the do-nothingness. If at least it was announced: nothing will be accomplished; this is your punishment. But plans and intentions are professed, and then everything falls through by default or incompetency. That is truly a mess. . . Friends with Colonel Keegan, the military governor; her hope to see him about Johnny's removal. (His *Fragebogen* was alright, but he was not to serve.)

The trip to the lake. Herreninsel (with another of Ludwig's fantastic castles), Fraueninsel (which we explored; old eighth-century church; unbelievable little village on isle; gardens, fishnets; barefooted children; one auto) and Krautinsel (garden for convent). *Grüss Gott!* The old man with Bavarian pipe mumbled at us in dialect. *Guten Tag*, I replied hesitantly. Evening trip back to Munich with Johnny and Princess-mother. Third Army territory (They told me I wouldn't see any more dirty boots, and non-saluting, and loose ties. . . things are going to be different.) (*Ach*, the new order comes to Bavaria.)

3 July 1945

Notes for a slipping memory.

The last days with Helma. The fear of getting hurt again. "It would be wonderful, really wonderful, I can't say, tell you how wonderful it would be to be in love, sincerely and completely. But think of what would happen, and so terribly soon! You'd be going away, and I would be here alone, left alone again. Then the hurt would be so much greater, and no, not even the sweet remembrances would help... Things have been so bad for so long, one can't risk being hurt so deeply again. Understand me and please forgive me. And don't think me cruel or vulgar if I say, find somebody else—you can and you should! Somebody warm and affectionate. I am afraid I am too cold and torn apart to be of much comfort and comradeship for you. Let's not even start. No, not even the slightest beginning, please... If I had known the awful consequences of the last time, I never would have had the courage, or is it foolishness, to start then. He was a Frenchman, and like now there was always the secrecy and the horrible anxiety, and the knowledge that as soon as 'things got better,' really, it was all over for us. Well, the war came to an end; happy, happy event. And I was alone again. Once more there was nothing. Dancing and the theater were gone, and now he was too... Can't you see it will be a repetition of something that has already wounded me once. It's a selfish reason, I am thinking only of myself, I know. But if I blame that on the war and what it has done to us, don't think it's a convenient thing to say. It is the truth. We live for so long in such ugly self-concern about our own skins, comforts, well-being, that nothing remains of character except what has survived in the blackout. *Bitte, Motty, bitte, bitte.*[90] It's not easy for me. I wanted to tell you last night and the night before. I'll never forget you, never in all of my life, and I'll make up little dreams of my own so often. But it can't be, it mustn't be. I am after all a German, and I know you are going to argue that I am putting in an unnecessary performance as a self-appointed martyr. But that too may be required of these times. I am a German; you are an American. Then there is the war, and the occupation, and the police, and the neighbors—and most of all there is you and I. It comes down only to that in the end. You will be going away, any day, and I will be alone and hurt again."

I had not the heart to argue with her. We said goodbye, with all the proper sentimental touches. I came by for her again in several days, and she knew I would come, had been expecting me. We smiled at each other shyly, for now there was another wrinkle to the sin, we were cheating on our own farewell. I never saw her after that.

The problem of identification—prompted by headline of Eisenhower's blast against Brass Hats. The real distortion of focus in our own era. Labels have been systematically confused. Our entire intellectual discourse involves endless cases of mistaken identification. We see anti-fascists where there are in reality none at all. We see monsters and ogres where in truth there is only an infernal machine darkened by our own spiritual shadow etc. etc. Recall: how the *Times* used to argue against socialism—why the socialism in Russia has produced an economic system which is so exploitative and class-prejudiced, why it's worse than capitalism even. (Ergo, let us preserve our own capitalism, with its equal economic blessings for all!) The sleight-of-hand of the labels.

And now the brass hats! Identity is missing. All of our identities are missing. To the General: "stay off our side." But that's precisely it. Society has ingeniously camouflaged its traditional front lines. Where are the boundary lines for the "sides"?

Week of 6 July 1945

Notes on a madness.

Aina, Friday. There is something fresh and charming about her. Perhaps it's the curious Nordic element, tawny-blonde hair, blue eyes, sunny-brown complexion; or perhaps the attractiveness of the stranger European body, fuller and in a not unpleasing way a little less formfull. But why dehydrate with dry analysis freshness and charm. It's the beauty of her face when she is sentimental and tender and glowing; the wonderfully formed expressions when she is curious or querulous or dreaming; the tones and inflections of her voice which catches so effectively all her mixed emotions ("But can we really be honest and sincere and loving with each other? But if there is no war with Russia—forgive me, darling, for bringing, it up again—but if there is no war, then I shall never go home again, I am exiled from Riga, from Latvia, from my whole life, forever! Oh, don't be a child. Pour me another few drinks, fast, fast. And let's go to your place..."). Memories of the first night. The dance, and the long flirtation across the floor. The playful sinfulness of cheating on the rules and regulations; the meeting on the veranda; the ride home, crowded, in the rain. The long unpersuasive talks about love. The bitterness and resentment about missing appointments. Finally, the long ride to Schloss Linderhof, the magnificent warmth of her hands and her touch and especially of her eyes and her smile—and to be sure, the sweet naiveté of her incredulousness at all the luxury and sybaritic richness of the Ludwig castle. Friday, to Westheim; and the mishaps with benedictine and the vermouth. The ride to Haunstetten, and the impulsive turn into the *Gasthof*. The last drinks. And to bed. What a fierce passion! Clawed and bitten and tossed about; the poor kid was beyond herself most of the time. She was very much embarrassed the next morning to see my eye, distinctly wounded, and the marks on my neck and body. We both made light of it however, and smiled at each other with no tension and doubt. Again: Aina, Monday. A little more sober, a little less wild; holding back her passion (unfortunately) with what was almost a desperation. For all the university veneer a simple peasant character (about love, emotions, bed) (the embarrassment in the morning about the condition of the room, and her pleading to wash the sheet before departure; I felt so ridiculous about the affair, I dozed off, and she worked on, happy about my "consent"). Auto difficulties: wrapping the bumper around an iron post in the middle of the night; stalling in the morning.

Helma, Sunday. Uneasy and anxious for no discernible reason at all; went back for additional cognac-and-cointreau, pacing up and down before the sunlit windows of the bar, and finally took off for Schwedenweg. The motor roared to a stop on the quiet street, and suddenly she came leaping out of the door. She could hardly believe it; apparently she had been hoping against hope for my return, and I of course except for this impulse had quite given up. She was as happy and pleased as a gurgling child. How wrong she had been, how stupid; I must remain with her, come back again and again, forget all the nonsense of the last time... We drove out, and she said yes to everything, to every absurd request. But why, why. We drove into the *Gasthof* yard, proceeded upstairs. She was still evidently overjoyed, and was enthusiastic and loving. This was really the first time; but as I knew, sweet and young, but skillful and thoroughgoing. Home after midnight, holding me, head on my shoulder, hair overflowing on to my cheek.

Lydia, Wednesday. Returned to Innsbruck and found her "out," but her agents spread the word about and she came bouncing along with more affection, more personal warmth than I had yet seen. We went on our old *Spazierfahrt*, along new routes. The Inn Valley was gray and invaded by odd formations of low-hanging clouds. I was hardly eager, but nothing of the sort could be said for her. How long would I stay? Would I stay with her? Why couldn't I spend a few nights here? Couldn't anything be arranged? I was, in part deliberately, rather casual, and it only prompted her. I was pleasant and reminisced about our old nights together, and regretted that there could not be others. She took the argument up. No night, then, but we have the afternoon? Cold as I was, the suggestion was too intriguing. At her apartment then, at three o'clock in the afternoon. And there we were. Undressing in broad sunlight, masked only somewhat by the sheer drapery over the window. There was on my part, I am afraid, something of a disinterested efficiency to the whole performance; but there it was, unbelievable, unforgettable. She was so yielding and so eager I felt almost miserable about my calculating (if romantic) objectivity. But still, there was something immensely satisfying about the experience, and I really hope for myself it is not the mere satisfaction of a bookkeeper adding sums.

No, it was a madness. A seizure of nerves and the passions. And also a desperate exercise in hidden intellectual prejudices. Remember that line somewhere from Stendhal—"This is the supreme triumph of your civilization. Out of love it makes ordinary affairs." My curse (if my single achievement) was that here I belonged not to this "civilization," and to know, to share it and live with it I would reduce, with all vulgarity and tastelessness, sentiment and affection and sex to the ordinariness and even sordidness of commonplace fornication.

So it was, and perhaps all this is an elaborate unsubtle rationalization to preclude the onset of a remorseful self-shame, an embarrassment before my own inner self. Perhaps...

[...]

10–12 July 1945

Rumors and gossip about troop movements again, and perhaps I could catch some units before it was too late. Left for the 103rd and Tenth Armored, and primarily (*selbstverständlich*) for Innsbruck and the core of the partisan story of the May days.

Found Colonel West on the Ammersee east of Landsberg, and had a brief talk. Once more: a bright, intelligent (as intelligence runs here) soldier, but quite without the understanding and depth required by the crises which came up. He spoke authoritatively, sharply, rather arrogantly of the resistance movement ("disorganized rabble"), and with the hopeless ignorance and blindness which is the hallmark of the great American military machine. Some details were clarified. He had been negotiating with the German command at Hungerburg when the Gruber committees took power below in the valley.[91] The command post was surrounded and the entire staff was captured—including Colonel West. He must have been treated a little roughly—Dr. Gruber later explained he was taken for a special German agent, a parachutist perhaps! That personal grievance did not serve very well ever to make for a rapprochement. He was rather objective about the achievement of the *Putsch*, although he was snappish about it. The HQ of the partisans was something out of "a cheap movie"—swarming armed civilians and assorted troops, runners dashing in wildly reporting flares in every which direction, hectic reports from the scattered town outposts... But they did contribute to the disruption of the last Nazi defenses, their radio propaganda prompting desertion, their successes pushing the chronic and fatal disorganization everywhere. They did "preserve order," although I am quite suspicious of that hoary virtue. And of course rendered service to the Military government, which to be sure rapidly managed to dispense with that gratuitous assistance.

Into the mountains, and into a fierce storm, and never saw the sun again for days. The rain was driving and miserable. Picked up a GI in Oberammergau and two Austrian women just below Mittenwald. Down into the valley we went to the tune of the local gossip—airplane crashes at the airports, Hofer the drunkard, the fear of the Russians and the French, the death of husbands on the eastern front, the speculation about an independent Austria, the fate of South Tyrol (Bolzano, Merano) and to the European hit parade (once again:

Rosamunde, In der Nacht ist der Mensch nicht gern alleine, Ich bin heute ja so verliebt, usw).

Found a room in the Hotel Kreid, with the last of the Americans in the Tyrol. The French had already taken over—new zone: Tyrol—Vorarlberg. Stupidities, stupidities, only stupidities. Austria is a problem, and the solution is always obvious: divide it up. Which leaves the US in Salzburg, the Russians in the east, and the French in the West, with the British sandwiched in somewhere.

[...]

Innsbruck, and I imagine all of Tyrol was none too happy about the new regime. Up at the Sonnenberghof, Lisl and Gretl had long faces as they waited on a crew of French women, apparently WACs of some sort, or hospital attendants. They sat there with me practically expressionless, eyes dropping and moving about meaningfully as loud screams or some crash and noise came out of the rooms and hallways. "Not very nice people. . ." The American regime was becoming a dream, a legend.

At the town hall, Dr. Gruber (tall, full head of straw-blonde hair) also had his grievances. He was quite realistic about it. There were troubles, difficulties with the Americans, but that now was the "golden age." The French were here, and a new crisis was setting in. Primarily: the economic question. The Americans were self-sufficient—they brought their own food and supplies, demanded nothing from the country. The French take their rations of milk, bread, cheese, cream, vegetables, etc., and then supplement their own national poverty with what existing machinery survived in Tyrol. Again: administrative seriousness is lacking. The Americans made their mistakes, but they worked in their offices and were in a real respect responsible. The French never turn up before eleven, are out most of the afternoon, and lose several days each week with parades and affairs of "honor." The Army officials impressed him as being curiously conservative (I explained a little about the relations of the Maquis and the Old Military, after Jean Casali in Lunéville), but nevertheless there was some saving grace of political hope, although he was cynical about it. The Catholics are optimistic, because everyone knows how strong Church influence is. The Communists are sanguine, for Russian orientations are powerful in Paris. The resistance was hopeful, for the French understand these things. The social-democrats were glad, for there was Blum and the great Socialist party of France. So something was salvaged.

The parade. The turbaned colonial troops everywhere, Moroccans and what-not, and I had my old feeling of resentment. Armies are evil enough, but the spectacle of a non-national force, an imperial-mercenary troop, quite revolts me. The exhibition was all American equipment, from the anti-tank weapons and artillery to the web equipment and shirts and pants. The flags were flying, which was a departure from US policy, but I am not sure it has political meaning. It may have been only for dress effect, and the commandant would certainly issue any directive to make the parade a success. The next morning another parade, more colonials, more music; probably rehearsals for the arrival of General Béthouart on the 14th and the Grand parade. Getting out of town and jeep getting caught in the middle of the formation! GI in the back (Kisslowicz from Brooklyn), shouting fraternal greetings at the un-understanding French troops, and mostly at the understanding Austrian girls—*Oh, baby! Oh, baby! Was ist los?* (And so it went for Kisslowicz didn't miss a trick from Innsbruck to Munich—*Oh baby, was ist los?*)

19 July 1945, Augsburg

Dear Meyer,[92]

As I mentioned the other day our headquarters are moving from Bavaria into the Rhineland for the occupation period, which means the imminent switch (this weekend) from Augsburg to Heidelberg. In some ways I regret it very much. The special opportunities of Munich I have found very attractive, and Bavaria itself was strikingly congenial. But, they all tell me, the terrible winter approacheth, and that's the main enemy; the only refuge seems to be the Neckar Valley (but then of course there are so many other obvious advantages of an untouched and for Germany flourishing university town).

I had only a few hours to say goodbyes in Munich the other evening, and I raced about making as many inquiries as I could. Both Hermann Usener and Max Foerster were in the city, and I noted their addresses but I couldn't reach them that evening nor the following morning. I checked through the University catalog with Prof. von Rintelen (philosophy and theology: Catholic), and I picked up some random comments. Foerster had been "betrayed" by one of his assistants, man named Spindler, who played his hand with the party and then took over his appointment.[93] The same kind of thing was being worked on old Karl Vossler, but with a little less success. Martin Heidegger is still living in Freiburg, and rather quietly. In the early years, I am told, he was quite a fanatic, and as rector of the university held regular and thorough purges. Hitler apparently went too far for him, and in the recent period since the war he has slowly moved himself out of politics. Jaspers is safe (at last) in Heidelberg, and von Rintelen visited him last month. His wife is Jewish, and all these years have of course been terrible for him. The University here, as you must know from other sources, is quite a wreck. The Ludwigskirche across the street is one of the few churches in the city intact. Everything else has been horribly destroyed. The Frauenkirche actually looks sickly; the two towers barely extend themselves upward, and with a kind of tubercular enfeeblement. Almost everything you would want to ask about, or for that matter everything you could locate on a town-plan, has been struck. Some of the visiting soldiers are putting little research questions aside for further investigation: there is as you know almost no war industry in Munich, and certainly none in the city proper; it was nevertheless devastated. There are to be sure plans for the reopening of the university but if our military government can be depended upon nothing will come of that insidious plot to seize power again. The whole regime is just stupid. There is so much foolishness, so much simple ignorance about in AMG circles it is hard for me to reclassify the American state policy in some more impersonal way. On the university matter what they have done is to check through the *Fragebogen*, and made an automatic elimination of all party members. Which leaves practically no faculty. Naturally if they want to be purists on the Party issue all well and good; it has virtues as well as obvious shortcomings. But in dozens of other activities they leave Party members and Nazis (well-known fanatics) in office on the grounds that they are for the time being necessary, their services are expedient. In the "minor" cultural matters they reserve for themselves to exercise complete anti-Nazi indignation. In Tübingen the French have appeared to me a little more sensible. Rector and staff were appointed, and they were made responsible for the elimination of the vicious among the faculty. It takes something less than political genius to understand that most of the university members were far from being real *Parteigenossen*. I have myself heard of so many cases where the card was issued almost at the point of the pistol. The estimate is that about sixty to seventy percent were in the NSDAP. Of the "independents," most were the old professors—men like Adolf Weber and Karl Vossler (here in München—both of whom, by the way, declined the appointment as rector of the new university age)—and a few were simply contrary (like Rintelen, who is a Catholic and without a family, and who would dare to call the *Gauleiter*'s hand). This broad party base did not make for the Nazification of the university, but to all intents and purposes the last vestige of independence had been eliminated. Students told me that in the last years it was a joke, a grotesquerie. In every way it was a terribly trying experience. Students in conference might begin grumbling against the regime, and what should one do? A word of sympathy, and the Gestapo might know of it in the morning. A feigned coldness and hostility, and one of the few remaining remnants of reasonableness might be alienated. Just a very few dared to work openly. Kurt Huber[94] (psychology-philosophy) became rather notorious as an anti-Nazi in the early years of the war. His students were writing *Nieder mit Hitler* on the blackboards, and Huber was "careless" enough to mention it to colleagues with some pride. He helped prepare the students' movement propaganda of 1942–43, and apparently was the counselor for the Scholl demonstration after Stalingrad in the early weeks of 1943. He, the Scholl brothers, Christine [*sic*] Probst,[95] and some fifteen others were hanged for treason. There was some mention of the desire to erect a memorial to Huber and the others when a new University is created. (Huber, by the way, was a Pg. too—the NSDAP had its Heideggers and its Hubers.)

I don't have very much else for you. Karl Barth, of course, left Bonn for Basel a long time ago (there never was a *Heil Hitler* permitted in his presence). Robert Curtius (very anti-NS) is still, most people think, in Bonn, although he may have as you indicate moved to Heidelberg. Alfred von Martin lives here in Munich, and I visited him for a few minutes the other morning. [...]

There isn't much more to add, except to say that I overlook the largest issue—politics and the intelligentsia—until another time. The Russian question is of course central to it. I have been quite amazed to discover that as deep and obsessive as the fears of the Russians are (for some it is the image of Mongolian hordes, for others ill-mannered peasants, for a great many others another more terrible totalitarianism which learned from and taught Nazism much), there is a considerable pro-Russian movement—the Russians as the *Volk der Zukunft*. The more of a failure America makes of its military achievement the more reconciled the German *Militarismus* and *Kleinbürgertum* become to the prospects of finding some opportunities only under an energetic force of communism.

Add: You must forgive the scantiness of these notes. I wish I had time to make serious inquiries: but always I have to manage a dozen things at once. I wanted to make a last search for books, and I did pick up two volumes of the *Handbuch der Philosophie* (*Die Grunddisziplinen: Logik, Erkenntnistheorie, Ästhetik, Metaphysik des Altertums-Mittelalters-Neuzeit; Staat und Geschichte: Philosophie der Sprache-Gesellschaft-Recht-Staat-Geschichte-Kultur-Technik*). Also: a work of Fueter in Below-Meinecke, Sombart, nineteenth-century Germany, and Loserth's *Huss und Wiclif*. I have some empty space in one of the Nelson boxes, and I'll stuff them into that, and in a month or so you'll be able to see them at Ben's,[96] if you have an interest in these or any of the other things. I'm making a carbon of this and sending it on to Ben. With best regards.

20 to 23 July 1945, Augsburg and Heidelberg

With Dr. Roeck,[97] and Ohlenroth, through old Augsburg. The Roeck house, eighteenth century, but most striking: the attachment, physical and spiritual, of a cultivated man for his house. The son, and the days of the freedom-movement; meeting the armored spearheads. The incident of the sergeant and the flak-girl; a sniper had fired; the sergeant was shot dead in return fire; the girl was ordered to mount and be taken back; she insisted she be shot, she feared nothing; the US officer insisted; she was adamant; shoot me; he fired once, twice, over her head, wide off the mark; she flinched a little, but her mind was made up; the officer was bewildered, almost helpless; he argued a bit more, and then shot her, in the face, she fell and died in an explosion of blood. Later the column was held up; the lieutenant could not manage to go on; he sat in a jeep by the side of the road and was uncontrollable; he broke down, from nervousness and tension and the realization that it was the first woman he had ever killed.

The tradition of Augusta Vindelicorum; the deep cultivated love of the city, its history, of Roeck and Ohlenroth. The latter had led many expeditions, and was responsible for the great Roman excavations in Bavaria (the old sunken churches by the Dom, the Imperial outposts from Verona to the Donau border). Now with the destruction of the accretions of later eras, the archeologist has an opportunity which would never have presented itself without the tragedy and destruction of War. Ohlenroth, for all his natural pacifism, could not disguise his enthusiasm. How many times he had passed a house, and cursed it for impeding the progress of a great favorite research! And now... The afternoon (Sunday) was warm and fine, and we made our tour—the Dom, St. Ulrich's (and Afra) Cathedral, the Fuggerei, the Rotes Tor, the town hall (a skeleton, and the Goldener Saal only a memory).

With Helma—a last evening, pleasant and sweet without sentiment although there were felt emotions. Playfulness almost wild (what with daylight and mirrors and utter soberness). With Aina—we had missed each other all week, and she was quite dispirited. That afternoon she had seen my car pull in and pull out in the distance, and she shouted and waved, but I of course could hardly hear or see her. I had only a very few minutes for farewells. She began to cry, red swollen eyes, and almost quivering lips. I promised to return later that evening. (The boxes were lugged, and I came back in a jeep.) She wanted to see or say nothing, go nowhere, only to be with me an evening. We sat and talked: I talked, she fought back tears. We went to Frau Ossmann's (Gasthof zur Sonne) and we were obliged to eat and drink, the inevitable maternalism. We drove home rather sullenly, after an hour in the courtyard (the Adler back was roomy), and she cried again and bit her lips fiercely. (I had been "so good to her"; why wasn't I like "so many of the others; it would have been so easy to say goodbyes then"; this was "the only light" in her life in Germany; "there is nothing else, nothing, nothing remains"; something nice "can become of my life, but not even the simplest pleasures truly remain for her..." So she sobbed. The last goodbye fairly dripped with sentiment, and a good measure of real tenderness. She had been a fresh, charming, affectionate creature, and I will never forget the twinkle of her eyes and the pursing of her lips—*Selbstverständlich, Mathias!*[98]—or her throaty loving "Mottisseel."

The long ride in the sunlight, via Stuttgart (lunch at the Schlossgarten, for an exchange of K-rations), and the Heidelberg *Kaserne*. Unpacking—the physical burden of historical scholarship! And the adventures of a Sunday. Two girls fleeing the French occupation in Pfalz. An old lady, weeping hysterically—she had "missed" her bus to Karlsruhe, and now every thing she owned was gone. We chased the bus, caught it, and learned that the MPs had put her off—overpacked passengers. We swallowed the illegalism, and waved cheerfully goodbye. They cheered us and thanked us in broken eloquent English and pidgin. Finding a garage.

The visit to the Jaspers. Mrs. Jaspers reading Goethe; dry remarks on Byron, "a very sick man" (my volume of letters). Conversations on the black days—she is a Jewess. The Russian question ("he understands the Russian question" was my subsequent introduction to the professor). A tall white-haired handsome man; looking rather ill, which he was. We talked briefly, and he returned to bed. I talked on with his wife, and two girls there. On American fairy-tales—Mrs. Jaspers had been curious about US folk-literature (the peace or violence of the German tales; the charm and culture of the Chinese). On the Army—the comic strips (for grown-ups! surprise)—the soldiers who carry doughnuts in their pockets and grease their uniforms—the "Gestapo" methods of the police—the flirtations from the street ("if you've got any guns or rifles, better hide them, the MPs are coming around in a regular search pretty soon!"). I left, to return in a few days for an interview with the professor. Mrs. Jaspers gave me a copy of Max Weber's letters to read. She had reminisced frequently about him; had quoted favorite remarks of his; had recalled how she followed him about the streets when she had been a student, and how much she loved him.

In the evening, the routine of adventure. Christy, by the Neckar. To the hotel, and a nice passionate night. Early exit in the morning. They had run away from the conscription of pretty young German women by the French officers, and now they were forced to find their way back. There were no opportunities in Heidelberg, esp. without passes, ration cards, etc. Perhaps they could still escape "the clutches of *der Kapitän*."

25 July 1945, Heidelberg

Wednesday evening, visit with the Jaspers.

Mrs. Jaspers, busy in the kitchen, green vegetables and so forth; so pleased about the foodstuffs, wine (salmon, cocoa, etc.).

The Professor and I retired to his study, a fine book-lined room, and we talked for an hour.

The difficulties of the last dozen years. His manuscripts—because since 1937–38, publication of his works very difficult.

In bookstores the display was always resplendent for the Nazi things, but very little sales; Nazis hardly read books, not even their own.

The request in Heidelberg continued for old and good things, Rilke, Weber, among others being often requested.

Many of the students were taken by the new trumpetry, and in many respects free university life, the free cultural spirit of the community died.

Recalls the address of Heidegger, then rector of Freiburg University, introduced as *Parteigenosse* Heidegger. So many trampled with their feet (old H. custom for approval) but others again came up and confessed to J., real views.

The story of Heidegger. Identification with the Nazi cause, but had his own private program for the party. Conducted purges of his faculty—fanatical, blind, stupid. Fast friends for many years—since 1920. Each year, the annual visit. But relations were broken sharply after that. Soon fell out with the polemical requirements of a Nazi Führer... His works were held up; unable to produce any really important or substantial things. In later years withdrew, and the stories of the last years were that he was an oppositionist; the war was lost; the party had to be put aside to make peace.

Would I have him in the university? Yes. Sometimes the line between political propaganda and free intellectual discussion is blurred. But I would have Heidegger in my university. Let there be a free and healthy clash of ideas. I can understand his proscription, however. In any case I would insist on the right to publication of his works. Either we are to be slaves, or we will be able to make a new beginning for free spirits.

Ernst Robert Curtius. Since '33 out of the university, living private life of scholarship in ancient and medieval times. Like von Martin, not without its significance for our crisis, but not in von Martin's direct political technique of anti-Nazi innuendo. Working on the principles of free culture, although that sounds like an awkward translation. The foundations of western civilization, the fundamental cultural tendencies, type-ideas in free and progressive communities. A series of brilliant and wise studies.

Meinecke: anti-Nazi too, but now old and pathetic in his eighty-second year. His money has been lost in the Russian bank situation in Berlin. His books, manuscripts, clothes, everything, was lost when a sniper shot an American officer in the vicinity of Würzburg, and the nearest building which happened to be a castle in which M. had been living (a huge beautiful thing with art treasures, Rubens etc.) was evacuated by the troops and burned to the ground. He now lives with a farmer in the country, an old man in a peasant's hut with nothing but his years. This is a portrait of the German scholar.

Jaspers himself. Connected with the university, but more and more persona non grata—his wife was Jewish, and very often had to flee to hiding-places. Social life was cut off. But continued his works... *Lebenswerk*: *Philosophical Logic*. First volume completed, manuscript, whiteness on the shelves—*Von der Wahrheit*.

Also a small manuscript, an essay, was completed in May with the first flush of liberation. *The Idea of a University*. But hopes for Heidelberg have cooled considerably (although Hartshorne[99] of Harvard has been around with some encouragement).

I talked some—the liberal mythos (so dangerous?) of the truth will triumph; so much has been lost in the past because of fond pretty illusion; the opportunities of the military historian; the details of war; the character of American and Allied occupation.

Left some pieces on politics, Max Weber. To return again, on his invitation, next Monday.

30 July 1945

Tuesday.

The city: the routine of this little metropolis (a small town, but still possibly the last real urban center in Germany!) is no longer strange and striking. The streets are crowded with shoppers, the store-windows trimmed with exhibitionist glitter, and trolley cars go hurtling by. The war, and sometimes even the occupation, is fled, gone, and for my own part recoverable only by special effort—or betimes by the accidental turn of a street-scene. Young German boys, without an arm or a leg, making their way down the avenue. Another former Wehrmacht soldier, hopping off a truck, dirty, weary, weighed down by the fantastic collection of front paraphernalia strapped to his back (blankets, gas mask, canteens, souvenirs), suddenly running into a girl, his sister perhaps, or his wife, and she screams and embraces him and kisses him and helps him with his pack. Two miserable pitiful boys wandering along in the square, their ragged clothes barely suggesting the field-gray of the army uniform, skinny, red-eyed, with the most terrible expression of emptiness and hopelessness and confusion on their faces. And yesterday: a young man, who looked Jewish, stuffing books into a little briefcase, and under his rain-coat you could see the zebra-striped jacket of the concentration camp, now neat and laundered. So the black days return for a moment.

But on the whole the new time has its own burning issues, and for the headquarters now ensconsced in a city, civilian metropolitan habits and urges flourish. Hollywood rules in each of the Heidelberg cinemas (and I deeply regret the absence of any German films: was *Mädchen in Uniform* the last available film really?). The best hotels and restaurants, if not all, are occupied by the US forces. The Molkenkur club on the mountaintop is for the entertainment of the conquerors. The officers race around in every variety of captured German vehicle, and the by-play of German misunderstanding of occupation, English titters through the park-grounds along the Neckar. Every GI has a girl, and if the evening is too early he is persistently whistling after each passing opportunity, or taking her hand, or reciting some carefully prepared introductory phrase, *Was haben sie vor heute abend, Fräulein?* I suspect, however, that the honeymoon is nearly over. Since the 15th when Eisenhower, in effect, repealed non-fraternization social life has taken on a feverish almost riotous pace. It does seem very curious, when one thinks of the quiet days of last February in France. The French were quite "available," but the mingling was limited if not nominal. True there was the business of the war, all the old urgencies. Still I suspect that the whole policy of non-fraternization gave a very fetching aspect of sin to social relations and now no one can bear to be alone any more. Denazification, reconstruction, military government—all this is play and side-issues, compared to the course of the way we have to live. The open season does appear to be over for now. The General (Haislip) addressed the officer staff the other afternoon, and seemed rather grim about the spectacle. He vowed "hard work" and "plenty of fun," but as for the Germans and their "damned meanness" well we could talk to them but he for one would not countenance entertaining them (lookit how many years of our lives we lost, and think of the tax burdens we'll have to carry for decades!). Yesterday the sirens were running: were the girls German, then they would have to step out of the car, it was now *streng verboten*. The new order is Non-nonfraternization, which is something quite different from the wholesale festivities of the current US-German relations. In a personal way for myself, this may not be too upsetting a turn. At least some of this mad competition for a busy social schedule will be eliminated. And in a little town like Heidelberg it is too vicious a whirligig. In Augsburg one could lose oneself in some private affair. Here every motion is a public adventure. (Except, and I am reminded to record at least this much of the evening, the wild party with Ilsa and Giselle which almost wound up in a swimming party in the moonlight in the Neckar; as Jordan drawled, "my old grandmother always used to say that if you're gonna go with people who aren't nice, go with nice people who aren't nice.")

The professor: went armed as usual to the Jaspers, carrying magazines, clippings, letters, and canned goods; cigarettes (soup, noodles, salmon, and coffee).

Marianne Weber was there, just leaving, and we were introduced and she consented to remain a while and talk with me. She is of course very old, thin and tall, and gray-haired. Her dress was long, and a black strawish hat sat gently on her head. Her long bony fingers played with the falling petals of the iris gathered in a vase on the table; and she talked of the difficulties of publication. The trials to get something of Weber printed during the Nazi years. The practical banning of the political writings, and although the scientific things were available, no further printings would be made. Thousands of volumes lay around in the publishers' houses, and needed only to be bound. But nothing would ever be done. Perhaps I could go to Tübingen and inquire about them. She had to leave early, but I could call tomorrow and we would talk some more. She borrowed the Schapiro-Gerth exchanges on her husband's *Politics*, and we said goodbye.

The Professor was quite excited about the copies of *Politics*. The spirit of controversy, of discussion, of the sharp clash of ideas was something which really put a light in his eyes. "How long it has been!" He promised to give some more detailed account of his reactions and comments some other time; for now I only learned how glad he was to read something like Macdonald's treatment on the responsibility of peoples, which he found fine and intelligent. He thought it in places a bit too sociological, and went on to suggest a few more moralistic and even theological implications of the problem. "Here were my friends and colleagues, my warmest and closest companions. Some happened to be Jews. And they fell afoul of the regime. They were beaten and tortured and killed. They had to fly like hunted animals, and they died... How could I stand by and watch? How could I sit and read and do nothing? I could do nothing, but I could run out into the streets and scream! That I could do, and that perhaps is what I should have done. They would have taken me too, and I would perhaps have become a martyr. But I didn't go out into the streets, and I didn't scream. I preferred to live, and there lies a guilt too! A different kind of guilt to be sure, but nevertheless a deep terrible sin. The original sin? Perhaps. The sin of wanting to live, of being unable to sacrifice oneself, foolishly or nobly, for an idea or a cause... But that guilt is guilt under God. And in most of the moralizing from the Americans or the British I can only see *Pharisäismus*."

(By the way: he noted in some of the pages a reference to an article by Hannah Arendt, and he inquired about her. It seems she was a favorite student of his; did a "fine doctorate" on Augustine; and he recalled fondly of last conversation with her, she in Paris, he in Luxembourg in 1938.)

News: Mannheim publishers is planning to print some of his manuscripts. First: *Die Idee der Universität*. Also: the Theological Faculty is reopening in the fall, and inasmuch as there will be no regular opening for Jaspers an opportunity is being made for him to teach philosophy in the Theology section. A little devious, but satisfactory. Must see Dr. Hartshorne who is the man here on the German universities; J. praised his work, and some article he had written. We talked on about books and figures. I felt curious giving an abbreviated review of the scholary situation in US and Britain. Brief mention of Dewey, Russell, Whitehead, Santayana, and new works. (What a difficult time explaining my grudging references to the Santayana autobiography; but the professor wanted to know why I mentioned the volumes with such a long face. And how will I ever collect the library which would be necessary to pick up the threads in the German scholarly community... His disbelief at the Fichte-Hegel-Marx-Nietzsche-Spengler line; that such rubbish could have taken hold where free ideas exist, that books were actually written! I borrowed his *Die geistige Situation der Zeit*.

31 July 1945, Heidelberg

To the old Weber house, 17 Ziegelhäuser Landstrasse. Marianne Weber expecting me. Talked for a while in the large wonderful sitting room. Above us there was apparently a portrait of the young Marianne, an engaging lovely oil. In the far corner a brown sculptured study of the professor. Some books lined the wall behind me: Mommsen, Eduard Meyer, Sybel, Burckhardt, Huizinga (*Herbst des Mittelalters*), and in between what were obviously two remnants of the Weber journey to America: a Tennessee edition of some life of Andrew Jackson (two volumes). Through the large windows leading out to the little balcony was a classic view over the Neckar, up to the castle, a brilliant red in the bright afternoon sunshine, and the Molkenkur mountain. Frau Weber had read the Schapiro-Gerth controversy, and was grateful in several different ways for having been able to read them. Of course: her natural interest in Weber literature. But also like the Jaspers a delight at reading critical and polemical discussions: and too at hearing from America and reading our periodicals. She spoke at some length of Max Weber's inner conflict—in some respects, between his heart and his head, his own ideology and the fund of his own heartfelt sympathies; in others, between his intellectual individualism and his strong cultural and social responsibility. I am not quite sure I caught all the nuances of her reminiscence, but I thought that after the fashion of Henry Adams here was a man who would be a socialist, with a new and whole and deep and liberating socialist philosophy, but something hidden in his tradition and character held him back. As for his nationalism, strong as it was, he never would have lasted a month of Nazism. He would have cried out, he would have protested and struck back; and they would have killed him. As it was Max Weber died under Nazism. His political writings were naturally very dangerous; and in what can be called the scholarship of the times what room was there for his critical method and his integrity? For the Mohr Verlag Frau Weber prepared a letter, and I wandered about the Weber library, the professor's study with his bookshelves. It was an exciting thing, simply reviewing the titles and leafing through volumes, without looking at the titles or glancing at the pages, simply feeling them, touching them. Ah, what sentimentalism! Here was Georg Simmel's *Goethe* (dedicated to "Frau Professor Marianne Weber"); here were Werner Sombart's own volumes on *Kapitalismus*, with an affectionate and respectful inscription to the professor. Here were Mrs. Weber's works in sociology, and of course her biography, standing with a handsome leather-bound complete edition of the master himself. I returned and we talked further. Of the emigrants, and of Thomas Mann (about whom she was sharp but with a gentleness and a wisdom: ". . . so to cut himself loose from his people and his tradition and his land. . ." Of world politics, and the developments in England, in Russian relations (on which I can say this much: in addition to the body of democratic anti-totalitarian grievances there remains a sense of Asiatic barbaric Russia, somehow apart and to be excluded from the European community. . . although this would not preclude a genuine friendliness for the people themselves—it remains the lingering nationalist-cultural indictment). Of American literature; she had been reading Van Wyck Brooks's *Flowering of New England* (with a dictionary to catch so many of the strange phrases), and I had to tell her something of Brooks, of *America's Coming-of-Age* and the biographies, and of the tendencies in American literary criticism. She listened carefully, occasionally with a kind of tender casualness correcting my German, constantly fingering her little leather bag, removing and replacing her handkerchief in busy nervous mannerism. (On the Manns, she recalled Golo, an earnest and able student in Heidelberg.) The news of the Gerth-Mills translations was new—only Shils and Parsons were known to her. She was becoming tired and I rose to say goodbye. She asked me to return soon, and extending invitation to attend meetings of her circle at which various papers were read. I promised, happily accepted—to attend *Faust & Prospero*, some time later this month.

12 August 1945, Heidelberg

Notes for a letter from Germany:

When we make a black endless crater and call it peace then perhaps the making of a mere desert scarcely calls for political or moral despair. These may yet prove to be golden days for the continent. In the shadow of the coming atomic destruction of Europe a nostalgia for this peaceful present begins to grow. How we must learn to cherish this epoch of simple rubble! We may be living our last moments before the fundamental disintegration of the earth. Once again, in the eternal recurrence of history, this recent war and peace has become society's "last romantic tragedy": to the fantasy of murder and destruction there was yet a theme of a lost, helpless humanity, to the very aspect of the standing ruins an ancient classic suggestion of the pathos and intimacy of suicide. Death was massed and mechanical and a product of technique, but still it was without the new dark depth, the impersonal mystery of an electronic bolt. The West has died, and we await now the disappearance of the desert.

For the moment, to be sure, the grimness of our modern situation is somewhat obscured. The American armies which, in the interesting formula, came as conquerors but not as oppressors, are living like conquerors, off what little remaining fat there is to the land. The hotels, the restaurants, the theaters, the clubs, the automobiles are all now in the service of American comfort and entertainment. The military machines have become domestic. General Patton's Third Army is in Munich which is only a massive shell of its former self but nevertheless a curious and exciting city.

15 August 1945, Heidelberg

The University Medical School.

The morning was miserable with the rain and humidity of Neckartal August days, nor was the Ludolf Krehl Klinik easy to find. A huge Technicolor sign—SEVENTH ARMY LIGHT VEHICLE REFUELING STATION—almost covered the front entrance and I passed it by twice. Through the clinic via the garden lines of people were making their way to the *Hörsaal* which was a typical European medical auditorium, with its steeply graded seating arrangement and amphitheatrical focus on the rostrum. The chamber was soon packed with men and women of all ages, and the brief ceremony began.

The old rector of Heidelberg university, a small silver-haired distinguished man, began. The remnants of the faculty which remain had come in somewhat earlier—the tall gaunt figure of Karl Jaspers, the jolly Alfred Weber (whom I recognized from the portrait which hung in Max Weber's library) among others.[100] The audience rose, and the rector made his opening remarks, cut back with a brief resume in English (thanking the American military government officers fulsomely) and then proceeded to introduce the new rector. The remarks were appropriate to the Latin dedication, and of course the taking of the Latin oath and the transfer of the golden rectorate chain which lay shimmering across his shoulders. The audience rapped on the long slender deskboards in applause, and Dr. Bauer[101] accepted. The old rector stood as the new rector reviewed, with eloquence and sincere praise, the achievements of the last quarter-century through two wars and endless dark days. The achievement was faith in the university, in its free cultural and scientific responsibilities, and this faith could now renew itself with the opportunities of the new freedom—a freedom which we could not create ourselves but which the Americans have now made possible for us. He spoke with shame and sadness of the past years, but the *Drang nach Wahrheit* would once again dominate German intellectual life. The wars are over, but the *geistige Kampf*, the war of the spirit, is just beginning. In a world which has been unified by its need for a common international order and peace, we must turn now to the youth in whom the future is entrusted. They must light up the world with minds dedicated to a reconstruction of civilization. "The fire has been rescued—light up your torches!"

Professor Jaspers, pale and a trifle unsteady, sat on a stool on the platform and read his remarks although with a clear and almost conversational directness. This is our New Beginning, but it is not as simple as picking up the threads of '33. Too much has happened, the catastrophe has struck too deeply. He spoke of National Socialism, its triumph, and the lives that were lost in the heroic resistance against it. Men and women who sacrificed themselves for their ideals, for the spirit of freedom which remained only in their gesture of defiance. For others who knew the horror fully as well death perhaps contributed nothing practical to the cause, or perhaps it was only that we preferred to live, to suffer the barbarism and to hope. So we shared in the shame of these twelve years. *Dass wir leben, ist unsere Schuld!* He reverted at this point to the issue of the Medical Faculty and insisted that a Faculty without a University, without the Idea of a university, becomes a mere technical school for specialists. Medical research, considered by itself, is a pure and independent activity, freer from the relentless social issues which dominate other pursuits. Still, no one can look back over what has happened in the last decade and not face the treason of medicine, the same treason which betrayed all of Germany to the Nazi darkness. A medical faculty rests on the foundation of two great principles which control the whole of intellectual and spiritual life—Science and Humanity. Medicine betrayed both under National Socialism. It betrayed Science with its swindles of race theory and biological superiority, with its eugenics for Nordic domination. It endorsed the barbaric destruction of the Jewish people in our midst, it gave support to the war and fanaticism of the Hitler regime. And it betrayed also Humanity. For Medicine like Law or Theology or Philosophy, is a creature without hope when it is not dedicated to the creative possibilities of a free individual life. It is the life of the individual, the expanding culture and freedom of his self, which is the ideal of civilization. We have ourselves created the barbarism when we lose that purpose. It is to such a rededication of our University that we must now address ourselves. To renew it with the strength of our past, with the spirit of our noblest souls—Goethe, Hölderlin, Lessing—with a faith in the real true destiny of our people and fatherland. To build it with an Idea—and to fashion with our own ambitions and our own individual spiritual achievements a new culture and a new society, a new Germany devoted to human rights and individual freedom. So we will find our path to science, to humanity, to god, in the mission of a university.

The rapping on the desks was loud and persistent. Professor Jaspers stepped down from the platform—he had not lectured at the university since 1937. I glanced around but I knew full well I would not find Mrs. Jaspers. As a Jew she had been hunted; as the husband of a Jewess Professor Jaspers had been humiliated and driven to despair. He hid her and comforted her. They both had carried sufficient poison on their persons to make suicide possible at any moment, and often they stood only a hair-line away from the final decision. Frau Jaspers was bereft and without hope. She had lost everything, faith, love, the university, Heidelberg, homeland. Germany existed no longer for her. But this is not Germany, Professor Jaspers insisted. "I am Germany..." She wept (as she told me) when he said that, she wept with a wild confusion of renewed faith and disbelief. "Karl Jaspers was one Germany: would that he were all of it!" Now that the Hitlerism has perished the conditions of life have become bearable and normal. But for Frau Jaspers the return is unmanageable. She refuses to mingle in the streets from which she was only yesterday an outcast, refuses to go to the theater or the university whose doors for so long had been shut to her, refuses to take up once again with the people who, whether by default or design, had participated (historically) in the persecution. It is a touching personal attitude, a strange and significant policy of "non-fraternization." Naturally: Mrs. Jaspers was not there. I am afraid she would have wept again.

16 to 21 August 1945, Berlin, via Kassel, Göttingen, Braunschweig, Hannover

The land bears curious witness to the character of the American victory. Everywhere the lingering tokens of the Nazi epoch, ignored by the thoughtlessness of the new regime preoccupied with every formality of administration except those of significance and real social content. In Mannheim, on the corner of Leibnizstrasse: "*NIE WIEDER ein 9. November 1918!*" Down the avenue, in even bigger whitewash staring out from the rubble: *Führer befiehl, wir folgen!* Throughout the area: Only Germany can save Europe, the victory is inevitable, the struggle is relentless and unending, the loyalty of the people is undying... On the road to Darmstadt: the huge *Hakenkreuz* of the NSDAP *Ortsgruppe* headquarters. And then the challenges, as it were, of the American sign-painters—THIS WAR IS OVER. NO ORDNANCE PARTS WILL BE ISSUED WITHOUT A SIGNED AND AUTHORIZED REQUISITION. —SLOW DOWN!

EUROPEAN JAYWALKERS! A whole host of adaptations of American highway billboards, counseling the wisdom of cautious driving and the innumerable advantages of the nearby service station.

Into Frankfurt. The Main was a turbulent muddy red and the sun was brilliant over the city. The Bahnhofsplatz was crowded with pedestrians for all the world oblivious to the devastation which stretched away. But to a point. The ruins cease abruptly. At the next corner—one could pick up a shattered brick of a little house now gutted and almost reach it—stands the IG Farben building, its thousand windows glistening in the noon-day.[102] The military police are in kid gloves and white scarfs and under apparent instructions to perform as a palace guard for the US headquarters. One was somewhat embarrassed, but as the fullness of the spectacle unfolded deeply ashamed. Why was this not also broken from the sky, burned and destroyed and returned to uneven earth? Why should this have escaped the terrible equality and justice of total tragedy? For a moment one could almost order its demolition, blast all the windows out, rip apart in a vicious irreparable jangle the fabulous escalator-elevator system now running with an efficiency which defied the logic of the war, blast the fountains and the gardens, burn the rich dining rooms and their vast draperies... But no. The devilish evil of our time destroys even its most understanding antagonists. In the end, I feel sure, all the so-called ironies and accidents of War will piece themselves together!

The autobahn north. The landscape of the countryside is constantly in exhibition. As if the highways were constructed to make a showcase of the land, and it is a land, truly, of such unmitigated beauty, of such endless scenic variety and delight, that for hour after hour I could resort mentally only to the clichés of the romanticists of nature. We ran into storms and raced out of them, and finally late in the afternoon the city of Kassel loomed in the distance. We could see it in the slight valley and as we approached, we had a strange uncontrollable feeling of excitement. We were moving into north Germany at last, and after a long day to discover a city. I knew from the first how foolish, how hopelessly romantic our expectant mood was. But there we were, alone, wandering about the foreign soil, and we would explore what lay ahead. We crossed an intact bridge across the Fulda and moved through the city. The grass was growing through the rubble. A trolley car passed, empty. Kids were on the mounds of ruins and shouted "chewing gum" at us as we passed. The streets and avenues were chewed up, ghostly with ugly gutted buildings and shells of neighborhoods. Kassel was dead. The setting sun was playing havoc with contrived shadows and darknesses—it was quite unbearable! The Third Division, which had lived in castles and mansions, were now quartered in battered houses that somehow missed the heavy strokes of the terror bombing. On the heights, towards Wilhelmshöhe, I stopped a woman and made inquiries. The city was "gone," early as '42 and '43, the beginning of the end of "such a pretty town!" Once one hundred and seventy-five thousand people lived here. Thousands have fled, thousands lay buried under the ruins, thousands live with them in cellars and makeshift gutted quarters. I had to leave! And in the hour before dark we made Göttingen, across the boundary of the British occupied zone.

This was the university town, intact, practically untouched, and I recalled with no little sentimentalism that first contribution of mine, "The Ghost of Göttingen," which was printed in *The Nation* for 1937.[103] We found a hotel; there were no sheets and no running water, but there were children playing before all the front doors, trees lined the streets, there were shop windows along the avenue—this was civilization! We wandered through Göttingen. The old church had burned, but little else was touched. We window-shopped and moved through the street-corner groups of young people busy with noisy flirtations. The cinemas were open and we saw half of a German film (*Circus Renz*) and half of an American (*Thousands Cheer*, the usual flat musical revue). Finally—after a wine party, a song fest (Gertrude and Inge), to bed in my sleeping bag (Hotel Stadt Hannover)... wondering for a moment if anything exciting lay before us. At the Thirtieth Infantry plans were being made to raid a DP camp. Gangs were making depredations on the countryside, and several companies were to be moved out to pick up machine guns, rifles, grenades, and the crew of snipers who had been picking at US guards. More relevant: one officer just returned, after some six weeks in the Russian zone. He had been picked up, held, imprisoned, questioned, searched, suspected as a spy, and at last released. I fell asleep dreaming of a convenient adventure with the Russian GPU (six weeks only!).

Friday. A gray dripping sky. To the music store, and at long last a record: Berlioz-Chopin (there were also Strauss's *Japanische Festmusik*, which I thought grimly appropriate to the times, but it was unavailable). To Frau Oncken's,[104] and delivered the Jaspers' greetings and letter. Friedrich Meinecke had recently arrived at their house and was living there now; a distinguished house of historians. Some brief talk about the University which was to open shortly, all three faculties! The British, she felt, knew what they were doing in Germany, but the Americans were in so many ways "unclever" (she of course had particularly in mind the formal exclusion of all PGs from the faculty, without regard to the actual political complexion of the picture).

On the road. The British Zone: "Diversion" signs for "bypass." Over a Polish DP camp—WE DEMAND THE IMMEDIATE RETURN OF A FREE POLAND!; THE POLISH PEOPLE WANT TO WORK ONLY IN POLAND. The ultimata were nailed on to the barbed-wire supports which fenced the camp around. In the distance, in the approaches to Braunschweig (I am embarrassed: it was several hours before it dawned on me that this was "Brunswick"), a gigantic smoking industrial plant! The fury returned. The impulse toward indiscriminate destruction was tied in together with the shame and indignation which one could not help feeling. These were the Hermann Goering Works.[105] Perhaps there had been an ingenious electrical-smoke screen, or something, which effectively protected the plant from the ravages of air power. But everywhere there were farmhouses in ruins, little communities of dwellings wrecked. But smug and defiant on the horizon were the stacks of the Goering Works. A sense of the swindle and corruption of the war mounted, and even as an unbeliever I felt humble and humiliated before the broken stones of the foreign land. Into Braunschweig, where the rubble, the mud, the bricks were still sprawled on to the streets. Another skeleton of a city.

In Braunschweig (Brunswick) to the British canteen at the Lorenz Hotel. An English officer was coming out, three tennis rackets under his arm (precious image! a touch out of Renoir's *Grande Illusion*). Yesterday's London press was available and the dispatches carried the details of the Japanese farce. The Tokyo radio is quoted as saying: "We have lost but this is temporary..."; the Emperor shed tears, and "all those present were impelled to weep aloud at his inexpressible generosity." In the hollowness of our era even the imperialism of old has lost its character, its personality. It once had the confident vicious strength of a giant striding the earth; it now too is a colorless soulless machine, without the courage even of its own motives (I mean to be sure the Anglo-Saxon world dominion).

The boundaries were entangled and the signs became more frequent. Finally at the border: a huge stand stretching across the autobahn, flying a dozen red banners. Russian sentries stood on their side of the fence, below three great portraits facing toward Berlin—Stalin, Molotov, and Zhukov, in technicolor. The victors. The heroes. (Was nationalism always such a mean thing of vulgar cheap sentiment? Here again I suspect a richness and independence of social character has gone out of the historic movements of our times—nationalism, socialism, imperialism: all are lost corrupted orientations. They have roots only in the apparatus of power, and their vigor is without tone, without style.) The road-signs were all repainted, and where exactly we were became a mystery of undecipherable Russian characters. Guards waved their yellow and red flags at passing vehicles, saluted sharply, and returned to their little tables (often protected by a gay parasol) and a solitary bottle perched and opened. Under a bridge to the table (with the bottle, inevitably) add a bed and a gray blanket. At road junctions a special guard with a long flowing cape and the muzzle of a machine gun peeping out... In the distance, to the right (south) lay Magdeburg, its twin-towered cathedrals, its pattern of industrial plants outlined against the sky. The stacks were smoking, and the designs of steel were familiar.

This was almost another Germany. The face of the land, the horizon too, was something quite different. The flatland stretched away for hundreds of miles. The settlements had an aspect of brutal efficiency about them. Pittsburgh!

A hitch-hiker. Helena. From Budapest. En route to Königslutter, with foodstuffs of the hospital. Admires Italian and Hungarian soldiers. They have so much courage! Reviewed the gossipy details of recent Hungarian politics to Nicholas Horthy, "a fine man. . ." The Germans, she found, were intelligent and very, very clean, but too egoistic. She didn't quite believe that I was a Russian, but when I spoke some she almost seemed convinced. I quite agreed that *dubra* was not correct Russian for *dubja* (good) (I believe), that we south Russians have a rather different accent. I asked about what liberties there were in Hungary, but no progress was made. She didn't know the German word *Freiheit* at all, which may or may not be significant, probably not. She left us at Königslutter, and called back *Arrivederci!* to McCabe,[106] whom I had introduced as a fabulous Italian patriot, Benito Valentino. Mac disappointed me. "What the hell does she want now? Ain't this the right town?" I assured him it was, and waved back to Helena.

Friday evening into the suburbs of Berlin, and dinner at Zehlendorf headquarters. Table-talk to my right—those very amusing Russians and the sale of watches in the black-market. Found a hotel (Nestler, Beerenstrasse and Lindenthaler Allee) and for the rest of the night there were only the mad tales of the Russians and the Market. "Listen!" the GIs were good enough to inform us, "you can really make a fortune! Clean up I tell you! We got here late, they only moved us guys from the Eighty-Second Airborne in last month. But the Second Armored sure made a killing. You musta read that story in *Stars & Stripes*—the boys got paid a million and over four million were sent home! It's getting a little rougher now. MPs clamping down a bit—there was a raid down there downtown this afternoon, but you can still do plenty of good business! Watches will bring you a couple of hundred dollars, and if it's a black-face with a sweep-second hand, Christ! You ought to be able to beat some Russian out of seven or eight hundred dollars! If it's gotta loud tick you've got it made. That's what they go for. . . Hell, it ain't hard to figure out. The Russkies haven't been paid in maybe six years. Beaucoup fighting and nothing to buy, nowhere to spend. Now they get all their pay and they can't take back no more than a couple hundred marks. So any goddamn little trinket you got you can turn in for a fortune. Shit, Manhattan is being sold and resold a hundred times every day down there by Unter den Linden! But watch out. They'll try and dump a thousand-mark note on you. Don't take it. It's no good. But all the rest of the currency is okay. Same as ours as a matter of fact only it's gotta dash in front of it, and ours gotta a zero. . . If you want to you can get rid of your PX ration, but that's where the MPs come in. They can't do nothing, not a goddamn thing, so long as you sell your own stuff. Hell, it's my personal property! What can they do? You gottem beat there. But with cigarettes and candy, and things like that, you can swing your price, but I don't know they may catch up with a guy... Boy, you think we're shittin' you, but wait'll you take a look tomorrow! I gotta a stack of mark that thick. I know that we won't be able to get rid of all of it, but I'm playing it smart. Putting it away in diamonds. That's always stable. But fella, you can let those Russkies have anything! One of the boys made a neat little pile selling rubbers! Don't laugh, but the German girls are smart and won't let the Russkies fuck 'em unless they wear rubbers, so now they gotta have them. That's where our pro kits come in, and boy what a riot that caused. Getting five and ten dollars for a couple of condoms—what a world!"

The Black Market lived up to its fanfare. Cigarettes were selling for ten and fifteen dollars a package. Watches were going for five thousand marks. Crowds of German civilians, American soldiers and officers, Russian veterans, male and female, milled around in the greenery out from Brandenburger Tor along the Charlottenburger Chaussee, and did a happy business. The Russians wanted to get rid of the money, the Americans were out to take all they could get, and the Germans caught in between hoped to salvage a smoke, something to eat, a bar of chocolate, a cake of soap. (A Russian would order a suit of clothes and if he were "broke" get it for free, and if he were "flush" he would pay ten thousand marks! So what German shopkeepers there were in Berlin had their own pockets stuffed with Allied currency.)

Glimpses of the city. Suburban communities demolished, the houses one by one wrecked. On the flat-faced fronts, still visible, the nationalist bronze plaque with the stern visages of Soldier and Eagle, both in profile. The scene was curiously unmoving: the House of the Angry and the Ambitious had fashioned its own destruction. (But only here could one say it coldly.) Fragments of conversation: "Them Russians sure are busy and plenty sharp-eyed. By god, they must send home fifty percent of everything they lay their eyes on! Christ, railroad trains with whole crews have disappeared. And sure as shootin', spot a double-lane railroad and one rail is missing..." Street-corner propaganda: everywhere the Stalinist billboards, with texts from the master—

"*Die Erfahrungen der Geschichte besagen, dass die Hitler kommen und gehen, aber das deutsche Volk, der deutsche Staat bleibt.*" (Stalin) "*Die Rote Armee ist frei vom Gefühl des Rassenhasses. Sie ist frei von solch einem entwürdigenden Gefühl, weil sie im Geiste der Gleichberechtigung der Rassen und der Achtung der Rechte anderer Völker erzogen ist.*" (Stalin)... On Hauptstrasse: the swastikas on a battered *Kraft durch Freude* office front. The huge movie-house display for Sergei Eisenstein's *Iwan der Schreckliche*. At the Springer Verlag: Linkstrasse was almost completely demolished, but the books miraculously escaped. The Russians, however, had removed some sixteen million volumes from stock—

mainly in engineering, chemistry, physics, medicine, etc. I searched for *Sozialwissenschaft*, but found nothing. Delivered letter of Prof. Jaspers, and went away with not a volume.

The ruins of Berlin. The city is unbelievable, and magnificent even in its destruction. There is little rubble, and strange how the impression persists that it is a clean city. The great avenues and boulevards stretch flatly away on a dead level and there is still everywhere the sense of immense and palatial buildings, of a great and systematic metropolis. The thoroughfares were crowded with pedestrians and vehicles and the view of massive architecture was inescapable. You look at Berlin and you see traffic and real estate. Devastated as it has been BERLIN BLEIBT BERLIN (as one poster remarked, advertising I believe some local musical comedy). Its vast area has every pattern of shambles. The varying ruins of Darmstadt, Kassel, Nuremberg, Augsburg, Munich could all be set down within the city limits of Berlin, and their own patterns matched. In the north and east ends the buildings are gutted and hopeless and are the very image of Darmstadt's ghostliness. Leipziger Strasse has the burned-out massiveness of Ludwigstrasse in Munich, and here and there there are whole areas as twisted and broken as the stones of Nuremberg. Berlin lies before you like a tortured giant, limp on the wrack, a blinded mortally wounded cyclops. The face of the city is black, its eyes poked and burned out.

Everywhere in Germany there is a certain feeling of age and patience, and I almost fancied that I was being told: Berlin was destroyed before, in the Seven

Figure 11. Posing in front of the Brandenburg Gate, Berlin, © Lasky Center, Munich.

Years' War of Frederick the Great, in the Napoleonic campaigns... *Doch das Leben geht weiter!* Cinemas all had lines of anxious movie-goers, the newspapers were being sold quickly at little and for the most regular stands. I noted a half-dozen cafés on Potsdamer Strasse, jammed with soldiers and girls, noisy with music, laughter, the breaking of glasses (the wine, the point three-two beer were abominations). The Café Weber: lemonade was the favorite, most of the girls were still alone (it was only nine o'clock). The Schwarzer Adler: an American flag was in display, the music was jazz styled in New York fashions, and the intimacies were public with the pace and promiscuity of Paris. The Femina: one ball-room still intact, and a sergeant sat at the bar, staring over my shoulder at a blonde: "Laugh, you silly bitch! Seven hundred and fifty marks for a bottle of lousy schnapps! Goddamn hangover poison, that's what it is! Hang 'em all! Shoot 'em all! Shit, the Russians have the right idea all right! Hit 'em on the head, that's what they deserve..." The crowd was a little more upper, the girls were women, smart-set whores. On the street again: a US traffic sign pinned up, half covering a text of Stalin (needless to say, in the American area). The radio was blaring (AFN, Berlin): *I Learned English Just For You*, "If there's a knock on the door (knock, knock) it's not the Gestapo".... GIs were mimicking the German lyrics, and humming along, fondling the girl brashly as the chorus came up again.

[...]

Affair on Claudiusstrasse. They came down slowly along the avenue. The drizzle was depressing, and I must have barked "get in!" They loaded their huge and heavy bag of black-market purchases into the jeep, and we drove them home. I knew nothing of them, could hardly see them. We chatted carelessly, and then started to move out. They suggestively remarked in the farewells to have fun, a remark whose word-structure or grammar I finally pretended not to understand. After several futile pointless repetitions and elaborations, they moved back into the car. We sat huddled together, protecting each other from the cold and the rain, and making friendly conversation to match the intimacy of our bodies. Mac was in a wrestle before I quite worked out of my mood, and I squirmed to disguise his pace. Their names were Inga (later: Irene) and Lisl, and mine was quiet, in a way sweet and sincere. I kissed her, at length, with no real desire except the compulsion of what seemed to me the natural, and most comfortable, course of events. She whispered for me to come tomorrow, which would be such a lovely evening. I said I would, reassured her with an honest promise that I would. She leaned back in, her face suddenly cold and wet from the rain, and kissed me goodnight. We waved, and drove off wondering who could ever locate that street and number again.

I might as well run on to the next installment. We circled around the neighborhood like anxious vultures the next night, and found them waiting.

They were, it happened to be, attractive and lively. Shrewd independent blackmarket operators, I presumed. They owned the apartment house, and every trip up or down involved a check of some little rental detail or the posting of some new housing bulletin. They were young, and if only Inga's wildness was really useful to Nazism both must have been good children of National Socialism. "You have to understand our background and education," they explained casually. "In Berlin it is a little different, but in East Prussia if one would ever say 'Good Morning' the frowns were universal and vicious. *Heil Hitler!* they growled back at you. And that's the way we were brought up... This was our Germany, and the war, for all its horrors, was something that had to be and certainly had to be won. For without victory all was lost. That was the way we always felt. We never could believe for a single moment that the war could actually really be lost. All our friends, so many German officers, had faith right to the spring of this year. It is impossible, they always said, for there to be any other outcome! As for the Russians, their threats to be in Berlin were just ludicrous! Russians in Berlin! It was a joke. Unthinkable! How bad the defeats truly were in the East was more or less covered up, but we knew ourselves that the Russian bombings were light and almost inconsequential. When the word spread during the first alarm that the Americans were coming—it was time to write out your testament... And they were something terrible. In the last year we never troubled to run into the cellar any more. We were sick of it, tired of it. We stayed in bed, and if we were hit that was all, it was over, finished with!" In the course of their remarks several things occurred to me—the truly stunned attitude of so many sections of the North German population, a strong bewildering feeling of disbelief. The coming of the Russians. The death of Hitler. The end of the propaganda, the reassurances, the lies, the vague mystical corrupt reassuring national hope, the security (yes security) of the constantly lurking menace. Now there was a strange emptiness, a nothingness, a blank freedom. Then it seemed to me, too, that another war had been fought here. Berlin was a Russian target, the first city really that had been in the combat orbit of the Eastern front. Not even Munich had quite the same atmosphere. The girls told of the first period under the conquerors: with the familiar inflection of contempt of the Slavic peasant. He came and stole and plundered. He grabbed jewelry, trinkets, wrist-watches (*Uhrie, uhrie...*). Furniture was dumped out of the windows. Everything was taken and moved, even to the simplest crudest chair. Perhaps, it was admitted, all armies loot—"but such primitiveness, ugh!" Then again it might even be symbolic that my first contact with young German nationalists should be in the North, in Berlin no less. (But I suppose I should know that Berlin is far from being "northern" or "Prussian"; it was always a highly political center, a fortress of the working-class movements, an independent disaffected area under the Nazis.) The real shame now, Inga and Lisl went on, is the Collaboration. As women the social fraternization was the political treason which hurt most deeply. (I listened in amazement!) Girls were now to be seen with the Russians; yesterday enemies to the death, tonight perhaps lovers. "How shameless..." Amazement is scarcely the word. For a moment the girls were caught in their old pattern of thought and prejudice. I glanced round, with obvious burlesqued attention, at the apartment, at the soft lights, at the drinks on the table, at the radio playing dance music. Inga laughed. "Well," she said, taken aback only slightly, "well, I suppose we shouldn't be talking!" We all laughed. (Some time during the evening I had fingered my pistol. Inga remarked that if they had had one, we wouldn't be here now. With some alarm, but more curiosity, I asked what in the world she meant. They would have fought the Russians in the streets. We had made our decision. Resist to the last. They would have shot it out as guerrillas, and would have died. I stared hard at her. Was it the wine? I wondered.) More and more the inner style of National Socialism seemed to be becoming clearer to me. It established a community, a unity of believers, a comradeship of struggle. But the faith and fanaticism which was its greatest strength—and at some points seemed foolishly to some observers to share the virtues of ideal fraternity—taught its young nothing of real dignity. Where was their pride, any form of character? The believers were schooled in formulas of intensity, and while the heat and the urgency of the prejudice lasted, the emptiness of their souls remained disguised. Now in the new disjointed time the props of martyrdom were exposed. The Nationalist personality had no roots in an aware self-fashioned discipline. Its philosophy was a twisted artificial thing, its purposefulness a neurotic and prompted compulsion. Here before me two middle-class girls were returned to their real mean life: the flight from the petty-bourgeois realities to fanatical fancies of a fascist Fatherland was over. The touch of dedication had fled, the cheapness remained.

The way back: GIs from the Eighty-Second Airborne, conversation bounced between what they called "daytime jumpin'" and "nighttime humpin'," or how to come down from the sky and get yourself a woman for a bar of candy (chocolate) or a couple of cigarettes.

In the morning: through the city, avenue by avenue. In the Russian area: the wreckage greater, the rubble propaganda thicker. Horst-Wessel-Strasse is now Karl-Liebknecht-Strasse, and the H. W. Haus, burned and gutted, has a new red-banner face, FOR A FREE, DEMOCRATIC GERMANY IN THE SPIRIT OF KARL LIEBKNECHT, ROSA LUXEMBURG, ERNST THÄLMANN.[107]

Two-story cartoons on walls of buildings caricaturing the destruction of Nazism. Banners draped on monuments. Russian convoys—battered trucks with elaborate embroidery and upholstery inside, portraits of Lenin hanging over the windshield. I stopped to take some snapshots. "What!" a young handsome German whispered to me. "Oh these dirty Russians!" (He referred, I think, to their soiled uniforms.) Small annexes to the Black Market. Russian soldiers fitting themselves in long black coats, fingering the silk of pink and green ladies' lingerie. A crowd at an intersection, a bicycle smashed against the curb, the limp figure of an old man on his back in the middle of the avenue. The plates of his teeth had been knocked almost half a block down, a pool of blood lay a little over his left shoulder, his sallow cheeks were sunk down into his mouth in terrible hollows. "A car came speeding along," I overhear, "and it knocked him over, killed him instantaneously. And they didn't even stop. . . Oh, these Russians!" How did they know it was Russians? Oh, they had seen it all, they could see it was Russian soldiers.

An hour free in the early evening (Sunday) and I ran to catch the last performance of *Iwan der Schreckliche*. Direction and script by Sergei Eisenstein, photography by Tisse, music by Prokofiev, with Nikolai Cherkassov in the title role. And it proved to be a film of great special power and even originality! In many ways it seemed to me to be the climax of all the progressive and retrograde tendencies in Soviet cinema. The wheel of art had come to a full turn since the early revolutionary days of Eisenstein-Pudovkin experimentation with the liberating images of a free humanity. This, too, was a triumph, an undeniable Stalinist triumph. Berlin was taken and in return the Kremlin offered its own unique solicitude. This was a German edition: not mere captions or dubbed-in dialogue, but acted out, spoken for German distribution. I couldn't help squinting around me in the dark theatre. How were the responses going? The question grew especially acute as the battle scenes developed. The Russian forces against the (Eastern) invaders (incidentally, the only real mass scenes in the film)—the tension was carefully developed. But still I wonder if the Germans were, as was the subtle intention, becoming emotionally involved in the Russian national orientation. The deep contradictions of Kremlin policy were nowhere more evident than in its propaganda. Here was the mystique of nationalism *in extremis*, the exaltation of everything peculiar in the Russian psychology for the advantage of a unified State. The passionate violent Ivan tears himself to pieces on the altar of Holy Russia, as if the prickly penetrations of the frontiers constituted psychiatric grounds for the wounds and tortures of his soul. I should venture to say that the film was bad propaganda, a surprising political failure. More likely than not it reinforced the German sense of the Russian as Stranger, a figure of primitive depths and resources. Fear rather than any kinship of confidence is instilled. But that too is a Stalinist contradiction, and his message might well stand: you have nothing to fear. . . so long as you fear us! Equally as striking is the technical production of Eisenstein-Tisse. The cinema returns almost twenty and thirty years to the time when words were unspoken and captions unsatisfactory, and only the

Face was the means to express the gamut of action and emotion. Here the facial imagery of royal intrigue and national politics is almost Shakespearean in its power and variety. The actors are superbly controlled, and nothing appeared to me to be overdone where an untoward hair in the movement of an eye-lash might render an entire climax ludicrous. In the very focus of the camera, too, there is Stalinist history. The mass is gone, the million-miened people, restlessly driving, spreading across the city, establishing itself in full and historic justice. Only one face remains, the face of a god and a father, and in his grimace, in the resolution of his fierce-burning eyes in the exultant strength of his tortured brow and spirit, the Russian identity is to be found. Eisenstein and Tisse have symbolically demonstrated the expropriation of the Soviet masses. How better can their tragedy be put than in the terrible image of facelessness?

Metropolitan notes: "Berlin was a great city," someone volunteers, "but never a beautiful one! Its efficiency was awesome and depressing. Its openness and constant light became monotonous. Everything was solid, nothing was fragile or dark. There were no narrow crooked old streets, but only thoroughfares systematically marked out. [...]

I look down Leipziger Strasse and I say to myself: nothing much has happened. The insurance companies and banks used to fail, and now their buildings have failed. I look at their massive blank faces, and see the visage of a broker after desperation and hopelessness have wrung his life-blood away. You think me perhaps a bit too cynical. Mechanical and heartless, no? Berlin, I am afraid, never moved me, neither in life nor now in death. You must know the history of the city. Capital created it, the new wealth and nationalist vigor of the Wilhelm-Bismarck era. It was always as clean as a Prussian bookkeeper's desk, as solid as a bank president. Now the market has collapsed, the whole market. Look! Berlin real estate! The bottom has dropped out of it!"

Yet it was not so cold and simple as that. The bottom dropped out of something deeper, more fundamental.

30 August to 3 September 1945

REVISIONS: By-pass in Frankfurt to 23 Grosshirschgrabstrasse. Reconstruction work beginning on the Goethe-Museum, the busts of the parents, and one of Lessing already standing on mantel-pieces, as pieces of the walls were being put together and the floors rebuilt. Next-door the ruins of the birth-house remained. In the midst of the rubble the handsome sculptured face of the young Goethe (Greek version) had been set down, as if in an old fantasy of the surrealists (classicism and death). A few de-labeled food-cans held bunches of flowers. A small unobtrusive note read: *Neues Leben blüht aus den Ruinen.*

Figure 12. Posing in the rubble of Goethe's birth house, Frankfurt, © Lasky Center, Munich.

Braunschweig: at the Lorenz Hotel, a pleasant English military government officer, who had something of an adventure in the Russian zone. Had been almost to Hamburg by noon when the Russian guards swarmed over him and refused to let them to the frontier. They quickly complied with instructions and cut back to British territory—although all papers were in order. Strange... The eerie shadows of the streets, now a romantic black-out as Tommies wander around and the girls exchange fierce lingering glances with them. A tall blonde didn't quite have her dog under control—it was almost nine o'clock—and I made a playful political issue of the obvious canine anti-Americanism. She laughed and I walked along with her, barely missing the huge craters in the streets. The house was badly hit, but not sufficiently wrecked as to be uninhabitable. Anneliese's sister and the evening's conversation: a round of catchwords—*prima, egal, usw.* (I could hear American echoes: "Swell!" "Same difference.") The curious cynicism about the war and the terror. The constant jokes about *amerikanische Gangster*. The story of how she painted a white cross on the roof of her house. But do you think that helped? They listened carefully for the planes the next day and hoped maybe their neighborhood might manage some new immunity. Down came the bombs and the whole block almost disappeared. No respect at all for sacred things—not even a white cross! Anneliese walked me back to the main thoroughfare, and we lingered on the corner. Every five minutes I made her repeat her series of lefts and rights which constituted my explicit directions for making my way through Braunschweig in utter darkness. We couldn't let each other go. I promised to return in a few days. She kissed me quickly and ran back down the street. I walked slowly on (wondering now and then what did happen to the dog).

The landscape of the North German plain again. Magdeburg in the distance—what a hateful horizon! The city lifts itself up against the sky in a small far-away silhouette, and for a moment I could not help speculating whether the destruction of these ugly things man has built on the horizon in the name of civilization is truly as disastrous as we in our despair conveniently believe. But no! True, our current efforts (4241 BC to 19– AD) on the earth to create a world for man have achieved something only slightly removed from total miserable failure. Still . . .

Into Berlin, and the problem of the Russians.

Monday.

Moved west and south again. Last glimpses of Berlin—tanks and guns lying about in the parks and on the avenues, vestiges of the siege. An isolated grave in a vacant lot (huge red star). Sidewalk cafés in spared neighborhoods. Thousands of blondes, cheap, hopeless little girls walking the streets. We were lost somewhere in the Berliner Ring, circled around Potsdam twice, cut for the autobahn at Brandenburg, almost overran a flock of chickens, and decided to ask for some eggs. There were none. This farmer had "lost" fifteen thousand hens to the Russians. (The difference between the Russian and the British zones: some eggs, a few hens, are still to be found.) Add differences: at the Helmstedt frontier, conversation re: the Russians and the Black Market. "Don't you see how it is? They pay those blokes all their back salaries for years and then deny them the right to spend it at home! So they let you chaps have it for practically nothing. Whatever they get for a bloody German mark is all to the good. Well, you know they've got to keep the working-class down over there. Or the whole Soviet system will simply go to pieces. Don't you see, Uncle Joe knows what he's doing. . ."

Brunswick: flat tire, to the Yorkshire Division. Hanover: "The city is wrecked, believe us, completely wrecked. We have just been out making a try at shopping, and why we have looked for hours and in vain for a simple pair of ordinary walking sticks!" Among the ruins: announcement from Goebbels for *eine Botschaft des Führers*, the placard could still be read on the town hall wall. Marburg: the bombings of the east end, the destruction of the iron-works. The university on the mountain-side. The university bookstore, shut tight by American orders. (The old man and woman were terrified at the prospect of my simply walking in through the back and looking around. The American officer had warned them that if they had so much as put their foot into the store, they would all be thrown out. An infuriating situation! For if they were suspects, remove them, and if they were not, why terrorize them? Ah, our liberators of Culture!)

In Heidelberg again: there were flowers on the dinner-table, music was being played, the meal was full, royal. Out on Hauptstrasse some women were sweeping the store-front sidewalks, and here and there a window was being washed to a glister. The houses stood intact in an endless array from the town hall to Bismarck-Platz. The avenue was crowded with people and vehicular traffic. The American Sales Stores had new window displays, featuring a garish display of cosmetics, silk niceties, household conveniences, elegant cloths, rich leather-goods, and civilians passed by (not without a long pause). A German girl (in a sweater) passed by and GIs began calling out from all sides, *Oh, vass iss lohs, bebbee?* I returned to the Bayerischer Hof, went up to my hotel room. I was beginning to feel a little sick.

10 and 11 September 1945, Heidelberg

I heard a woman's laugh from a room down the hall and my curiosity was irrepressible. I knocked on some pretense or other (I mumbled, disguising it even from myself) and then peeked in. It was Maria. She was slouched on the bed, still laughing. Beside her was Eggers, doughy and sullen in his usual fashion; and characteristically inconsequential across the room was Walp. For a moment I was distressed, but apparently it was only something of a social conference. Gregerson I discerned in another corner. "Oh, do come in, Lieutenant Lasky!" she sang out with arch gaiety, "unless, of course, my company continues to be undesirable for you!" I was stunned. I never had particularly cared for her, from the time of our very first meeting, but then again I had never been anything less than polite and friendly, and even at times when Jordan and I were out together rather on the warm side. I protested, and she apologized half-heartedly. The chatter resumed and I stood at the door scarcely knowing what to do. Finally I asked whether I could see her alone for a few minutes. "Naturally you can, Lieutenant Lasky! Naturally you can! Shall we go to your room?" The irony in her voice continued to be uncomfortable. I escorted her out of the room, trying to maintain my reserve and aloofness with gestures of formality. And she strolled down the hall, humming a tune, tossing her head about to clear her long hair from her eyes.

I met her for the first time in Augsburg. Jordan and I burst into the store and we caught her attention because apparently she had been busying herself raptly in a book which demanded more quiet than we were prepared to allow that sunny afternoon in June. After a spell we made our full round and came past her again, and she stared at length at us. I went over brashly and rummaged among the articles in her section. She was still staring and I couldn't decipher whether it was interest, resentment, boredom, or dreaminess. *Haben sie gar nichts hier für uns?* "Nothing at all," she replied in English, with a careful schooled accent. *Gar nichts?* I pleaded. "Not a single thing. There are articles for women only, and I am rather sure they would not interest you." *Vielleicht*, I replied. *Wahrscheinlich*, I added. We swung out through the door and hopped into the auto. We were about to leave when she appeared out in front. Her arms were clasped before her bosom, and she stared at us. This was becoming just a little embarrassing, and more than a little challenging. "Shall we go, Jordy," I asked, "or shall we look into it?" Might as well. Jordy refuses a woman as often as a bee passes by a flower. *Ist etwas los?* I began. *Haben wir etwas unangenehm* [sic] *gesagt oder getan?* —*Nein, nein*, she answered, . . .*bestimmt nicht . . . Aber ist es verboten, Sie anzusehen?* The difficulty was over. Why no, she could look at us all she wanted, provided she was registering no grievance. Not at all, and she smiled coyly. She was not a very pretty girl, but there was an attractive robustness about her, and her mercurial changes of mood were stimulating. She turned out to be a Latvian, would be very glad to see us later that evening. When we returned, I unobtrusively abdicated my *jus primae noctis* (as Lord of the languages: Jordan speaks no German), and watched the romance flower. They held hands in the front seats of the jeep; I sat alone in the back, weathering the bumps, ignoring the exchanges of intimacies. But the affair with Maria was not something I could easily escape. I had always to straighten out Jordan, drunk on my cognac, en route uncertainly to her apartment. There were constantly chance meetings with her on the streets in Augsburg and pressing inquiries as to where he had been last night, or last weekend. What could I say? God knows whom he had met now!

[. . .]

I sat on my bed and listened to Maria. "You know how I am! I was like a child with him. I believed everything he said. I trusted everything he did. I knew it couldn't last forever, but then I never thought I could ever be as unhappy as I am now. They all say, forget him, but I have tried and I cannot. What should I do? Laugh and sing and be gay? You see for yourself how forced and insincere it is. I am so miserable I weep all the time. How could he be so cruel to me? Why doesn't he sometimes come and visit me? Has he then so many other girls that he never finds a single second? Sometimes I am afraid the whole thing was a lie. He never cared for me, not for a fraction of an evening. But I remember the first night. He was honest with me, and I was so taken by it. He showed me a picture of his wife and his little boy. I liked that so much. But now! I saw him last week and he said of course he loves me, but work work work. He said he was going to Kassel, and then my girl friends tell me the gossip that he spent the weekend with Rita. If it is all over—do you really think it is over, gone with?—why doesn't he tell me? He is always lying. And about the baby too! He says now he never knew—'Should I go around asking girls whether they're pregnant?' he says so meanly. And believe me! I didn't want him to know. I wanted it a secret. But I now know that he was told about it! When we were all still in Augsburg. How terrible, how terrible life has become! I never knew so much misery could exist. I think so often of my mother and father. They were fine wonderful people, and they gave me so much love, so much affection. I felt in moments a bit of shame, but then I was so happy how could I deny myself. And now I am a murderess. Really, really. I killed the baby, my baby, and nothing will ever be the same again."

I am not sure whether Jordy ever really knew anything about her condition. I have never pressed him directly on the subject, but as I piece together the crisis which developed, it took him quite by surprise. And at that time there was nothing for him to do except to reassure her again and again that he did not hate her for having murdered his child. But what a fall was there from the gossamer fantasy of their earliest romanticism!

[...]

She sat there before me sobbing as if the collapse of the world had not been something she had been fearing since the very beginning. But I suppose with every broken heart there is this terrible nostalgia for tragedy. It had been once pure divinity, and now there was only hate and despair. The real colors of the emotions involved were something less brilliant than that; still here were the strange materials of a Dreiserian European tragedy.

"So many cruel things have happened. Just today Rita showed up with little trinkets and what not that Ed has apparently given her. There went more terrible gossip. I don't care about the gifts, but it cheapens her so, and it cheapened Ed and then I begin to feel that there was something wrong and shameful about everything from the very beginning. I never wanted things or anything he could give me, and if I received them, it would not make any difference. But now I have to be hurt every day because she treasures so a piece of goods or something to make a coat or a dress. God knows where he manages to find all those items he is always having around... Oh, he finds time for everything. You say he waited all evening to see me. But I was here, and still we missed each other. Oh, I can't believe it, I can't believe anything anymore. Don't you think he told me he loved me still the other day? You say it is all over. I know it, I know it too, but my heart can't accept it that way. Every memory is such a deep wound."

[...]

It was getting very late. I could listen forever, but the hurt which was inevitable could not be relieved. I know Jordy too well not to believe that he had cared for her, and sincerely, that he had tried to please her in every way. Of all the transient lovers in this army of playboys, who has so much goodness and generosity and affection and determination to share pleasures and happiness?

But once again—it is the failure of the undeveloped heart. Not even love is possible without training, without the achievement of a personal discipline which can exercise a measure of control over all the emotional recklessness involved in the lives of two people. We strolled back down the hall together. It was quiet. Eggers was gone, Walp was asleep. Who would take her home? We dropped into Greg's room, and he blinked at us from behind blue pajamas. We had a few drinks. She began to whine about getting back—there was no transportation and she dared not venture out alone for curfew was several hours gone. We tried to figure something out. But she listened to nothing, but only bemoaned her fate. I told her to sleep on Greg's couch. She jumped up and down and grabbed my arm and I had to sit down with her again. What to do? We had a few more drinks. Nothing developed. She began to be very irritating and more than a little unsympathetic. It was well past midnight and annoyance was mounting. Weary and mad I finally made for the door. She could remain here or be thrown out. I shouldn't have said it. But there it was and I slammed the door. A moment later I peeked back again and mentioned to Greg to take care of her, smiling foolishly. The next morning, he told me she had left about six in the morning. Last night I saw her riding about with somebody in a jeep, her hair flying in the wind, and she sang out—"Oh, there you are? And how are you darling?" I waved back to her, and her chatter was lost in the noise of the Hauptstrasse traffic.

17 September 1945, Heidelberg

Monday. Notes of a weekend.

Another half-rainy dismal Neckartal afternoon, left for Bavaria. A long trip but uneventful except for slight mechanical troubles (ignition wiring) in Stuttgart area, and for the singular excitement of Augsburg on the horizon, the quiet urban landscape against the horizon, an industrial tower or two, but the quiet emphases of the Dom and the St. Ulrich's tower. "Life," the magnificent manufacture of sentimentalisms! Brief visit to Schwedenweg. Helma busy with a dance performance; left words to Haunstetten. The embarrassing affections of Frau Ossmann at reunion. To Heimbaustrasse, and Aina: lustrously outdoors as ever. Waited for her, alone, in her neat self-decorated room, and then to our Gasthaus zur Sonne. A few dishes (cold cuts, tomato salad), a few drinks (the old Liebfraumilch, '37), and to bed. My God! Passion at a fierce intensity, sweetness and affection till it hurt (physically). Her old self, she left at three in the rain... In the morning to town: small items at the tailors, Bavarian trousseau, lunch at the Kaiserhof, snap-shots of remembered avenues and sights. Out again for Aina, and my God! In bed all afternoon until exhaustion, satisfaction, delight, the sunlight filtering through the shutters and dancing its rays on our bodies (and on the floor in wonderful patterns)—plus the time schedule—called it quits. She was happy and sad by turns, and touching and tender always. It had been almost two months since the last goodbye—how long it might be since! I could not bear to be honest with her. I promised and promised. She was so heartbreakingly sincere I couldn't cut her off from her only hope and prospect. I left. And changed my plans. Perhaps it was only fatigue. But then I hadn't the courage to spend my planned evening with Helma. I dropped in, greeted the family (little Kareenela was delightful with her new repertoire of English phrases intermixed senselessly with French and kindergarten songs). Helma had been obviously quite busy these last weeks, but was "sweet" and "loyal." We wrestled with what minute after minute became a genuine frustration, but I had to leave. Once again: the faithful wait... The colors of the countryside were unbelievable, the rich picturesque greens against the multi-streaked sky. The sun sank quickly (we had lost an hour that weekend) and trouble once again with the little Adler. Who was to know that it was only an empty gas tank? We were about to strip the carburator, change tires, rewire the ignition, and I choked and throttled the motor for twenty miles. Finally we came to a halt. Hailed a German truck, which unfortunately had three trailers attached, one of which jack-knifed and sent us into the ditch—however, only a fender was wrecked. All apologies, the German crew triumphantly located the empty gas tank (the gauge read half-full!) and had a few laughs (which served to save face for the accident). I drove on to Stuttgart, half-asleep at the wheel, stayed over. In the morning (Monday), through Bruchsal (foolish, foolish! I had read of the castle and dreamed of a town, but it was a ruin!), to Heidelberg. Two Swiss UNRRA girls, one from Lausanne (spoken: French), one from Berne (spoken: Swiss German).

To the CP, happy to find Mooney back (at long last!). Naturally he had been operating on a grand scale. Borrowed a jeep and kept the driver in Mulhouse. *L'Affaire* Camille. Into Switzerland, and an accountant would be needed to add things up. There was the French girl in the bar, and the dozen telephone calls to get out of a series of wild parties. There was Herta and the mansion and the fabulous engagement party at a lavish celebration which was an utter bewilderment. There was Anne Harrison, the ambassador's daughter at a diplomatic shindig trying to kiss him. The American consulate financing him with Swiss francs to get back into the country from Mulhouse to visit the pining fiancée. The anxiety about the Colonel who was furious and was setting the MPs on his trail. Finally, finding the driver again, set up romantically like all faithful chauffeurs, and back to Heidelberg. We sat in the bare newly-painted rooms, our eyes smarting, drinking Liebfraumilch at ten in the morning, screaming our hilarious tales at each other, marveling at our corrupted souls.

[...]

October 1945

Dear Dwight,[108]

This is a letter from "a sick man in Germany," and if you will you may take that symbolically. I am lying here in an efficient hospital just a stone's throw away from the magnificent IG Farben American headquarters, and these structures may perhaps be the only things standing in this devastated city. I don't know for sure because Frankfurt was a city I've sedulously avoided. I hated it that first evening last April when I crossed the Main and found a gray, sullen, deathly ruin. Since then, I am afraid, it has become even more depressing.

[...]

It was then with no little alarm that I found myself required to leave Heidelberg a few weeks ago. One had found an oasis of normalcy there. The town was untouched, and it was indeed "beautiful," when untroubled by chronic Neckartal rain. I had made friends, visited the university often, discovered things in bookstores, attended public functions (e.g., the re-foundation of trade-unionism, a spirited meeting which began with Beethoven, went through a long Marxian analysis of working-class history, since Lassalle, and finished with Mozart). I can't tell you how forbidding the move was for me.

[...]

The next morning my orders were to leave again. I repacked wearily (in seven minutes) and raced for the airport. The usual opera-bouffe goes on there hour after hour. Nobody knows what planes are coming in or going out, if only (please) you would wait.

And what a waiting room! Immaculate brass of military government officers (always in greens and pinks), curiosities in kilts and monocles from foreign armies (our allies who never fail to amuse the red-eyed sleepy GI, and I am glad for him: he needs to laugh), all kinds of chattering women from the loud noisy USO entertainers to the Red Cross (what in hell do they do?), to the innumerable insufferable others who manage to wangle themselves on to the continent.

[...]

We finally left that evening from the railroad station. The sheds are battered, and there isn't very much to give one a sense of an operational line. But a train would leave for Bremen that night from the central track (the other tracks were crowded with reserved special cars respectively for certain American generals and old corporate executives), and so we mounted one of the several dispatched Allied coaches and waited. The station was in one of its daily usual mob scenes. Thousands of tired, desperate people, with luggage and strapped baggage, all were trying to make the train. There was, of course, only room for so many; or I should say a few more than that too: I saw the unbelievably packed cars. I walked down through to the first of the German section in the hope that I might wander along and strike up some conversations. The barrier was impassible. Several arms, heads and legs jutted out from the German car into the train partition, and no face I could locate was in a position, or mood, to talk. The smell was fishy and foul. I turned away, and opened the wrong door. It was the latrine. Two girls came out with their valises, frightened and anxious. I went back to the compartment and from the window on the other side of the track people were pleading for a ride from Americans. "She's not too bad," someone would say. "Might be a good thing for tonight..." And they would string the tearful girl along for a while. In front of my own window a tall young girl was making her plea in a bad English, which I stopped, and she went on to tell me how her father was a prisoner of the Russians and her Swedish mother had been killed in the "terror-bombings" and how she had to find her brother in Hamburg and maybe find her way to Scandinavia again. "Say, she is pretty nice!" someone interrupted. "You've really got something here!" I opened one of the side doors, and stuffed her into the corner of an empty compartment.

The trip to Bremen was uneventful except for the long conversations with Karen, who was cold, intense, and bitter. For twenty minutes she indicted the German people for characterlessness, spinelessness, spiritlessness, that would have come badly from anybody else's mouth. She didn't think of herself as German, but was part of the tragedy. What was most infuriating—this may interest you—was the fraternization. For her it was not a question of politics, parties, ideologies. It was a matter of personal pride and dignity. "Here are these women. Their husbands have been away for a long time. And naturally that gives them license to sleep with the first man who makes a pass, a not very unlikely situation with an occupation army swarming! The poor boys fought long and loyally, what difference in what misguided cause, some one told them they had to fight, and now that kind of loyalty, that kind of simple character is nowhere to be found! I find the women shameless and vulgar and corrupt. Where else in the world but in Germany can you see such a disgusting spectacle? It wasn't so in France, nor in Scandinavia! How far would an invader get with occupational social amenities in America? You can blame it on the War—that this is what it has done to all of us. But maybe because I'm not really German I can see it for what it is. No one thinks of their life anymore—

what it means, what it should add up to. The pride in living, the dignity of believing in something, that's part of the ruins too."

I was quite surprised. She wanted to talk more—provided of course I would take no offense if she spoke frankly—but she was embarrassed by her stomach rumblings: she had had nothing to eat that day. While she devoured one of my ration boxes, I leafed through a little book of hers which some old lady had given her at the station in Munich—Nietzsche's *Unzeitgemäße Betrachtungen*. Her estimates of the American and British representatives in Europe were shrewd and witty. I have yet to hear a civilized remark on Europe and Europeans from an American, a remark with half the intelligence and discipline, which were controlling this girl's passion. The crisis came on the subject of the Bombing. I played the devil's advocate. (You know my own real sentiments—one of these days, I trust, the whole rotten mess of stupidity, ignorance, inadequacy, narrow-mindedness and barbarism, which inspired the aerial destruction of Germany, will be exposed.) But her eloquence and the justice of the case simply left me defenseless. None of them could understand why entire cities were demolished, why libraries, cathedrals, homes, monuments, hospitals, the whole of a culture, was burned to the ground, burying populations in the ruins. What could one tell them? Who started? She wasn't interested in tit-for-tat military strategies. What mattered was the moral responsibility for a terror such as the world has never known, terror day after day, night after night, in shaking cellars, with only the ultimate devastation as the relief and the end. I made no defense, only looked at her. She was possibly twenty, tall but still a little on the awkward side, blonde with a Scandinavian handsomeness. She sat huddled up in a corner, trembling somewhat, peering out the window at the various stops, sight-seeing Germany. I left her when we reached Kassel, and worried about her not a little when a long line-full of GIs clambered aboard. But nothing untoward happened. When we reached Bremen in the morning she was gone.

I never looked at Bremen carefully enough to know whether it was like all the others. In one section of the town (one always automatically and conveniently calls it the "industrial section") there are endless square blocks of shattered ruins. In the center the old town had a bit of its own personality. The Dom had been badly burned but it was standing, and not very much of the town hall was serviceable except the *Ratskeller* (now a handsome Army mess set amidst the eighteenth-century wine kegs). There was still some of the *Hansa* [*sic*] about Bremen, I felt, but I found no more of it when I went out to the docks. There was a considerable resumption of maritime activity, and in the jangle of iron and steel and gigantic cranes a great port (this is Bremerhaven) was recovering. There was much lore about the *Europa* and how she was camouflaged, and the *Bremen*, and where she used to dock, etc. I found myself interested only in the sea. I shan't be melodramatic or allegorical. I simply stared out into the sun which seemed to give the whole perspective a tone of golden serenity. The North Sea was very quiet and lovely that evening. We returned to the ruins, and met another party coming into the improvised hotel. One couple was Belgian and we talked a bit. He and she both agreed: it pleased them, it pleased them very much, immensely! to see the wreckage of Bremen, to see all of the German cities in such condition! She was a pleasant-looking sweet-faced woman and she said: "The more ruins, the more devastation I find the better I like it!" I stared at her and walked through the door. May God burn her eyes out! I cried to myself angrily. She is already too blind to see.

The street was dimly lit but not without its sights and interest. It had previously been Richthofen-Strasse, and the new signs poignantly read: FRIEDRICH-EBERT-STRASSE. (The next morning at breakfast some of our military administrators of Germany thought it deucedly clever of me to know and note little things like that!) Some woman came by for the third time looking for an address; I offered to help her, but was characteristically sidetracked on the subject of black-market commodities. I was sorry: I had no coffee, and didn't quite care enough for schnapps. There were some kids hanging around the street-lamp on the corner, some boys and girls, teasing each other, abusing each other playfully. One boy was seventeen, wore army boots, had served on the eastern front for three years; one girl wore a black patch over an eye which had been blinded by an artillery splinter in the April assault. We chatted amiably about the movies, about Johannes Heesters and Marika Rökk and Zarah Leander. They sang: *Du und ich im Mondenschein—das könnte so romantisch sein!* I returned with *In der Nacht ist der Mensch nicht gern alleine*. And we all laughed and said good-night.

[...]

I find myself not reporting a wealth of incidents and conversation simply because there is a physical limit to the composition which an arm wounded with hypodermic punctures can manage. I do want to go on, however, to Stockholm and Berlin—if only fleetingly.

Sweden was fabulous. The capital was an inexhaustible toy for a week—the brilliant lights, the taxis, the theaters, restaurants and hotels, the glistening shop-windows, the women... "They are a very clever people," Norwegians had told me. "You'll find the Swedes much cleverer than we... really shrewd businessmen." Perhaps that's what it was. Shrewd business which brought brilliant and gay Stockholm through the war. I tried snooping around the story of the neutrality, but it truly is a long-range historical research. In part, small-nation fear; in part, shrewd business; in part, traditional neutrality. I know that when the German Embassy was seized here by American forces, the Swedish government had already had two weeks to check through the files. There, for my musty mind, went a hundred and fifty beautiful footnotes on Nazi-Swedish deals. George Axelsson (of the *Times*) knew the story as well as anyone, but you know newspapermen... "It'll make a good think-book for people who are interested in things, in ideas, but it won't make a cent." Naturally: what makes cents makes sense, and it was senseless to go on. I frankly got very little from high-level journalistic summary of political movements and economic tendencies. The kind of thing I used to take for information, I now feel is stuff you ought to have when you don't really want to know anything! And it is after all (in most cases) purveyed by people who as a matter of actual fact do not know anything. (Of a new and higher type of journalism, there were no indications, a humane literate journalism, full of the world's sounds and ideas, alive with a personal and humble sense of the experience of history, moving with the warmth and details of everyday life. There was still the shallow and empty notion of news, the story, the routine dispatch which unfolds the turn of great events with a terrible irrelevancy. Meaning perhaps is there, but real urgency? The passion of the play is missing.

I should really write nothing more about Stockholm for what remains is only a romantic interlude, the course of which made me into a partisan of the delights, conveniences, beauties and luxuries of Stockholm. An enchanting city! Copenhagen, although ordinarily much merrier and faster, seemed tired and old. Most Americans there were however taken by the metropolitan pace, which after the ruins of the continent is a liveliness unbelievable. This was the "Paris of the North," they had heard, and there was prowling of the streets all night, every night. From my own window I could hear the spirited street-corner chatter. Americans at last had discovered Europe, *a Europe* at least, something with a historic tone.

But for Americans in Europe, 1945, the old historic tones are all missing. Of the large attitudes and myths which once used to take the American mind, nowhere have I found even a vestige. Once we believed Europe was old, America was young, Europe was the past, the US the youthful energetic future. Once there was the cult of the civilized Europe and the crude America. Latterly there were notions of the mature continent (e.g., politically). None of these have I found abroad. The contradictions of our time are too cruel a burden for any formula and so we survive with none. For the Jamesian seekers of European polish there was the death house of foulness and cannibalism. For the politico there was a continent of irresponsibility and frantic prejudice. For everybody there was the vast ruin with its hateful rubble and dispirited victims.

No, the large impulses are gone. The twisting of emotions and ideas has been so persistent, so daily and unrelieved, no one seems to have perceived how we have been cut off from our very souls. But then soullessness is the very tone of our time, and perhaps that will be our discovery.

How poignant the peace is! What a cataclysmic end for the world of the international middle class, the fine heroes of the nineteenth century! It is, I must confess, even for me something of a forbidding world: I have become too devoted to the past. I knew where I was when people believed in education, in the schools which would defeat ignorance and backwardness: when people believed in industry, in the march of modern life, and the moral improvement of the race with its mechanical refinement: when people believed in people, in the brotherhood of men and in the perfectibility of the neighbors. This is, after all, the classic faith of the modern world, the song of "humanity." But the German test-case tore it apart irreparably and who is there who has remarked the issues or the consequences? No one believes in education for Germany, partly because also the educators have no faith in themselves, and rightly. The old liberal formula of the for-good and for-bad alternative has finally been abandoned—industry here has no capacity for good, and even the machine, thus, has come to inherit an original sin: the evil belongs to it! And the machine is broken, destroyed. Much, too, as the people are broken, and as so many spokesmen would like to have them destroyed. The imperfectibility of man, the incorrigibility of the wayward soul—inscribe those doctrines in your middle-class credo—the honeymoon with faith has long been over. Make no mistake about these times. This is not cynicism, or disillusionment, or some other variant of an expedient current turning away from belief and purpose. This is not a spectacular barrenness of a wasteland. This is a deep, organized, systematic, humdrum emptiness. This is the twentieth century with its throat cut and looking only slightly pale. This is the world of the new generation, not lost, not to be pitied, only aimless and flat. And where now will we be able to find points from which to begin? To move ourselves out from under the weight of this murderous nothingness? I make no pretense at a certain answer. Certainly not in political terminology or moralizing, not in art or literature or even intellectual clarity. I have tried laughing and crying and understanding—nothing is enough. I have tried studying the ruins of all history, I have tried perspective, indignation, passion, pathos, pity. Everything is more, or less, than what I need. Is this only a private obsession? Oh, we can live effectively enough with our poses and masks. Still—we will have to find a way to talk, a way to look, or we shall never even draw ourselves up from the flatness of the devastation to see the real expanses of our tragedy.

But this is far from the traveler's report. In this connection I want only to add as a footnote that I looked with some intensity for a Bristol hotel, in Oslo and in Copenhagen, but I couldn't recall which it was, which had burned down and when, where the celebrated confusion about L. T. occurred, or any of the details of the whole Moscow scandal![109] I knew only "Bristol Hotel" and a curiosity—symbol perhaps of the amnesia of the last decade.

The sight of Berlin for the fourth time was not so affecting—the war refuses to grant one even the satisfaction of a consistent depression. Along Potsdamer Strasse citizens were chopping down trees which lined the avenue. In the Tiergarten the Black Market had blossomed forth again, and civilians, Russians, GIs were swarming over each other exchanging currency, cigarettes, watches, and odd consumer goods furiously. Along Unter den Linden some Russian peasant girls, led by a Soviet hero on horseback (fourteen years old, machine gun strapped to his back), were driving a convoy of several hundred cows past the University buildings towards the Dom and the Old Museum. In Alexanderplatz the barter-business flourished as of old, with only occasional interruptions from surly, screaming Red Army corporals, and wedges of German police squadrons. The rubble stretched away everywhere. Nothing but Berlin's own peculiar formation of massive burned-out ruins. I had once thought I would cry. It seemed to me that if one were truly honest and sincere and could manage from the complex of our masks and falsities one direct simple emotion we should stumble and fall among the broken stones and sob till some of the sickness of our heart and soul was relieved. Have we built and achieved so much that the devastation of the formal physical Civilization of a great city is merely a matter of pity and regret? From one point of view, this is all we have done in our thousands of years! Now nothing was left. What will they do with his ghastly chunk of real estate? If time could be accelerated, I could see the ruins slipping into the earth and in a fast century or so, like the accumulated layers of ancient eras, a new city lives above on new levels. Failing that, Berlin will have to move out. Somewhere on the plains toward Magdeburg or Frankfurt an der Oder a planning commission will mark out a new town-square and the radiation of avenues, and on the pleasant insignificant flatlands good burghers will re-expropriate the countryside.

A good deal of the excitement of the streets seems to have disappeared. A note of pre-winter grimness hit me, at least. I recall how last summer there was a newness and eagerness everywhere. In the newspapers and the long lines waiting for the latest issues. In the get-rich-quick frenzy of the airborne troops occupying the city. In the tales of the strange Russians. Life in the rubble seems to have settled down. There is still, to be sure, a vigorous journalistic community, but I noted one significant change, a slight item perhaps, but it may obviously mean much more. The *Neue Zeit*, which had been so popular and resourceful some months ago, was a small sheet now and almost lifeless. Its large format, I learn, was suddenly and arbitrarily reduced. The editor (a Christian-Democrat) is under regular fire from the *Deutsche Volkszeitung* (CP) and the *Tägliche Rundschau* (Red Army). The staff members complain of the harshness of Soviet censors, and the claim was that as much as thirty-five to forty percent of the editorial content is sometimes removed. There has been little opportunity to publish news of "western" orientation, and the editors have been increasingly forced to publish in prominent places materials supplied by the Soviets. I note too that the burgeoning of American literature has wilted somewhat. *Die Amerikanische Rundschau*, whose ten thousand copies flooded what few German bookstores remain, has been something of a flop. (It featured "stale" articles by MacLeish and Benét.) Scarcely more success was met by *Heute*, an ersatz *Life*: its flashy illustrated features sold copies, made no readers. Similarly, the Black Market is rather soberer. The Tiergarten is alternately fair grounds and a police trap. Sometimes you see British tanks sitting in the middle of the park. Other times: Russians fingering green women's lingerie, measuring themselves in long outmoded German overcoats, buying brightly colored cloth. In the Russian zone the exchanges go on, but the prices have gone down, and the old tricks and ruses are somewhat played-out. It was nice being able to stack a cigarette-carton full of paper and take a thousand marks for it. But at the next turn when you received vinegar and water for Moscow's best vodka—well, it was time for a renewal of honesty and a restoration of business confidence before the whole market's throat was slit. So: the cigarettes go for ten dollars a package (somewhat more for king-size Pall Malls), the watches for two or three hundred dollars (depending on how loud the tick is, and how well you can lie about the number of jewels). On the Russian situation generally, surprise, shock, amusement, revulsion, affection, camaraderie, and all manner of propaganda, have hardened into cool casual prejudices, and that wondrous sense of exploration of last summer is gone. I miss it. "America" discovering "Russia" was a precious spectacle! Not the fake literary discoveries of survey-history readers and purchasers of the Pushkin Modern Library giant. But the earnest and real-life collision of curious national creatures. Americans unmoved and baffled by the Technicolor agitprop in Russian areas. Russians distressed by the violent efficiency of American night guards. Americans amazed at the childishness and crudity of the plain soldier. Russians contemptuous of American caution: "Are you afraid to die," one said, after he had taken an A-20 up in a slow roll after a two-minute briefing with his instructor aghast down on the field. Americans perplexed by the Russian mass complex: a Russian had been run over and killed by a jeep, but no we needn't worry ourselves about it, it was only one man after all, and he wasn't an officer anyway! Russians so envious of Yankee ingenuity: they would have slugged the fuel-line all night with a hammer in order to get some speed into the vehicle; all that was wrong was that the choke had slipped out and everything was flooded. Americans growing to dislike and fear the Russians—the "menace" consisting of the disagreeable necessity of always having to carry a .45 when they're around, of the constant anxiety about your person, your property, your girl, of the occasional political distress prompted by the systematic Kremlin encroachments into the west, of the inability to share any experience easily, freely, together. The explorers, as I say, are rather jaded. Still there is much to be seen. Shots still ring out wildly in the northeast. It upset me more than a little one night, as did the sight of furniture being flung out of some window above me. Girls will still hail your jeep and plead for protective escort. (In the US zone you see girls, women, pedestrians, making their way along the streets briskly, and with no apparent concern that it is after curfew.) I do hear, however, that the food situation has generally improved. On the whole, I think the Stalinist high command must have been somewhat surprised by the simple "orderliness" and "efficiency" introduced by effete, degenerate powers. Their fetish of their own dynamism betrayed them somewhat. Their propaganda to the contrary, the great and heroic Red Army made no converts. On the contrary, they found every little detail (the ignorance of the peasant hosts, the carelessness of uniform, the violence of backward elements) of the organizational bottom-levels serving to depress their international political position. I expect many "internal reforms." A drive is currently on to apprehend the thousands of Russian AWOLs in Berlin, and they have admitted, actually, the high desertion rate among their elements, both officers and men. A new facet of the Red Army!

30 October 1945

Paragraphs from a letter (Hannah Arendt):

I had been away from Heidelberg, and in fact from Germany (for the first time in six months) and it was something of a reunion to come back to the Jaspers'. I hadn't seen them in a month. As always, it was the *Küche* first, and as always the professor was there with his passionate curiosity, opening all the boxes, examining the canned goods, asking me for the translations of the instructions on the shaving-cream tubes, etc. I have been managing to draw some special rations around army bureaus, and as Frau Jaspers says, I arrive as a *Weihnachtsmann*. Your packages have been happily received; it has been a pleasure for me to deliver them. My only regret is that my German is so poor it really is a task for me to sit in the professor's study and patiently work through some kind of critical introduction to each of the volumes received (the Niebuhr, the Koestler, etc.). Both he and his wife, I should report, are fairly well. For a while they were planning to go to Switzerland on invitation from the university at Basel. It would have been far more comfortable and agreeable: no small thing. There would have been warmth and food and more peace than it is possible to have anywhere here. But there was the probability that the philosophy faculty would be opening shortly. And after all these years it was not very easy to "walk out." So they remain in Heidelberg. The food situation, with help, is improving. Apparently they have enough coal to keep a room or two heated throughout the winter. (Carefully, Frau Jaspers explained to me, trembling in the living room, that they can't really begin the winter until the middle of November.) The psychological situation is less good. The visitors to 66 Plöck are constant and wearying. So many are looking to the Jaspers for advice and help: Mrs. Jaspers as a proud respected Jewess, the professor as a spiritual force. It must really try them, wear them out to listen to the tales of woe all day long, and the stories of AMG stupidity or foolishness. What could I tell them when they broached the matter of permanently moving to Switzerland? What a paradise it would really be for them! All the simple things of civilization, now fabulous luxuries, would make these years for them richer and happier. The manuscripts could be published. The anxiety about the new threats to personal and spiritual freedom (chaos in Germany; Russia) considerably relieved. We talked, but you and I both know that in Heidelberg and in Germany they will remain.

I am really sorry I myself am so "put out" these months I have been unable to write anything, much less revealing reports about the German or European situation. I have written a note here and there, something to Lionel Trilling on the Heidelberg opening (I learn that Margaret Marshall in the *Nation* is running a few paragraphs: I suspect it will be of interest to you), a few pages to Dwight. But in terrible ways I find the literary faculty simply paralyzed. Perhaps it is only my nervousness (to survive this apparatus one turns into a high-powered wreck). Maybe it is a subtle reluctance to record anything for fear that these terrible days will actually be taken for history. What a naive and hopeless method of protesting harsh realities!

The month I mentioned previously was spent, and very happily, in Scandinavia. There was a little bit of work in Oslo, with our task force in Norway, and then there was a glorious week in Stockholm (a city of cities!), and a brief nice visit to Copenhagen. We came back via Berlin where I took sick and spent a week in a local hospital recovering from what was essentially just fatigue. Lying in a bed day after day I finally got a glimpse of a perspective of my life this last year. What an unbelievable unreal adventure! I wished so hard I could find powers within me some time to come to terms with my own experience, my own past. And I wondered whether the changes in me—really: the way I talk and walk and think and read, the tone of one's ambition, the range of one's confidence and sensitivity—were as deep, as I sometimes in a fit of autobiographical terror, suspect. But then these personal confessions are of small interest or relevance.

How I long to write something about Berlin! I have been into the city several times now since August, and in a trip of a few days one can only gather scattered impressions. But "impressions" have always been sold short, and it makes me angry to think of all the intellectualistic fakery in abstractions. How can you know what a city is unless you take three hours and drive through it street by street until you sicken at the sight of broken burned stone? How can you know the tragedy here, its pathos and cheapness, until you pick up some girls on the avenue and listen to them talk and sit with them in their homes (cave-dwelling primitivism of the twentieth century) and see them dream (or watch them, dreamless). And what sense of international politics can one have until you've seen a Russian soldier (one Red Army hero, no more, a single solitary Soviet native, that is all that is required!), watched him in the Black Market (insisting on watches with loud ticks and sweep-second hands), followed him (not a little anxiously) into the clubs in the Russian zone. (I was intrigued by the dispatch sent from Berlin to the London *Daily Worker*, a copy of which I found in Copenhagen, which denied vehemently all the "slanders" about the Soviets in Berlin, demanded a single date, incident, witness. The next night we tiptoed down towards Unter den Linden, wild shots ringing out into the night, furniture coming out of windows, shaking off girls who wanted our protection, finally locating our vehicle, and shortly thereafter escaping with our lives from some drunken madman who had temporary control of the jeep on a dark road leading out of the city at the point of a pistol.

But after all these are only "impressions." They have no other virtue other than they actually happened.

But the paper is gone, and I am afraid my line of thought too.

11 November 1945, Frankfurt

Dear Cap[110],

I was in Berlin a few days ago and had a post-card all prepared for you—but then my Norwegian issue having flopped so badly, I withdrew it. It was, however, quite nice: a pleasant view looking down Unter den Linden towards Brandenburger Tor and the Tiergarten. No sooner had I bought the cards than I turned the corner of Friedrichstrasse and was on the boulevard itself, a gray dismal avenue of ruins, its ugliness relieved only be the glassy polish of the wet streets. The spectacle was intriguing. Down towards the Dom, passing the university buildings, was a long convoy of cows, hundreds of them. Surrounding the cows were a half-dozen stout smiling homely peasant creatures, supervised by a young Russian on horseback, machine gun strapped to his back, his stern mien scarcely disguising his fourteen years of age. But then I couldn't get the whole story on the back of a post-card, so we'll let it go (Unter den Linden, a Russian supply route for Brandenburg cows).

The Scandinavian tour was a glorious two weeks, but no, it wasn't a holiday, at least not formally. I was supposed to take a run up to Oslo and catch the American task force before it left, check through their records, patch up their histories, etc. Left with a major, and had some serious intentions. But he happens to be the goddamnest sightseer who ever laid hands on a guide-book, so off we were à la Cook. Up through museums, past monuments, into theaters, over landmarks. Till I thought I would go mad. Finally, I escaped by sneaking across the border into Sweden. Wound up in Stockholm with fake papers and a free day on my hands. I couldn't get a plane out in a week, which gave me eight days in a fabulous wonderland of a city. Oh, that's probably an exaggeration. But you have no idea how the normal virtues of a metropolis become inflated almost to the point of becoming the Good Life. I saw nobody, spoke to nobody, learned nothing. I fell in love, spent a fortune, was as happy as I could be.

But, Cap, that hardly constitutes what you must want as "news." Some time late in September the Army program began to fizzle out. I began to get deeply annoyed and irritated and simply couldn't do a job on either research or writing. I finally left with four pages of manuscript completed and the army-historian frantic. From there, pick it up to Oslo. But I suspect so many things have changed. The running gag of the office happens to be that one never meets nice plain people anymore, only Characters, Characters! And it is true. The frenzy of keeping oneself half-way adjusted (or happy, but maybe it is only high-spirited) is a hothouse of idiosyncrasies and irresponsibilities. You simply can't keep to a straight line of work or ambition, and ideas like ethics and habits become quite lost in the adventurism of personality. You do discover new resources of confidence, and in many ways you develop an inner power. But what happens to an individual, like what happens to a nation or an army or a whole people, is not something that can be easily grasped. I am more and more convinced that nobody rightly understands what has happened to the way human beings live and die here. I am afraid no one will be able to catch what is happening to isolated young men.

Strictly speaking, I am supposed to be concerned with the history of the occupation in Europe. A nominally fascinating assignment and every now and then I get caught up in a burst of enthusiasm and want to see and understand so much my mind would break. Usually one paces oneself slowly, gives in to hopelessness and resignation easily (there is no end to stupidity and incompetency, you know), and finds release in some recklessly contrived escapade. The themes of the history are so clear and overwhelming perhaps we don't dare to face them. So many scandals, so much cheapness and ignorance, so little fineness and clean vigorous spirit, so deep a disease of the heart and mind.

But the "new," the "news." Last night we drove out to Wiesbaden, a little town about thirty kilometers north and west of here, and spent an evening at a bar. The town was hit badly in spots, but there were still attractive avenues with trees and upright architecture. We made our usual round of vicious cynical jokes about the aerial destruction, the "terror-bombing" as the Germans have taught some of us to say. What was here? Some nice hotels, baths, clubs. . . and an airfield some distance off. Well, somebody must have thought it a bright idea to kill off some of the rank which possibly congregates in a little resort wonderland. So a few hundred planes came over and knocked it half-way to hell. You ride down a street and in the middle of it what must have been two handsome old nineteenth-century homes are sprawled all over the real estate in broken stones and twisted iron. In the middle of a park a great monument is bent and battered into almost a comical design. Oh, no doubt, the mission was very successful! But I wonder who believes it. None of us did last night, or for months now, and we have been over the ruins of Germany. We don't believe in the Mission, formulate it as you will. It was hypocrisy, duplicity, stupidity, and most of all barbarism. The war, or maybe it is really the postwar, has taught that lesson: the barbarian is our brother. . . We sat around the bar and swapped tales. The same old round of war stories. (Have they ever been told in the States? How nobody ever took prisoners after the German offensive failed last winter: how the stockade for Wehrmacht PWs remained constant although great units were being captured and were surrendering: how you simply get rid of them, and feel a little better about it if the son-of-a-bitch was wounded. "I remember one time a new green kid came up with five krauts. We told him the PW cage was five miles back, and to hurry up about it, he had only five minutes. They must have gone back a thousand yards into the woods, when we heard that old M-1 barking. The kid made it, with a few minutes to spare. . ."). We all must have gotten a little drunk. The *Weinbrand* wasn't too bad, and the house (property of an IG Farben director) was on the magnificent side. We got home rather late, after some delay on the part of our fräulein hitch-hikers who didn't quite like the idea of our thinking they were too young.

Not much "news," Cap, but the themes (always!) are so simple, so clear.

20 November 1945

Unexpected trip back to Heidelberg. An uneventful dull ride; two boring Polish officers were no help. The sight of the city again was, by contrast, quite stimulating. A significant, screaming change: the ubiquitous Pro Station signs. On every avenue, almost at every turn, the green light and the conspicuous plainly-lettered posters. The Army's battle against VD continues (the other day one of the local battalions declared an extra holiday: a reward from Division for going an entire week without a new case!) American culture taking root.

Somewhat on the more engaging side: an evening in the Laterne (*Kleinkunstbühne*), and the performance went on from half past six almost till ten. The café was crowded (ten marks entrance) and smoky, and neither the tea, coffee or beer was very good. Still there was something extremely attractive about the show. Perhaps it was a subtle feeling that people were here enjoying themselves who had been without that kind of casual slight entertainment for terrible eternities. Too, there was a nice freshness about some of the performers and their skits. There was also an occasionally sharp note to some of the fun, and encouraging it was to this rather perverse political taste.

[...]

Then there was the magician, who borrows of course some jewelry from the audience. The promise is passionately made to replace every piece of it if something goes awry. Replace a watch? He checks himself, and with dripping merriment confesses: of course, just as soon as things become normal again, and stares at the ceiling as if he could already glimpse that happy time two decades or so hence! Finally of course a burlesque on the occupation-Esperanto, with flirtations and affairs conducted in a pidgin-French-English-German (a delightful dance by Charlotte Poppe). The evening's farewell: an invitation to return, and the reassurance that there are only two places in all of Europe where romance and gaiety still thrive—Budapest... and Heidelberg. Everybody laughed. Most everybody shuffled out of the Laterne and returned to their cold empty houses.

22 November 1945, Frankfurt

Dear Dwight,

Your brief note of the twelfth came the other day, and to it for now I reply with a) there was nothing really wrong (the hospital affair), only sheer fatigue: I had been down to Munich and back, to Konstanz on the Bodensee and back (and for nothing, only to see the Swiss horizon), up to Norway and through Scandinavia and back via Berlin: I simply dropped; b) use my name, do what you want with the letter: only, my god, it was very hastily written, and if you think my name should go with that kind of rather careless composition all right, but do do some editing like a good boy, a faithful friend, an old critic. By the way I dispatched a fourth (or fifth) and final installment, which I trust you've received.

On the food situation, it is strange to find somebody really morally disturbed about it. The disease of "moral atheism" is too deep and chronic. Here I know nobody, except Mooney here with me, who evinces any distress. He's a curious boy and I should write something about him some day. The only soldier I know who has grown and learned things. I suppose, frankly, he has taken a good deal from me. But then I am so changed in many ways I don't quite recognize the borrowings. He was a simple enthusiastic high-school boy who was making his way with his Firm. But there was a fine passion about him, a strange gusto which made him want to see and hear. And the result as of these days is something of a spectacle. The other day on the road to Kassel he was burning to give everything up and do Something. Do something about the madness of a world where people are starving, after thousands of years of civilization to have nothing to eat and die of it, where people have to be afraid of a passing stranger, after civilizations of "law and order" to tremble for your person! He for one was ready for a Crusade. But what could I tell him to fight for, and whom with, and where? We sat around the other evening waiting for one of our boys to return. The sergeant has been working with me interviewing German generals (reconstructing the Great Game of World War II): he's a German-American, but with a family in Württemberg, somewhere near Stuttgart. We got him a pass, lent him our jeep and scraped together some rations to take south with him. He came back and I wish you could have heard his story. The zone is French, and as he walked through the door, he saw the troops going through the house, ransacking all the drawers, picking out what they liked (jewelry, linen, gloves, what-not), and tossing it into a sack. He turned white and furious. He grabbed one and tossed him; he screamed that unless they got out, he'd shoot them all. He was beside himself. This was after all his house, he had been born here, this was his mother and his family. Well, the homecoming was not too pleasant. His mother and relatives had almost nothing to eat. Occasional expeditions were made deep into Bavaria, to the Allgäu (three hundred kilometers!) to scrape together some food. When he took out a little bag of sugar, his mother held it out in her hand and wept, "staring at it as if it were a bag of gold-dust." They had managed to get an egg that month, and he sat around and listened to the debates as to how they should cook it and eat it. Finally the theory which won out dictated that it be put into some hot water and utilized as egg drops. This made for the maximum good. And also they could have the egg for a week, a whole week. When he was leaving his mother fondled her son's leather briefcase and told him sadly, "You know, Gottfried, if we had a briefcase like this we could get an entire pound of butter..." He didn't want to make her feel badly, and so he came back: "My gosh, I forgot completely. You know I brought it down to give to you, I don't need it and thought it might be useful here." He left her as he found her, weeping.

I wrote my folks this story earlier this evening, mainly because their notes to me have been so alarming on the German question. I had no idea of what the main newspaper-headline trend was until some one showed me something from the *Times* and *Tribune*. The *Tribune* spoke of the "symptoms of a potential German rebellion," "German unwillingness to accept the consequences of defeat." The *Times* was in a similar vein, with some reference to the infiltration of Nazi ideologies among Americans via fräulein girl friends. What nonsense and stupidities! You know, of course, what the explanation is for this line (which seems to be persistent and organized, because it appears in American items constantly). The Army wants to maintain its force and it is feeding the chair-borne correspondents with a distorted picture of the "menace," the security threats here. I happen to know what the police story is. Occasionally a GI is beat up, occasionally a jeep is stolen, or somebody monkeys around with some equipment. But that's the usual police-blotter stuff around any precinct. Why for somebody to carry a pistol around in the streets of Germany (in Frankfurt, or Heidelberg, or Mannheim, or Augsburg, or Munich) is absurd, laughable. There are no German rebels, and as for Nazism among the girls, that too is a joke. Politics, on the old themes, is gone. And the relations between Americans and German girls, I daresay, never even skirts the issues of war, peace, and politics. What is really sickening—my father spoke of being sickened at the thought that the Germans are not "sorry," have not learned the meaning of the war—is how little people understand about the real situation here. How little sense they have of the ordinary taken-for-granted details of Germany and the European peoples in these terrible days. The picture here is of a ruined poverty—stricken animalized people, with little to eat, everything to fear, nothing to hope for. Triumphant civilization is going back to its historic beginnings: we reach higher levels when we complete the transformation of the Germans into domesticated animals. Oh, there are some half-Nazi criminal characters around, many ambitious businessmen (the big boys in the Ruhr are classic), many unscrupulous young gangsters. But that isn't what we have grown to call the big picture, that isn't the people, the mass. They are beaten, shabby, docile, acquiescent—and nowadays, thank god, a little more independent, more prepared to offer native criticism of our corrupted occupation policies. (The *Frankfurter Rundschau* slammed the city Mayor the other day in flaming editorials—the poor goof who was appointed by US (and this is November!) was an out-and-out Nazi, who had endorsed the *Führer-Prinzip*, and was a favored administrator in the hey-day of imperial conquest. A nice scandal!)

[...]

On the personal side, I have been on the whole well. I am fortunately or unfortunately low-point-man on the totem pole, which should keep me here until the spring. I wish I knew how to use the time constructively. I wish I could make up my mind about the future. I'm twenty-five now, I say to myself (almost constantly), twenty-five... and have less courage to face the future than ever before. What do I want to do? It is not so much that I am "aimless," rather I seem to have lost a focus. Where do I want to work and live (in Europe, in NY, on a world-junket route) and how (busying myself in the details of some work-job, corresponding free and leisurely, in say "creative thoughtfulness")? But again, enough for now.

My best regards to you, Nancy, the growing family, and friends you may happen to see.

Also: I would like some letters from you.

Yours,

29 November 1945

Morning: hasty visit to Oberursel. The dispensary building has been cleaned out, and the Institute begins to take shape.[111] Some six generals have been moved in. "Solitary confinement" is now just a bad memory. They had been removed from the cells and transferred to "Alaska," where conditions were livable and even sociable. Little groups could assemble to talk and exchange views. Major Schramm, for example, was gathering information from some of the others on "fraternization" and also completing his own manuscript on the Collapse of the German Military Power.[112] We all stood around and talked in the mess hall one morning; the General officers were once again in "class A" uniform, and that perhaps made them feel somewhat brighter—all they have is memories of glory, memories of a human dignity. When the enlisted men came in for lunch—the table was magnificently set, and the irony was obvious to all, I thought—we all filed out quickly. So the house is being organized, and in a very interesting way it is "convenient" and "comfortable" even for us. Our first visits were to the cells in A-wing. A burly dirty GI guard dangled his keys in the corridors and took us to our doors. He would go in first himself. "Get up!" you could hear him screaming: the door was partially open, "Get up, I said! Get your clothes on!" One could look in and see the general stumbling out of his cot, fumbling for his shoes, and trying to button his shirt and pants. Bewildered, and not a little frightened. All of them except for Hitzfeld were slight and quiet men. The guard was mean and angry and for no ostensible reason in all the world. "Get up there against the window and turn around! An American officer is coming into the room!" I felt hotly ashamed. I looked at Hornung, but we averted each other's eyes. The general continued to stumble around. He understood very little English, tried opening the window to appease the guard. Of course that was wrong and the guard seized and lifted him violently around, and grunted final approval. We were admitted. I said, *Guten Tag, Herr General*, and we all tried to pretend that nothing had happened.

Now, to be sure, we have our own house. No particular measures of security are going to be taken: there is no threat of escape at all. There is a nice dining room-kitchen where the meals should be considerably better than soup and bread twice a day—all the man have lost thirty, forty, fifty pounds in the last six months or so. They live on cots in separate rooms. There is good light, some furniture, a pleasant little garden in the back. I found most of them tidying the place up. General Mellenthin was clearing a table to make a writing desk. General Waldenburg and von Wagener were dusting shelves, cleaning windows. General Hitzfeld was sweeping small piles of dust and dirt together and carrying them on pieces of paper to the garbage can.[113] He smiled at us warmly and we all laughed as we took in the walls of his room plastered with pin-up girls. An unexpected luxury. The General dissented somewhat. Oh, one or two of these girls are fine, but this mass of feminine pulchritude was a little upsetting for an old man. We all laughed again... The interrogation briefs can now be organized, and slowly we will be able to piece together the thrusts and failures of the German Wehrmacht in the Western Front as seen by the Generals who knew their hopes, their strength, the real strategy and course of events. The Great Game of War! And so I find myself playing Landlord to the German General Staff. PS. The problem of the Geneva Convention comes up again and again. Without a doubt the solitary confinement and general conditions of imprisonment of previous periods were flagrant violations of "international law." There was no good reason, the prison-officers themselves confessed, for the situation. The generals came in and there they were installed. Iron rations. Fleeting two minutes a day for the latrine functions, in crowded hurried stalls—("General, with terrible case of GIs,[114] just gets his pants down, and comes the knock on the door to get out..."). Solitary. ("Four hundred hours—for four hundred hours I have been looking at these walls"—Gen. von Wagener). Latest wrinkle: the question of pay, which has been ignored. Trying to round up a German paymaster from the Seventh Army.

30 November 1945, Stuttgart

We spent most of the afternoon with Dr. James Kerr Pollock[115] (political adviser to General Clay in Berlin). I remembered him vaguely from Michigan campus days—he was professor of political science and a vigorous advocate of intervention against Germany. Well, here is one academician at least who has moved to accept the responsibility. He is here and active. Oh, to be sure, from the front-office little tidbits of gossip come through revealingly. Apparently the good Doctor is on a Cook's tour of Europe like most everybody else: "if only he'd stop running around in France and Switzerland we might get something done!" He has been out of Berlin now for weeks, tied up here with the Württemberg-Baden crisis. This administrative monstrosity in the American zone has been almost unmanageable. The French have the southern sections of two old traditional provinces; the US took everything north of the autobahn, which is a convenient line on a map but which has twisted economy and procedure into a hopeless mess. Pollock, I suppose, is to salvage something out of the botches of power-politics.

We had just begun our conversations when an unfortunate interruption held us up. Some cartons of cigarettes had been stolen from the house. That almost ended the Occupation of Germany for that day. The Doctor was distressed, made a quick trip up the hill (Stuttgart, as usual, lay foggily in the valley), and we sat around while the sleuthing continued. Finally, over a drink in the handsomely furnished living room—without a sufficient number of requisitioned mansions there would be no Occupation!—we reviewed the problems before us.

In the final analysis, his frank summing-up of the American record included four major points of failure or error—

1. The Zonal Division of Germany. When the country was divided into four parts, which apparently was a personal decision of Roosevelt at Yalta, it made any kind of Occupation policy for Germany impossible. Only confusion and chaos could conceivably be served. After almost a year (half) serious progress is being made towards building from four zones, four Germanies, back to a single controlling agency. This does not necessarily mean at this time, or at any other time, before or after, that a German nation or state exists. The systematic destruction or the sedulous revival of the country could be the purpose. Only earnestness and efficiency is involved. That is precisely what has been lacking. There are four economic committees, and agriculture and industry are neither saved nor sacked. There are four political attitudes, and no coordinated blows can be administered to the lingering Nazi structures in the community. There are four images of the Conqueror, and to the general despair there is added only the intrigues of international hothouse politics.

2. France. The inclusion of the French influence was a "horrible mistake." Once again, the personal weight of Roosevelt. They were built up into a major power, given the authority to pose and perform like a Big Fourth. Their vindictiveness, their chauvinism, their poverty, were given free reign. They looted Germany mercilessly, and refused to allow the growth of even a single element of law and order; it does not exist in their own zone, and on a national scale, they have sabotaged all efforts at zonal collaboration. The specter of a united Germany haunts them. So any construction of central government departments becomes out of the question. More than that, to the power and glory which we had propped up we now had to cater to sensitively! The French con-

sidered it essential to expand their zone to a respectable size—the so-called Koblenz bridgehead (which gave them some of the greatest wine-growing country in the world)—to keep some part of Württemberg-Baden (the terrible loss of prestige in finally moving out of Stuttgart!)—to move into a corner of Berlin. None of which facilitated efforts to arrive at a new workable policy for post-Nazi Germany. (To be sure, this kind of inadequacy, incompetency, and vicious stupidity is not a national monopoly of the French—when the US demanded so much of the British zone to form a Bremen enclave much the same narrow-minded process was at work; the Navy wanted, insisted on useless banks of the Weser which no one had ever seen. And when one American Army (Patch's) had to move out of their administrative zone (Bavaria) in order to make room for new forces (Patton's) which in all reason should have been assigned the western military district. So two months after the Occupation had begun, things were back at scratch again.)

3. The lack of policy. The Morgenthau shadow from Quebec on. The hatchet-policies of hate Germany and destroy Germany via Colonel Bernstein.[116] The pastoralization of the whole land. The American program: the preservation of chaos! No resumption of normal social activities. Paralysis. And now no small share of the responsibility for winter burdens in Germany—which we ourselves want so much to avoid—is on American hands. They prevented Germans from taking measures to insure sufficient food and warmth (clothes, etc.) for the future. Textile factories were shut down, etc. The crisis which is coming could have been averted. But until after Potsdam, no line on Germany was available. July and August went by before anybody had a considered serious directive on the large principles governing the destruction and reconstruction of post-Nazi Germany.

4. The failings of an Army in postwar struggles. The curse of homesickness: who could be earnest "sweating out points"? Soldiers without real morale—who had oriented them on the Mission to Germany? Combat troops, accustomed to having their own way from the commander to the patrol, wrestling against the growing hamstrings of civil order and reconstruction—the tactical commander wants to give the orders. The general tourist-unsettledness of the Americans—the French have their families, the Russians, the British fly home... The rather naive sensitivity of military non-political Americans in political Europe—how could we appoint a magnificently equipped Secretary-General to office when some sergeant in CIC dug up the information that he had written (no less!) somewhat critical articles of President Roosevelt—or how could we keep in office a splendid *Regierungspräsident* (in Ansbach) when it was discovered he had once held high position in a bureau (advertising) which had National Socialist functions?

[...]

29 November to 1 December 1945

Random notes on the Stuttgart trip.

The argumentative excitement of the American Occupation of Germany informs every detail of the developing situation. In Karlsruhe the other day, I hear, a new American movie-house was inaugurated, the Palace; and for its premiere the military exhibitors showed *The Maltese Falcon*! What a storm! "Poor taste and exceptionally poor judgment," was only one mild comment by American critics, sorely distressed. "At this stage of the occupation of Germany such a film is entirely out of line. German propaganda during the war has stressed that America was a land of gangsters among other things. This film, distributed by DSCC Film Control, showed: the leading man flaunting the authority of the police; the leading lady as an underworld character; three murders taking place with the police unable to apprehend the criminals."

Nor are the Germans without protest these days. In Karlsruhe too, a few Sundays ago, the Kulturbund gave a Concert and Theater program. The seventh number of the program was selection from Bert Brecht's *Dreigroschenoper*, which is apparently being systematically revived (I missed a performance in Berlin). Before and during the number there was a mounting commotion in the theater. There was no mistaking the disturbance: people shouted, stomped on the floor, whistled. After a few minutes the performers managed to re-establish quiet and order. The announcement was made that the police were being summoned, and those who did not care for the music would please leave the auditorium. The estimate is that about a quarter of the audience departed. The performance continued. My informant finds it "interesting to note that the disturbance was caused by the younger people of the audience," and attributes the demonstration to some kind of political reaction on the ground that Brecht "is supposed to have definite communistic tendencies, which is written into his music." We know, of course, something about Brecht, but I don't know the *Dreigroschenoper* and so am in no position to know. But from the people I talked to about the incident, the situation would appear to be somewhat different. One girl I engaged in conversation was quite firm on the issue. She had seen the film version and knew the work. She denied that politics or communism had anything to do with it. "The opera is a piece of dirt and filth. The music? It goes something like this—How nice were the Years I spent in a Bordello!—and—For this World People are Not Bad Enough—and so on. It is something out of the past and it cuts across the sentiments of new generations. Our young people simply have a radically different taste than the Brecht of 1928! The older folks may smack their lips and roll their eyes, but for us it is disgusting and corrupt, the least we can say: unsuitable."

The rising crime rate: the arming of the German police in particular areas.

The rise of juvenile delinquency: forbidding under-eighteen after dark.

The growth of Communist "Community Clubs" in small towns. (CP tempo determines political pace!)

Night of 14 November—Crailsheim posted appeal from German Red Cross for whereabouts of the two children of a local Jewish parent who had been confined in a concentration camp. The appeal was defaced, the word *Juden* stamped on it.

The community of Nazis—strengthened by the systematic political persecution of Occupation.

Continuing poster campaign against fraternizing German women.

I append the texts of two posters.

The relaxation of restrictions of fraternization has been followed by a definite increase in civilian associations with American troops billeted in the community. Resentment against those German women exhibiting friendliness toward American soldiers is becoming increasingly apparent and has finally provoked expression in the form of a leaflet commonly known as "The Chocolate Whore," reproduced below. Noticeable is the lack of accusation or insinuation against the American soldiers. The writer remains unidentified. A Second leaflet, prose in form but similar in theme, entitled, "What we don't like," is attached as Annex "A" to this report:

"Ode to a Whore [117]
Whether you're married
or go singly about
your whoring goes on
day in, day out
chocolate bars are all you crave
while you're giving out what little you have
Your men fell with the weapons they bore—
—and you are enjoying it all the more
Your bridegrooms are missing, or dead, or lost
And you—you are forgetting so fast.
Six long years we bled and fought—for you
Six long years we suffered and thought—of you
—and you? Are you so cruel, so abandoned, unkind
to have the taste of chocolate on your mind?"

ANNEX "A"—TO WEEKLY INTELLIGENCE REPORT

Have you ever seen all those nice ladies, how they stand on the corners and wander in the woods? Every age is represented from schoolchild to Mama, some are very much embarrassed, and others are of the opinion that they are now giving peace to the world openly and importantly. Yes, that would be all right, but hear what we don't like: For a pound of coffee, for a chocolate bar, for a little bag of black tea, for oranges, candy, biscuits, or what have you, these nice ladies give everything. Not only do they give their entire womanly honor to the activity in question. We don't care about them personally. However, to what will it lead, if they do as they please, if they are even proud of the role they play. Look: here is our danger: Not only the rest of our women, but we Germans all will suffer under these claws which the devil of whoredom spreads slowly but surely to suppress us in the world. Therefore, let us tell those chicks how matters really stand. It's true: the war is lost, and the Third Reich has vanished. But we have taken an oath. Regardless how deep the dirt, regardless how great our suffering, regardless how hard our lot which costs us not only all our joy but also many tears, if even our whole future lies dark ahead, our honor will be saved! For he who smashes that gem forgets that our dead, who gave their lives for us, are watching us and shuddering turn their faces silently away. Therefore, let us warn these ladies publicly and in the name of all. If you don't stop this whoredom in private as well as in public, we are through with you—you will be nothing more to us. True, the war is lost, but we have our honor still, and we must not forget: Germans we are and will remain.

29 September 1945

Still clearing the rubble, and now progress is being made with the conscription of former Nazis for street-cleaning.

In Pforzheim the job is still Augean. One sees in Stuttgart bright efficient trolleys, and most of them bear the legend—donated by the city of Pforzheim to relieve the crisis of Stuttgart traffic. (Or: "You at least have streets left. As for us, it will be months before we even find the pavements, much less the tracks!")

The children are going to school again. Mornings and afternoons you can see little groups marching along carrying their bags of books. The onset of the cold weather threatens further cessation of education. No fuel. Plans to keep them open are ingenious and desperate—contributions in kind by the children at the rate of one stick of wood per day per child, is the most revealing and pathetic.

By and large: the business of military government and new German administrators. The stage in the Occupation has apparently been reached where both parties are looking towards the assumption of full responsibility of self-government by the German people.

The activities of the Communists: Reconciliation with nominal Nazis? Recent speeches have been distinctly stressing the right to vote for "Everybody"!

30 November 1945, Augsburg

Friday evening.

We left hurriedly, checked out of the Graf Zeppelin Hotel, raced for the filling station just outside Stuttgart before it closed and the trip was out. Gas and oil, and into the cold we went. The weather was clear, the stars were out, until the Swabian Alb, and then there was snow on the autobahn and ice on our windows as we drove through a foggy invisibility. Hour after hour, and finally Augsburg. Dropped AG at the Kaiserhof, and I managed to lose only about a half-minute before I took off again for Haunstetten.

I was naturally anxious and disturbed. It had been more than two months— possibly she had decided in favor of repatriation, perhaps they had moved to new homes. It was almost eleven when the jeep pulled in front of 13 Heimbaustrasse. All the houses were dark, and I could almost hear people waking up as I felt my way around and overcame hesitation to rap on all the doors and walls. Some one came. They said they would call her. In a few minutes a trembling sleepy surprised girl came out, was stunned, repeated my name in wonder, and finally embraced me slowly and sat down with me and continued to whisper her surprise.

Reunion at the Ossmanns—Frau Ossmann greeted me almost fulsomely. We sat around drinking champagne, politely declining offers of dinner or midnight supper. She busied herself with the preparation of a room for the two of us that night. Aina could only say, "Three months... my god, three long terrible lonely months! How I missed you! I simply couldn't bring myself to believe that you had gone to America. I couldn't understand not hearing from you... O, my darling, how glad I am that you are here again. But by tomorrow, by the next day, I'll be trying so desperately to recall how it was, what it was to see you and hear you, to have you here..." I could only say, really, it was only two and a half months.

We drank more than we should have (or did we), and both of us a little high we went to bed and had no sleep. She left (her old simple prudish self) some time before daylight. I never heard her go. In the morning the jeep wouldn't start. We heaved and pushed and finally... I saw Aina briefly again. She was controlling her tears. At last I managed to dump some supplies for her, food, and clothes, and toilet articles. She put her hands up over her eyes; she was embarrassed by the gifts, embarrassed by her tacit acceptance. I kissed her again and again in futile efforts to say goodbye. I was in town again by ten, picked up AG, found by good fortune a Bavarian jacket for me at the tailor's, and we began our journey back.

The fog was settling in again and we could hardly make out the last sign— YOU ARE NOW LEAVING AUGSBURG—WHY NOT LEAVE ALL YOUR WORRIES BEHIND—PRO-STATION.

5 December 1945, Frankfurt

Wednesday.

There is an American Frankfurt, with its quiet restricted area and its interesting aspect of rubble in the distance beyond the IG Farben buildings, with its regular headquarters routine and slight stimulation from imported cultural variety (a newspaper, a movie), with its close-lived boredom from bureau to mess-hall to billet, with its empty-mindedness-in-Europe or its hardness of heart...

There is also of course the German Frankfurt, largely unknown, the great metropolis trying to hide itself in its own ruins, its people like somnambulists, except nothing can make a pretense of the ache of cold and hunger, distressed and trembling in bare rooms, scarcely losing themselves in a crowded uncomfortable cinema, barely consoled by strange vigorous words in the newspaper, a helpless folk lost without the pillars of their society.

Then there is a Frankfurt in which the two worlds meet, a narrow twilight zone of our times, a new-born city made out of the rubble, the violence, the sordidness of the War.

By the station vague crowds milled about. In front there were GIs and German girls mutually accosting each other, and they lingered under the dim street lights as if to fake a certain sociability to the affair. In the station itself the large waiting-rooms were filled with travelers and refugees. They stood by the walls resting their packs, they sat huddled about in groups singing or munching on dark bread crumbs, or lay together in family circles under folds of blankets sleeping through all the noise and trespassing. In the cellars the German Red Cross had set up a warmed refuge for mothers and children. The old women were exhausted, the young women were frail and sick, the babies bawled and screamed all night. Old and young slept together in cribs, others found an old army stretcher, or took advantage of the nicely carpentered wooden benches, line after line of which stretched over the underground vastness of the station. Upstairs on the far side some US Army trucks were parked up to the side entrances. Fräuleins had been loaded. One truck had fifteen, with some of the Negroes hanging out the back to give the impression of a packed troop movement. (In a subsequent raid their barracks yielded twenty-four girls, who had been living there in some cases for weeks, rather comfortable with the usual GI luxuries.)

The day's rain had made the city wet and quiet. We wandered out through the outskirts, but apparently inclement weather had given it a measure of peace. The café where the German policeman had shot two Poles ("killed them, and with a little .25!" the MP told me in wonder) was closed. Across the square another little café was bright and warm with beer-drinkers and small parties. What few Poles were there left suddenly when a blue-clad round-up squadron came round and told them of what was apparently a big blow-off in their own camp. They all went out like a shot. The innkeeper spoke an obsequious English and was rather nice. He offered us wine, beer, inquired whether his sign was all right—it read: No DISTURBANCES IN THIS CAFÉ PLEASE (TAKE THEM OUTSIDE). (And, by the way, he was having fewer disturbances since the authorities have been docking DPs a pack of cigarettes every time they miss bed-check!) In the outskirts, too, all the official American clubs were quiet. At the AEF—hundreds and hundreds of troops, sitting around small softly-lit tables going through their endless tales of repple-depples, crooked point calculations, tyrannical corrupt officer cliques, kraut chicanery, etc. The beer cellar below was foul with the odor they love. At the Palmgarten—ping-pong and billiards and old copies of *Time* and the *New Yorker*. There were no girls, except for a rare civilian-worker or a WAC.

There are "whoring houses," but very few whore-houses, and the distinction is historical and important, for there does seem to be a good deal in the press about prostitution. There is, to be sure, no end of what the troops call "shacking up," but it is something far different from prostitution, from the commercialized fornication in normal society. There is no "market" in women, because the tragic loneliness and terrible frustrations of the bad years have made all of German femininity available. The extensive willingness of the surrender underlines one other aspect of our life here which the press consistently distorts. The large picture of US-German relations is not the "resistance of Germans" but the "acceptance of the Americans." They have been taken into their beds. If middle-class morality is outraged—they should have been taken into the homes—be it known there are no homes, and the middle-class image of proper social life, the host and guests in a pleasant living room, has been shattered brutally (and by the middle-class genius for industrial efficiency).

I could hardly follow the turn of streets as we responded to a radio call indicating trouble. It was somewhere in the vicinity of Kaiserstrasse, or it could have been Elbestrasse, but at any rate there we were, and everything was still. We prowled about, and finally, back in the station, we pieced the whole story together. Two of the girls had turned a third in for the "clap." She spent long expensive weeks in the hospital, and on her release turned in the other two girls. The smears will also probably show VD, and the round of revenge is complete. The next call was somewhat on the more violent side. Some airborne troops were wrecking the house. The girls apparently wouldn't quite agree to oblige them as they demanded. Their special passion rebuffed, they proceeded to smash the beds, beat the women, rip open pillows. By the time our MP car came along the place was a shambles. Rather on the more orderly side was M's raid, in another section of the city. There was kicking on the doors and rattling of the locks and gates, but the blonde opened up. Everybody scurried for cover, nude, flimsily clad. A few GIs were caught. One officer (if he had known what kind of a place she had he would never have come up). The girls milled about, preparing a defense. They began to smile and said, according to M's non-German ear, *Du schlaffen mit mir? Ish gut fuckin'.* . . (Do you want to sleep with me? I fuck well.) The place was searched, under beds, and into closets, and up through the bombed-out floors, where the odor of perfume mingled with the foul outdoors to make an unearthly smell.

4 December 1945, Frankfurt

Items for the evening.

Picking up girls, to the VD center for five-day check.

At the "booking office" an attractive well-dressed wife of a former German Army officer (who knows where any of them are now). Had been sleeping with a Negro soldier. She had been en route from Mainz to Heidelberg to see her daughter. On the way a girl informed her she might stay at some of her American friends' place. Accepted, and was escorted to the Negro barracks in Offenbach. She received food, a warm room, a bed (where she was found). She was asked if she knew that social intimacy not to mention sexual relations with Negroes was normally frowned on. She replied—"I don't see anything wrong. They're Americans. Same as you—are they not? Your democracy says all men are the same. I see nothing wrong. . ."

Sentence: VD check, fine for violation of curfew and trespassing on American property.

More from the Negro barracks: twenty-four "white German fräuleins" in a raid. Shacking-up. Luxurious—rations, soap, candy. Stayed on until lovers were redeployed, then found somebody else.

The pitched-battles—factory nearby secured by Twenty-Ninth Infantry guards, and sniping is a regular attraction. . . and with rifles, pistols, schmeissers, and even machine guns. The infantry is getting "sick of it" and soon "somebody is going to get hurt." The story: the Negroes get drunk, start shooting, raising hell. "I think," one MP's explanation ran, "they're just trying to show off to their white girl-friends living with them." One night: five in front of the gate of the MP stockade. Drunk and wild and violent. "Come on out and get us you MP bastards!" They left shortly after, however.

Conversation piece: "You know, Boss, I'm gonna get killed six months after I hit the States! I know it, I know it. I'm just gonna get killed." Why? "I just loves that white meat I've been getting. Those fräuleins have sure been good to us. I just loves that white meat and I'm gonna look for more of it when I get back to the States. . ." Said the MP—"You just watch your step, boy! That kind of stuff won't get you very far back home. You'll last about six minutes."

Fragment: "What a job! I moved four goddamn blocks of Germans out today. They're makin' room for DPs coming in. Shit, they couldn't take a thing, just some personal belongings. No furniture, no pictures, no nothing. A few tried to pick up some extra stuff. We made 'em put it back. Krauts, krauts, and more krauts, old men, women, children, everybody. . ."

"Jesus, you're just like the Gestapo! How do you like being the Gestapo?"

"Yeah, look at me, fellows, I'm a Gestapo man. . ." Laughter.

"Yeah, but they should have thought of that six years ago. They all got it coming to them. If it wasn't for them bastards we wouldn't have to be over here. Fuck 'em!"

The drunken paratrooper, picked up by the military police in a café. In brawls. Had backed some German up against the wall. They seized him. Did he have a gun? No. They searched him. Inside his jacket: a P-38. Mad and mean, soldier shouting—"I know who turned me in, that no-good cocksucker. It was that kraut son-of-a-bitch. I beat him up tonight, but tomorrow I'll kill him! I'll kill him. The no-good German bastards, I hate every one of them. I'll kill 'em. . ."

Later: whimpering—losing chance at redeployment. Too bad, too bad.

16 December 1945, Frankfurt

[. . .]

Braunschweig: Our old stop at the Lorenz Hotel. The canteen was noisy and crowded with British troops, and very warm in the special ways that never fail to be impressive. The hotel and canteen are administered by a combination of local and official army personnel, all Jewish. And one notes the Star of David conspicuously everywhere—on the sign posting the "JHC" canteen, on brooches which the clerks and waitresses wore. How strange for an American soldier, for certainly nowhere in the US military community can a Jewish institution function and serve the general troops with such independence and dignity (albeit with no little self-advertisement, but that may be precisely the point).

We sat at the little bar and I talked with some of the Jewish women. They were, so far as they knew, the last of the Braunschweig community—there were once more than a thousand families. . . now eight people remained. They had come back from their camps in Poland, to a city which no longer really existed, to a home which they would never call their own again. "You boys," the old lady said to me softly, "are surprised and distressed at the ruins, at all the rubble. For us there is not yet enough!" She said it softly and her eyes were turned away from us sadly, as if somewhere in her a measure of embarrassment for her hardness of heart was welling up. "Would more ruins help?" There was an intransigent bitterness through all her quiet tones, she was simply speaking her soul and there was no argument. "Help, it wouldn't," she agreed. "But how can we feel otherwise? They wiped out homes and families and children, they broke and tortured and destroyed our whole people!" And they wiped out also (I added) sympathy and pity and generosity and humanity and love... After all, did all of them serve in the ranks of the murderers. "Oh, no, oh, no! There are here, as everywhere, *viele anständige Menschen*, good decent citizens. Still the crime went on. No one helped. No one cried out..." Very few helped, very few cried out. They were silent in order to live. They wanted to live, not to die, they wanted to go on from day to day rather than challenge the brutal blackness, they were weak and average and human. In order to live. A not very worthy or inspiring motive, but still who should be so thoughtless as to make point and purpose of an accusation against masses who fail to rise to heroism. Perhaps they should have martyred themselves for justice. But they wanted to live. Perhaps we should be generous and understanding and loving. But we are hateful and vindictive in order to release our bitterness and suffering. Again, a weak and human thing. But so is the course of the tragedy pushed along. Each of us wields the measuring rod of the gods. None of us adds a cubit to his own stature. The cause of human justice is served best in the trials of the present active moment, in the shaking moral decision of the here-and-now, but our justice is retributive and in sadness and pity we lose our way.

Berlin: I saw Brigitte[118] again, and she was anxious and distraught as usual. Her father had disappeared. I had seen him last in November. We had sat together and talked during the evening celebrations of the October anniversary—the shots were ringing out, and he pooh-poohed my concern. A few days later he was told to report to the *Kommandatura* at Alexanderplatz. He was, to be sure, a PG; and I think I know the family story. He and Brigitte and in fact the whole family had trouped for many years under Jewish management and in the ways of the theater and were in intimate association with elements that poisoned one's reputation and standing under the Nazis. With the outbreak of the war the crisis was renewed, and the old man joined the party. Nor could he keep in good standing. On tour in German-occupied Poland and Russia they discovered old friends and ran into new disfavor by kindnesses and help for them. But now there is the new era of total denazification. He reported three weeks ago, and hasn't been heard of since. Brigitte and her mother went down to the Alexanderplatz *Kommandatura*—reputed, they say, to be the worst in the zone—but there was nothing to be had. No news, no promises, no hope, nothing but evasions and vague threats if their distress continued to constitute an official annoyance.

But for a while we managed to forget. She was warm and lovely, and charming in her bright energetic manner. She worried about the champagne, but it made her gay and flushed her face. She teased me and taunted me, but was sweeter and tenderer than the girl I had known before. She was more alone, more hopeless, than she ever was before. She had greater need now to be happy in fitful moments. Remember the girl who wished she could fall into a dreamlike sleep and wake like the princess in the fairy-tale to find the world full of color and beauty. How could one live out one's youth in this terrible broken wasteland! But then, she thought sadly, one would be sleeping and dreaming away one's youth, and in ten years one would be old and everything would be gone... That was almost six months ago, in a pleasant summer evening when we could still play with fancies. Now we came back again and again to baseness and despair.

"I know I should work, but where and how? To dance in the German places is impossible. They are cold and inconvenient, there is just no point to it. And now with the days so short I don't dare to walk home in the dark. To dance in the American clubs is—well, it's not for me. I had an offer a short while ago. They would call for me in their car. They would pay me well. They would fix it so I wouldn't need to worry about rations. There was only one catch—the manager said, I would of course dance naked. I must have practically screamed—What! He saw no reason for me to become angry. That was why they were giving me 'a good deal' I think he called it. I went on to tell him how I felt. If they wanted a dancer and would let me use my own music—my God! they want me to use something 'Allied,' something English or some American jazz, for my 'old-hat' Strauss and things!—I would be happy to perform. If they wanted something else, they had better import some specialist from America who can give them what they want. Of course, there is always a way out. The managers can be so very nice about everything. All you have to do is sleep with them. But if it comes to whoring one might as well work the streets—there is some little dignity to having a profession of one's own! But these people don't want me, they don't want a dancer. Why the fat baby-faced little girls who used to sit at a desk year after year in the theatrical agencies are now stars on the American circuit—why they never moved their legs, they never knew an hour of practice, there weren't even ordinary hoofers in the line. But that's our times, our pleasant cozy world community... So I find myself more and more alone. Your old friends you now find silly and vulgar—they want only to run to the cinema and on the street almost break their necks looking backwards at passing men. Whatever hopes you had for your life you might as well bury in the rubble. And hopes for Germany or for ideals?—let's be honest and earnest. We are cold. I sit in my room and shiver and tremble and count the days in December and then in January and then in February until the winter is gone. If I ask why, you tell me the Ruhr is shattered and give me statistics and explain the policy of feeding the Europeans whom we robbed in order to be warmer and more comfortable all these years—but everybody knows you can get coal on the black market, and all you want! We are sick to death of terror and secret police and Gestapo methods. Any knock on the door still frightens us. But you know that if the people who were in concentration camps are out, those who were out are now in. Some were criminals, many are simple ordinary persons who are the eternal victims of society. Whoever is on the seat of power, these poor folk lie prostrate under it. This is not reconstruction, and this is certainly not Justice. Or at least still the same old phoney goddess with her eyes blindfolded and her scales fixed."

We talked until we could bear to hear no more. She smiled at me, with a curious note of tolerance on her lips, as if she regretted burdening me with a trouble which was not my own. She put her arms around me with a wonderful graceful affectionateness, rested her head against me, her hair falling softly all over her face.

On the way back: a GI along Unter den Eichen, coatless, hatless, waving his arms in the driving rain. I picked him up. "Oh, I got drunk," he explained. "And I must've gone to sleep. When I got up a little while ago all the fellows and girls were gone, and so was my hat and coat and half a bottle of cognac which some son-of-a-bitch stole! But what the hell! I've gone through almost three thousand dollars in the last month. No sense worrying about a few fuckin' marks worth of that rat-poison... Yeah, those Black Market days were really something. I didn't put too much away. I got the folks to send me a couple of cartons of cigarettes every week or so, and so before they clamped down I soaked five or six thousand dollars away. One friend of mine dumped thirty-odd thousand in his bank—but then he worked in the kitchen, you know, and he had sugars and spice and just everything nice."

On the roads: old men, and young kids, waving hundred-mark bills at passing Allied vehicles, hoping for some bargain on cigarettes or chocolate or sugar or breakfast-dinner-supper rations, or anything. In the city: the furious commotion prompted by a jeep parking on a street-corner or side alley—everybody within blocks begins to run and pushes and tugs to make some kind of purchase. The prices have gone up again now that the American troops find it impossible to make overseas remittances. Cigarettes at 150 marks... In Alexanderplatz: more *Kommandatura* military police, and heavier armament. One chap we ran into was swinging a light machine gun over his shoulder: law and order reigned.

Along the Charlottenburger Chaussee, in the Tiergarten now a bestumped denuded barrenness—the new Red Army memorial, with hundreds of colored flags and banners, wreaths and flowers, two stony motionless guards, the gigantic image of a Soviet hero. The victory is now, I suppose, complete. To the east, just beyond the Brandenburger Tor a huge portrait of Stalin graces Unter den Linden. To the west, the French tricolor flies from the Siegessäule. To the south, the armored entrance into the Berliner Ring is memorialized with the silver-plated First Tank on a pedestal with identification: *Ewiger Ruhm*.

What a sickening spectacle! How these empty vanities of nationalist sentiment and prestige disgust me! These endless eternal symbols of corrupted loyalties, this vicious round of the breaking of stones and the making of monuments and the demoralization of images and ideas. But perhaps I should control my reactions to an innocuous remark on the pathos of the avenue.

[...]

We poked our cameras around the Russian guards at the Victory Shrine and one boy began to giggle somewhat breaking his frozen stance at attention. We rode down the avenue past the Siegessäule and cut for the Kurfürstendamm. All the way to Potsdam we speculated on a) how long the Shrine would stand—consensus gave it eight years, b) the manner of its destruction—atomic power was almost unanimous, only one holding out for some protonic death formula, c) how valuable before and after pictures would be... But this last pleasant collector's thought vanished somewhere along the autobahn past Magdeburg. Our own fate was sealed. There must be thousands of lists on which our names were conspicuously recorded. And then, too, we were all on

Figure 13. Victory Shrine and the bombed out Reichstag, Berlin, © Lasky Center, Munich.

the Mandatory-Death OT (Occupation Troops) roster. That fixes us. How nostalgic only last month became—why at the time we were picking out cells for ourselves. In a decade or so we could see ourselves in Cells Fifty-Six and Seven, solitary confinement with soup and bread twice a day. We were not planning it, but then neither did those German generals who are the current occupants in the camp cells at Oberursel dream in their darkest moments that after a lifetime of professional soldiering they would find themselves in dark dirty cold dismal corners of a prison classified as the scum of the earth. No, we would join no organizations, hold not a single membership card, avoid all lists, gather road-maps of the entire planet, bury caches of supplies on all continents, make friends in the international community of clerks and typists (our lives may hang on the ribbon-thread of a typographical error), resign ourselves fiercely to the imminent devastation and barbarization of the earth. At the Helmstedt frontier we cursed the French whose vehicles clogged every passage, scowled at the Russian guards, cursed the British who politely declined to give us gas, muttered to ourselves angrily all the way to Braunschweig where some hot tea and butter-rolls at a pleasant Jewish canteen (run by eight survivors of the thousand-family community) took us momentarily out of the depths.

On the road: two columns of German soldiers, black sick faces, dirty torn field-green uniforms, barely putting one foot in front of another. Two white-banded civilians were helping one man along, who sunk to his knees with every movement of his legs. People paused for a moment on the street and slowly watched the procession. The road back.

19 December 1945

Downtown across the Main to the hospital, and in one clinic—the sign in a red crayon GI scrawl read: VENEREAL DISEASE—we found Dr. X. who went through his records and brought in some interesting cases. On the floor below an old shabby scrawny woman was handing some bread and cheese to a nurse for her daughter who was somewhere inside. When she left the doors were carefully locked again. In our little case-history chamber we met Katharine Uhl. She came in with natural and obvious nervousness, dressed in an attractive silk kimono with a silk nightgown underneath. In her hands, tightly clutched, was a small portfolio crammed with letters.

Her medical record, Dr. X. told us after a while—we had the story a little wrong—showed negative results on the VD smear. She was not sick at all, was apparently a "respectable middle-class woman," and a mistake had been made. She had been turned in last week. One morning the American MP came to her house. "Are you Katie?" he asked. He didn't know her last name. She said yes. "You're sick," he said. No, no, she denied it, it must be some mistake. Oh, no, he said, a soldier gave us your name and you have to come along. He was very nice about it. He agreed to pull his jeep around the corner so that the neighbors wouldn't see her leave under arrest. The story as our questioning—Mooney, Hornung, the Dr., and I—revealed it was a touching and instructive lesson in contemporary history—not the history as it unfolds in the reports of state and press headlines, not the history of the Logic of Events, but the history which Happens to people.

Last May, with the war's end, Katie returned to Frankfurt to see whether her house had been destroyed, whether she had anything left. Her apartment was still intact but inhabited by a platoon or so of American troops. There were no difficulties about it—they consented to give up the place and move elsewhere in the building. In the course of time, she got to know several of the Americans, learned to love one of them. He was a man of about thirty-four—she was somewhat older. They lived together for about a week in May, and he was transferred to Innsbruck and Czechoslovakia for occupation duty. They corresponded regularly through military channels—a friend delivered his letters and posted hers. He returned for weekends in June and July, and for several days in August. Two months ago he returned to the States. They had made plans and agreements: he was to come back one way or another, as soldier or as civilian, to marry her if possible or to live with her. He wrote her every day, sent packages frequently. A crisis came up, however, when the intermediary source departed. A new man was designated, but he had a condition—if she didn't sleep with him, there would be no more mail, no more packages! She refused. He came around and showed her the backlog of correspondence. One night the blackmail worked—26 November. She slept with him. He gave her the mail and packages. When she called at his billet the following week to ask for the new deliveries, he became angry and refused. "I know there was mail for me there, and that he was receiving everything—he works as a mail clerk in the Army APO.... One of the girls there (she turned to the doctor: *siebzehn Jahre alt, armes Kind!*) told me she had seen the batches in his pocket and on his desk. He was very mean. He threatened me, said he would kill me with his revolver if I bothered him. I knew that the whole gang of them in the house—Huff with Boyle and Clark—were busy in the black market and the little things that were being sent to me were going into their loot. One time I saw in their house hundreds and thousands of medical pills from Weinheim. (She turned again to the doctor: 'They're supposed to abort pregnancy...') What could I do? I was frightened and stayed at home. And then the MPs came. It was terrible. Tossed into a cell in the jail like a criminal."

She was no longer frightened and was telling her *Geschichte* freely. She was nicely philosophical about the week in the VD clinic—there was another girl downstairs who was turned in by the same chap. The doctor raised an eyebrow and made a note of it. What a club the GI has to wield over the fräuleins! What a tyranny he can establish over the streets! (The story of tyranny in Europe, some one cracked softly, from *lettre de cachet*, to *lettre de coucher*.)

In her own circle, she readily admitted, the American in the beginning was distinctly persona non grata. She insisted, however, that her friends get to know her lover and with acquaintance came respect and friendship. They had little parties and gatherings back in the so-called non-fraternization days of June. It was very pleasant, and she was very happy. Arrangements were made then for her to divorce her husband (who was a foreman in a factory and who was still living with her parents and fourteen-year-old son). He was loyal and affectionate and she not only felt it was a case of true love, she knew it. To be sure, their time together was not very extensive and they didn't have too much time to talk about general subjects. I had inquired about political issues, the bombings, and similar themes.

"I didn't want to bring up those subjects. After all we were so guilty, we had started the whole thing, how could I really complain about the destruction of Germany... But when we did talk about things what was right I had to concede to in his argument and I insisted on keeping in my own! To bomb factories and things like that is a matter of war and it has to happen. But the wholesale elimination of all our homes!—that was something else. But he talked like an American..." We smiled and pressed her further. "But how an American talks is precisely what we want to know..." "Oh, he said that after all when a plane drops a bomb nobody can ever exactly determine where it's going to fall."

We had been talking for about an hour. There was a lull in the conversation. She was still clutching her portfolio of letters tightly against her breast. She was a nice-looking woman with a sensitive embarrassed smile. She had told her story and was looking wistfully off into the spaces beyond the corner of the floor. There was, as often during the time we were talking, traces of tears in her eyes. We thanked her and she left. We thanked the doctor and he promised us some special cases next time, several very eloquent prostitutes and a curious matter of a mother and a daughter. We promised we would be back if we could at all manage a few free minutes, and we left the hospital wondering how much the makers of history—the men who write the orders and issue the vast directive for masses—how much they know of the history as it happens to people.

Notes

1. Lasky misunderstands the expression: *sage-femmes* are midwives, not fortune-tellers.
2. Major James T. Hamilton. Administration and Research, Seventh Army Information and Historical Section.
3. Sergeant Howard S. Dyer, Seventh Army Information and Historical Section.
4. The Rundstedt or Ardennes counter-offensive was the final German counter-offensive in northwest Europe launched in December 1944.
5. First Lt. Edgar S. Mooney, Seventh Army Information and Historical Section.
6. First Lt. Arthur Gottlieb, and Capt. Keith Eggers, Seventh Army Information and Historical Section.
7. The Colmar Pocket was a bridgehead west of the Rhine held by the Nineteenth German Army at the end of 1944. The pocket was eliminated by Allied forces in February 1945.
8. The "Maison Rouge story" refers to the skirmish Lasky researched as part of his official duties as a combat historian.
9. Tauchnitz was a German publishing house based in Leipzig. Its English-language Tauchnitz Editions comprised a collection of British and American authors.
10. The personnel and equipment of the University of Strasbourg had been evacuated to Clermont-Ferrand following the outbreak of World War II in 1939. The University returned to Strasbourg in 1945.
11. Jean-Marie de Lattre de Tassigny (1889–1952) commanded the French First Army. Jacob Devers (1887–1979) was commander of ETOUSA since 1943 and commanded the Sixth Army Group since 1944.
12. Joseph de Goislard de Monsabert (1887–1981) commanded various African forces of the French Army, including the Ninth Regiment of Algerian Tirailleurs.
13. British Army Field Marshal Henry Maitland Wilson (1881–1964) succeeded Dwight D. Eisenhower as supreme Allied commander in the Mediterranean in January 1944.
14. Antoine Béthouart (1889–1982) commanded the First Corps of the French First Army since 1944.
15. Henri-Honoré Giraud (1879–1949) was commander-in-chief of the French forces in Africa in 1942. Due to his disagreements with Charles de Gaulle he was stripped of his position in 1944 and chose to retire.
16. British Army Field Marshal Harold Alexander (1891–1961) succeeded Henry Maitland Wilson as Supreme Allied Commander in the Mediterranean in November 1944.
17. On 22 June 1941 the German forces invaded the Soviet Union.
18. "Dr. Friedrich" was the pseudonym of Rudolf Heinrich Daumann (1896–1957). His radio talks at the German *Radio Paris* were an integral part of the German propaganda and from 1941 to 1943 also appeared in print.
19. The GPU was the secret police agency of the Soviet Union from 1922 until 1923.
20. William Ganoe (1881–1966) was a United States Army colonel and military historian with the ETOUSA from 1943 to 1945.
21. Jagdpanther was a type of German tank.
22. Walter Livingston Wright was the civilian head of the Army's Historical Branch.
23. Hans Wallenberg (1907–1977) was a German journalist, who left Germany in 1937 first for Czechoslovakia. In 1938 he went to the United States and joined the US Army in 1942.
24. The Ludendorff bridge which spanned the Rhine at Remagen near Bonn was captured by the troops of the United States First Army on 7 March 1945, when the Germans failed to

destroy it. It allowed the Americans to establish a bridgehead at the eastern side of the Rhine. After five divisions had crossed, the bridge collapsed on 17 March.

25. Courtney Hodges (1887–1966) commanded the First Army during most of the campaign in northwest Europe.

26. The B-24 Liberator was an American heavy bomber used by the Allied forces since 1941.

27. Hans Fritzsche (1900–1953) headed the radio department at the German ministry of propaganda. He was best known for his radio broadcasts *Hier spricht Hans Fritzsche*.

28. The idiom "going postal" acquired its modern meaning in the 1980s in the context of stress-induced bursts of violence in the workplace shootings at the US Postal service. Here it simply refers to preparing material to be posted.

29. Jacques Doriot (1898–1945) founded the fascist party Parti populaire français in 1936 and from 1940 collaborated with the Germans during the occupation of France.

30. The Maquis were a French guerilla resistance movement during the German occupation of France from 1940 until 1945.

31. Albert Kesselring replaced Gerd von Rundstedt as commander-in-chief of the German forces on the western front on 10 March 1945 as a direct result of the seizure of the Ludendorff bridge at Remagen by the Americans.

32. Kurt Dittmar (1891–1959), a German Army general, was a military commentator on German radio.

33. "Long Tom" was a name used for the 155mm M1 cannon used by the United States Army.

34. First Lt. Edward E. Jordan ("Jordy"), Seventh Army Information and Historical Section.

35. The Gebietsführerschule der Hitlerjugend (Langemarck) in Stemwede was a schooling facility of the Hitler Youth leadership, operating from 1936 to 1945. "Langemarck" refers to a battle in World War I.

36. Sam Sloan (1905–1940) and Charles A. Pearce "Cap" (1907–1970) were two of the three founders of the New York-based publishing house Duell, Sloan, and Pearce.

37. Wade H. Haislip (1889–1971) was a United States Army general and commander of the Fifteenth Corps of the US Army.

38. Frank McCarthy (1912–1986) was a United States Army colonel and George Marshall's secretary of staff.

39. Lucian K. Truscott (1895–1965) was a United States Army general and commander of the Fifth Army.

40. The Monuments, Fine Arts, and Archives program was a section of the United States Army established to mitigate combat damage to historical structures and help protect works of art in war areas.

41. The Cheka was the first secret police organization of Soviet Russia, established in 1917. Although the organization had not operated under that name after 1922, the term was still generally used to refer to the Soviet secret police.

42. Karl Schilling (1889–1973) was a NSDAP member of the German parliament from 1941 to 1945.

43. Jakob Sprenger (1884–1945) was the governor of Hesse from 1935 to 1945. In March 1945 he fled to Austria and committed suicide.

44. "Pro Station" refers to a prophylactic station for the prevention of venereal diseases.

45. Martin Blumenson (1918–2005) was an officer in the United States Army Historical Section between 1944 and 1946 placed first with the Third Army and later with the Seventh. He would become the official biographer of General George S. Patton.

46. Sergent Edwin Carter was on temporary assignment with the Seventh Army Information and Historical Section in April 1945.

47. Technician Donald E. Maske was on temporary assignment with the Seventh Army Information and Historical Section in April 1945.

48. First Lt. Robert H. Weinstein, Editorial Team of the Seventh Army Information and Historical Section.

49. Carl Neinhaus (1888–1965) was first elected mayor of Heidelberg in 1929 and stayed in office until 1945. He joined the NSDAP in 1933. From 1952 to 1958 he was mayor of Heidelberg again.

50. Operation Dragoon was the code name for the Allied French Riviera landings in August 1944.

51. The battle in the Forest of Parroy near Lunéville in October 1944 lasted several weeks and was characterized by the difficult wooded terrain.

52. "Der Fuehrer's Face" was the song featured in the animated propaganda short of the same name (Disney, USA 1943).

53. In the military context the abbreviation T/O can stand for "table of organization" or "theatre of operation." Here it is clearly used figuratively.

54. Robert d'Hooghe (1903–1987) had owned a bookshop in Darmstadt since 1937. After the city was bombed on 11 Semptember 1944, he salvaged a small part of his book stock in a cellar in Darmstadt.

55. The Reichskulturkammer was the professional organization of German artists in Nazi Germany. Membership in the organization was compulsory for anyone who wanted to work in the arts.

56. *Gau Westmark* was an administrative division of Nazi Germany, comprising the present-day German state of Saarland and part of the occupied Lorraine in present-day France.

57. The National or Bavarian Redoubt was thought to be one of the last Nazi strongholds in the mountainous areas of southern Germany and Austria. It was later proven to have been mostly myth.

58. Second Lt. William Sutton, Seventh Army Information and Historical Section.

59. Paul Reynaud (1878–1966) had been prime minister of France in 1940, when he was arrested by the Vichy regime and transferred to Germany, where he remained in custody until the end of the war. Maxime Weygand (1867–1965) was a French Army general and successor of Maurice Gamelin as the supreme commander of French forces during the battle of France in 1940. He became defence minister in the Vichy government, but he was arrested—allegedly because of his anti-German views—in 1942 and imprisoned in Germany. Maurice-Gustav Gamelin (1872–1958) was a French general and commander-in-chief of the French Army from 1935 to 1940. After the fall of France, he was arrested and tried by the Vichy regime, then imprisoned by the Germans. Along with Paul Reynaud and Maxime Weygand, he was freed by US forces from the Itter Castle in Tyrol on 5 May 1945.

60. The Braunes Haus (Brown House) was the NSDAP headquarters in Munich. It was destroyed in an air raid in 1944.

61. Jefferson Caffery (1886–1974) was an American diplomat and the US ambassador to France from 1944 to 1949.

62. Georg Groscurth (1904–1944) was a German physician active in the resistance against the Nazi regime. He was arrested in September 1943 and executed in May 1944.

63. Rupprecht Gerngroß (1915–1996) and Ottheinrich Leiling (1910–1990) were leaders in the FAB, a resistance group which tried to overthrow Nazi rule in Munich in April 1945.

64. Alexander Schmorell (1917–1943) and the siblings Sophie (1921–1943) and Hans Scholl (1918–1943) were students of Munich University and members of the resistance group Weiße Rose. They were arrested and executed after the group was discovered in February 1943.

65. Franz Sperr (1878–1945) was the Bavarian delegate to Berlin. He was arrested in 1944 and executed in 1945 in connection with 20 July assassination attempt on Hitler because of his contacts to protagonists of the plot.

66. *Fasanenjagd* was FAB code for their attempt to overthrow the NS government of Bavaria. It took its name from *Goldfasane* (golden pheasants) the colloquial expression for high-ranking Nazi officials.

67. The Nationalkomitee Freies Deutschland, founded in 1943, aimed to undermine the German war effort. While it used conservative German symbolism to appeal to members of the Wehrmacht, it was operated from the Soviet Union.

68. The Vienna-based resistance group, O5, maintained contact to the American secret service and to the Soviets since 1944. However, the plan to overthrow of the NS military command of Vienna in April 1945 was discovered and thwarted.

69. Robert Murphy (1894–1978) acted as General Eisenhower's political adviser during the North African campaign. At the end of the war, he was SHAEF's political adviser on German affairs.

70. Bruno Riedenauer (born 1910) was the FAB member responsible for radio broadcasts. After the war it came to disagreements between him and Rupprecht Gerngross.

71. Hanns Jacobsen (1905–1985) was associated with the FAB, but he was not a member.

72. Franz Xaver Schneider (born 1901) was a member of the Munich resistance group O7. The group sought contact to FAB in April 1945.

73. Lothar Rohde (1906–1985) owned a radio technology company. He was arrested in 1944 on grounds of radio contacts with Great Britain. In April 1945 he escaped from Dachau concentration camp and joined the FAB.

74. Franz Ritter von Epp (1868–1947) was an active member of the NSDAP since 1928 and prefect of Bavaria from 1933 to 1945. He was arrested on orders of the NS leadership in Bavaria for his involvement with the FAB, although he had refused to participate.

75. *Panzerfaust* was a German anti-tank gun.

76. According to the archives at Dachau, this may refer to Jakob Lutz, a former SS-Sturmführer who was sentenced for cruelty against prisoners at Dachau in 1949.

77. Curt Riess (1902–1993) was a German author and journalist who left Germany in 1933 and settled in the United States. He returned to Europe during the war as a correspondent.

78. Klaus Mann (1906–1949), was a German author and the son of Thomas Mann. Leaving Germany in 1933, he lived in the United States from 1936 on. In 1945 he returned to report for *Stars & Stripes*.

79. Nikolaus Puhl (1883–1954) was the NSDAP's commanding officer at Wasserburg near Munich during the bloodless capitulation on 28 April 1945.

80. Rudolf Hübner (1897–1965) was a German Army general appointed commander of Munich on 28 April 1945.

81. Hans von Seißer (1874–1973) was police president of Bavaria during the Weimar Era. From May to August 1945, he was the police president of Munich.

82. Heinrich von Srbik (1878–1951) was an Austrian historian and from 1942 to 1945 the president of the Historical Commission of the Bavarian Academy of Sciences.

83. All these men participated in Hitler's 1923 coup in Munich. Emil Maurice (1897–1972) was an early member of the NSDAP and one of the first members of the SA. Robert Wagner (1895–1946) another early member of the NSDAP. In 1933 he became the *Gauleiter* of Baden, and, in 1940, Head of the Civil Government in Alsace. Hermann Kriebel (1876–1941) was a German officer and the military leader of the 1923 coup. Friedrich Weber (1892–1955) was a

German civil servant. He served in various positions in the NS government including, from 1941, as undersecretary of the Interior.

84. Vidkun Abraham Lauritz Jonssøn Quisling (1887–1945) was a Norwegian politician and key Nazi collaborator, who headed Norway under German occupation (1942–1945).

85. The Renner government was the first postwar Austrian government, established in April 1945. The government was headed by the Socialist Karl Renner. It was unilaterally recognized by the Soviet Union and Communists held one third of the cabinet positions.

86. All Austrian chancellors between 1920 and 1934 had been members of the conservative *Staatspartei* which refers to the Christian Social Party (Christlichsoziale Partei). It was closely associated with the Heimwehr, a nationalist paramilitary group.

87. First Lt. Hans Wallenberg, Psychological Warfare Branch (see note 23).

88. Fritz Schäffer (1888–1967) became the first postwar Bavarian prime minister in May 1945. He was removed from office in September 1945 due to his reluctant attitude towards denazification.

89. Paul Giesler (1895–1945) was *Gauleiter* of Munich-Upper Bavaria from 1942 to 1945.

90. "Motty" was endearing version of Lasky's birthname "Matthew."

91. Karl Gruber (1909–1995) was a leader of the resistance movement in Tyrol and subsequently in 1945 interim governor of Tyrol.

92. Meyer Schapiro (1904–1996) was a Lithuanian-born American art historian who taught at Columbia University. Lasky knew him from campus as well as from *Partisan Review* and from socializing in the circles of the New York Intellectuals.

93. Theodor Wilhelm Max Förster (1869–1954), a German scholar of English and professor at Munich University (1925–1934 and 1945–1948). His student and protegee Robert Spindler (1893–1954), a member of the NSDAP since 1933, turned against him and played a crucial part in Förster's removal. Spindler then took Förster's chair and headed the department until his own removal in 1945 (he returned to university teaching in 1950).

94. Kurt Huber (1893–1943) was professor of psychology and music at Munich University since 1926. He was arrested and executed in 1943 as a member of the resistance group Weiße Rose (see note 64).

95. Christoph Probst (1919–1943), a student at Munich University and a member of the resistance group Weiße Rose was arrested and executed in 1943. Lasky mistakenly refers to him as "Christine."

96. Benjamin Nelson (1911–1977), who had studied at the City College of New York and taught at Columbia University, had become a friend and mentor to Lasky.

97. Morton McDonald Roeck, MD (1893–1978), had bought the historic rococo house in 1927. Ludwig Ohlenroth (1892–1959) was a German archeologist who had been *Gauheimatpfleger* of Augsburg and in 1944 had initiated a commission to survey and record all the demage caused by air raids to historical buildings.

98. Mathias is the German version of Lasky's birthname Matthew.

99. Edward Y. Hartshorne (1912–1946) was an American sociologist and former secret service officer. As education officer in the American Military Government he oversaw the denazification and reopening of the German universities in the US occupation zone after the war.

100. Alfred Weber (1868–1958), the younger brother of the sociologist Max Weber, was professor of economics at Heidelberg university from 1907 until 1933. After the war, he was reinstated as professor and took an active part in the reconstruction of the university.

101. Karl Heinrich Bauer (1890–1978) was a professor of medicine, a surgeon, and the first rector of Heidelberg university after its reopening in 1945.

102. The IG Farben was a German chemical company. Their chemical plants produced Zyclon B, one of the components for the gas chambers. The company headquarter in Frankfurt became the US Army headquarters in March 1945. Today the building is used by Frankfurt University.

103. Elvin [sic] J. Lasky, 1937, "The Ghost of Göttingen," *The Nation* 145(3): 84.

104. Margatete Oncken (1876–1954) was the wife of the German historian Hermann Oncken (1869–1945).

105. The Hermann Goering Works were an iron and steel industrial conglomerate in Salzgitter in Lower Saxony. It was named for NSDAP leader Herman Göring who had been instrumental in the mergers that created them in 1937.

106. Technician Thomas B. McCabe was on temporary assignment with the Seventh Army Information and Historical Section from April 1945.

107. From 1933 to 1945 the Horst-Wessel-Haus was used by the SA and the Gestapo. Before, from 1926 to 1933, it had been the Karl-Liebknecht-Haus and the headquarters of the German Communist Party. After the war, renamed again Karl-Liebknecht-Haus, the building was used by the East German Communist Party.

108. Dwight Macdonald (1906–1982) was an American journalist and editor of *Partisan Review* (1937 to 1943) and of *Politics* (1944 to 1949). After a letter from Lasky was printed in *Partisan Review* in 1938, the two men continued to correspond for many years. Lasky considered Macdonald, who also introduced him to the social and intellectual circles around *Partisan Review*, a mentor.

109. Hotel Bristol was a hotel in Copenhagen. During the first Moscow Trial in 1936, one of the defendants testified that he met with Leon Trotsky in 1932 at the Hotel Bristol and received from him anti-Soviet instructions. It was soon discovered, however, that the hotel had burned down fifteen years earlier, in 1917.

110. Lasky regularly corresponded with Charles A. Pearce "Cap" (1907–1970) of Duell, Sloan, and Pearce publishing since 1942 (see note 36). In 1944 Pearce had written a very generous reference for Lasky recommending him as a candidate for officer training.

111. Immediately after the end of the war, the US Army established a detention and interrogation center at Oberursel, a small town near Frankfurt. A number of high-ranking German army officers and NSDAP officials were detained there.

112. Percy Ernst Schramm (1894–1970) was a German historian who served as an officer of the German army in the war and was imprisoned by the US Army from May 1945 to October 1946.

113. Otto Hitzfeld (1898–1990), Friedrich Wilhelm von Mellenthin (1904–1997), Siegfried von Waldenburg (1898–1973), and Otto Wagener (1888–1971) were German generals imprisoned by the US Army from 1945 to 1947.

114. Here military slang for diarrhea.

115. James Kerr Pollock (1898–1968) was an American political scientist. He was special political adviser to the United States military government in Germany from 1945 to 1949 and subsequently to the United States High Commissioner in Germany.

116. Bernard Bernstein (1908–1990) was an American public official and a United States Army officer. In 1945 he was financial adviser to the United States military government in Germany. A proponent of the Morgenthau plan, he advocated for and a harsh occupation policy towards Germany.

117. Lasky also includes the original German: *Hurengedicht*.

118. Brigitte Newiger (1926–2014) would become Lasky's first wife in 1950.

Appendix A
List of Primary Literature in the Diary

Throughout the diary Lasky refers to works of literature, politics, culture, and philosophy, often in fragmentary manner or in translation. This list (appendix A) attempts to give the full titles and the years of the first publication. Moreover, where applicable, it includes the year of the first publication of the relevant translations.

Appendix B adds to the collection by providing information on the names from history, literature, politics, and culture that appear in the diary but are not central to the immediate events related.

These collections provide an interesting overview of the cultural frame of reference Lasky operated with when writing his diary.

Adams, Henry. *The Education of Henry Adams* (1907).
Albrecht, Karl (1897–1969). *Der verratene Sozialismus* (1938); French trans. *Le Socialisme Trahi* (1943).
Augustine of Hippo. *City of God* (ca. 1470).
Boissonade, Prosper. *Du nouveau sur la Chanson de Roland* (1923).
Brecht, Bertolt. *Dreigroschenoper* (1928).
Bromfield, Louis. *The Rains Came* (1937); German trans. *Der grosse Regen* (1939).
Brooks, Van Wyck. *The Flowering of New England* (1936).
———. *America's Coming-of-Age* (1915).
Buck, Pearl. *A House Divided* (1935); German trans. *Das geteilte Haus* (1936).
———. *The Mother* (1933); German trans. *Die Mutter* (1934).
Cather, Willa. *My Antonia* (1918).
Cervantes Saavedra, Miguel de. *Don Quixote* (1605).
Cohen, Hermann. *Logik der reinen Erkenntnis* (1902).
Cronin, Archibald J. *The Stars Look Down* (1935); German trans. *Die Sterne blicken herab* (1935).
Czech-Jochberg, Erich. *Deutsche Geschichte. Nationalsozialistisch gesehen* (1933).

Dilthey, Wilhelm. *Von deutscher Dichtung und Musik* (1933), published posthumously.
Eliot, T. S. *The Waste Land* (1922).
Elster, Hanns Martin, ed. *Der deutsche Genius* (1926).
Fisher, H. A. L. *Paul Vinogradoff: A Memoir* (1927).
Fueter, Eduard. *Geschichte der neueren Historiographie* (1911), edited by Georg von Below and Friedrich Meinecke.
Gerth, Heinrich. "Max Weber's Politics—A Rejoinder," *Politics* (March 1945).
Gide, André. *Voyage au Congo* (1927); English trans. *Travels in the Congo* (1929).
Goethe, Johann Wolfgang von. *Aus meinem Leben. Dichtung und Wahrheit* (1833).
———. *Die Leiden des jungen Werther* (1774); English transl. *Sorrows of Young Werther* (1779).
Grimm, Jacob and Wilhelm. "Wilhelm Tell," *Deutsche Sagen* (1818).
Grote, Hans. *Das Schicksalsbuch des deutschen Volkes. Von Hermann dem Cherusker bis Adolf Hitler* (1933).
Halévy, Daniel. *Histoire d'une histoire esquissée pour le troisième Cinquantenaire de la Révolution française* (1939).
Hitler, Adolf. *Mein Kampf* (1925).
Hughes, Dorothy. *Fallen Sparrow* (1942).
Huizinga, Johan. *Herfsttij der middeleeuwen* (1919); German trans. *Herbst des Mittelalters* (1924).
Jaspers, Karl. *Philosophical Logic—Von der Wahrheit* (1947).
———. *Die Idee der Universität* (first published 1923; heavily revised versions in 1946 and 1961).
———. *Die geistige Situation der Zeit* (1922).
Lewis, Sinclair. *Babbitt* (1922).
Loserth, Johann. *Huss und Wiclif. Zur Genesis der hussitischen Lehre* (1925).
Macdonald, Dwight. "The Responsibility of Peoples," *Politics* (March 1945).
Macduff, J. R. *Sunsets on the Hebrew Mountains* (1862).
Maeterlinck, Maurice (1862–1949). "Sensations d'automobile," *Les Annales politiques et littéraires* (29 December 1901).
Mann, Thomas. *Unordnung und frühes Leid* (1925); English trans. *Disorder and Early Sorrow* (1926).
Marshall, Samuel Lyman Atwood. *Island Victory* (1944).
Martin, Alfred von, ed. *Coluccio Salutati's Traktat "Vom Tyrannen." Eine kulturgeschichtliche Untersuchung* (1913).
McGiffert, Arthur Cushman. *A History of Christian Thought* (1932 and 1933).

Melville, Herman. *Billy Budd* (1924), unfinished manuscript published posthumously
Milton, John. *Paradise Lost* (1667); German trans. *Das verlorene Paradies* (1682).
Mitchell, Margaret. *Gone with the Wind* (1936); German trans. *Vom Winde verweht* (1937).
Mommsen, Theodor. *Gaius Julius Caesar* (1940), reprint of *History of Rome Vol III* (1891).
Montesquieu. *Cahiers* (1716–1755).
Moore, Frank. *The Civil War in Song and Story* (1865).
Moore, George. *The Coming of Gabrielle* (1920).
Nietzsche, Friedrich. *Unzeitgemäße Betrachtungen*. 4 Volumes (1873–1876).
Novalis. *Die blaue Blume* [= *Heinrich von Ofterdingen*] (1800).
Oppenheimer, Franz. *Der Staat* (1908).
Pater, Walter Horatio. "Pascal," *Contemporary Review* (February 1895).
Pyle, Ernie. *Here Is Your War* (1943).
Rilke, Rainer Maria. *Brief an einen jungen Dichter* (1929); French trans. *Lettres à un jeune poète* (1937).
Rosenberg, Alfred. *Der Mythus des 20. Jahrhunderts* (1930).
Schapiro, Meyer. "A Note on Max Weber's Politics," *Politics* (February 1945).
Sombart, Werner. *Die deutsche Volkswirtschaft im 19. Jahrhundert* (1903).
———. *Sozialismus und soziale Bewegung im 19. Jahrhundert* (1896).
Stendhal. *Le Rouge et le Noir: Chronique du XIXe siècle*. Paris: A. Levasseur (1830).
Wells, John Edwin. *A Manual of the Writings in Middle English, 1050–1400* (1916).
White, Bouck. *Book of Daniel Drew* (1910).
Wister, Owen. *The Virginian* (1902).

Appendix B
List of Names in the Diary

Adams, Henry (1838–1918), US-American historian and author
Albrecht, Karl (1897–1969), German author
Aquinas, Thomas (1225–1274), Sicilian philosopher and Catholic theologian
Arndt, Ernst Moritz (1769–1860), German historian
Aue, Hartmann von (ca. 1160–1220), mediaeval German knight and author
Axelsson, George (1898–1966), Swedish-born US-American journalist
Bach, Johann Sebastian (1685–1750), German composer
Baedeker, Hans (1874–1959), German publisher, head of the family's travel guidebook company from 1925 to 1943
Balzac, Honoré (1799–1850), French author
Basset, René (1855–1924), French linguist
Beethoven, Ludwig van (1770–1827), German composer
Below, Georg von (1858–1927), German historian
Benét, Stephen Vincent (1898–1943), US-American poet
Berlioz, Louis-Hector (1803–1869), French composer
Béthouart, Antoine (1889–1982), French general
Bismarck, Otto von (1815–1898), Prussian politician, first chancellor of Germany from 1871 to 1890
Blum, André Léon (1872–1950), French socialist politician, three-time prime minister (1936/37, 1938, 1946/47)
Böhme, Jakob (1575–1624), German philosopher and theologian
Boissonade, Prosper (1862–1935), French historian
Bonaparte, Napoleon (1769–1821), French military leader and politician, emperor from 1804 to 1814
Botticelli, Sandro (1445–1510), Florentine-Italian painter
Brand, Max (1896–1980), Austrian-American composer
Brecht, Bertolt (1898–1956), German poet and playwright
Bromfield, Louis (1896–1956), US-American author
Brooks, Van Wyck (1886–1963), US-American literary critic and biographer
Brown, Ada Scott (1890–1950), US-American blues singer

Buck, Pearl (1892–1973), US-American author
Bukharin, Nikolai Ivanovich (1888–1938), Russian bolshevist, political theorist, and author
Burckhardt, Jacob Christoph (1818–1897), Swiss historian of art
Byron, George Gordon Lord (1788–1824), English poet
Calderón de la Barca, Pedro (1600–1681), Spanish poet
Caruso, Enrico (1873–1921), Italian opera singer (tenor)
Cather, Willa (1873–1947), US-American author
Cervantes Saavedra, Miguel de (1547–1616), Spanish author
Chamberlain, Arthur Neville (1889–1940), English politician, prime minister from 1937 to 1940
Chamson, André (1900–1983), French author, active in the resistance movement
Chaumet, André (1914–1983), French politician and journalist, leader of the fascist *Parti populaire socialiste*
Cherkasov, Nikolay (1903–1966), Soviet actor
Chopin, Frédéric François (1810–1849), Polish composer
Churchill, Winston (1874–1965), British prime minister from 1940 to 1945 and from 1951 to 1955
Clark, Mark Wayne (1896–1984), US-American general
Claudel, Paul (1868–1955), French Catholic poet and diplomat
Clausewitz, Carl von (1780–1831), Prussian-German general and military theorist
Clay, Lucius D. (1898–1978), US-American general, military governor of US-American Zone in Germany from 1947 to 1949
Cohen, Hermann (1842–1918), German philosopher
Cram, Ralph Adams (1863–1942), US-American architect of Gothic revival buildings
Cromwell, Oliver (1599–1658), English general and head of state during republican interlude
Cronin, Archibald Joseph (1896–1981), Scottish author
Curtius, Ernst Robert (1886–1956), German literary scholar
Czech-Jochberg, Erich (1890–1966), Austrian journalist
Da Vinci, Leonardo (1452–1519), Italian painter, architect, and scientist
Daladier, Édouard (1884–1970), French socialist, prime minister of France from 1938 to 1940
Dante Alighieri (1265–1321), Italian-Florentine poet
Darlan, Jean Louis Xavier François (1881–1942), French admiral, prime minister of Vichy government
Déat, Marcel (1894–1955), French politician, founder of the *Rassemblement national populaire* and a member of the Vichy government

de Coulanges, Numa Denis Fustel (1830–1889), French historian
Degas, Edgar (1834–1917), French painter
de Gaulle, Charles (1890–1970), French general, head of Provisional Government of the French Republic from 1944 to 1946 and president of France from 1959 to 1969
de Lagarde, Paul (1827–1891), German orientalist
Devers, Jacob Loucks (1887–1979), US-American general
Dewey, John (1859–1952), US-American philosopher
Dilthey, Wilhelm (1833–1911), German philosopher
Dreiser, Theodore (1871–1945), US-American author and journalist
Duhem, Pierre Maurice Marie (1861–1916), French physicist and historian of science
Dürer, Albrecht (1471–1528), German painter
Ebert, Friedrich (1871–1925), German Politian (Social Democrat), president of Germany from 1919 to 1925.
Ehrenburg, Ilya (1891–1967), Soviet author and journalist
Eisenhower, Dwight David (1890–1969), US-American general and politician, president from 1953 to 1961
Eisenstein, Sergei (1898–1948), Soviet filmmaker and director
Eliot, T[homas] S[tearns] (1888–1965), US-American author and playwright
Elster, Hanns Martin (1888–1983), German author and editor
Éluard, Paul (1895–1952), French surrealist poet, active in the resistance movement
Erasmus, Desiderius (1466–1536), Dutch philosopher
Eschenbach, Wolfram von (ca. 1160–1220), mediaeval German knight
Ferber, Edna (1885–1968), US-American author
Fichte, Johann Gottlieb (1762–1814), German philosopher
Fisher, Herbert Albert Laurens (1865–1940), English historian
Foch, Ferdinand (1851–1929), French general
Frederick the Great [Frederick II] (1712–1786), King of Prussia from 1740 to 1786
Freytag, Gustav (1816–1895), German author
Frick, Wilhelm (1877–1946), German politician, NSDAP minister of the interior from 1933 to 1943
Fueter, Eduard (1876–1928), German historian and author
Galli-Curci, Amelita (1882–1963), Italian opera singer (soprano)
Gibbon, Edward (1737–1794), English historian
Gibbs, Philip (1877–1962), English journalist
Gide, André Paul Guillaume (1869–1951), French author

Glotz, Gustave (1862–1935), French historian
Goebbels, Joseph (1897–1945), German politician, minister of propaganda for the NSDAP
Goethe, Johann Wolfgang von (1749–1832), German poet and playwright
Göring, Hermann (1893–1946), German politician, leading member of NSDAP
Gottfried von Straßburg (died ca. 1210), German-language poet
Gouraud, Henri Joseph Eugène (1867–1946), French general
Gracchus, Gaius Sempronius (ca. 153–121 BCE), Roman politician and reformer
Gracchus, Tiberius Sempronius (ca. 163–133 BCE), Roman politician and reformer
Grady, Henry Woodfin (1850–1889), US-American journalist
Grey, Zane (1872–1939), US-American author
Grillparzer, Franz (1791–1872), Austrian author and playwright
Grimm, Jacob (1785–1863), and Wilhelm (1786–1859), German authors and collectors of folktales
Grote, Hans (1896–1946), German military officer and author
Guérin, Charles (1873–1907), French poet
Guizot, François Pierre Guillaume (1787–1874), French historian and politician
Gustavus Adolphus (1594–1632), King of Sweden from 1611 to 1632
Halévy, Daniel (1872–1962), French historian
Handel, Georg Friedrich (1685–1759), German-British composer
Haydn, Joseph (1732–1809), Austrian composer
Heesters, Johannes (1903–2011), Dutch-born German actor and singer
Hegel, Friedrich (1770–1831), German philosopher
Heidegger, Martin (1889–1976), German philosopher
Herodotus (ca. 484–425 BCE), Greek historian
Hess, Rudolf Walter Richard (1894–1987), German politician, leading member of NSDAP
Himmler, Heinrich (1900–1945), German politician, leading member of the NSDAP, head of the SS
Hofmannsthal, Hugo von (1874–1929), Austrian author
Hölderlin, Johann Christian Friedrich (1770–1843), German poet
Horthy de Nagybánya, Miklós [Nicolas] (1868–1957), Hungarian general, regent from 1920 to 1944
Hughes, Dorothy (1904–1993), US-American author
Hugo, Victor (1802–1885), French author and playwright
Huizinga, Johan (1872–1945), Dutch historian

Hutten, Ulrich von (1488–1523), mediaevel German knight and author
Jackson, Andrew (1767–1845), US-American politician, president from 1829 to 1837
James, Henry (1843–1916), British-American author
Jaspers, Karl (1883–1969), German philosopher and psychiatrist
Jeritza, Maria (1887–1982), Moravian opera singer (soprano)
Johnson, Harold Ogden (1891–1962), US-American comedian
Kafka, Franz (1883–1924), Czech author
Kamenev, Lev Borisovich (1883–1936), Russian bolshevik revolutionary, Soviet politician
Kant, Immanuel (1724–1804), German philosopher
Karl der Grosse [Charlemagne] (748–814), King of the Franks from 800 to 814
Kesselring, Albert (1885–1960), German general
King, Henry Churchill (1858–1934), US-American congregationalist theologian
Klopstock, Friedrich Gottlieb (1724–1803), German poet
Koestler, Arthur (1905–1983), Hungarian author
Komorowski, Tadeusz "Bór" (1895–1966), Polish general, prime minister of Polish government in exile from 1947 to 1949
Krehl, Ludolf (1861–1937), German physician
Lasalle, Antoine Charles Louis, Comte de (1775–1809), French general
Laski, Harold (1893–1950), British politician and political scientist
Lassalle, Ferdinand (1825–1864), German socialist and philosopher
Lawrence, David Herbert (1885–1930), English author
Leander, Zarah (1907–1981), Swedish actress and singer
Lenin, Vladimir Ilyich (1870–1924), Russian/Soviet politician and philosopher
Lessing, Gotthold Ephraim (1792–1781), German author and philosopher
Lewis, Harry Sinclair (1885–1951), US-American author and playwright
Liebig, Justus (1803–1873), German chemist
Liebknecht, Karl (1871–1919), German politician
Lot, Ferdinand Victor Henri (1866–1952), French historian
Ludendorff, Erich (1865–1937), German general and military politician
Luther, Martin (1483–1546), German Reformation theologian
Luxemburg, Rosa (1871–1919), Polish-German politician and antiwar activist
Macduff, John Ross (1818–1895), Scottish author and theologian
Machiavelli, Niccolò di Bernardo dei (1469–1527), Italian-Florentine political philosopher
MacLeish, Archibald (1892–1982), US-American poet

Maeterlinck, Maurice (1862–1949), Belgian poet and essayist
Mann, Golo (1909–1994), German historian and author
Mann, Thomas (1875–1955), German author
Marshall, Margaret Alice (1900–1974), US-American journalist
Marshall, Samuel Lyman Atwood (1900–1977), US-American military journalist and historian
Martin, Alfred von (1882–1979), German historian and sociologist
Marty, André (1886–1956), French communist politician and journalist
Maugham, William Somerset (1874–1965), English author and playwright
Mauriac, François (1885–1970), French author
Maurois, André (1885–1967), French author of historical fiction
McGiffert, Arthur Cushman (1861–1933), US-American theologian
Meinecke, Friedrich (1862–1954), German historian
Meister Eckhart [Eckhart von Hohenheim] (1260–1328), German theologian
Melanchthon, Philip (1497–1560), German Reformation theologian
Melville, Herman (1891–1891), US-American author
Meyer, Eduard (1855–1930), German historian
Michelangelo di Lodovico Buonarroti Simoni (1475–1465), Italian-Florentine sculptor
Michelet, Jules (1798–1874), French historian
Milton, John (1608–1674), English poet
Mitchell, Margaret (1900–1949), US-American author
Molière [Jean-Baptiste Poquelin] (1622–1673), French playwright and actor
Molotov, Vyacheslav (1890–1986), Soviet Russian politician, foreign minister from 1939 to 1949 and from 1953 to 1956
Mommsen, Theodor (1817–1903), German historian
Montesquieu (1689–1755), French philosopher
Moore, Frank (1828–1904), US-American journalist
Moore, George (1852–1933), Irish author
Morgenthau, Henry (1891–1967), US-American politician, treasurer from 1934 to 1945
Mörike, Eduard (1804–1875), German poet
Mozart, Wolfgang Amadeus (1756–1791), Austrian composer
Müntzer, Thomas (1489–1525), German theologian
Niebuhr, Reinhold (1892–1971), US-American Reformed theologian and author
Nietzsche, Friedrich (1844–1900), German philosopher
Novalis [Friedrich von Hardenberg] (1772–1801), German author and philosopher
O'Daniel, John Wilson (1894–1975), US-American general

Olsen, John Sigvard (1892–1963), US-American comedian
Oppenheimer, Franz (1864–1943), German sociologist
Papen, Franz von (1879–1969), German diplomat and politician, vice-chancellor from 1933 to 1934
Parsons, Talcott (1902–1979), US-American sociologist
Patch, Alexander McCarrell (1889–1945), US-American general
Pater, Walter Horatio (1839–1894), English essayist and art critic
Patton, George Smith (1885–1945), US-American general
Paul, Jean (1763–1825), German author
Pearce, Charles A. (1907–1970), US-American editor and publisher
Pershing, John Joseph (1860–1948), US-American general
Petchorine, Dimitri (1908–1957), Russian-born French lawyer and author
Pieck, Wilhelm (1876–1960), German politician, later president of the GDR from 1946 to 1950
Prokofiev, Serei (1891–1953), Soviet composer
Puccini, Giacomo (1858–1924), Italian composer
Pudovkin, Vsevolod (1893–1953), Soviet filmmaker and director
Pushkin, Alexander Sergejewitsch (1799–1837), Russian poet
Pyle, Ernie (1900–1945), US-American war correspondent
Ranke, Leopold von (1795–1886), German historian
Ratzel, Friedrich (1844–1904), German geographer and ethnographer
Renoir, Pierre-Auguste (1841–1919), French painter
Reynaud, Paul (1878–1966), French politician, prime minister from March to June in 1940
Rilke, Rainer Maria (1875–1926), German poet
Rintelen, Fritz-Joachim Paul von (1898–1979), German philosopher
Rökk, Marika (1913–2004), Austrian actress and singer
Rommel, Erwin (1891–1944), German general
Roosevelt, Franklin Delano (1882–1945), US-American politician, president from 1933 to 1945
Rosenberg, Alfred (1893–1946), German author and propagandist of NS-ideology
Rubens, Peter Paul (1577–1640), Flemish painter
Rundstedt, Gerd von (1875–1953), German general
Russell, Bertrand (1872–1970), English philosopher
Sagnac, Philippe (1868–1954), French historian
Saint-Saëns, Camille (1835–1921), French composer and pianist
Santayana, George (1863–1952), Spanish-born US-American philosopher
Schiller, Friedrich (1759–1805), German poet and playwright
Schleiermacher, Friedrich (1768–1834), German theologian and philosopher
Schopenhauer, Arthur (1788–1860), German philosopher

Schubert, Franz (1797–1828), Austrian composer
Shakespeare, William (1564–1616), English playwright
Shelley, Percy Bysshe (1792–1822), English poet
Shils, Edward (1910–1995), US-American sociologist
Sickingen, Franz von (1481–1523), German knight
Simmel, Georg (1858–1918), German sociologist
Slezak, Walter (1902–1983), Austrian actor and singer
Sloan, Samuel (1904–1945), US-American editor and publisher
Sombart, Werner (1863–1941), German sociologist
Spengler, Oswald (1880–1936), German philosopher
Stendhal [Marie-Henri Beyle] (1783–1842), French author
Storm, Theodor (1817–1888), German author
Strauss, Richard (1864–1949), German composer
Sybel, Heinrich von (1817–1895), German historian
Tacitus, Publius Cornelius (ca. 55–115 CE), Roman historian and rhetorician
Thälmann, Ernst (1886–1944), German politician, leader of the Communist Party from 1925 to 1933
Thierry, Jacques Nicolas Augustin (1795–1856), French historian
Thucydides (ca. 460–400 BCE), Athenian historian
Thurber, James (1894–1961), US-American author and cartoonist
Tieck, Ludwig (1773–1853), German author and editor
Tisse, Eduard (1897–1961), Soviet cinematographer
Treitschke, Heinrich von (1834–1896), German historian and political theorist
Trilling, Lionel (1905–1975), US-American literary critic and author
Trotsky, Leon (1879–1940), Ukrainian-Russian Marxist, political theorist, and politician
Truman, Harry (1884–1972), US-American politician, president from 1945 to 1953
Tserclaes, Johann, Count of Tilly (1559–1632), Catholic commander in the Thirty-Year War
Usener, Karl Hermann (1905–1970), German art historian
Vossler, Karl (1872–1949), German Romanist
Wagner, Richard (1813–1883), German composer
Waldo, Peter (ca. 1140–1218), French preacher and founder of the Waldesians
Waller, Fats (1904–1943), US-American jazz pianist and composer
Weber, Adolf (1876–1963), German economist
Weber, Alfred (1868–1958), German sociologist and economist
Weber, Marianne (1870–1954), German historian
Weber, Max (1864–1920), German sociologist

Wells, Herbert George (1866–1946), British science fiction author
Wells, John Edwin (1875–1943), US-American English scholar
Wessel, Horst (1907–1930), SA paratrooper, turned into martyr by NSDAP propaganda
White, Bouck (1874–1951), US-American author and clergyman
Whitehead, Alfred North (1861–1947), English mathematician and philosopher
Willis, Nathaniel Parker (1806–1867), US-American poet
Wister, Owen (1860–1938), US-American author and historian
Wolfe, Thomas (1900–1938), US-American author
Zetkin, Clara (1857–1933), German socialist and women's rights activist, Communist politician
Zhukov, Georgy (1896–1974), Soviet general

Appendix C
Names and Ranks of Lasky's Fellow Soldiers

Full names and ranks of Lasky's fellow soldiers in the 7th Army 6th Information and Historical Section. Listing taken from ETOUSA Historical Division Records 1941–46. NARA Record Group 498 File No. 161.

April 1945

Lt. Col. William Goddard
Major Joseph D. Duncan
Major Charles S. Davis
Capt. Warran E. Waters
Capt. James D. T. Hamilton
Capt. Keith X. Eggers
1st Lt. John D. Walp
1st Lt. Edgar S. Mooney
1st Lt. Arthur Gottlieb
1st Lt. Lenthiel H. Daws
1st Lt. Edward. E. Jordan
1st Lt. Robert H. Weinstein
2nd Lt. William H. Ferguson
2nd Lt. Melvin J. Lasky
2nd Lt. William A. Sutton

Of the personnel attached on temporary duty he also mentions:

2nd Lt. Martin Blumenson
S/Sgt. Howard S. Dyer
T/4 Thomas B. Mc Cabe
T/5 Donald S. Maske

Index

Aachen, 104, 180
abortion, 259, 295
Adams, Henry, 213, 216, 239, 303, 305
Adlerwerke (factory), 222
Afghanistan, 26
AFN, 250
Africa, African, 55, 73, 92, 95, 297n12, 297n15, 300n69
African Americans, 21, 55, 58n7, 138, 187, 286, 288
Agfa, 22, 177
Air Force (US), 77, 177
Alabama (US state), 138
Albrecht, Karl, 95, 303, 306
Alexander, Harold, 94, 183, 297n16
Algeria, Algerian, 55, 94, 297n12
Allach, 181
Allgäu, 276
Alps, Alpine, 181, 188, 203, 213, 223
Alsace-Lorraine, Alsatian, 14, 22, 50, 73, 76–78, 82, 84–85, 87–88, 93, 95, 108–09, 102, 110, 113–14, 121, 124, 129, 191, 299, 300n83
American Military Government (AMG). *See* occupation: government
American Sociological Review, 11
Amerikanische Rundschau, 269
Ammersee (lake), 228
Ann Arbor, 11–12, 24, 59, 279
Ansbach, 281
anti-American, 255
anti-Communist, anti-communism, 1, 16, 59–60
anti-fascism, 174, 177, 209, 219, 225; anti-Nazi, 63, 95, 132, 152, 191, 194, 199, 223, 231–232, 235
anti-Semitic, anti-Semitism, 30, 71, 138, 172, 211, 223, 230, 236, 238, 242–43, 283

anti-Soviet, 95, 203, 302n109
anti-Stalinist, 11, 95
Aquinas, Thomas, 83, 169, 306
Arendt, Hannah, 14, 18, 56, 60, 238, 270
arms, 72, 75, 81, 86, 92–94, 98, 101, 109, 112–113, 118, 129, 134–135, 137–38, 140–41, 144–145, 149–51, 178, 189, 194–95, 207, 215, 229, 231, 234, 242, 245, 246, 252, 256, 268, 272, 277, 283, 288, 289, 292, 300
Army: British, 148, 229, 245–46, 255, 264, 269, 281, 289, 294, 297n13, 297n16; French, 55, 72, 86–87, 92–94, 109, 144, 177, 206–7, 209, 228–31, 234, 276, 280–81, 294, 297nn11–12, 297nn14–15, 299n59; German, 51, 77, 82, 100–02, 116, 120, 125, 129, 133, 142, 148, 152, 178–79, 182, 184, 186, 189, 190, 198–99, 215, 236, 274, 279, 288; Soviet (Red), 94, 229, 268–70, 272, 292–94, 300n68
Arndt, Ernst Moritz, 172, 306
art, 5, 20n18, 59, 69, 90, 92, 124, 141, 144, 154, 163, 166, 171, 180, 202, 216, 222, 235, 253, 267, 298n40, 299n55, 301n92
aryan, 85, 163
Asia, Asian, 31, 240
Atlantic, 55, 61, 73
atomic (bomb), 35, 240, 293
Aue, Hartmann von, 173
Augsburg, 16, 22, 24, 177–81, 200, 213, 215–17, 222, 230, 232–33, 237, 249, 257–60, 277, 285, 301n97
Augustine of Hippo, 113, 238, 303
Austria, Austrian, 57n3, 130, 177–78, 187–88, 195, 200, 202–3, 206–9, 228–30, 298n43, 299n57, 300n82, 301nn85–86; Austro-fascism, 207–10

autobahn, 134, 141, 157, 178, 183, 222–23, 244, 246, 256, 280, 285, 293. *See also* transport
Axelsson, George, 266, 306

Bach, Johann Sebastian, 173, 216, 306
Bad Kissingen, 151
Baden, 280–81, 300n83
Baedeker, Hans, 202, 306; travel guide book, 16, 22, 202, 204
Balzac, Honoré, 81, 89, 306
bank, banks, banking, 101, 162, 175, 235, 254, 292
Barth, Karl, 232
Basel, 232, 270
Basset, René, 71, 306
Bauer, Karl Heinrich, 36, 241–42, 301n101
Bavaria, Bavarian, 129, 144, 175, 177, 187, 189–190, 192–197, 199–200, 213, 221–224, 230, 233, 260, 276, 281, 285, 299n57, 300nn65–66, 300n74, 300n81, 301nn88–89
BBC, 174
Beachhead News, 167, 210
Beethoven, Ludwig van, 122, 128, 172–73, 262, 306
Belgium, Belgian, 21, 163, 171, 187, 223, 265
Bell, Daniel, 2, 11–12, 59–60
Below, Georg von, 232, 304, 306
Benedictine, 214, 226
Benét, Stephen Vincent, 269, 306
Berchtesgaden, 176, 179
Berlin, 1–2, 4, 10, 14–18, 25, 29, 53, 60, 64, 95, 148, 171, 179, 185, 191, 201–3, 218, 235, 243, 246–54, 256, 265, 268–72, 275, 279–82, 290, 292–93, 300n65
Berlioz, Louis-Hector, 245, 306
Bern, Berne, 15, 261
Bernau, 183
Bernstein, Bernard, 281, 302n116
Béthouart, Antoine, 94, 230, 297n14, 306
bible, 100
bicycle, 132, 146–48, 188, 213, 253
Bismarck, Otto von, 126, 131, 172, 254, 306
black market, 201, 211, 247–48, 250, 253, 256, 265, 268–69, 272, 292, 295

Blitz, 183
Blum, André Léon, 229, 306
Blumenson, Martin, 159, 298n45
Bodensee, 275
Böhme, Jakob, 172, 306
Boissonade, Prosper, 115, 303, 306
Bolshevism, Bolshevik, 81, 95
Bolzano, Bozen, 228
bomb, bombs, bombing, bombed out, 18, 22, 35, 78, 80, 111, 118, 134, 142, 146, 153, 161–63, 173, 176, 180, 186, 188, 192, 196, 211, 222, 240, 244, 251, 255–56, 263–64, 274, 288, 293, 296, 299n54; bomb shelter, 83
Bonaparte, Napoleon, 61, 72, 106, 178–79, 250, 306
Bonn, 114, 232, 297n24
books, 9–10, 18, 22–23, 36, 45, 60, 64, 68, 70, 83, 103, 113, 144, 156, 160, 172–73, 178, 202, 207, 232, 235–36, 238–40, 248, 284
bookshop, 15, 23, 73, 88, 96, 115, 160, 171, 220, 235, 256, 262, 269, 299n54
border, border crossing, 125, 141, 177, 233, 246, 273
Borneo, 162
Botticelli, Sandro, 220, 306
bourgeois, petit bourgeois, *Kleinbürger*, 35, 152, 220, 232, 252. *See also* middle class
Bourke-White, Margaret, 22
Brand, Max, 160, 306
Brandenburg Gate, 248–49, 272, 293
Braunschweig, Brunswick, 63, 243, 245–46, 255–56, 289, 294
Brecht, Bertolt, 282, 303, 306
Bremen, 148, 262–65, 281; Bremerhaven, 264
Brenner (mountain pass), 203, 206
Brickner, Richard M., 31
Britain, British. *See* Great Britain
Broadway, 162
Bromfield, Louis, 160, 303, 306
Brooklyn, 21, 24, 187, 230
Brooks, Van Wyck, 22, 240, 303, 306
brothels, 15, 84–85, 137, 204, 282, 287. *See also* prostitution
Brown, Ada Scott, 88, 306
Bruchsal, 261

Buchenwald (camp), 24, 184, 195, 202, 211, 218
Buck, Pearl, 160, 303, 307
Budapest, 247, 275
Bukharin, Nikolai Ivanovich, 95, 307
Bund Deutscher Mädel (BDM), 223. *See also* Hitler Youth
Burckhardt, Jacob Christoph, 239, 307
bureaucracy, 23, 27, 105–6, 109, 111, 155, 216, 221
Byron, George Gordon Lord, 156, 173, 234, 307

Caffery, Jefferson, 181, 299n61
Calderón de la Barca, Pedro, 83, 307
camera, 3, 13, 15, 22, 87, 137, 177, 224, 254, 293
Canada, Canadian, 193
capitalism, capitalist, 36, 219, 221, 225
car. *See* transport: car, jeep
Caribbean, 31
Carrefour (magazine), 109
Carter, Edwin, 161–63, 167, 169–70, 298n46
cartoon, caricature, comic strips, 72, 209, 211, 213–14, 234, 252, 313
Caruso, Enrico, 188, 307
cathedral, 15, 53, 73, 75, 77–78, 160, 178, 180–81, 214, 216, 233, 246, 260, 264, 268, 272
Cather, Willa, 156, 303, 307
Catholicism, Catholic, 139, 159, 180, 190, 194, 200, 216, 229–31
censorship, 15, 107, 160, 268
Central America, 31
Cervantes Saavedra, Miguel de, 104, 303, 307
Chamberlain, Arthur Neville, 207, 307
Chamson, André, 109, 307
Chaumet, André, 95, 307
Cheka, 147, 298n41
Cherbourg, 168
Cherkasov (Cherkassov), Nikolai, 253, 307
chewing gum, 71, 167, 205, 244
Chiemsee (lake), 223–24
children, childhood, 4, 9–10, 21, 54, 57n3, 59, 71, 80, 82, 84–87, 96, 107, 113–14, 124–27, 131, 136, 141–42, 157, 166, 174–75, 181, 183–84, 186–88, 198, 205–6, 211, 216–18, 222–24, 244–45, 251, 258–59, 265, 269, 283–84, 286, 289–90, 292
China, Chinese, 71, 131, 148, 224, 234
chocolate, 21, 52, 71, 85, 114, 122, 126, 157, 205, 248, 252, 283–84, 292
Chopin, Frédéric François, 245, 307
Christianity, Christendom, Christian, 67, 83, 187, 216, 268, 301n86, 304
Christmas, 43, 95, 98, 108
church, 85, 100, 109, 113, 118, 124, 139–41, 163, 180, 183, 190, 202, 205, 211, 216, 224, 229–30, 233, 245
Churchill, Winston, 71, 104, 183, 307
CIC, 189–91, 195, 203, 208, 281
Cicero, 80
cigarettes, 52, 83, 87, 122, 129, 175, 178, 196, 214, 218, 237, 248, 252, 268–69, 280, 287, 292
cinema. *See* film
Civil Affairs Division, 29, 127, 131, 140, 175, 203
Clark, Mark Wayne, 41, 106, 179, 307
class, 26, 71, 152, 225, 251–52, 256, 262, 267, 287, 294
Claudel, Paul, 109, 307
Clausewitz, Carl von, 106, 307
Clay, Lucius D., 279, 307
Clermont-Ferrand, 83, 86, 109, 297n10
coal, 125, 271, 292
Coca Cola, soda, 178, 214, 222
Cohen, Hermann, 67, 303, 307
collaboration, 51, 81–82, 85, 110, 112, 119–20, 130, 207, 218, 252, 280, 298n29, 301n84
collective guilt (*Kollektivschuld*), 3, 21, 33, 142, 176, 204, 211–13, 218, 238, 242, 296
Colmar, 43–44, 81, 96–98, 101, 113, 297n7
Cologne, Köln, 22, 63, 103, 114, 129, 132, 175, 180
Commager, Henry Steele, 38
Common Sense (magazine), 1
communication, 47n3, 71, 77, 127, 140, 162, 170, 175, 179, 214, 221
Communist Party, Communism, 34–35, 71, 173, 185, 187, 191, 193–95, 202–03,

209–10, 229, 232, 268, 282–84, 301n85, 302n107
Como (lake), 22, 177
concentration camp (KZ, Konzentrationslager), 16, 24, 30–31, 45, 87, 92, 95, 102, 163, 179, 181, 183, 186, 192, 207, 209, 221, 236, 283, 292, 300n73
Congress for Cultural Freedom (CCF), 1, 16
conqueror, 3, 30, 50, 126, 131, 158, 183, 215, 219, 237, 241, 251, 280. *See also* occupation
Conscience, 74–75, 115, 156, 168, 216, 219
conscription, conscript, 25, 39, 73, 110–11, 117, 131–32, 137, 171, 186, 190, 220, 234, 284
conservative, conservatism, 191, 221, 229, 300n67, 301n86
Control Post (CP), 72, 81, 118, 145, 261
Copenhagen, 15, 21, 187, 266–67, 271–72, 302n109
correspondents. *See* journalism
corruption, 27, 35, 73, 112, 147, 170, 197, 200, 211, 218, 246, 251, 263, 277, 282, 287
counter-intelligence, 132, 148, 193
countryside, 76, 78, 82, 86, 88, 105, 112–13, 125, 141, 157, 176, 183, 188, 213, 217, 220, 223, 244–45, 261, 268. *See also* landscape
Crailsheim, 283
Cram, Ralph Adams, 216, 307
Cromwell, Oliver, 67, 307
Cronin, Archibald Joseph, 159–60, 303, 307
currency: Reichsmark, 140, 175, 215, 247–48, 250, 256, 269, 275, 292; US Dollar, 139, 247–48, 269, 292
Curtius, Ernst Robert, 232, 235, 307
Czech-Jochberg, Erich, 173, 303, 307
Czechoslovakia, Czech, 128, 177, 183, 295, 297n23

D-Day, 39
d'Hooghe, Robert, 171, 299n54
Da Vinci, Leonardo, 97, 307

Dachau, 22, 177, 179, 181, 195–98, 202, 204, 207–8, 211, 218, 221, 300n73, 300n76
Daily Worker, 272
Daladier, Édouard, 179, 207, 307
Damron, Harry, 210
Dante Alighieri, 83, 307
Danube, Donau (river), 178, 233
Darlan, Jean Louis Xavier François, 92, 307
Darmstadt, 15–16, 23, 45, 54, 141–46, 149, 151, 153, 155–57, 161, 164, 166, 170–76, 211, 243, 249, 299n54
Das Reich, 133
Daumann, Rudolf Heinrich, 95, 297n18
Davis, Charles S., 51, 58n7, 92, 105, 138, 167, 179
DDT, 181, 185
Déat, Marcel, 95, 307
de Coulanges, Numa Denis Fustel, 78, 308
Degas, Edgar, 115, 308
de Gaulle, Charles, 71, 93–94, 297n15, 308
Deggendorf, 53, 181
de Lagarde, Paul, 172, 308
Demilitarization, 30, 32, 36
democracy, democratic, 11, 35–36, 71, 148, 165, 209, 221, 240, 252, 288
democratization, 31–33
denazification, 2, 30–34, 36, 37n1, 223–24, 231, 237, 290, 301n88, 301n99
Department of War (US), 13, 40, 44, 73, 155
deportation, 54, 87, 96
Der Monat, 16
desertion, 101–2, 182, 190, 194, 199, 228, 270
destruction, 3, 23, 35, 53, 74, 76, 97, 108, 112, 124, 145, 152, 158, 180, 189, 211, 218–19, 233, 240–42, 246, 248–49, 252, 256, 264, 274, 280–81, 293, 296
Deutsche Volkszeitung, 268
Devers, Jacob Loucks, 92, 139, 180, 297n11, 308
Dewey, John, 10, 239, 308
dictatorship, 153, 187, 192, 203, 210
Dieppe, 183
Dilthey, Wilhelm, 172, 304, 308
diplomacy, diplomat, 3, 26, 36, 261, 299n61

Disney, Walt, 299n52
displaced person (DP), 22, 30, 62–63, 132, 137, 141, 162, 170, 174–75, 183, 190, 204, 218, 245, 287, 289
Dittmar, Kurt, 116, 298n32
Dixie, 26, 192
Doriot, Jacques, 109, 298n29
Dos Passos, John, 24
Dr. Friedrich. *See* Daumann, Rudolf Heinrich
Dreiser, Theodore, 259, 308
Duhem, Pierre Maurice Marie, 115, 308
DUKW ("duck"), 118, 134–135
Dürer, Albrecht, 220, 308
Dutch. *See* Netherlands
Dyer, Howard S., 73, 80, 161, 167, 169–70, 181, 297n3

Eastern Front, 228, 251, 265
Ebert, Friedrich, 265, 308
Eggers, Keith, 80, 167, 257, 260, 297n6
Ehrenburg, Ilya, 202, 308
Eighty-Second Airborne (US), 52, 247, 252. *See also* Air Force (US)
Eisenhower, Dwight David, 30, 41, 47n8, 101, 106, 126, 161, 171, 177, 190, 225, 237, 297n13, 300n69, 308
Eisenstein, Sergei, 248, 253–54, 308
elections, 284, 299n49
Eliot, T(homas) S(tearns), 22, 26, 36, 91, 136, 174, 216, 304, 308
Elster, Hanns Martin, 172, 304, 308
Éluard, Paul, 109, 308
England, English. *See* Great Britain
Epp, Franz Ritter, 195, 300n74
Erasmus, Desiderius, 83, 308
Eschenbach, Wolfram von, 173
espionage, 127–28, 148
ETOUSA, 74, 297n11, 297n20
eugenics, 242
Europe, European, 1–3, 9–10, 12–17, 21–22, 24, 26–27, 34–36, 38–40, 44, 49–50, 52–54, 56, 57n4, 60–62, 73, 95, 109, 114, 137–39, 141, 152, 154, 156, 158, 171, 173, 179, 192, 208–9, 211, 213, 216, 224, 226, 228, 240–41, 243–44, 259, 264, 266, 271, 273, 275, 277–79, 281, 286, 292, 296, 297n4, 298n25, 300n77

FAB (Freiheitsaktion Bayern). *See* resistance against NS rule: in Germany and Austria
fanatism, fanatic, 32, 63, 82, 109, 119, 130, 132, 138, 147, 149, 151–52, 157, 187, 197, 216, 223, 230–31, 235, 242, 252
Farrell, James T., 10
fascism, fascist, 22, 31, 128, 152, 173, 177, 208–9, 252, 298n29
father, fatherhood, 9, 81–82, 85, 120–21, 127, 153, 157–58, 164–65, 185, 211, 214, 218, 222, 254, 259, 263, 277, 290
Ferber, Edna, 67, 308
FFI (Forces Françaises de l'Intérieur). *See* resistance against NS rule: in France
Fichte, Johann Gottlieb, 160, 239, 308
film, 10, 79, 89, 96, 112, 115, 131, 183, 228, 236, 245, 248, 250, 253, 265, 282, 286, 291
Finland, Finnish, 53
Fisher, Herbert Albert Laurens, 160, 304, 308
flags (and banners), 86, 92, 125, 150, 230, 246, 292, 183; Austrian (red and white), 188, 203, 208; Bavarian (white-blue), 199; French (tricolor), 78, 92, 101, 110, 137, 293; German (NS-flags), 144, 152, 183, 203, 208, 243; red, 246, 252; US-American (stars and stripes), 21, 85, 250; white, 114, 125, 175, 183, 196
Foch, Ferdinand, 106, 308
food, 29, 35, 61, 82, 101, 110, 131, 140, 155, 175, 183–84, 191, 195, 204, 208, 229, 234, 247, 254, 270–71, 275–76, 281, 285, 288
forced labor, 30, 127
Förster, Theodor Wilhelm Max, 230, 301n93
Fort Totten, New York, 1, 67–69
Fragebogen (questionnaire). *See* denazification
France, French, 9, 13, 15, 24, 32, 39, 43, 50–51, 53, 55, 70–72, 74, 77–78, 80, 82, 84–88, 92–96, 101–2, 106, 109–112, 115, 120–27, 134, 137–38, 140–41, 144, 148, 162–63, 177, 183, 186, 190, 206–7, 209, 211, 213, 215, 218, 222, 225, 228–

31, 234, 237, 261, 263, 275–76, 279–81, 293–94, 297nn11–12, 297nn14–15, 298nn29–30, 299n50, 299n59, 299n61
Frankfurt (Main), 1, 15–16, 53, 61, 145–46, 149, 151–52, 159, 163, 177, 180, 211, 244, 254–55, 262, 272, 275, 277, 286, 288–89, 295, 302n102, 302n111
Frankfurt (Oder), 268
Frankfurter Rundschau, 277
fraternization, 51–53, 55, 92, 124, 134, 144, 148, 158, 161, 167, 237, 252, 263, 278, 283. *See also* nonfraternization
fräuleins, 54–55, 58n6, 127, 237, 274, 277, 286, 288, 296. *See also* women
Frederick the Great (Frederick II), 126, 250, 308
freedom. *See* liberty
Freiburg, 230, 235
Freimann, 199
Freytag, Gustav, 172, 308
Frick, Wilhelm, 182, 308
Fritzsche, Hans, 108, 114, 179, 298n27
Front National, 71, 94–95, 108
Fueter, Eduard, 232, 304, 308
Führer. *See* Hitler
Fulda (river), 244

Galli-Curci, Amelita, 188, 308
Gamelin, Maurice-Gustav, 179, 299n59
Gangster, 136, 215, 255, 277, 282
Ganoe, William, 97–98, 297n20
Gemütlichkeit, 159
generation, 4, 26–27, 59–60, 91, 109, 117, 113, 165, 186, 201, 219, 282. *See also* youth
Geneva Convention, 279
Gerngroß, Rupprecht, 188–89, 191, 193–96, 198–200, 299n63, 300n70
Gerth, Hans Heinrich, 238–40, 304
Gestapo, Geheime Staatspolizei, 63, 85, 87, 92, 95, 102, 111–12, 120, 132, 147, 149, 152, 160, 172–74, 179, 184–85, 187, 189–190, 194–97, 200, 210, 214, 231, 234, 250, 289, 292, 302n107. *See also* police
GI, 1, 12, 15, 17, 22, 34, 47n8, 50, 52–53, 55, 63, 74, 78, 88, 93, 98, 101, 103, 109, 124, 127, 137, 145, 161, 164, 175, 185,
196, 199, 201, 207, 211, 218, 228, 230, 237, 247, 250, 252, 257, 262, 264, 268, 277–79, 286, 288, 292, 294, 296
Gibbon, Edward, 80, 308
Gibbs, Philip, 160, 308
Gide, André Paul Guillaume, 67, 81, 304, 308
Giesler, Paul, 224, 301n89
Giraud, Henri-Honoré, 94, 297n15
Glotz, Gustave, 88, 309
Gmünd, 176–77
Goebbels, Joseph, 100, 114, 133, 147, 152, 166, 171, 179, 203, 256, 309
Goethe, Johann Wolfgang von, 9, 16, 61, 81, 83, 95, 125–26, 146–47, 160, 172, 220, 234, 240, 242, 254–55, 304, 309
Göring (Goering), Herman(n), 83–84, 171, 246, 302n105, 309
Gotha, 148
Gottfried von Straßburg, 83, 309
Göttingen, 243, 245, 302n103
Gottlieb, Arthur, 80, 134, 167, 297n6
Gouraud, Henri Joseph Eugène, 84, 309
GPU, 95, 192, 210, 245, 297n19
Grady, Henry Woodfin, 138, 309
Great Britain, 32, 101, 106, 147–48, 160, 163, 171, 183, 186, 189, 200, 207, 209, 211, 229, 238–40, 245–46, 255–56, 264, 269, 281, 289, 291, 294, 300n73
Grey, Zane, 160, 309
Grillparzer, Franz, 172, 309
Grimm, Jacob and Wilhelm, 172, 176, 304, 309
Groscurth, Georg, 185–86, 299n62, 309
Grote, Hans, 173, 304, 309
Gruber, Karl, 228–29, 301n91
Guadalcanal, 93
Guerilla, 130, 252, 298n30
Guérin, Charles, 71, 309
guilt, 72, 74–75, 79, 98, 142, 155, 168, 176, 201, 207. *See also* collective guilt
Guizot, François Pierre Guillaume, 95, 309
gun. *See* arms
Gustavus Adolphus, 169, 309

Haislip, Wade H., 138–39, 237, 298n37
Halévy, Daniel, 115, 304, 309

Hamburg, 21, 188, 255, 263
Hamilton, James T., 58n7, 72–73, 75, 77, 90–91, 105, 138, 168, 176, 297n2
Handel, Georg Friedrich, 173, 309
Hannover, Hanover, 148, 243, 245, 256
Harrison, Anne, 261
Hartshorne, Edward Y., 236, 238, 301n99
Haunstetten, 226, 260, 285
Haydn, Joseph, 173, 309
Heesters, Johannes, 265, 309
Hegel, Friedrich, 172, 220, 239, 309
Heidegger, Martin, 230, 232, 235, 309
Heidelberg, 3, 15, 23, 33, 36, 131, 133, 152, 155, 157–59, 162–63, 178, 181, 222, 230, 232, 234–237, 239–41, 243, 257, 260–62, 270–71, 274–75, 277, 288, 299n49, 301nn100–101
Heil Hitler. *See* Hitler salute
Heilbronn, 176–77, 211
Heiligenberg, 157
Heimwehr, 210, 301n86
Helmstedt, 256, 294
Heppenheim, 155
Herodotus, 106, 309
Hershey bar. *See* chocolate
Hess, Rudolf Walter Richard, 84, 200–201, 309
Hesse, 152, 155, 174, 176, 298n43
Heute (magazine), 269
Himmelfarb, Gertrude, 60
Himmler, Heinrich, 100, 309
Hindenburg, Paul von, 126, 158
Historical Section (US Army), 8n8, 13, 15, 17, 23, 42, 23, 30, 39–56, 72, 79–80, 105, 166–67, 273, 294
history, 3–6, 10–13, 15, 18, 21–24, 26, 35, 38–56, 59, 61, 67, 71, 73–79, 84, 88, 90, 95, 97–99, 105–07, 112, 115, 119, 133, 136, 143–44, 151, 164–66, 172–73, 177, 195, 209, 214, 219–20, 234, 254, 262, 271, 273, 295–96; military, 14–15, 38–56, 61, 72, 104, 106–07, 167, 216, 236; oral, 47n7, 99
Hitler, Adolf, 13, 21, 32, 60, 63, 72, 97, 100–101, 109, 116, 127, 130–33, 136, 144–47, 152–53, 164, 166, 172–73, 179–80, 186–88, 190–93, 195–98, 200–201, 207, 211, 213–14, 218, 223–24, 230–31, 235, 242–43, 248, 251, 256, 277, 300n65, 300n83, 304
Hitler salute/*Deutscher Gruß*, 82, 84–85, 152, 185, 195–96, 207, 211, 232, 251
Hitler-Stalin Pact, 187
Hitler Youth (Hitlerjugend), 21, 82, 85, 127–29, 157, 298n35
Hitzfeld, Otto, 278–79, 302n113
Hodges, Courtney, 104, 298n25
Hofmannsthal, Hugo von, 172, 309
Hölderlin, Johann Christian Friedrich, 242, 309
Holland. *See* Netherlands
Hollywood, 117, 236
Holocaust, 4, 16, 24, 62–63
Homburg, 125, 174
homosexual, 169
Hook, Sidney, 10, 18
Horthy de Nagybánya, Miklós (Nicolas), 247, 309
Houssen, 101, 113
Howe, Irving, 59
HQ, 13, 43, 51, 72, 74–76, 81–82, 85, 87, 93, 96, 105, 107, 110, 115–16, 120, 125, 127, 131, 135, 141, 158, 166, 189–91, 193, 197–98, 200, 204, 207, 228, 230, 236, 243–44, 247, 262, 286, 299n60, 302n102, 302n107
Huber, Kurt, 231–32, 301n94
Hübner (Huebner), Rudolf, 198, 300n80
Hughes, Dorothy, 156, 304, 309
Hugo, Victor, 81, 309
Huizinga, Johan, 239, 304, 309
human rights, 243
Hungary, Hungarian, 247
Hunger, 30, 34, 67, 141–42, 144, 155, 184, 194, 198, 217, 219, 276, 286
Hungerburg, 203, 205, 228
Hutten, Ulrich von, 160, 172–73, 310

IG Farben, 244, 262, 274, 286, 302n102
Ill (river), 84, 98
imperialism, imperialist, 53, 108, 219, 229, 233, 246, 277
infantry, 24, 45, 81, 93, 97, 101, 103, 106, 135, 161, 178, 181, 245, 288
Infantry Journal, 106
Inn (river), 196, 203–4, 211, 227

Index

Innsbruck, 15, 179, 203–4, 206–8, 227–30, 295
international law, 279
interrogation, 51, 129, 218, 279, 302n111
Iraq, 26, 60
Ireland, Irish, 25, 183, 185
Iron Cross, Eisernes Kreuz, 142
Isar (river), 181
Italy, Italian, 73–74, 83, 125, 130, 138, 156, 167, 177, 179, 198–99, 204, 207, 211, 220, 247

Jackson, Andrew, 239, 310
Jacobsen, Hanns, 195, 300n71
James, Henry, 62, 91, 153–54, 156, 266, 310
Japan, Japanese, 148, 245–46
Jaspers, Gertrud, 56, 61, 230, 234, 236–37, 239, 243, 245, 270–71
Jaspers, Karl, 17–18, 22, 61, 230, 234, 236–39, 241–43, 245, 249, 270–71, 304, 310
jazz, 250, 291
Jeanne d'Arc (Joan of Arc), 78
Jebsheim, 81–82
jeep. *See* transport: car, jeep
Jeritza, Maria, 188, 310
Jew, Jews, Jewish, 4, 9–10, 12, 16, 21, 24, 59, 63, 71, 138, 147, 183–88, 193, 196, 211, 223, 230, 234, 236, 238, 242–43, 271, 283, 289–90, 294
Johnson, Harold Ogden, 183, 310
Joint Chiefs of Staff (JCS), 1067, 30, 32, 34
Jordan, Edward E. ("Jordy"), 22, 25, 51, 126, 144, 149, 151, 167, 177–78, 237, 257–58, 298n34
journalism, 3, 10, 15, 18, 22, 27, 38, 43–46, 52, 59, 61–62, 79, 99, 103, 108, 155, 157, 191–92, 196, 199, 266, 268, 277, 297n23, 300n77, 302n108, 312

Kafka, Franz, 163, 310
Kaiserslautern, 30, 45, 124–28, 131, 134–35, 137, 141, 144
Kamenev, Lev Borisovich, 95, 310
Kant, Immanuel, 169, 172, 310
Karl der Grosse (Charlemagne), 172, 310
Karlsruhe, 157, 162, 234, 282

Kaserne, caserne (barracks), 70, 72, 105, 122, 124–27, 137, 144, 149, 158, 161, 165, 178, 198, 234, 286, 288
Kassel, 185, 243–44, 249, 258, 264, 276
Kesselring, Albert, 109, 116, 148, 180, 298n31, 310
Kiev, 132
King, Henry Churchill, 160, 310
Klopstock, Friedrich Gottlieb, 173, 310
Koblenz, 281
Koestler, Arthur, 270, 310
Komorowski, Tadeusz "Bór," 183, 310
Königslutter, 247
knight. *See* medieval
Konstanz, 275
K-ration. *See* food
krauts, 88, 93, 116, 118–19, 171, 274, 287, 289
Krehl, Ludolf, 241, 310
Kremlin, 95, 209, 253, 270
Kriebel, Hermann, 201, 300n83
Kristol, Irving, 59–60
Kunheim, 54, 81, 87, 113
Kulturbund, 282

labor union, 262
Landsberg am Lech, 200–202, 228
landscape, 52–53, 76, 176, 190, 217, 223, 244, 256, 260. *See also* countryside
Landstuhl, 139
Langemarck, 130, 298n35
language, 5–6, 9, 11, 22, 32, 61, 101, 103, 144, 148, 151, 169–70, 189, 258, 297n9
Lasalle, Antoine Charles Louis, Comte de, 71, 310
Laski, Harold, 189, 310
Lasky, family, 4, 9–12, 14, 16, 32, 60, 276–77; sister (Floria), 9, 35
Lassalle, Ferdinand, 262, 310
Latin, 73, 80, 241
Latvia, Latvian, 226, 258
Laufen (camp), 21, 183, 187
Lausanne, 261
Law for Liberation from National Socialism and Militarism (Befreiungsgesetz), 33, 37n1
Lawrence, David Herbert, 69, 310
Le Figaro, 109

Leander, Zarah, 265, 310
Lebenau, 183
Lederhose. *See* traditional dress
Leica. *See* camera
Leiling, Ottheinrich, 189, 195, 198, 200, 299n63
Leipzig, 166, 297n9
Lenin, Wladimir Iljitsch, 192, 211, 252, 310
Lessing, Gotthold Ephraim, 83, 146, 242, 254, 310
letters, writing letters, 5, 11, 13–16, 18, 23, 35, 38, 50, 58, 62, 68, 82, 89, 91, 95, 107–08, 114–15, 125, 127–28, 156, 162, 164, 167, 175, 185, 234, 237, 239, 240, 245, 249, 262, 270, 272, 275, 278, 295–96, 302n108
Lewin, Kurt, 31
Lewis, Harry Sinclair, 159–60, 304, 310
L'Humanité, 94
liberalism, 1, 23, 60, 79, 95, 165, 190, 219, 267
liberation, liberators, 13, 16, 22, 25, 30, 51, 71, 85, 91–92, 102, 108, 119, 124, 131, 137, 153, 160, 166, 172, 174, 187, 196, 200, 203, 207, 209–10, 236, 256, 298n26
liberty, 3, 13, 25, 31, 39, 55, 60, 77, 84, 131, 137, 153, 160, 172, 189, 192, 200, 208, 210, 219, 232, 242–43, 247, 251, 271; statue of, 11
library, 9, 15, 23, 38, 67, 70, 73, 81, 83–85, 140, 147, 160, 171–73, 176, 199, 202, 224, 239, 241, 264, 269
Liebfrauenmilch, Liebfraumilch (wine), 168, 170, 176, 260–61
Liebig, Justus, 176, 310
Liebknecht, Karl, 252, 302n107, 310
Life (magazine), 142
Linderhof (castle), 16, 203, 226
Linz, 206
literature, 5, 9–11, 23, 27, 59, 61–62, 73, 80, 91, 104–06, 109, 117, 160, 172, 234, 239, 240, 267, 269, 303–05
Łódź, 9, 16, 60, 184
London, 14–16, 61, 120, 161, 186, 189, 201, 209, 246, 272
looting, 25–26, 72–73, 122, 127, 140, 144, 156, 162, 174, 183, 209, 215, 218, 251, 280, 295

Lorraine. *See* Alsace-Lorraine
Lorraine (magazine), 96
Loserth, Johann, 232, 304
Lot, Ferdinand Victor Henri, 88, 115, 310
Ludendorff bridge, 103, 108, 114, 297, 298
Ludwig, Ernst, 144, 149
Ludwigshafen, 63, 128, 132, 162
Luftwaffe (German Air Force), 142, 178, 181, 186, 223
Lunéville, 13–14, 51, 70–75, 79–80, 86, 89, 103, 112, 119, 122, 139, 159, 167, 229, 299
Luther, Martin, 172–73, 176, 180, 216, 310
Luxembourg, 238
Luxemburg, Rosa, 252, 310

Macdonald, Dwight, 9–11, 14, 16, 18, 26, 52, 58, 156, 238, 262, 271, 275, 302n108, 304
Macduff, John Ross, 160, 304, 310
Machiavelli, Niccolò di Bernardo dei, 115, 310
machine gun. *See* arms
MacLeish, Archibald, 269, 310
Maeterlinck, Maurice, 110, 304, 311
Magdeburg, 256, 293
Maginot-Line, 132, 164
Main (river), 131, 145, 262, 294
Mainz, 114, 135, 288
Maison Rouge (report), 44, 82, 84, 89, 90, 97–98, 113, 216, 297
Manhattan, 9, 247
Mann family: Golo, 311, 240; Klaus, 196, 240, 300n78; Thomas, 156, 204, 240, 300, 304, 311, 240, 300n78
Mannheim, 128–29, 131, 133, 158, 162, 238, 243, 277
Maquis, 109, 112, 222, 298
Marburg, 256
Marseille, 94, 137, 168
Marshall, George, 41, 138–39, 298n38
Marshall, Margaret Alice, 271, 311
Marshall, Samuel Lyman Atwood, 106, 304
Martin, Alfred von, 232, 235, 304, 311
Marty, André, 94, 311
Marx, Karl, 239; Marxism, 189, 262, 313
Maske, Donald, 161–62, 170, 299n47

Index 325

mass, 79, 147, 222, 254, 290, 296, 177, 263.
  See also people
Maugham, William Somerset, 67, 311
Mauriac, François, 109, 311
Maurice, Emil, 201, 300n83
Maurois, André, 96, 311
McCabe, Thomas B., 247, 302n106
McCarthy, Frank., 139, 298n38
McCloy, John J., 38, 40
McGiffert, Arthur Cushman, 67, 304, 311
medals, 92–93, 119
medieval, 72, 83, 90, 139, 159, 171, 216, 235, 305–07, 310, 313
Mediterranean, 196, 297n13
Meinecke, Friedrich, 232, 235, 245, 304, 311
Meister Eckhart, 172, 311
Melanchthon, Philip, 83, 311
Mellenthin, Friedrich Wilhelm von, 279, 302n113
Melville, Herman, 67, 156, 305, 311
Meran, Merano, 228
Merck (factory), 146
Messina, 108
Metro-Goldwyn-Mayer, 211
Metz, 109
Meyer, Eduard, 239, 311
Michelangelo, 144, 216, 311
Michelet, Jules, 95, 311
middle class, 16, 26, 71, 152, 220, 252, 267, 287. *See also* bourgeois, petit bourgeois, *Kleinbürger*
Milan, 22, 177
militarism, militarist, 34–35, 37, 195, 199, 200, 215, 232
military government. *See* occupation: government
military police (MP), 73, 86, 134–35, 189, 215, 234, 289
Milton, John, 160, 305, 311
Mississippi (US state), 91, 138
Mitchell, Margaret, 160, 305, 311
Mittenwald, 228
Molière, 83, 311
Molotov, Vyacheslav, 246, 311
Mommsen, Theodor, 220, 239, 305, 311
monarchy, 183, 193, 200, 204, 223, 254, 308–10

Monsabert, Joseph de Goislard de, 94, 297n12
Monte Cassino, 109
Montesquieu, 115, 305, 311
Mooney, Edgar S., 51, 53, 79–80, 86, 89, 96–97, 100, 102–03, 105, 108, 115, 126, 130–31, 134–135, 142, 154, 161–63, 167, 171, 178, 179, 215, 216, 261, 275, 295, 297n5
Moore, Frank, 160, 305, 311; George, 83, 305, 311
Morgenthau, Henry, 281, 302n116, 311
Mörike, Eduard, 172, 311
Morocco, Moroccan, 229
Moscow, 95, 125, 132, 209, 253, 267, 269–70, 302
Moselle (river), 88, 102, 105
mother, motherhood, 43, 54, 96, 98, 112, 120, 126, 144, 184, 186, 199, 221, 223–24, 259, 263, 276, 286, 290, 296, 303
movie. *See* film
Mozart, Wolfgang Amadeus, 173, 188, 214, 262, 311
Munich, München, 15, 35, 53, 148, 176–177, 179, 181–82, 188–91, 193–97, 200, 215, 220–21, 223–24, 230–232, 241, 249, 251, 264, 275, 277, 299n60, 300n72, 301n89
Müntzer, Thomas, 173, 311
Murphy, Robert, 193, 220, 300n69
music, 10, 26, 85, 88, 106, 117, 122, 128, 132–33, 160, 166, 173, 192, 203, 205, 214, 216–17, 230, 245, 249, 250, 252–53, 257, 261, 282, 291, 299n52, 301. *See also* jazz
Mussolini, Benito, 22, 177

Nancy, 13–14, 50, 53, 88–89, 102, 109, 116, 118, 123, 139
Nation (magazine), 245, 271, 302n103
National Socialism, Nationalsozialismus, 3, 9, 13, 16, 32–35, 37n1, 54, 58, 71–72, 75, 78, 83, 85–86, 88, 95, 100, 108–09, 111–12, 116, 118, 120–21, 125–127, 129–30, 132–34, 136, 144, 146–49, 152, 157–58, 163, 170–74, 179–81, 183, 185–86, 188, 190–91, 193–205, 207–209, 211, 218–23, 228, 231–32, 238–39, 242–43, 251–

52, 266, 277, 280–81, 283, 299nn55–57, 299nn62–63, 300n66, 301n84
Nationalkomitee Freies Deutschland, 191, 300n67
Natzweiler, 87
Nazi, Nazisms. *See* National Socialism
Neckar (river), 157–58, 162, 176, 230, 234, 237, 239, 241, 260
negroes. *See* African Americans
Neinhaus, Carl, 162–63, 299n49
Nelson, Benjamin, 232, 301
neoconservatism, 60, 64–65
Netherlands, 141, 162, 223, 308–310
Neuenheim, 157–58
Neue Zeit, 268
Neues Deutschland, 194
Neuf Brisach, 82
Neustadt, 74
neutrality, 265
Neu Ulm, 178
New Deal, 45, 164–65
Newiger, Brigitte, 290, 302n118
New International, 10
New Leader, 11–12, 59, 62
New Republic, 10, 11
New York (US state), 1, 67–69, 222
New York City, 9–12, 14, 16–18, 24, 38, 51, 59–62, 222
New Yorker, 287
New York Herald Tribune, 277
New York intellectuals, 1, 11, 59–64
New York Review of Books, 62
New York Times, 9, 266, 277
newspapers, 4–5, 9–10, 45, 85, 95, 109, 130, 149, 155, 166, 171, 174, 176, 191, 204, 209–10, 246, 250, 266, 268, 276, 286–87, 295. *See also* journalism
Niebuhr, Reinhold, 270, 311
Nietzsche, Friedrich, 220, 239, 264, 305, 311
nonfraternization, 34–35, 45, 52, 55, 57. *See also* fraternization
Normandy, 161
North Africa. *See* Africa
Norway, Norwegian, 265, 271–272, 275, 301n84, 310
Novalis, 172, 305, 311
NSDAP, 32, 33, 194, 199, 231–32, 235, 243, 298n42, 299n49, 299n60, 300n74, 300n79, 300n83, 308–09, 314. *See also* National Socialism
Nuremberg, Nürnberg, 22, 166, 177, 179, 180, 211–213, 218–19, 249; Trials, 32

Oberammergau, 97, 203, 211, 228
Oberursel, 278, 294, 302n111
occupation (general), 13, 15, 26–27, 50, 55, 111, 127, 131, 163, 174, 176, 196, 200, 202, 206, 208, 215, 218, 220, 221, 224–25, 230, 234, 236, 237, 263, 273, 275, 280, 282–84, 294–95
—by Germany, 86, 102, 110, 120, 298nn29–30, 301n84
—government (Allies in Germany), 2, 15, 17, 21, 25, 29–36, 219, 221, 131, 140, 142, 155, 170, 173–75, 188, 190, 203, 208, 210, 220–24, 228, 231, 237, 241, 255, 262, 271, 277, 284, 301n99, 302nn115–16, 307
—zones: British, 245, 256; French, 32, 229, 276, 280–81; Soviet (Russian), 255, 269, 272, 290; US-American, 32, 229, 270, 280, 301n99, 307
Odelzhausen, 222
Oder (river), 268
Ohlenroth, Ludwig, 232–33, 301n97
Olsen, John Sigvard, 183, 312
Oncken, Margarete, 245, 302n104
Operation Dragoon, 164, 299n50
Oppenheimer, Franz, 220, 305, 312
Oslo, 267, 271, 273

Pagny-sur-Moselle, 88, 102
Palatine (Pfalz), 234
Palermo, 108
Panther. *See* tank
Papen, Franz von, 166, 312
Paris, 14, 24, 74, 81, 84, 121, 123, 159, 166, 206, 210, 229, 238, 250, 266, 297n18
Paris Herald Tribune, 135
Parsons, Talcott, 240, 312
Partisan Review (magazine), 10–11, 18, 24, 59, 62, 64, 156, 301n92, 302n108
Patch, Alexander McCarrell, 41, 92–93, 106, 128, 133, 178–79, 181, 281, 312
Pater, Walter Horatio, 67, 305, 312

Patton, George Smith, 7n4, 41, 71, 81, 106, 128, 131, 139, 145, 148, 171, 241, 281, 298n45, 312
Paul, Jean, 172–73, 312
peace, 26–27, 34–35, 37, 58, 104, 114, 116, 140–41, 152–53, 158, 162, 166, 174, 176, 178, 204, 210, 220, 234–35, 240, 242, 267, 270, 277, 284, 286
Pearce, Charles A. "Cap," 135, 272–74, 298n110, 302
people, 44–45, 108–109, 121, 149, 295–96; French, 86, 121, 222; German, 3, 16, 30–31, 33–34, 36–37, 62, 121, 125, 132, 147–48, 153, 186, 202, 213, 218–19, 284; Jewish, 242, 290; Russian, 95. *See also* mass
Pershing, John Joseph, 106, 312
Pétain, Henri Philippe, 72
Petchorine, Dimitri, 95, 312
Pforzheim, 284
Philadelphia, 24, 175, 184
Pieck, Wilhelm, 95, 312
pistol. *See* arms
Pittsburgh, 247
Podhoretz, Norman, 60
Pogue, Forrest, 17, 39–40, 45–46, 47n7
Poland, Polish, 9, 24, 60, 85, 174, 183–84, 189, 218, 224, 245, 266, 289, 290, 307, 310
police, policing, 51, 55, 91, 119–20, 132, 144, 160, 166, 196–97, 200, 210, 221, 225, 234, 268–69, 277, 282, 286, 300. *See also* Gestapo; military police (MP)
Politics (magazine), 156, 238, 302n108, 304–05
Pollock, James Kerr, 279–80, 302
Pompey, France, 88
Potsdam, 256, 281, 293
POWs, 42, 97, 100–01, 109, 118, 121, 125, 126, 129, 131–32, 137, 142, 148, 155, 171, 178, 181, 183, 186, 198, 263, 274
press. *See* newspapers
priest, 163, 190, 202
Probst, Christoph, 232, 301n95
professor, 13, 17, 20n18, 38, 44, 73, 86, 234, 237–40, 242–43, 270–71, 279, 301n93–94, 301n100
Prokofiev, Serei, 253, 312

proletariat, proletarian, 187, 190
propaganda, 27, 41, 44, 71, 95, 97, 100–01, 108–09, 142, 147–49, 152, 173, 185, 189, 191, 194–95, 198, 202–03, 228, 231, 235, 248, 251–53, 269–70, 282, 297, 298n27, 299n52, 309, 314
prostitution, 15, 85, 137, 128, 204, 207, 250, 283–84, 287, 291
Pro-station, 158–59, 274, 285, 298m44
Protestantism, protestant, 180
Prussia, Prussian, 175, 251, 254, 306–8
Psychological Warfare Branch (PWB), 100–01, 301n87
Puccini, Giacomo, 188, 312
Pudovkin, Vsevolod, 253, 312
Puhl, Nikolaus, 196, 300n79
PX, 220, 247
Pyle, Ernie, 43, 98, 305, 312

Quebec, 281
Quisling, Vidkun Abraham Lauritz Jonssøn, 208, 301n84

racism, 55, 58, 94, 130, 138, 242, 288. *See also* anti-Semitic, anti-Semitism
radio, 117, 122, 130, 153, 167, 191, 193, 195, 197, 199, 201–02, 209–10, 228, 246, 250, 252, 287, 297n18, 298, 300
Ranke, Leopold von, 43, 166, 312
Ratzel, Friedrich, 172, 312
Reader's Digest (magazine), 168
reconstruction, 29–33, 36, 108, 141, 156, 166, 191, 194, 202, 221, 237, 281, 292, 301n100
Red Army. *See* Army: Soviet
Red Cross, 72, 147, 262, 283, 286
reeducation, 2, 31–33, 36–37, 50, 54, 161
Reformation, 159, 173, 310, 311
refugees, 32, 62, 95–96, 109, 118, 132, 143, 162, 184, 187, 194–95, 202, 218, 234, 236, 286. *See also* displaced person
Reichstag, 201, 293
religion, 91, 100, 113, 128, 180, 190, 216. *See also* church
Remagen bridge, 103, 297n24, 298n31
Renaissance, 139
Renner, Karl, 209, 301n85
Renoir, Pierre-Auguste, 246, 312

resistance against NS rule: in France, 43, 87, 94–96, 109, 112, 119–20, 229, 298n30, 307–08; in Germany and Austria, 189–194, 199–200, 228, 242, 299nn62–64, 300n68, 300n72, 301n91, 301n95. *See also* anti-fascism: anti-Nazi revolution, 70, 115, 153, 155, 179, 189, 195–96, 198, 209, 222, 253
Reynaud, Paul, 179, 207, 299n59, 312
Rhine (river), 13, 75, 81, 85, 94, 103–04, 110, 112, 114, 116, 118, 124, 126, 128, 134, 141, 162, 168, 174, 176, 194, 223, 230, 297n7, 297n24, 298n24
Rhône (river), 167
Ribeauville, 76
Riedenauer, Bruno, 194, 198–99, 300n70
Riess, Curt, 196, 198–99, 300n77
rifle. *See* arms
Riga, 226
Rilke, Rainer Maria, 115, 220, 235, 305, 312
Rintelen, Fritz-Joachim Paul von, 230–31, 312
Roeck, Morton McDonald, 232–33, 301n97
Rohde, Lothar, 195, 300n73
Rökk, Marika, 265, 312
Rome, Romans, 15, 73–74, 130, 159, 180, 199, 213, 305
Rommel, Erwin, 109, 312
Roosevelt, Franklin D., 40, 60, 154, 164–65, 280–81, 312
Rosenberg, Alfred, 172, 305, 312
rubble, 3–4, 16, 22, 35, 61–62, 64, 75, 77, 113, 114, 124, 142–43, 145–47, 153, 176, 178, 180, 191, 211, 216–17, 240, 243–44, 249, 252, 254, 255, 266, 268, 284, 286, 289, 291. *See also* destruction
Rubens, Peter Paul, 235, 213
Ruhr (river), 166, 277, 292
Rundstedt, Gerd von, 76, 80, 100, 116, 175, 182, 297n4, 298n31, 312
Russell, Bertrand, 239, 312
Russia, Russian. *See* Soviet Union

Saar Basin, 124
Sabotage, 92, 100, 127, 186, 189, 201
Sagnac, Philippe, 88, 312
Saint-Saëns, Camille, 110, 312
Salzach (river), 188
Salzburg, 15, 179, 188, 229
Santayana, George, 239, 312
Sarrebourg, 78, 86
Sarreguemines, 124
Saverne, 78, 86
scandal, 106, 196, 267, 273, 277
Scandinavia, Scandinavian, 5, 52–53, 263–64, 273, 275
Schäffer, Fritz, 221, 223, 301n88
Schapiro, Meyer, 18, 230, 238–39, 301n92, 305
Schiller, Friedrich, 83, 125, 172–73, 312
Schilling, Karl, 152, 298n42
Schleiermacher, Friedrich, 172, 312
Schmorell, Alexander, 189, 299n64
Schneider, Franz Xaver, 195, 300n72
Scholl, Hans and Sophie, 189, 194, 232, 299n64
Schongau, 202
school, 10, 12, 23, 38, 43, 73, 81, 82, 91, 96, 128–30, 141, 151, 170, 172, 184, 186, 197, 202, 206, 242, 267, 276, 284, 298n35
Schopenhauer, Arthur, 172, 312
Schramm, Percy Ernst, 278, 302
Schubert, Franz, 172, 313
Schwäbisch Gmünd. *See* Gmünd
Scotland, 14, 310
Seißer, Hans, 200, 300n81
SHAEF, 177, 300n69
Shakespeare, William, 81, 83, 160, 160, 254, 313
Shelley, Percy Bysshe, 156, 313
Shils, Edward, 240, 313
Sicily, 108, 138
Sickingen, Franz von, 135, 173, 313
Siegfried line, 116, 118–19, 125, 132, 164
Simmel, Georg, 240, 313
singing, songs. *See* music
slavery. *See* forced labor
Slezak, Walter, 198, 313
Sloan, Samuel, 135, 298n36, 302n110, 313
Slovakia. *See* Czechoslovakia
sniper, 118, 134, 208, 232, 235, 245
Socialism, Socialist, 10–11, 59, 95, 195, 211, 225, 239, 246, 301n85, 303
Sollors, Werner, 23

Sombart, Werner, 220, 232, 240, 305, 313
South Tyrol. *See* Tyrol
Southern states (US), 22, 58, 91, 138
Soviet Union, Soviet, 2, 6, 17, 21, 26, 34–36, 59, 95, 126, 129, 131–33, 141, 147–48, 160, 174, 176, 178, 187, 192, 196, 198, 204, 206–07, 210–11, 221–22, 225–26, 228–29, 234–35, 240, 245–48, 250, 252–56, 263, 268–72, 281, 290, 293–94, 297n17, 298nn41–42, 300nn67–68, 301n85, 302n109, 307–08, 310–14
Spaulding, General Oliver L., 40–41
Spengler, Oswald, 239, 313
Sperr, Franz, 189–99, 300n65
Speyer, 180
Spindler, Robert, 230, 301n93
Sprenger, Jakob, 152, 298n43
Springer Verlag, 248
Srbik, Heinrich, 200, 300n82
SS, 95, 118, 132, 149, 152, 183, 186, 190, 192–93, 198–99, 207, 211, 224, 300n76, 309
St. Dié, 74–75, 113
Stalin, Joseph, 59–60, 94–95, 187, 192, 203, 211, 246, 248, 250, 293; Stalinism, Stalinist, 11, 59–60, 71, 192, 248, 253–54, 270
Stalingrad, 232
Stars and Stripes (magazine), 22, 103, 154–155, 157, 162, 165, 196, 210, 247, 300n78
Stendhal, 24, 27–28, 61–62, 69, 227, 313
Stockholm, 15, 53, 265, 266, 271, 273
Storm, Theodor, 172, 313
Strasbourg, 13–14, 21, 73, 76, 77, 83–84, 86–87, 164, 175, 297n10
Strauss, Richard, 245, 291, 313
strike, 183, 199
Struthof (camp), 87–88
students, 10–11, 18, 84, 172, 184, 189, 192, 231, 235, 299n64
Stuttgart, 177, 234, 260–61, 276, 279, 280–82, 284–85
suicide, 179, 195, 241, 243, 298n43
surrender, 29–30, 32, 34, 57, 100–01, 114, 118, 128, 131, 133, 158, 169, 171, 179–80, 195, 274

Sutton, William, 81–82, 96.97, 118, 161, 167, 178, 216, 299n58
swastika, *Hakenkreuz*, 21, 85, 172, 223, 243, 248
Sweden, Swedish, 53, 263, 266, 273, 306, 309–10
Switzerland, Swiss, 186, 191, 194, 261, 270–71, 279
Sybel, Heinrich von, 239, 313

Tacitus, Publius Cornelius, 104, 313
Tägliche Rundschau, 268
tank, 62, 71, 77–78, 82, 97–98, 113, 124, 126, 134, 142, 145, 164, 229, 256, 269, 293, 297n21, 300n75
Tassigny, Jean-Marie de Lattre de, 92, 297n11
Tauchnitz, 83, 297n9
Taylorist, 23
terror, 19, 43, 71, 84, 92, 97, 106, 108, 127, 132, 134, 151–52, 188, 190, 208, 210, 244, 255–56, 263–64, 271, 274, 292
Thälmann, Ernst, 252, 313
The Hague, 101
Thierry, Jacques Nicolas Augustin, 95, 313
Thucydides, 39, 85, 105, 313
Thurber, James, 214, 313
Thuringia, 148
Tieck, Ludwig, 172, 313
Tilly, Johann Tserclaes, Count of, 169, 313
Time Magazine, 287
Tisse, Eduard, 233, 253–54, 313
Tokyo, 84, 246
totalitarianism, 172, 208, 232, 240
traditional dress, 94, 144, 189, 213, 229, 262
train. *See* transport: train, railroad
transport: car, jeep, 26, 36, 46, 53, 75–78, 81, 86, 102–03, 105, 125–26, 134–35, 138–39, 142, 144–45, 148, 176, 178, 181–83, 192, 195, 199, 204, 208, 221–23, 230, 233, 236–37, 249–50, 253, 258, 260–61, 263, 269–70, 272, 276–77, 285, 287, 291–92, 295; train, railroad, 71, 125, 135, 142, 162, 184, 191, 198, 221, 248, 262–63; truck, 24, 70–71, 77, 82, 93, 103, 124–25, 131, 135, 137, 141, 175, 178, 181, 202, 221, 236, 252, 261, 286

treason, 232, 242, 252
Treitschke, Heinrich von, 172, 313
Trilling, Lionel, 10, 60, 62, 271, 313
Trotsky, Leon, 95, 192, 109, 267, 302n109, 313; Trotskism, Trotskyist, 10–12, 59
Truman, Harry S., 60, 154, 164, 176, 313
Truscott, Lucian K., 139, 298n39
Tserclaes, Johann. *See* Tilly
Tübingen, 231, 238
Tunisia, 92, 109
typewriter, 1, 3–4, 6, 13–14, 46, 106, 175
Tyrol, 228–29, 299n59, 301

Ulm, 178
unconditional surrender. *See* surrender
uniforms, 21, 53, 74, 86, 90–91, 94, 125, 129, 132, 137, 183, 185, 188, 204, 217, 234, 236, 237, 253, 270, 278, 294
United Service Organizations (USO), 262
United States High Commissioner for Germany. *See* occupation: government
university, 15, 226, 236, 242–43; Berlin, 268, 272; Brunswick, 256; City College of New York, 10–11; Columbia, 11, 13, 38, 44, 202, 301n92; Freiburg, 235; Harvard, 73, 236; Heidelberg, 36, 158–59, 230, 235–36, 241–43, 245, 262, 301nn100–01; Leipzig, 166; Michigan, 11, 24, 31, 36, 59; Munich, 189, 193, 220, 230, 231–232, 299n64, 301nn93–95; Strasbourg, 83–84, 86, 162, 175, 297n10
Usener, Karl Hermann, 230, 313

Vatican, 216
Velden (camp), 195
venereal disease (VD), 55, 274, 287–88, 294, 296, 298n44
Verona, 233
Vichy, 72, 83, 92, 95, 112, 299nn59, 307
Vienna, 15, 148, 191, 195, 207, 300n68
Völkischer Beobachter, 222, 224
Vorarlberg, 205–06, 207, 229
Vosges (mountains), 72, 76, 81, 113
Vossler, Karl, 230–31, 313

Wagner, Richard, 9, 110, 313
Wagner, Robert, 201, 300n83

Waldenburg, Siegfried von, 279, 302n113
Waldo, Peter, 67, 313
Wallenberg, Hans, 27, 52, 100, 217, 287n23, 301n87
Waller, Fats, 88, 313
war crimes, war criminals, 154–55, 218, 221, 290
Washington, DC, 13–14, 38, 41, 60
Wasserburg, 193, 196, 300n79
weapons. *See* arms
Weber, Adolf, 231, 301n100, 313
Weber, Friedrich, 201, 300n83
Weber family: Alfred, 241, 313; Marianne, 22, 56, 237, 313; Max, 22, 220, 234–36, 238–40, 301n100, 304–05, 313
Wehrmacht. *See* army: German
Weinheim, 295
Weinstein, Robert H., 162, 167, 176, 299n48
Weiße Rose (White Rose). *See* resistance against NS rule: in Germany and Austria
Wells, Herbert George, 168, 314
Wells, John Edwin, 83, 305, 313
Werwolf, Werewolf, Werewolves, 152, 194–95
Weser (river), 281
Wessel, Horst, 206, 252, 302, 314
Westphalia, 197
Weygand, Maxime, 179, 299
White, Bouck, 221, 305, 314
Whitehead, Alfred North, 239, 314
Wiesbaden, 273
Willis, Nathaniel Parker, 160, 314
Wilson, Edmund, 22
Wilson, Henry Maitland, 94, 297n13
Wister, Owen, 160, 305, 314
Wolfe, Thomas, 67, 314
women (incl. girls), 17, 24–25, 34, 49–58, 63, 68, 81, 84–85, 87–89, 93, 95, 102, 111, 115, 119–22, 125, 131, 137, 142, 144, 157–58, 160–161, 166, 169, 175, 178, 180–81, 183, 185–187, 191–92, 197, 204, 207, 210–11, 213–15, 218–19, 222–24, 226, 228–30, 233–34, 237, 244, 248, 250–52, 255–59, 261–263, 265, 268–70, 272, 277, 279, 283–88, 291–92, 294–96. *See also* fräuleins

Women's Army Corps (WAC), 229, 287
workers, 74, 111, 161, 194, 199, 208, 272, 287
World War I, 40–41, 47, 164, 223, 298n35
Worms, 45, 114, 135, 142, 144, 170, 176
Wright, Walter Livingston, 40, 99, 297n22
Württemberg, 129, 276, 280–81
Würzburg, 175, 235

Yalta, 280
Yankee, 138, 269
youth, 2, 9, 87, 91, 96, 114, 137, 147, 174, 207, 242, 266, 283, 291. *See also* children, childhood; generation; Hitler Youth (Hitlerjugend)
Yugoslavia, Yugoslavian, 125, 192

Zamość, 184
Zetkin, Clara, 95, 314
Zhukov, Georgy, 246, 314
Zurich, 15

Milton Keynes UK
Ingram Content Group UK Ltd.
UKHW021847070824
446670UK00021B/229